PRODUCTION MANAGEMENT AND BUSINESS DEVELOPMENT

PROCEEDINGS OF THE 6TH ANNUAL INTERNATIONAL SCIENTIFIC CONFERENCE ON MARKETING MANAGEMENT, TRADE, FINANCIAL AND SOCIAL ASPECTS OF BUSINESS (MTS 2018), 17–19 MAY 2018, KOŠICE, SLOVAK REPUBLIC AND UZHHOROD, UKRAINE

Production Management and Business Development

Editors

Bohuslava Mihalčová, Petra Szaryszová & Lenka Štofová
Department of Management, Faculty of Business Economics with seat in Košice, University of Economics in Bratislava, Slovak Republic

Michal Pružinský & Barbora Gontkovičová
Department of Commercial Entrepreneurship, Faculty of Business Economics with seat in Košice, University of Economics in Bratislava, Slovak Republic

CRC Press
Taylor & Francis Group
Boca Raton London New York

CRC Press is an imprint of the
Taylor & Francis Group, an **informa** business
A BALKEMA BOOK

CRC Press
Taylor & Francis Group
6000 Broken Sound Parkway NW, Suite 300
Boca Raton, FL 33487-2742

First issued in paperback 2020

© 2019 by Taylor & Francis Group, LLC
CRC Press is an imprint of Taylor & Francis Group, an Informa business

Typeset by V Publishing Solutions Pvt Ltd., Chennai, India

No claim to original U.S. Government works

ISBN-13: 978-1-138-60415-5 (hbk)
ISBN-13: 978-0-367-73261-5 (pbk)

Visit the Taylor & Francis Web site at
http://www.taylorandfrancis.com

and the CRC Press Web site at
http://www.crcpress.com

Table of contents

Preface

Humankind has entered the third millennium, the conditions of massive development, but also the conditions of increasing and difficult to solve problems. We are all expected, in particular executives in all spheres of human activity, to make swifter, more effective, fairer and wiser decisions about the use of both proven and new tools to ensure the increase of people's well-being, the preservation and development of the environment and the protection of human health and safety.

There are several reasons why management studies are so important as they gradually bring new knowledge. Management is essential to business. Management teaches to understand how people behave in organisations, and the nature of power, influence and leadership. Whether one aims to be self-employed, an entrepreneur, head one's own company; or to work for private business, not-for-profit organisations or government agencies—Management provides the tools for success!

The conference proceedings "Production Management and Business Development" is a collection of scientific papers by researchers from several countries and presents the latest developments in management science. Each of the studies was presented at the 6th International Scientific Conference "Marketing Management, Trade, Financial and Social Aspects of Business" (MTS 2018), which was held from 17th–19th May 2018 (17th–18th May 2018 in Košice, 19th May 2018 in Uzhhorod). All research is original and brings the latest knowledge of the investigated areas.

Our special thanks go to both the Program and the Organizing Committees for their responsible work and assistance in the realisation of the conference, also in putting together these proceedings.

We believe that the outcome of the conference as well as the contributions published will be useful and motivating to organize future meetings and for the scientific development of researchers.

Editors

Production Management and Business Development – Mihalčová et al. (Eds)
© *2019 Taylor & Francis Group, London, ISBN 978-1-138-60415-5*

Competitiveness at regional level: Managerial and institutional impact

V. Andryshyn, V. Serzhanov & O. Butusov
Faculty of Economics of the Uzhhorod National University, Uzhhorod, Ukraine

ABSTRACT: The concept of regional competitiveness has become much discussed between economists and researches abroad. Moreover, regional competitiveness is frequently used by policy-makers, as a key indicator of the success or failure of policy. The problem is that according to some opinions, the Ukrainian regions do not have the same level of economic independence that is inherent in the regional systems of EU countries. The competitiveness increase of any territory is possible in the conditions of providing the regions with the necessary resources and creation of an effective system of local self-government. Only in this case regions can compete for providing favorable economic conditions, establishing international economic relations, attracting foreign direct investments. This paper seeks to find out if latest processes of power decentralization, modernization of regional policy and empowerment of local authorities regarding the development of territories really influence the level of regional competitiveness and local business performance in Ukraine.

1 INTRODUCTION

Nowadays, the term "regional competitiveness" is still causing a number of reservations, since the term "competitiveness" has started to be used to characterize and understand the activities of firms, and then it has been expanded and designed at the national and regional levels. Because of this, the main contradictions and misunderstandings surrounding the competitiveness of the region relate to the main differences and to the fact that they are common, both at the firm level and at the regional level.

In economic literature, the notion of "competitiveness" is analyzed and interpreted in different ways, depending on which economic object it is used to: the national economy as a whole, the region, industry, enterprises and products.

We can distinguish two main approaches to the interpretation of the regional competitiveness. According to the first approach, regional competitiveness is considered as an aggregate indicator of the competitiveness of local firms, according to the second—as a derived function of the indicator of macroeconomic competitiveness.

2 DEFINING REGIONAL COMPETITIVENESS

2.1 *Competitiveness as microeconomic productivity*

The first approach is based on the fact that the region is considered as a set of independent, autonomous economic entities, which, as a result of their activities, can both improve and worsen the economic attractiveness of a particular region. According to this approach, the competitiveness of the region directly depends on the competitiveness of enterprises located in it. However, in order to attract and retain profitable companies, enterprises in this territory, it is necessary to create favorable conditions, which is an indicator of the influence of external and internal factors of competitiveness.

The regional competitiveness depends not only on the presence of a critical mass of (qualified) organizations within its boundaries, but also on its capacity to coordinate the actions of these organizations (Boschma 2004).

The existence of SMEs is of crucial importance in terms of regional competitiveness. These companies usually use local resources and their profit remains in the region, so it can be used to make further investment (Mrva & Stachova 2014).

Spatial economics which does not incorporate entrepreneurship factors may fail to understand and identify key sources of regional development with regions that are open and creative able to attract human capital and enjoy more dynamic entrepreneurship (Huggins et al. 2013). In a competitive environment, entrepreneurs will be alert to opportunities and contribute to regional economic growth. However, changes in levels of entrepreneurship and contributions to regional economic development will take time to emerge, and as such, any effects are only seen in the long term. Alternatively, regions can be uncompetitive and lack entrepreneurial dynamism because they lack the key strengths which make leading regions prosper and develop.

Indeed, there are various grounds for questioning both the universality and strength of the region-firm competitiveness nexus. In some instances the competitiveness of firms in the region might be altogether disconnected from the region. This is certainly the case with multinational enterprises, the competitiveness of which might reflect conditions in the parent country as much as the host one (Bristow 2005).

Some researchers find that the main difference in competitiveness between firms and regions is that the region, unlike the firm, is not eliminated, it does not disappear from the market due to competition and unsuccessful activities (Vuković et al. 2012).

Regions really compete differently from firms. A major difference between the evolution of firms and regions, however, is that firms enter and exit markets in contrast to regions. That is, market selection forces do not drive out regions (i.e. they do not disapear), like firms go broke. Since regions do not exit, they always carry with them a past that may affect the competitiveness of firms either positively or negatively. In this case, it would be more meaningful to conclude that some regions perform better than others (Boschma 2004).

On the contrary, once a place has a reputation as a thriving center for a particular industry or service then it becomes a prime place to locate for newcomers who want to communicate with businesses and individuals (Thompson & Ward 2005). The most famous example of this phenomenon is Silicon Valley, a globally recognized center in the IT industry in California.

2.2 *From national to regional competitiveness*

The second approach to the interpretation of regional competitiveness as a derivative of macroeconomic is based on the assumption that firm productivity is a necessary, but insufficient condition for regional competitiveness. An adequate level of productivity of firms does not necessarily ensure sustainable development of the region, which is determined by the level of income per capita, the level of unemployment, a favorable and healthy living environment. Within the framework of this approach, the view of the regional competitiveness as a macro-prime dominant factor dominates, while the same factors can be recognized as the driving forces of competitiveness of both states and regions. The region is competitive if it succeeds in creating favorable conditions for the growth of added gross value, increasing standards of living and welfare of the population (Storper 1997).

The consequences of regional competition are similar to the result of the competition between countries: the standard of living, employment and wages increase in the successfully competing regions, new investments appear, talented and creative young people, businessmen move there, etc. (Lengyel & Rechnitzer 2013).

However, the concept of national competitiveness cannot be fully designed at the regional level. Governments have more power, macroeconomic tools and mechanisms for influencing the private, public and non-profit sectors, the entire economic system as a whole, than regional governments. Some laws managing the economics of international trade do not operate at the sub-national level. Unlike nations, exchange rate movements and price-wage flexibility either do not work properly or do not exist at the regional level. To the contrary, interregional migration of mobile factors, capital and labour, can be a real threat to regions. In the absence of such macro-economic adjustment mechanisms, the concept of macroeconomic competitiveness cannot be fully applied to the regional level either. That is why regional competitiveness is a concept that is "stuck in the middle" (Martin 2003).

Cellini and Sochi believe that the regional competitiveness is not a simple interpretation or macroeconomic, microeconomic competitiveness that regions cannot be analyzed either as a simple set of companies, either as a simplified model of the national economy (Cellini & Soci 2002). The authors consider the regional competitiveness considerably wider than the potential growth of export or trade balance. Considerable attention, researchers suggest, should be given to such important issues as the efficiency of the real estate market, transport and communications, which are topical issues of regional policy. Thus, the authors emphasize that the social component is a fundamental element of the competitive position of the region, unlike the national level and the level of the enterprise.

R. Akhunov also emphasizes that in contrast to the micro level, the macro (meso) level of competitiveness has not only economic but socio-economic character. The scientist points out another significant, in our opinion, difference in competitiveness on the meso-level from the microeconomic level—its spatial binding, continuity with the territory. Separate business entities have mobility. Though with considerable costs, in other equal conditions, they can radically change their location, place in business-friendly places, replace staff, relatively quickly master the new technological system and thereby significantly improve their competitiveness. The region, obviously, no matter how competitive it has, cannot leave its territory and cannot fundamentally replace its human resources (Akhunov 2014).

3 INSTITUTIONAL IMPACT

Regional competitiveness is determined by skilled labor, investments and other resources of the region, which leads to the emergence of comparative advantages of the region and promotes attraction and retention of firms and new industries (Mongkhonvanit 2014). Thompson & Ward believe «that place matters. Economic growth needs a combination of factors to come together in the same place. These factors include having the right labor force and infrastructure, as well as skilled and knowledgeable people who can make it happen (Thompson & Ward 2005).

Regions can compete due to low wages, low labor qualifications, low taxes, but such a kind of competitive strategy only entails and affects the inability to economic development on the basis of high qualifications and income. Conversely, the right competitive strategy based on the use of knowledge and support for entrepreneurship can lead to positive results and is beneficial both in economic and social terms. Thus, the development of entrepreneurship, as the main source of prosperity, is a key element of regional development (Huggins et al. 2013).

In sum, regions accumulate different institutional environments over time, which act as incentive and selection mechanisms. Institutions affect not only the intensity and nature of relations and, thus, the degree of interactive learning between agents in a regional context, but also the capacity of regions to upgrade, transform or restructure specific institutions (such as specific laws) required for the development of new economic activities. What matters is whether institutions are flexible and responsive to change when required: the implementation and diffusion of novelty often requires the restructuring of old institutions and the establishment of new institutions. This dynamic capability of institutions affects the long-term competitiveness of a region considerably (Boschma 2004).

Enterprises can now not be considered completely independent—they rely on a variety of factors, such as research institutions and universities, cultural influences, knowledge dissemination organizations, government policies and a network of other firms operating in the same locality.

Effective management of the competitiveness of the region's economy involves identifying sustainable factual and potential competitive advantages. The regional authorities themselves should actively form the conditions of economic activity in the region and ensure the competitiveness of the regional economy.

Mongkhonvanit clarified the role of government and regional authorities in cluster-based economic development by explaining the four interrelating and influential roles of government in competitiveness.

Roles in factor conditions: to create specialized education and training programs; to establish local university research efforts enhancing cluster-related technologies; to support cluster-specific information gathering and compilation; and to improve specialized transportation, communications and other infrastructure required by such clusters.

Roles in context for strategy and rivalry: to eliminate barriers to local competition; to focus on efforts to attract foreign investment around clusters; to focus on export promotion around clusters; and to organize relevant government departments around clusters.

Roles in demand conditions: to create pro-innovation, regulatory standards encouraging demand conditions (i.e. reduce regulatory uncertainty, stimulate early adoption of regulation, and encourage innovation or new products and processes); to sponsor independent testing, product certification and rating services for a cluster's products and services; and to act as a sophisticated buyer of the cluster's products/services.

Roles in related and supporting industries: to sponsor forums to bring together cluster participants; to attract suppliers and service providers from other locations; and to establish cluster-oriented free trade zones, industrial parks or supplier parks (Mongkhonvanit 2014).

4 DECENTRALIZATION AS STRATEGIC MANAGERIAL TOOL

At the present time, Ukraine has a sufficient regulatory framework for regulating relations between the state, regions and united territorial communities. However, this process needs further improvement, especially in the context of the implementation of decentralization reform.

Porter stresses on the need for much of economic policy to be decentralized to the regional level. Since many of the essential determinants of economic performance appear to reside in regions, national policies will be necessary but not sufficient. The importance of regions may explain why countries with greater economic decentralization, such as Germany and the US, have been historically successful. It may also explain why countries such as India and China are making notable economic progress in particular states or provinces relative to others (Porter 2003).

Regions of Ukraine, when declaring the market basis for their management, under the conditions of a unitary state, are actually limited in their rights to use such market mechanisms as taxation, credit policy, and system of economic privileges that can form motivational levers of competitiveness. In other words, the regions do not yet have the same level of economic independence that is inherent in the regional systems of EU countries.

It is believed that the term "regional competitiveness" is expedient only in relation to countries with a federal state structure. In this case, the regions are characterized by real rivalry at the federal level for providing favorable economic conditions, establishing international economic relations, attracting investment.

European experience convincingly proves that raising the level of competitiveness of the territory is possible in the conditions of giving the regions the necessary powers and resources and creating an effective system of local self-government. At the same time, Ukrainian regions today do not have the necessary conditions for effective policy, which is related to the inconsistency of the existing model of regional management with real needs of the regions. The dominance of the role of central government and the inadequate capacity of local state administrations and local self-government bodies to create conditions for economic activity, the formation of the necessary technical and market infrastructure, and the implementation of development programs significantly hamper the processes of increasing the competitiveness of the regions.

Priority issues require such as decentralization of power, modernization of regional policy and the expansion of powers of local authorities regarding the development of territories. To make effective management decisions on the effective solution of these tasks, it is essential to develop advanced methodological approaches to monitoring and assessing the socio-economic development of regions with the use of an objective and adequate system of indicators that would ensure the accuracy of the assessment. Taking into account the tendencies of changes and giving an opportunity to carry out forecasting of regional development, the result of this policy should become:

– The ability of regional authorities to create conditions for local enterprises to achieve and maintain competitive advantages.
– Ability of the regions to provide production of competitive goods and services.
– The ability to realize the existing potential of the region while at the same time contributing to sustainable development, solving environmental and social problems.
– Ensuring high social standards and living standards for the population, including at the expense of not only creating new jobs, but also due to the high level of their quality.

The problem of using decentralization as a tool for increasing the efficiency of functioning of regional power, and as a result—regional competitiveness, has long been of interest to Ukrainian scientists and experts. This is due, in particular, to the successful realization of the principles of decentralization in practice in most of the EU states. Decentralization means that way of defining and differentiating tasks and functions, in which most of them move from the level of central bodies to a lower level and become their own tasks and responsibilities.

Decentralization is closely linked to the organization of public administration system. It promotes the building of an effective relationship between the central government and local government level. That is, decentralization is an extension and strengthening the rights and powers of local and regional self-government in relation to the independent decision-making and execution delegated by the state authorities. The transition to decentralized management is a characteristic feature of a large number of highly developed and developing countries. This process is explained by the desire of countries to improve the efficiency of public services, eliminate macroeconomic instability and accelerate the process of economic growth.

Increasing local budget revenues by stimulating local self-government to regional self-development through decentralization of financial resources is an important task for improving the competitiveness of the regions.

Decentralization, on the one hand, is an important condition for the self-development of regions, with another—can be a threat to both regional development and the integrity of the state: the risk of reducing the coordination between levels of government in the delegation of functions; increasing the level of conflict and contradictions between central government and local self-government bodies through power; inhibition of the implementation of state programs against the background of giving greater importance to local political priorities; attempts by central authorities to avoid responsibility for providing public services to the population, the removal of central governments from the solution of urgent issues; inconsistency of delegated authority and responsibilities with resources to perform public functions.

Uncertainty of strategic programming tools for socio-economic development at the regional and local levels, and the limited powers of local authorities in the field of international cooperation is an obstacle to the use of competitive advantages of the regions of Ukraine. The consistent decentralization of decision-making and empowerment in this process of regional and local authorities, as well as the improvement of the institutional base, should become a strategic reference point for state policy to strengthen the competitiveness of

Ukrainian regions. Decentralization contributes to strengthening the structures of local and regional authorities, both in terms of completeness of managerial capabilities and resource provision, ensures that local and regional communities are adequately accounted for, effectively implements the internal potential of the region, including local initiatives, the introduction of effective management through a clear separation of functions and the powers of managerial units of all levels.

5 CONCLUSIONS

Consequently, decentralization is a key element in the transition from a command economy to a market economy. There are two ways to achieve sustainable economic development in the region: either through external support, redistribution of funds between regions, or by mobilizing internal forces. Foreign experience shows that developed economies use market mechanisms for the influence of central government on the economic development of certain territories. In many countries, which are characterized by stable economic growth and which have undergone a stage of fiscal decentralization, effective and flexible mechanisms are adapted to change the economic situation.

Institutional support for regional development is a basic condition that forms the institutional basis for the development of a civilized democratic state. In our opinion, it is important to ensure institutional support to the development of various forms of self-organization of the population, to establish effective cooperation in the framework of the regional authorities—business structures— the public, support of various forms of public activity in order to effectively address the problems of regional development through the development of civil society and public consensus achievement.

REFERENCES

Ahunov, R.R. 2014. Vzaimosvyaz konkurentosposobnosti i vosproizvodstvennogo potentsiala regiona, *Izvestiya Irkutskoy gosudarstvennoy ekonomicheskoy akademii* 5(97): 79–89.

Boschma, R. 2004. Competitiveness of Regions from an Evolutionary Perspective, *Regional Studies* 38(9): 1001–1014.

Bristow, G. 2005. Everyone's a 'Winner': Problematising the Discourse of Regional Competitiveness, *Journal of Economic Geography* 5 (3): 285–304.

Cellini, R., & Soci, A. 2002. Pop Competitiveness, *Banca Nazionale del Lavoro, Quarterly Review* 55 (220): 71–101.

Huggins, R. et al. 2013. Regional Competitiveness: Theories and Methodologies for Empirical Analysis, JCC, *The Business and Economics Research Journal* 6(2): 155–172.

Lengyel, I., & Rechnitzer, J. 2013. The competitiveness of regions in the Central European transition countries, *The Macrotheme Review* 2(4): 106–121.

Martin, R. 2003. *A Study on the Factors of Regional Competitiveness.* Cambridge: University of Cambridge. Retrieved from http://ec.europa.eu/regional_policy/sources/docgener/studies/pdf/3cr/competitiveness.pdf.

Mongkhonvanit, J. 2014. *Coopetition for Regional Competitiveness*, Springer Briefs in Education.

Mrva, M., & Stachova, P. 2014. Regional development and support of SMEs—how university project can help, *Procedia—Social and Behavioral Sciences* 110: 617–626.

Porter, M. 2003. The Economic Performance of Regions, *Regional Studies* 37: 549–578.

Storper, M. 1997. *The regional world.* New York: The Guilford Press.

Thompson, N., & Ward, N. 2005. *Rural Areas and Regional Competitiveness.* Newcactle: Newcastle University upon Tyne. Centre for Rural Economy.

Vuković, D. et al. 2012. Defining competitiveness through the theories of new economic geography and regional economy, *J. Geogr. Inst. Cvijic* 62(3): 49–64.

Production Management and Business Development – Mihalčová et al. (Eds)
© *2019 Taylor & Francis Group, London, ISBN 978-1-138-60415-5*

Regional aspects of the development of municipal waste

M. Bačová & M. Stričík
Faculty of Business Economics with seat in Košice, University of Economics in Bratislava,
Košice, Slovak Republic

ABSTRACT: There was 19.67% of municipal and construction waste recovered in Slovakia in 2009, 77.65% was disposed and 2.68% was temporary stored in place of origin. It was disposed by landfill 77% of waste. In 2016, 33.20% of municipal and construction waste was recovered, 66.03% was disposed and 2.68% was temporary stored in place of origin. It was disposed by landfill 77% of waste. This contribution defines municipal waste construction waste and management of municipal and construction waste according to the applicable the Act of the National Council of the Slovak Republic No. 79/2015 on waste. This contribution also analyses the development of the amount of municipal waste and construction waste, with emphasis on the development of mixed municipal waste, and analyses the management of municipal waste—recovery, disposal, separation, waste temporary stored in place of origin in 2009–2017 in Slovakia and in eight Slovak regions.

1 INTRODUCTION

Municipal waste is defined as a household waste generated in the territory of a municipality during the activities of natural persons and waste of similar nature and composition originating from legal persons or sole traders, with the exception of waste generated during the immediate performance of activities which constitute the subject of business or activity of the legal person or sole trader, household waste is deemed to be waste from property serving for the individual recreation of natural persons, such as gardens, cabins or cottages or serving for the parking or storage of vehicles used for household purposes, especially garages, garage spaces and parking spaces due to Act no. 79 from 17th March 2015 on waste and on amendments to certain acts in Slovakia. Municipal waste also includes all waste which is generated in a municipality during the cleaning of public roads and places which are in the property or in administration of the municipality, as well as for the care of public greenery, including parks and cemeteries which are in the property or in administration of the municipality, and other greenery on the properties of natural persons. Mixed municipal waste is defined as an unsorted municipal waste or municipal waste after the components of municipal waste have been sorted out.

The municipalities are responsible for the management of municipal waste generated in the territory of the municipality, and minor construction waste generated in territory of the municipality.

Municipal waste management is an important part of the circular economy.

Peri (2018) states, that municipal solid waste management is a challenging issue. This problem needs to be addressed in order to achieve a sustainable urban policy. European directives and, subsequently, national standards set minimum standards for recycling and preparing for re-use of materials contained in municipal waste. Nevertheless, landfilling as a method of disposal continues is used to a considerable extent.

Recycling means a recovery operation by which waste materials are reprocessed into products, materials or substances either for the original or other purposes. It includes the reprocessing of organic material but it does not include energy recovery and the reprocessing into materials that are used as fuels or for backfilling operations. For example the recycling rate in Japan was roughly the same in 2007 (20.5%) as it was in 2002 (19.9%). It appears that recycling rates have reached some sort of steady state. The relevant policy question is whether the steady state is socially optimal (Kinnaman 2010).

Kinnaman (2014) pointed out the issue of socially optimal recycling rate of municipal waste. He notes that the socially optimal level of municipal the recycling rate is the level that minimises the overall social costs of managing municipal waste.

Preparation for re-use means checking, cleaning or repairing recovery operations, by which products or components of products representing waste are prepared so that they can be re-used without any other pre-processing.

Waste recovery means an operation where the principal result is waste serving a useful purpose by replacing other materials in production activities or in the wider economy, or waste being prepared to fulfil that function.

Waste disposal means an operation which is not recovery even where the operation has as a secondary consequence the reclamation of substances or energy. Landfilling means the deposition of waste at a landfill.

Waste prevention, preparing for re-use, recycling, other recovery and disposal (including landfilling) represent the hierarchy of waste management. (Directive 2008/98/EC of the European Parliament and of the Council, Act no. 79/2015 Coll.)

2 MATERIAL AND METHODS

The object of the research is the handling of MSW in the Slovak Republic.

Based on data from the Statistical Office of the Slovak Republic this contribution analyses the development of the amount of municipal waste and construction waste, with emphasis on the development of mixed municipal waste, and analyses the management of municipal waste—recovery, disposal, separation, waste temporary stored in place of origin in 2009–2017 in Slovakia and in eight Slovak regions.

3 RESULTS & DISCUSSION

The total municipal waste generated in the Slovak Republic in 2017 amounted to 2130 thousand tonnes. There were made some analysis over nine years in Slovakia with the result of increasing total quantity of waste of 22%. The amount of waste produced in this analysed period increased, with the exception of 2011, 2012 and 2013 when there was a decrease in waste generation (Figure 1).

Table 1. The basic characteristics of Regions in Slovakia in 2017.

Region	Person Number	Area Square km
Bratislava	646,365	2053
Trnava	561,764	4146
Trenčín	588.090	4502
Nitra	679,735	6344
Žilina	690,900	6809
Banská Bystrica	650,648	9454
Prešov	823,068	8973
Košice	798,660	6754

Source of data: Own processing according to Statistical Office of the Slovak republic 2018a.

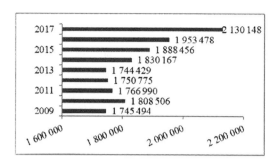

Figure 1. The development of municipal waste generated in Slovakia (in tonnes).
Source of data: Own processing according to Statistical Office of the SR 2018c.

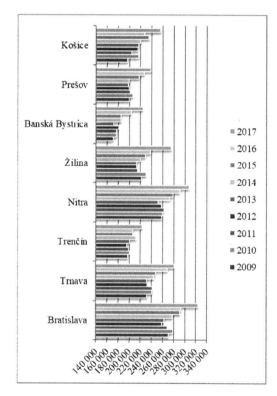

Figure 2. The development of municipal waste generated in regions in Slovakia (in tonnes).
Source of data: Own processing according to Statistical Office of the SR 2018c.

Figure 2 summarises the amount of municipal waste generated in eight regions in Slovakia. It demonstrates that in all region the total quantity of municipal was produced increased—in Bratislava region (20.05%) during analysed nine years, Trnava region (21.18%), Trenčín region (12.18%), Nitra region (19.16%), Žilina region (24.22%),

Banská Bystrica region (31.66%), Prešov region (19.36%) and Košice region (30.33%).

The analysis of the development of municipal waste generated in Slovakia and within Slovak Regions shows that during the analysed eight years, the amount of waste generate (kg per capita) in 2016 as compared to 2009 increased in Slovakia (38.02 kg per capita – 11.82%), in Bratislava region (25.28 kg per capita – 5.82%), Trnava region (65.67 kg per capita – 15.91%), Trenčín region (22.27 kg per capita – 6.79%), Nitra region (60.58 kg per capita – 16.54%), Žilina region (28.15 kg per capita – 8.87%), Banská Bystrica region (49.96 kg per capita – 19.09%), Prešov region (27.89 kg per capita – 11.27%) and Košice region (32.64 kg per capita – 12.93%). The development of municipal waste production (kg per capita) is illustrated in Figure 3.

Figure 4 shows an overview of structure of municipal waste in Slovakia and in Slovak regions in 2009.

Figure 5 shows an overview of structure of municipal waste in Slovakia and in Slovak regions in 2017.

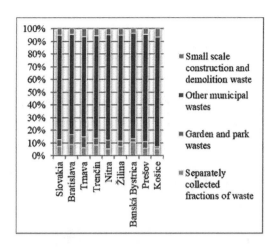

Figure 4. The structure of municipal waste in Slovakia and in Slovak regions in 2009 (%).
Source of data: Own processing according to Statistical Office of the SR 2018c.

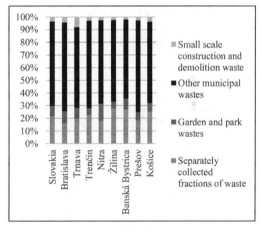

Figure 5. The structure of municipal waste in Slovakia and in Slovak regions in 2017 (%).
Source of data: Own processing according to Statistical Office of the SR 2018c.

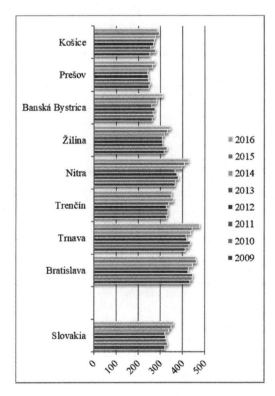

Figure 3. The development of municipal waste generated in Slovakia and in Slovak regions (in kg per capita).
Source of data: Own processing according to Statistical Office of the SR 2018d.

Comparison of Figure 4 and Figure 5 shows that the amount of separately collected fractions of waste is increasing and the volume of other municipal wastes is decreasing. It is a positive phenomenon. At the present, the pace of change is not enough.

Other municipal waste includes the mixed municipal waste.

Figure 6 shows the development of mixed municipal waste in Slovak regions. It demonstrates that from 2009 to 2017 in total only in Bratislava region the amount of mixed municipal waste

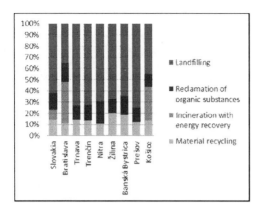

Figure 6. The development of mixed municipal waste generated Slovak regions in 2009–2017 (in tonnes).
Source of data: Own processing according to Statistical Office of the SR 2018c.

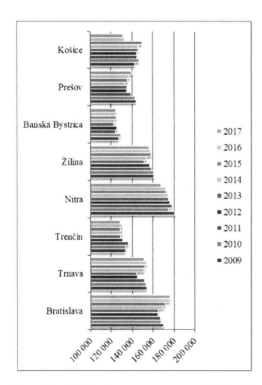

Figure 7. Municipal waste management in Slovakia and in Slovak Regions in 2017 (%).
Source of data: Own processing according to Statistical Office of the SR 2018b.

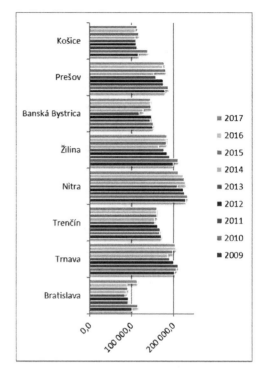

Figure 8. The development of amount of municipal waste sent to landfill in Slovak regions (in tonnes).
Source of data: Own processing according to Statistical Office of the SR 2018b.

increased (3.75%) and in other regions the amount of mixed municipal waste decreased—Košice region (−8.04%), Nitra region (−6.99%), Trenčín region (−3.66%), Prešov region (−2.97%), Žilina region (−2.69%), Banská Bystrica region (−1.78%) and Trnava region (−1.64%).

Figure 7 shows the municipal waste management in Slovakia and in Slovak Regions in 2017.

The amount of material recycling of municipal waste in Slovakia was 14% and in regions from 11 to 20%.

There are two incinerators in Slovakia The amount of municipal waste sent to incineration in 2017 are in Bratislava region 37%, in Košice region 30%, in other regions less than 1% and in Slovakia only 9%.

The amount of landfilling in 2017 was 61.6% in Slovakia, 35% in Bratislava region, 73% Trnava region, 72% Trenčín region, 69% in Nitra region, 67% in Žilina region, 65% in Banská Bystrica region, 75% in Prešov region and 45% in Košice region.

Figure 8 shows the amount of municipal waste sent to landfill.

4 CONCLUSION

There was generated 2130 thousand tons of municipal waste in 2017 in Slovakia. The total quantity of municipal waste production increased of 22% from the year 2009 to 2017. The total quantity of municipal waste production increased from 12 to 32% in Slovak regions. The largest share of the total amount of municipal waste produced in Slovakia is mixed municipal waste, which is gradually decreasing. The rate of decline is insufficient for Slovakia to meet the requirements of the European Commission. The amount of separated waste is growing. The problem is that more than 60% of the municipal waste ends in landfills.

ACKNOWLEDGEMENT

This contribution is a partial output of VEGA project no. 1/0582/2017 "Modeling the economic efficiency of material and energy recovery of municipal waste" addressed at the Faculty of Business Economics of the University of Economics in Bratislava with seat in Košice.

REFERENCES

Act No. 79/2015 Coll. on waste and amendments to certain acts.

Directive 2008/98/EC of the European parliament and of the Council of 19 November 2008 on waste and repealing certain Directives.

Kinnaman, T.C. 2014. Determining the socially optimal recycling rate. *Resources, Conservation and Recycling* 85: 5–10.

KinnamanT.C. 2010 The Optimal Recycling Rate. *Other Faculty Research and Publications.* Paper 6.

Peri, G. et al. 2018. Greening MSW management systems by saving footprint: The contribution of the waste transportation. *Journal of Environmental Management* 219: 74–83.

Statistical Office of the SR 2018a Population Density—SR, Areas, Regions, Districts, Urban, Rural [om7015rr].

Statistical Office of the SR 2018b. Municipal waste and small construction waste from municipalities according to the waste treatment categories (in Tonnes) [zp1005rs].

Statistical Office of the SR 2018c. Quantity of municipal waste according to the waste subgroup (in Tonnes) [zp3001rr].

Statistical Office of the SR 2018d. Relatively indicators from the area of treatment with municipal waste [zp3002rr].

Production Management and Business Development – Mihalčová et al. (Eds)
© 2019 Taylor & Francis Group, London, ISBN 978-1-138-60415-5

Mineral planning policy and investment mining projects in Slovakia

V. Bauer
Technical University of Košice, Košice, Slovak Republic

ABSTRACT: In the mining sector, the growing trend of investing in the extraction of industry minerals, especially on prospective deposits of minerals, can be observed throughout the all the world. With the limited movement of financial capital, investors and creditors, investment opportunities with lower risk profiles and stable returns on investment are being sought. Proposals for new mining projects are strictly monitored by both professional and incompetent public, and therefore, when assessing them, they often encounter conflicts of interest. In Slovakia, however, there are several prospective investment mining projects for deep mining, selected energy and non-ferrous construction materials. A separate problem is the preparation process, possibly also the implementation of a new investment mining project, which is currently subject to a number of administrative approval procedures, as well as to the strict supervision of the public and non-governmental organizations.

1 MINING OF MINERALS AND SUPPORT OF THE STATE RAW MATERIAL POLICY

Reliable setting of the state raw materials policy (SRMP) is very problematic in Slovakia's existing social and economic conditions. In Slovakia, there is a long-term failure to prepare a rational and practical concept of raw material policy, which would allow the realization of a selected prospective mining project. Frequently inconceivable legislative constraints shift the competence of the mining sector into almost inconceivable situations. Nevertheless, the Raw Material Policy of Slovakia represents the most appropriate tool for assessing the significance and usability of specific types of mineral resources located in our territory. Although the Slovak Republic is to a larger extent only "the poor owner of minor sources of minerals", there are also economically significant sources of raw minerals in our territory. In the long run, uranium and talc, can bring significant economic profit, while optimally adjusting socio-economic relationships and healthy economic and environmental system are predominantly prospective for mining. The particular importance is the economic potential of talc deposit, which is expected to have a more pervasive international penetration of world's raw materials markets.

The economic feasibility of these raw materials is directly related to the extraction process, which is technologically and economically formalized by the mining project for the mining process, until the complete extraction of the deposits on the deposit. An outreach project requires a consider-able amount of investments. Summarized investments directed to the mining project are almost always risky, and the investment risk rate is usually estimated in specific cases. In assessing the riskiness of the investment, account is taken in particular of the state of knowledge of the quality of the mineral in a given volume of mineral resources on the deposit, which is the basic economic parameter determining the economic value of the deposit and it is the greatest importance for potential investor in terms of the realization of the mining project. The mining project under consideration is then evaluated by the investor using standard tools, including the following economic studies:

- Expertise review (expert decision making), processed for level initial economic assessment of the project.
- Pre-feasibility study, (preliminary project feasibility study), it is prepared for necessary to confirm or challenge the project's intentions.
- Feasibility study (detailed feasibility study), intended for the detailed description of the mining project that is decisive from the perspective of the investor.

The investment mining project is preceded by a number of administrative and political processes, and also by the lobbies that a potential investor must undertake in order to allow access to raw material reserves on a particular deposit. These processes include some "necessary environmental practices" that are a standard part of the preparation of a new mining project when it is introduced into the implementation phase. These may be for potential investors or multinational investment groups, worldwide controlling the mining industry, certain complications, and causing considerable problems in project enforcement. Nevertheless, the mining companies' interest in some commodities is currently high, varying depending on the stock exchange or the commodity market. The overwhelmingly large mobile financial capital available for the extraction and trading of raw materials sector is mainly used by transnational, mostly monopolistic, mining companies that annually launch and implement several new mining projects on different continents of the world (Bauer 2013).

2 PROCESSES RELATED TO NEW INVESTMENT MINING PROJECTS

The preparation and implementation of a new investment mining project is a lengthy process that takes place in a certain time sequence derived from the scope of the project. This is mainly due to the optimal adjustment of its technological parameters, which are strongly influenced by the mining and mining conditions. In view of the expected economic results of the project, it is therefore very important to assess the impact of the key technical parameters as well as the efficiency indicators of the mining project. At present, there is no uniformly used methodology that would comprehensively evaluate the project in its technical, social, environmental and economic parts, so this problem is not adequately addressed. Several methodologies are mainly aimed at assessing the economic risks of the mining project, taking into account investments with lower risk profiles and stable investment returns. What is important is the number of financial resources needed to implement the project, which is most often reflected in capital expenditures and total costs. Projective proposals for a specific mining project will be reflected in the expected economic results and indicators that are very important for alternative investment decisions.

When creating a mining project for a new deposit site, several processes are taking place in a sequence of steps, which are approved and documented by the relevant administrative institutions of the state administration. The sequence of the process steps (see Figure 1), in terms of the mining business in Slovakia, is essential as follows:

1. Development of a geological survey according to the geological law.
2. Determination of the protected deposit area.
3. Determination of the mining space.
4. Development of the project preparation of the bearing mining.

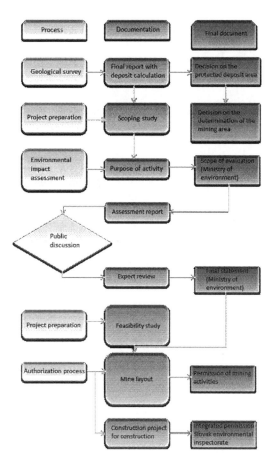

Figure 1. Sequence of steps prior to the start of mining (Herman 2017).

5. Assessment of the environmental impact of extractive activities.
6. Demonstration of necessary mining rights and design activities.
7. Processing of the opening, preparation and mining project.
8. Preparation of public procedure and work with the public in relation to the project.

It is necessary to implement the final evaluation parameters of the aforementioned processes, as well as the technical and economic evaluation parameters of the efficiency of the mining business, which determine the extent of the costs and determine the level of the investment resources in the short and the long term. The following evaluation economic instruments are used to finance the mining project:

– **Cash—flow** as the sum of all financial flows resulting from investment in the project and its factors.

- **The payback period PBP** – the payback period, monitored for the entire project, regardless of cost and revenue developments.
- **Return on investment ROI** – to assess the economic efficiency of the investments made.
- **Internal Rate of Return (IRR)**, evaluates the current effective return on investment for the entire project.
- **Net Present Value** assesses the current difference between the expected earnings and capital expenditure values.

For all these instruments, the mining project also takes into account mining project design tools, starting with expert review to feasibility study, which take into account important aspects of the mining project (type of deposit, volume and quality of mineral reserves, raw material treatment, infrastructure building, investment and operational etc.), and which play an important role in financial decision making in the process of securing financial capital. When conducting a feasibility study it is necessary to evaluate the basic project indicators based on the results of the cash flow, cost and revenue analyses of the final financial plan, but also the financial efficiency and feasibility of the project, the risk factors and the objectives of the technical and economic study (Bauer 2013).

The feasibility study is based on the baseline technological characteristics of the project, taking into account its projected outcomes and expected benefits. At the same time, the following socio-economic parameters of the project are assessed:

- Economic evaluation of mineral reserves.
- The technical and technological solution of the project.
- Impact on the environment, socio-economic impact.
- Admission and operating costs.
- Financial plan of the project.
- Risk analysis.
- Assessing the effectiveness and sustainability of the project.
- Reliability and financial profitability of the project.
- Analysis of conflicts of interest in the implementation and realization of mining.

Also, a well-prepared feasibility study may, in a new mining project, create a conflict of interest in its enforcement and implementation, as the permitting process is subject to a more complex process and often conflicts with nature conservationists and non-governmental non-profit groups. There are some major deposits of gold, talc and uranium in Slovakia that is of interest to a potential foreign investor (usually a supranational mining company), so it is important to assess these minerals in a comprehensive way, including the design of an investment mining project.

3 EVALUATION OF MINING PROJECTS ON SELECTED DEPOSITS OF MINERALS

From the point of view of foreign investors, there are currently three—four mining projects in Slovakia with varying perspectives of their mining. Specifically, there are two standard gold deposits at Biely Vrch near Detva and Kremnica—Šturec, one unique uranium deposit at Kurišková—Jahodná near Košice and one very important deposit of talc in Gemerská Poloma. In the case of all the listed deposits, the processes related to the preparation of the mining project have been initiated in the recent past, with the intention to obtain and process the raw material. However, over the course of a few years, there has been a complete lack of implementation of gold and uranium mining projects, due to unresolved conflicts of interest between interested communities and various conservation associations. In the case of gold and uranium mining projects, unprecedented barriers to their legitimate enforcement have emerged in the preparatory processes. And despite the economic profitability of projects, defined by IRR, Real-Time Ratio (PBP), and Net Profit (NPV), which is a key factor in bank and lending decision-making processes when providing finance for a planned project. These two projects clearly demonstrated the impact of a very strong emphasis on the environmental aspect of the mining project, which prevails in the general public's awareness. In assessing projects, they are almost unrecognized and do not take into account the social aspects of the mining project.

In the promotion of selected mining projects to the realization, therefore, the main effort of investors is to approach the unqualified public in such a way that the social and environmental benefits of the future mining are felt by the municipality and the city and their inhabitants, in which there are locations with important deposits of minerals (Csikósová et al. 2013). In relation to the public, the existing methodologies emphasize all four aspects of the mining project, ie it must be social, environmentally acceptable, economically and technologically and technically perfectly mastered, even in the last detail (Fig. 2).

When assessing the environmental aspects, the location of the deposit is taken into account, i. the place where the potential mining project will be carried out, the expected streams of interest, finding solutions and setting up measures to eliminate the environmental impacts of mining. Similarly, it is necessary to evaluate the technical aspects of

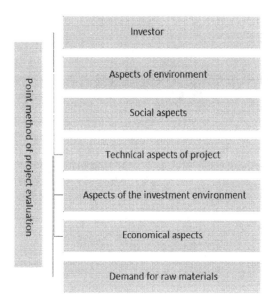

Figure 2. Project evaluation by selected criteria (Herman 2017).

the project in terms of the level of project design, the condition of the bearing review and the operational risks of the project. Aspects of the investment environment are mainly given by issuing/not issuing the permits and authorizations, site infrastructure, and time attributes of the project. The economic aspects of the project are measurable by IRR, NPV and PBP values and are supported by real demand for raw materials on world commodity exchanges.

The final evaluation criteria for the mining project must be relevant for non-governmental non-profit organizations, environmental protection groups, and mining of affected municipalities and towns. Building the complex criteria for the mining project evaluation, which would be acceptable to non-governmental non-profit organizations

or conservationists, however is a very difficult task. Mainly because the miners of the mining projects submit their negative arguments at the stage when a potential investor submits his intention to subsequently submit it to the public with the worst possible scenario that can occur during mining. In the subjective assessment, they point to all the negative aspects of the mining project with the main goal of getting the affected public as well as the surrounding area, often by way of petition, to their side.

4 CONCLUSION

At present, the practice is that many mining projects are influenced by the subjective view of the third sector and are totally halted, respectively are suspended for a long time. A new investment mining project may have some hope for success only if the lay public develops a view of the project and takes account of several aspects of the project, using appropriate assessment criteria, when accepting an investor. Basically, there is no other alternative with currently set rules.

REFERENCES

Bauer, V. 2013. *Planning of minerals industry extraction.* Košice: Technical university.
Bauer, V. 2013. *Mining technology and processes.* Košice: Technical university.
Bauer, V., & Herman, M. 2014. Expected structural changes of brown coal and lignite mining industry at Slovakia. In *Górnictwo węgla brunatnego,* 8. International brown coal mining congress, Belchatow, 7.–9.5.2014 (pp. 35–42). Krakow: ART-TEKST.
Csikósová, A., Čulková, K. & Antošová, M. 2013. Magnesite industry in the Slovak Republic. *Gospodarka Surowcami Mineralnymi,* 29(3): 21–35.
Herman, M. 2017. Proposal of methodology to support the implementation and implementation of mining projects. In Dissertation, TU Košice FBERG.
Rybár, M. et al. 2000. *Oceňovanie ložísk nerastných surovín.* Košice: TU F BERG.

Production Management and Business Development – Mihalčová et al. (Eds)
© 2019 Taylor & Francis Group, London, ISBN 978-1-138-60415-5

Neuromarketing for evaluating new technologies in marketing management

J. Berčík, J. Paluchová & J. Gálová
Faculty of Economics and Management, Slovak University of Agriculture in Nitra, Nitra, Slovak Republic

ABSTRACT: Thanks to modern technologies, retail is changing at an incredibly fast pace, which is visible in everyday shopping. All these changes are taking place in accordance with the development of information and communication technologies. In general, basic retail trends can be divided into two groups. Within the first, trends are inspired by the past, while the second group includes trends that arise and are developed based on current technological solutions and predictions of future consumer behavior. The paper highlights new possibilities of exploring the perception of modern technologies in retail, as there is an increasing need for their implementation. The aim is also to point out the different aspects of the perception of these technologies at an implicit and explicit level. The paper concludes proposals and recommendations based on a survey for the marketing management of retail stores as well as the economic practice.

1 INTRODUCTION

Fast, interactive and convenient shopping with a scanner in hand where the customer places goods directly into the bag, all essential information are in one place in a mobile application, fast self-service cash registers, interactive information displays, always up-to-date electronic price tags, or even monitoring and analyzing the behavior of people while they are moving in a store, as well as a detailed analysis of data from the store (data mining), on which the decision-making of marketing management and sellers is based, these all serve primarily to improve the comfort and experience of shopping as well as to predict behavior. It is clear that in a challenging competitive environment, marketing management seeks to perceive and focus on customer needs and wants, but also to monitor the development of modern technological possibilities as well as the activity of competition. In this case, however, it is important to correctly decide to what extent new technologies are beneficial to particular purchase segments, in order to achieve the desired effect in the form of making purchases more attractive and simpler. This means that, in addition to understanding the needs and wishes of their customers, it is also essential for business success to focus on how these customers change due to lifestyle changes that have been initiated also by smart mobile devices (smartphones), Internet access, as well as information access and, last but not least, the phenomenon of social networks. Not only younger consumers want everything fast and ideally right now. When they do not get it, they lose

patience and go to the competition. At the same time, if the technology is not easy to control, they lose interest very quickly. Regardless of the complexity and functionality of each technology, they have an increasingly important role, and marketing management is therefore important to address the extent to which their implementation is particularly beneficial in terms of customer perception and cost.

2 THEORETICAL BACKGROUND

Consumer goals play an important role in determining how consumers perceive the retail environment and management and various retail marketing mix elements (Mark & Reynolds 2003). Goals such as entertainment, recreation, social interaction, and intellectual stimulation (Bielik & Horská 2008, Mravcová 2015) also affect the way consumers proceed through the stages of the consumer decision process. Greval et al. (2009) present, that retailers manage systematically undertake in-store activities (e.g., taste tests and demonstrations) to increase consumer involvement and purchase. Retail environmental factors, such as social features, design, and ambience, can result in enhanced pleasure and arousal. Butler (2008) explains, neuromarketing is concerned with the general nature of natural laws because it has been defined as understanding human behavior in the specific context of markets and marketing exchanges in order to achieve a fuller understanding of consumer behavior. Neuromarketing—or consumer neuroscience resorts to methods and research insights regarding the human brain, seeking to learn and solve problems in the marketing field. When neuromarketing communicates with the fields of psychology, neuroscience, and marketing, it reveals the interdisciplinary face of scientific knowledge (Khushaba et al. 2013, Cruz et al. 2016). Consumer neuroscience is an emerging interdisciplinary field that combines psychology, neuroscience, and economics to study how the brain is physiologically affected by advertising and marketing strategies Madan (2010), Prokeinová & Hanová (2016). Ohme et al. (2009) introduce the change in the human brain signal, denoted as Electroencephalogram (EEG), and its main spectral bands of Delta (0–4 Hz) Theta (3–7 Hz), Alpha (8–12 Hz), Beta (13–30 Hz), and Gamma (30–40 Hz) is observed to examine consumers' cognitive or affective processes in response to prefabricated marketing stimuli. New innovation technologies in business provide benefits for both consumers by supporting the decision-making process and retailers by providing updated information on client's behaviors and market trends. On the one hand, these technologies allow consumers to (a) achieve information and customized contents on favorite products, services, sales, promotions, etc., (b) compare and choose among alternatives, (c) search for items, and (d) calculate total purchases, by providing more convenient experiences in terms of time saving and providing entertainment. On the other, these technologies provide constantly updated information on market segments, preferences, needs, while shopping, etc., which can be exploited for the development of more efficient (direct) marketing strategies (Pantano et al. 2013). As Kowatsch & Maass (2010) present, to improve the traditional points of sale by enriching the provided information through the most recent advances in 3D graphics, as well as to provide retailers with information on consumers' in-store behavior. To date, the most powerful innovative technologies are RFID (Radio Frequency Identification) systems (reader and writer for providing additional information on products), storefront displays enriched with virtual reality elements (i.e. virtual mannequins), smart shopping trolleys capable of supporting consumers during the in-store experience, and recommendation systems for mobile. In Verhoef et al. (2009) paper, self-service technologies have been introduced to supplement the social environmental factor (i.e., employee component) in stores. The use of self-service technology (e.g., self-checkout and price scanner machines mounted on a shopping cart) can influence the consumer shopping experience. Sorescu et al. (2011) present, the customer interface design concerns the way in which a retailer structures the exchange process with its customers. Interface decisions require not only the positioning of the store in terms of pricing, assortment, and overall design (e.g., whether the store should be organized as a convenience store, specialty store, or themed brand store), but also require selecting the structure of the interface itself (e.g., kiosks, stores-within-a-store, catalogs, e-commerce, or mobile commerce).

3 MATERIAL AND METHOD

The survey was conducted in Slovakia from February to May 2017 through a personal survey of 3067 respondents. There were 1221 men (40%) and 1846 women (60%) participating.

In terms of age structure, 66% of people aged 18–24, 27% of people aged 25–49, 5% of people aged 50–64, and 2% of people over 65, took part in the survey. The survey was conducted through mobile devices (tablets, mobiles, iPads), because, in addition to explicit feedback, implicit feedback was recorded by measuring the reaction time. The commercially available iCode™ application from Neurohm in Poland was used to measure the reaction time, the development of which was preceded by several studies in the field of neuromarketing.

iCode™ reflects actual attitudes of consumers more precisely than just explicit opinions assessed only by traditional questionnaires. The time that consumers' brains need to produce an answer shows how certain consumers are and how likely their opinion will be translated into actual behavior. iCode™ has the form of a short online survey, where the Response Time measurement was applied to reveal instinctive reactions, enhancing our understanding of consumer behavior (iCode 2017).

Primary data processing was carried out using descriptive statistics (frequency, quantiles, averages and standard deviations) as well as inductive statistics (chi-squared test). This test is used to determine whether the difference between the observed and expected frequencies is only random (independent variables, due to sampling variation) or is too significant to be merely incidental (there is a relationship between variables) (Rimarčík 2015, Paralič 2013).

The assumptions in this test were defined as follows:

H_0: Variables are independent.
H_1: Variables are dependent.

Computing the test statistic was based on a contingency table (Table 1).

The value of the test statistic was computed using the equation (1)

$$G = \sum_{i=1}^{r} \sum_{j=1}^{s} \frac{\left(n_{ij} - n_{ij}^{\cdot} \right)^2}{n_{ij}^{\cdot}} \tag{1}$$

where …

The rejection of the null hypothesis was based on the chi-squared distribution. The null hypothesis is rejected if

Table 1. Contingency table.

	Variable 1 1st category	Variable 1 2nd category	...	Total
Variable 2 1st category	observed frequencies	observed frequencies	...	$n_1.$
Variable 2 2nd category	observed frequencies	observed frequencies	...	$n_2.$
Variable 2 3rd category	observed frequencies	observed frequencies	...	$n_3.$
...	...	...	...	$n_j.$
Total	$n._1$	$N._2$	$n._j$	n

$$n_{i.} = \sum_{j=1}^{s} n_{ij} \quad n_{.j} = \sum_{i=1}^{r} n_{ij}$$

Source: Paralič 2003.

$$G > X_{1-\alpha}^2 \left[(k-1)(m-1) \right] \qquad (2)$$

where ...

The chi-squared test for independence was computed using the RapidMiner software and MS Excel.

4 RESULT AND DISCUSSION

A survey conducted to perceive new technologies on a sample of 3067 respondents shows that almost all respondents (97%) have experience with new technologies. 2% of women and 1% of men responded that they had no experience with new technologies. Those who said "yes" most often mentioned the self-service cashier 89%, mobile applications 71%, interactive displays and large screens 51%, and self-scanning purchases 40%.

It is interesting to see the responses by measuring reaction time. It is a modern, implicit method that can capture a subconscious perception of a person, and hence whether or not he or she has a serious answer. Using this method when questioning whether they evaluate new technologies positively suggests very interesting findings. For those who answered yes (77.5%), a high reliability level can be found based on the measurement of reaction time (subconscious perception), as 57% of them actually identified themselves with this answer. An opposite example is moderate reliability for answers "no" (5.9%), because only 3% of them were really convinced by their answer. 16.6% of people were not able to comment at all.

From the results we can conclude that using multiple methods when surveying the same, we can get different answers. While on the basis of a traditional survey, most people clearly favor new technologies in the store with highly positive ratings, measuring their response speed with a special application, we find

that only 57% of them actually identified themselves with the answer. The reason is the fact that modern technology not always meets customer expectations. An example may be self-scanning of purchases, which is often associated with negative reactions, especially in the early stages (mainly in the case of non-packaged goods) and by random checks, which can even extend the length of the purchase itself.

It is certainly worth mentioning the question whether people would welcome more similar new technologies, for which most (54.6%), especially younger respondents, said "yes". Younger respondents were not able to comment at all or labeled the "no" response (14.8%) in this case.

In addition to evaluating respondents' opinions, we also focused on hypothesis analysis. In the first hypothesis, we assumed that there is a dependence

Figure 1. Measuring reaction time on how people evaluate new technologies.
Source: Export of the platform iCode™ (2017).
*Note: LSS – The Level Scoring System, HI YES – HI ANSWERS score.

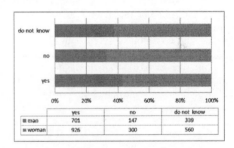

Figure 2. Dependence between gender and preference (by welcoming more) of new technologies.
Source: Own processing based on research in 2017.

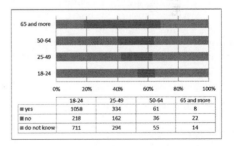

Figure 3. Dependence between the age and the preference of a store/shopping center/place that has modern technology.
Source: Own processing based on research in 2017.

between gender and preference (by welcoming more) of new technologies. The difference in preference based on gender is shown graphically in Figure 2.

This dependence was verified using the chi-squared test at a significance level of 0.05, and the hypothesis of the dependence of these attributes was confirmed.

We also wanted to verify whether the age is dependent on the fact whether the store/shopping center/place of preference is modern (Fig. 3). In this case, the hypothesis about the dependence of attributes tested at a significance level of 0.05 by the chi-squared test is confirmed.

5 CONCLUSION

Although technology has its importance and merit directly at the point of sale and it improves the convenience and speed of shopping, it must also serve customers, therefore should be tailored to be simple and user-friendly as much as possible. At the time when shopping is not just about meeting needs but also about experience, the implementation of new technologies can be very helpful. Marketing management should, however, prior to their actual implementation, consider various aspects, such as the perception of these technologies (not only through traditional research tools, where the answer may be distorted by the so-called desired response—the answer that is expected and common to them), but also the total costs associated with their implementation. The worst case scenario is a considerable investment with a relatively low impact on consumer comfort (e.g. complicated use). Even today, a very common thing, such as a self-service cashier, may take the form of a simpler and more complicated form depending on the manufacturer and the price, and therefore all aspects must be carefully considered. Neuromarketing is an area that offers marketing management more relevant information about real consumer perceptions, and can also provide valuable advice on the actual deployment and localization of particular technological solutions at the point of sale or provision of services. However, the consumer cannot feel the pressure that the seller wants to sell something immediately. When the customer is comfortable in the shop, he will gladly come back later and buy what he needs.

ACKNOWLEDGEMENT

The paper is part of the research projects KEGA 038SPU-4/2016 "Implementation of new technologies and interdisciplinary relationships in practical education of consumer studies" and VEGA 1/0570/18 "The Use of Consumer Neuroscience in the Implementation of Aromachology in Selected Sectors of the Economy", as well as part of the Grant Agency of the SUA in Nitra project 03-GA SPU-17 "Consumer neuroscience and its use in aromachology" solved at the Department of Marketing and Trade, Faculty of Economics and Management, Slovak University of Agriculture in Nitra.

REFERENCES

Benda Prokeinová, R. & Hanová, M. 2016. Comparison of selected econometrics tools of the consumer behaviour. *1st Business & entrepreneurial economics (BEE) conference.* Zagreb: Sveučilište u Zagrebu, 330.

Bielik, P. & Horská, E. 2008. Internalization at the Slovak agro-business: focused on competitiveness, territorial expansion and bringing values to customers. In *Agricultural market and trade: evidence and perspective of V4 region and its neighbour.* Wies Jutra, 10–42.

Butler, M.R. 2008. Neuromarketing and the perception of knowledge. *Journal of Consumer Behavior* (7): 415–419.

Cruz, C.M.L. et al. 2016. Neuromarketing and the advances in the consumer behavior studies: a systematic review of the literature. *International Journal of Business and Globalization* 17(3): 330–351.

Grewal, D. et al. 2009. Customer Experience Management in Retailing: An Organizing Framework. *Journal of Retailing* 85(1): 1–14.

iCode. 2017. Reveal Consumers' True Attitudes. Available at: https://icodetm.com/ [Accessed 2018, April 18].

Khushaba, R.N. et al. 2013. Consumer neuroscience: Assessing the brain response to marketing stimuli using electroencephalogram (EEG) and eye tracking. *Expert Systems with Applications* (40): 3830–3812.

Kowatsch, T. & Maass, W. 2010. In-store consumer behavior: How mobile recommendation agents influence usage intentions, product purchase, and store preferences. *Computers in Human Behavior* (26): 697–704.

Madan, C.R. 2010. Neuromarketing: The next step in market research? *Eureka* 1(1): 34–42.

Mark, A.J. & Reynolds, K. 2003. Hedonic Shopping Motivations. *Journal of Retailing* 79(2): 77–95.

Mravcová, A. 2015. Environmental challenges in rural development in the context of global education. In Mura, L., Bumbalová, M., Gubáňová, M. 2016. *Sustainability of rural areas in practice: Conference proceeding from international scientific conference.* Nitra, 416–426.

Ohme, R. et al. 2009. Analysis of neurophysiological reactions to advertising stimuli by means of EEG and Galvanic skin response measures. *Journal of Neuroscience, Psychology, and Economics* 2(1): 21–31.

Pantano, E. et al. 2013. Obsolescence risk in advanced technologies for retailing: A management perspective. *Journal of Retailing and Consumer Service*, 20: 225–233.

Paralič, J. 2003. Objavovanie znalostí v databázach. In *Elfa s.r.o.* Košice. 8.

Rimarčík, M. 2015. Opisné charakteristiky. Available at: http://rimarcik.com/navigator/och.html. [Accessed 2015, January 13].

Sorescu, A. et al. 2011. Innovations in Retail Business Models. *Journal of Retailing* 87(1): 3–16.

Verhoef, P.C. et al. 2009. Customer Experience Creation: Determinants, Dynamics and Management Strategies. *Journal of Retailing* 85(1): 31–41.

Production Management and Business Development – Mihalčová et al. (Eds)
© 2019 Taylor & Francis Group, London, ISBN 978-1-138-60415-5

Trends in FDI inflows in manufacturing support services

A. Bobenič Hintošová

Faculty of Business Economics with seat in Košice, University of Economics in Bratislava, Košice, Slovak Republic

ABSTRACT: The main aim of the present paper is to examine the trend in foreign direct investment inflows in conditions of selected manufacturing support service sectors in Slovakia covering not only traditional support service sectors (as transportation and storage; administrative and support services), but also shared service center sectors supporting new strategies for companies' functioning. The correlation analysis conducted for the period from 2009 to 2015 based on the data processed by National Bank of Slovakia showed that there are rather week interconnections among analysed sectors in attracting FDI inflows. Going out from the overview of new successful investment projects, Slovakia is becoming a hub attracting many financial, IT, accounting and other service providers.

1 INTRODUCTION

Generally, foreign direct investment (FDI) is characterised as an investment made by a company or individual of one country in business interests in another country, in the form of either establishing business operations or acquiring business assets in the other country, such as ownership or controlling interest in a foreign company. Increase in foreign direct investment inflows is usually considered a direct accelerator of economic growth and regional development. On the other hand, foreign direct investments may result in regional as well as sectoral and industrial disparities within national economy; hence, we will look more closely at foreign direct investment flows within service sectors.

Services are generally used throughout the manufacturing process and the manufacturing value chain. Some services are needed in the early stage of the chain (e.g. research and development); some are needed at the end (retailing, maintenance and repair); and some are needed at every stage (telecommunications and financial services) (Nordås 2010, Miroudot & Rouzet 2013). According to ECSIP (2014), when taking account of both direct and indirect linkages, the average service content of manufactured goods produced in the EU reaches close to 40% of the total value of final manufacturing goods produced. The bulk of these services are distribution services (15%), transport and communication (8%) as well as business services which ranges between less than 10 to even 20% and more across EU member states.

Within the present paper the analysis is conducted not only in conditions of traditional support service sectors (as transportation and storage; administrative and support services); however, in the center of our interest are also shared service center sectors supporting new strategies for companies' functioning. Their dynamic growth can be observed especially in the countries of Central and Eastern Europe (Ślusarczyk 2017). Knol et al. (2014) define shared services centers as half-autonomic organizational units that provide, previously dispersed services of support for the external clients within the organization, first, in order to lower the costs. These centers are not a uniform category; however, we can distinguish centers of BPO type (business process outsourcing) using a process approach and ITO centers (information technology outsourcing) focusing on information technologies (Ślusarczyk 2017). Thus, the paper deals also with information and communication sector and professional, scientific and technical activities.

The main aim of the present paper is to examine the trend in foreign direct investment inflows in conditions of selected manufacturing support service sectors in Slovakia. The quantitative analysis is supplemented by successful investment stories.

2 FOREIGN DIRECT INVESTMENT INFLOWS

The following part of the paper presents previous empirical findings dealing specifically with the topic of FDI in service sectors in Central and Eastern European countries followed by presentation of development of FDI inflows within selected manufacturing support service sectors in Slovakia and analysis of potential intersectoral relationship.

2.1 Previous empirical findings

Literature and previous empirical findings dealing specifically with the topic of FDI in service sectors in conditions of Central and Eastern European countries is rather limited. One of the few is a work of Capik & Drahokoupil (2011) who state that foreign direct investments in the service sector are widely attributed an important role in bringing more skill-intensive activities into the Visegrád Four (V4). This region relied heavily on FDIs in manufacturing, which was often found to generate activities with limited skill content. This contribution deconstructs the chaotic concept of "business services" by analysing the actual nature of service sector activities outsourced and offshored to the V4. Using the knowledge-based economy (KBE) as a benchmark, they assessed the potential of service sector outsourcing in contributing to regional competitiveness by increasing the innovative capacity. They also discussed the role of state policies towards service sector FDI. The authors argue that the recent inward investments in business services in the V4 mainly utilize existing local human capital resources, and their contribution to the development of the KBE is limited to employment creation and demand for skilled labour.

Another study by Melikhova et al. (2015) deals also with FDI in services within Visegrád economies. The authors try to answer the question what services appear to grow faster than the whole economy from inward FDI point of view. These are mostly the knowledge-intensive services: water and air transport in Hungary, post and telecommunications and financial intermediation in the Czech Republic. Real estate and business services grow faster than the entire economy in all V4 countries. Further, the authors revealed a strong correlation between the changes in services FDI and the variation in global tertiarisation effects. The growing inward FDI in services is related to the increasing use of both domestic and imported tertiary intermediates by the entire production systems of the V4 countries.

With the topic of foreign direct investments specifically in conditions of shared service industry in Poland is dealing the study by Ślusarczyk & Golnik (2015). The study provides and overview of Polish shared industry, as the area international investors search for savings and quality improvement for their companies and examines the trends in foreign direct investments and their current shape on the international market.

The broad study conducted by Duboz et al. (2016) explored FDI location determinants in service functions in the EU-28. They considered simultaneously three sectors and eight service functions for 271 European regions. Their fundamental findings are that service functions location choices are different according to sectors and that location determinants vary according to the service function considered.

Sass et al. (2018) in their most recent study analyzed the impact of FDI on the host economy in four selected service industries in two areas: export and employment. According to them FDI in the four selected service industries differ in terms of their vertical or horizontal nature: in business services FDI is predominantly vertical; in financial services and telecommunications it is predominantly horizontal; while in computer-related service activities both types can be found. Based to these results, the impact on the host economy differs in the four service industries. They found a positive and significant impact on exports in vertical business services and in horizontal telecommunications services, and on employment in business services and, to a lesser extent, in financial services. The positive impact either diminished or disappeared during the global recession of 2008–2009. The comparison of the four Visegrád countries demonstrates the heterogeneous intensity and significance of this impact, indicating their different specializations in the analyzed services industries.

The present paper aims to complement the existing empirical findings with analysis of FDI inflows not only in traditional but also in shared service sectors specifically in conditions of Slovakia.

2.2 Data and methodology

In this paper, description of FDI based on directional principle is used. Thus, inward direct investment is an investment by a non-resident direct investor in a direct investment enterprise resident in the host economy; the direction of the influence by the direct investor is "inward" for the reporting economy (RC). FDI statistics compiled according to the directional principle show inward investments taking into account also reverse investments (i.e. reverse investments of the reporting country are recorded as negative inward investments).

More specifically, in accordance with recommendation of OECD (2008) for the reporting country, inward FDI is summarised as follows: Inward investment = investments by direct investors abroad in direct investment enterprises in the RC *minus* reverse investments by direct investment enterprises in the RC in their direct investors abroad *plus* investments by fellow enterprises abroad in resident fellow enterprises where the ultimate controlling parent of the resident fellow enterprise is non-resident in the RC *minus* investments by resident fellow enterprises in fellow enterprises abroad where the ultimate controlling parent of the resident fellow enterprise is non-resident in the RC.

The overview of foreign direct investment inflows presented in this paper is based on input data (in thousands EUR) processed by National Bank of Slovakia for the period from 2009 to 2015 and covers following sectors (marked in accordance with NACE Rev. 2):

– Transportation and storage *(TS)*.
– Accommodation and food service activities *(AFSA)*.
– Information and communication *(IC)*.
– Financial and insurance activities *(FIA)*.
– Real estate activities *(REA)*.
– Professional, scientific and technical activities *(PSTA)*.
– Administrative and support services *(ASSA)*.

The graphical presentation of the input data is supplemented by correlation analysis using Pearson and Spearman correlation coefficients.

2.3 *Results*

The following Figure 1 shows development of FDI inflows separately within analysed sectors.

It is obvious that the total volume of inward FDI was the highest in 2011 influenced mainly by foreign direct investment inflows into financial and insurance companies. In 2014 the administrative and support service activities were most attractive for FDI inflows. In the following period, the inward FDI to these sectors did not show big differences. Based on the presented overview it cannot be concluded that shared service industries has attracted the highest volume of inward FDI within service sectors. However, especially within information and communication sector as well as transportation and storage sector the growing tendency of FDI inflows in the recent years are obvious. The negative signs of the inward FDI in particular sectors can be explained by reverse investments of foreign subsidiaries located in Slovakia. Following Table 1 presents simple statistics of the data used for further analysis.

Further Table 2 presents results of correlation analysis of intersectoral relationships of FDI inflows. Based on the values of Pearson correlation coefficients and p-values there is only one statistically significant negative relationship namely between FDI inflows into information and communication sectors and real estate activities. This was confirmed also by Spearman correlation coefficient which detected also rather nonlinear relationships between transportation and storage sectors on one hand and real estate activities as well as professional, scientific and technical activities on the other hand and also in case of administrative and support service activities and accommodation and food service activities. Surprisingly, no statistically significant relation was detected between total volume of inward FDI and inflows into particular sectors. We can conclude that there are rather week interconnections among analysed sectors in attracting FDI inflows.

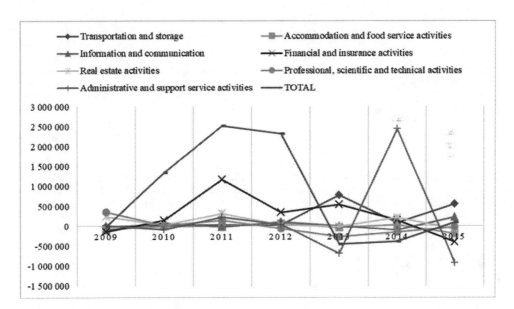

Figure 1. Volume of inward FDI in selected sectors and total in the Slovak republic (in thousand EUR). Source: Own processing according to data from National Bank of Slovakia.

Table 1. Simple statistics—inward FDI.

Variable	Mean	Std Dev	Median	Minimum	Maximum
I_TS	213.780	318.847	33.263	−5217	781.028
I_AFSA	−29.859	82.768	−10.982	−188.273	62.007
I_IC	27.272	117.696	1072	−100.158	220.348
I_FIA	258.438	505.923	152.308	−402.694	1168.021
I_REA	107.302	147.187	34.843	−71.013	320.517
I_PSTA	1129	203.665	−18.502	−272.275	350.634
I_ASSA	145.778	1094.642	21.854	−930.248	2435.077
I_TOTAL	774.080	1268.151	95.664	−454.968	2511.474

Source: Own processing according to data from National Bank of Slovakia.

Table 2. Pearson and Spearman correlation coefficients between sectoral inflows of FDI.

	I_TS	I_AFSA	I_IC	I_FIA	I_REA	I_PSTA	I_ASSA	I_TOTAL
I_TS	1	−0.50066	0.35896	−0.13044	−0.64162	−0.60540	−0.51866	−0.53932
I_AFSA	−0.07143	1	−0.43312	0.60258	0.37126	−0.23551	0.57100	0.44396
I_IC	0.42857	−0.07143	1	−0.32890	−0.79928**	−0.23333	−0.62525	0.24348
I_FIA	0.17857	0.60714	−0.17857	1	0.48809	−0.09473	0.11106	0.56677
I_REA	−0.71429*	0.32143	−0.78571**	0.32143	1	0.54720	0.57874	0.21969
I_PSTA	−0.85714**	−0.28571	−0.28571	−0.28571	0.60714	1	−0.10585	0.27986
I_ASSA	−0.32143	0.78571*	−0.57143	0.46429	0.75000*	0.07143	1	−0.11285
I_TOTAL	−0.46429	0.35714	0.32143	0.21429	0.32143	0.53571	0.25000	1

Note: The asterisks denote the statistical significance of coefficients on a level of 10% (*), 5% (**), and 1% (***), based on p-values. The Spearman's rank correlation coefficients are below the diagonal, while the Pearson's correlation coefficients are above the diagonal.
Source: Own processing.

3 SUCCESSFUL INVESTMENT STORIES

In order to attract FDI countries usually establish various investment promotion agencies and institutions. In the conditions of Slovak republic, it is The Slovak Investment and Trade Development Agency (SARIO) as a government-funded allowance organization that works under the supervision of the Ministry of Economy of the Slovak Republic. According to information provided by this agency successful investment projects from knowledge intensive business sectors point of view were within the period of 2002 and 2016 realised especially Shared Services & Business Process Outsourcing Centres (5%) and Information & Communication Technologies (3%). Hence, we will look more closely at some successful investment stories from these sectors based on information provided by SARIO.

Slovak republic developed Institutional Strategy for Business Service Centres Development in Slovakia that is aimed to maintain and develop the favourable conditions, which motivate foreign and Slovak investors to establish and expand Business Service Centres (BSCs) in Slovakia. BSCs not only contribute to stabilizing the operation of foreign companies, but also to increase their added value. They have a positive impact on employment and vocational training for young people. Currently, there are over 40 BSCs established in Slovakia employing more than 30,000 people with 10% annual average growth in employment. Therefore, Slovakia is becoming a hub attracting many financial, IT, accounting and other service providers. Thanks to the availability of qualified labour force and its performance, BSCs in Slovakia are evolving towards centres with higher added value with greater emphasis on quality of their services. On top of that, more and more BSCs aim at creating Centres of Excellence with specialized positions. Top companies currently operating in this sector are:

AT&T Global Network Services Slovakia (Bratislava) has operated in Slovakia since 1999. It has four centres in two cities, with a workforce of more than 3 000 that support high–quality communication services and solutions for multinational customers. In Slovakia, they continue to find great opportunities to match the requirements of global clients with a highly motivated and skilled workforce.

Dell came to Bratislava for the cost but stayed for the quality. The branch was established in early 2003 to support European operations. The ability to hire qualified and professional people, a strong track record of successful transitions combined with a stable economic environment lead the company to build the Global Support Centre with 1800 employees supporting various functions across the world.

Embraco decided to establish its branch in Košice for several factors including the position of the city as a promising hub services, its infrastructure and the people readiness through their educational institutions. Embraco in Kosice, just like around the world actively participates in building strong ties and long-term partnerships with local communities. Until now, a centre of services and innovation has been highly satisfied with local presence.

IBM International Services Centre (Bratislava, Košice) provide broad range support, through Business Process Services, CIO services, Digital Sales, Finance & Accounting, Sales Support and more that requires well educated employees with perfect foreign language and IT skills, and Slovakia has enabled IBM International Services Centres to grow from 100 to 5000 employees over the last 12 years.

LafargeHolcim European Business Services (Košice) started to provide its services from January 2014 and is currently supporting group companies in 13 countries in Europe. The key factor for choosing Košice was a combination of qualified, educated and available labour force, high potential of local universities and the overall government support of this sector in Slovakia.

T-Systems Slovakia is present in Košice for 10 years. They exceeded initial business case approximately tenfold, reaching 3600 highly qualified employees in both IT operations and business process outsourcing. They are particularly happy with a very close and productive partnership with the region, local middle schools and universities, who helped to propel them among largest ICT shared centres in Slovakia and the one with fastest growing value added.

Further sector that has a solid position in the Slovak economy is an information and communication technology sector that can be demonstrated not only by the presence of foreign companies (Dell, IBM, HP) that performed inward FDI but also strong domestic IT companies (ESET, Sygic etc.) that perform outward FDI. Top companies currently operating in this sector are:

Eset protects users in 180 countries. It is a global leader in security software development including award winning NOD32® Antivirus. Sygic developed most downloaded offline navigation in the world. It is a developer of GPS navigation software for mobile devices and solutions for business. Soitron developed a system for intelligent police cars Developer of IT solutions from integrated communication systems.

4 CONCLUSION

The paper presented overview of foreign direct investment inflows within selected manufacturing support service sectors in Slovakia. As the review of previous empirical findings showed there are not many studies dealing with the topic of inward FDI within service sectors in the conditions of Central and Eastern European countries. The increase of volume of FDI in service sectors was in the observed period of 2009–2015 driven by inward FDI to financial and insurance activities, followed by transportation and storage activities and administrative and support services. Based on the results of correlation analysis can conclude that there are rather week interconnections among analysed sectors in attracting FDI inflows.

Despite the fact that the data on FDI inflows did not show that shared service industries has attracted the highest volume of inward FDI within service sectors, the effort of the Slovak investment policy is aimed particularly at these sectors. Going out from new successful investment projects, Slovakia is becoming a hub attracting many financial, IT, accounting and other service providers. Companies established in these sectors (mainly based on FDI) have a positive impact on employment and vocational training for young people. The deeper analysis of the effects of FDI inflows in these sectors is on agenda of future research.

ACKNOWLEDGEMENT

The paper presents partial results of the research project VEGA No. 1/0842/17 "The causality links between foreign direct investments and firms' performance" in the frame of the granting program of the Scientific Grant Agency of Ministry of Education, Science, Research and Sport of the Slovak Republic and Slovak Academy of Sciences.

REFERENCES

Capik, P. & Drahokoupil, J. 2011. Foreign direct investments in business services: Transforming the Visegrád four region into a knowledge-based economy? *European Planning Studies* 19(9): 1611–1631.

Duboz, M.L. et al. 2016. Do foreign investors' location determinants in service functions differ according to sectors? An empirical analysis of EU for 1997 to 2011. *International Regional Science Review* 39(4): 417–456.

ECSIP 2014. *Study on the Relation between Industry and Services in terms of Productivity and Value Creation.* Vienna: ECSIP Consortium.

Knol, A. et al. 2014. A taxanomy of management challenges for developing shared services arrangements. *European Management Journal* 32(1): 91–103.

Melikhova, Y. et al. 2015. Trade in services and tertiarisation of the Visegrád four economies. *Post-Communist Economies* 27(1): 1–22.

Miroudot, S. et al. 2013. Trade Policy Implications of Global Value Chains. *OECD Trade Policy Papers* No. 161. Paris: OECD Publishing.

NATIONAL BANK OF SLOVAKIA. *Foreign Direct Investment.* Available at: <https://www.nbs.sk/en/statistics/balance-of-payments-statistics/foreign-direct-investment>

Nordås H.K. 2010. Trade in goods and services: Two sides of the same coin? *Economic Modelling* 27(2): 496–506.

OECD 2008. *Benchmark Definition of Foreign Direct Investment.* Paris: OECD Publishing.

SARIO. Available at: <http://www.sario.sk/en/invest/sector-overview>.

Sass, M. et al. 2018. The impact of FDI on host countries: The analysis of selected service industries in the Visegrad countries. *Post-Communist Economies* 30: 1–23.

Ślusarczyk, B. & Golnik, R. 2015. Poland's shared service industry as one of the fastest growing sectors of modern business services in Central Eastern Europe. *International Journal of Business and Globalisation* 15(2): 193–204.

Ślusarczyk, B. 2017. Shared services centres in Central and Eastern Europe: The examples of Poland and Slovakia. *Economics & Sociology* 10(3): 46–58.

Production Management and Business Development – Mihalčová et al. (Eds)
© 2019 Taylor & Francis Group, London, ISBN 978-1-138-60415-5

The SCP paradigm: Theory and findings in manufacturing support services

T. Bobenič & M. Bruothová
Faculty of Business Economics with seat in Košice, University of Economics in Bratislava,
Košice, Slovak Republic

ABSTRACT: The paper on the theoretical level presents the starting point of the structure-conduct-performance paradigm, followed by the critique of the traditional concept and overview of results of some empirical findings of the most frequently tested relationship within this paradigm, namely structure-performance relationship. Subsequently, the paper brings results of correlation analysis conducted to test structure-performance relationship within two most significant manufacturing support service sectors in Slovakia within 2009–2016 period. The results indicate that the fragmentation of transport and storage sector leads to higher performance from different indicators point of view. In case of information and communication sector, this is valid only for the relationship between number of enterprises and the level of earnings. Thus, we can conclude that the relationship of structure and performance seems to be sector or industry specific.

1 INTRODUCTION

The structure–conduct–performance (SCP) paradigm is based on neoclassical theory and it was first published by economists Edward Chamberlin and Joan Robinson in 1933 and then developed by Joe S. Bain (1959) who described this model in his book *Industrial Organization*. The SCP paradigm is considered a pillar of industrial organization theory, and it has been since its conception a starting point when analysing markets and industries, not only in Economics, but also in the fields of business management and controlling. The aim of the present paper is to introduce theoretical background of the SCP paradigm including elements and critique of the traditional concept and subsequently to test structure-performance relationship in conditions of selected manufacturing support service sectors in Slovakia.

2 THE SCP PARADIGM

The SCP paradigm is traditionally used as an analytical framework to explain relations amongst market structure, market conduct and market performance. Following its reasoning, an industry performance (which could be considered as the potential benefits to consumers and society as a whole) are determined by the conduct of the firms within the boundaries of this industry, which in turn depend on the structure of the market.

2.1 Elements of the SCP paradigm

Based on the work of Ferguson & Ferguson (1994) the delineation and short characteristics of the elements that the SCP paradigm consists of is presented below.

"Structure" describes the characteristics and composition of markets. At its most aggregated level, it relates to the relative importance (sizes and trends) of broadly defined sectors of the economy. It can also refer to the number and size distribution of firms in the economy as a whole. There could be far-reaching political and economic implications if such firms become progressively more dominant. More specifically "structure" also relates to importance and characteristics of individual markets within the economy. In this sense, it describes the environment within which firms in a particular market operate. The way in which markets fail to follow perfect competition conditions, depends on the degree of supply concentration, demand concentration, product differentiation and market entrance barriers. In addition, the structure of the market will always be determined by the nature of the product and the technology available.

"Conduct" refers to the behaviour (actions) of the firms in a market; to the decisions these firms make and to the way in which these decisions are taken. It thus focuses on how firms set prices, whether independently or in collusion with others in the market. How firms decide on their advertising and research budgets, and how much expenditure is devoted to these activities, are also typical considerations. These factors are often more difficult to identify empirically than either structural or performance characteristics.

"Performance" refers to outcome or equilibrium assessed in terms of allocative efficiency. It refers to economic results. The variables mostly used to measure performance are profitability and price-cost margin. The performance of a market is, however, a multi-dimensional concept, which encompasses effectiveness, productivity, efficiency, equity, profitability, quality, pricing and technological progress of the firms in the industry together with job opportunities and employment (Coughlan et al. 2006, Scherer & Ross 1990). In many papers, the use of efficiency measures is explored as a proxy for performance.

2.2 Critique of the traditional SCP paradigm

As stated by Ferguson & Ferguson (1994) the traditional SCP approach has been subject to widespread criticism. Some suggest that the relationships between structure, conduct and performance are more complex than originally envisaged. It has been argued that the technique is too loosely derived from its theoretical underpinnings, and this has led to various developments, including attempts to link SCP more rigorously (if more narrowly) back to neoclassical theory. Others have disputed the relevance of neoclassical microeconomics to the study of industry. They consider that the SCP approach gives too limited perspective on the operations of markets and that it provides a poor (and even misleading) basis for policy formulation.

In this regard, the SCP model stresses that the analysis should focus on the critical determinant of the profitability, as it mostly determines the performance of the industry. However, Porter (1980) and Scherer & Ross (1990) insist that from the strategy and business policy point of view, it is the firms that structured the industry that should be assessed as this leads to the conduct, which affects structure and performance in return (Faulkner & Campbell 2003). Thus, the single-direction of causality assumption within traditional SCP model has been challenged by many empirical studies (e.g. Kalirajan 1993) that presented a possibility of feedback from conduct and performance on structure.

There are currently two competing hypotheses in the SCP paradigm: the traditional "structure performance hypothesis" and "efficient structure hypothesis". The "structure performance hypothesis" states that the degree of market concentration is inversely related to the degree of competition. This is because market concentration encourages firms to collude. More specifically, the standard SCP paradigm asserts that there is a direct relationship between the degree of market concentration and the degree of competition among firms. This hypothesis will be supported if positive relationship between market concentration (measured by concentration ratio) and performance (measured by profits) exist, regardless of efficiency of the firm (measured by market share). Thus, firms in more concentrated industries will earn higher profits than firms operating in less concentrated industries, irrespective of their efficiency.

The "efficiency structure hypothesis" states that performance of the firm is positively related to its efficiency. This is because market concentration emerges from competition where firms with low cost structure increase profits by reducing prices and expanding market share. A positive relationship between firm profits and market structure is attributed to the gains made in market share by more efficient firms. In turn these gains lead to increased market concentration. That is, increased profits are assumed to accrue to more efficient firms because they are more efficient and not because of collusive activities as the traditional SCP paradigm would suggest (Molyneux & Forbes 1995). Thus, positive correlations between market concentration and profitability can be explained by the structure performance hypothesis or the efficient structure hypothesis.

3 STRUCTURE—PERFORMANCE RELATIONSHIP

In the following part of the paper, we focus on testing structure-performance relationship within conditions of selected manufacturing support service sectors. Services are generally used throughout the manufacturing process and the manufacturing value chain. Some services are needed in the early stage of the chain (e.g. research and development); some are needed at the end (retailing, maintenance and repair); and some are needed at every stage (telecommunications and financial services) (Nordås 2010, Miroudot & Rouzet 2013).

According to ECSIP (2014), when taking account of both direct and indirect linkages, the average service content of manufactured goods produced in the EU reaches close to 40% of the total value of final manufacturing goods produced. The bulk of these services are distribution services (15%), transport and communication (8%) as well as business services which ranges between less than 10 to even 20% and more across EU member states. This latter category includes services such as legal and accounting services, R&D, advertising and market research, engineering activities and ICT services. The remaining service activities, which represent a negligible share of the total, are non-market services. These numbers reflect a trend towards increased use of outsourcing of services by manufacturing firms. In this regard, we will in the following text focus on presentation of previous empirical findings regarding structure-performance relationship within manufacturing support service sectors and testing of this relationship in selected sectors in Slovakia.

3.1 Previous empirical findings

The most frequently analysed relationship within SCP paradigm is a structure-performance relation. Studies of the industry structure—performance relationship are numerous, beginning with the pioneering work of Bain (1951) who tested the major hypothesis that the profit rates of firms in industries of high seller concentration should, on average, be larger than those of firms in industries of lower concentration, and continuing with e.g. the work of Martin (2012) who examined the mainstream industrial economics view in light of recent studies of the market structure and market performance relationship in specific industries. In this regard, we can mention some recent works for example by Setiawan (2013) whose results suggest that there is a simultaneous relationship between industrial concentration, price rigidity, technical efficiency and price-cost margin with a positive bi-directional relationship between industrial concentration and price-cost margin. Ying & Tze-Haws' (2014) study tackled the endogeneity problem of conventional SCP with dual causal effects found between capital intensity and return on assets. Outreville (2015) in his study find support to the efficiency-structure hypothesis. The structure-performance relationship has been tested also in conditions of more broadly defined sectors /industries. In this regard, we can mention the work by Bobenič Hintošová & Hliboká (2015) who examined the relationship between industry structure and international competitiveness for a panel of 10 key industrial sectors over the period from 1999 to 2012 in the Slovak Republic. The results indicate that international competitiveness improves with a change towards a more concentrated industry structure.

From the production support service sectors point of view, some similar studies can be found majority of which is applied on banking or insurance sector (e.g. Maudos 1998). Shin & Kim (2013), for example pointed out that with increased concentration through bank consolidation and reduction the number of banks, competition is found to be higher, as banks are maximizing their interest revenues. Interesting results brings study of Bikker & Haaf (2002) who conclude that competition is strong among large banks—

operating predominantly in international markets—and weaker among small banks—operating mainly in local markets—while medium-sized banks take an intermediate position. In some countries, perfect competition has been found among large banks. Iannotta et al. (2007) pointed that a higher ownership concentration is associated with better loan quality, lower asset risk and lower insolvency risk. Mitchener & Wheelock (2013) even showed positive influence of banking market concentration on the growth of manufacturing industries that can be considered as important argument in favour of significance of the banking sector and its structure within the whole economy. Byeongyong (2005) tested the traditional structure conduct-performance model and the efficiency structure hypothesis to examine the relationship between market structure and performance in property-liability insurers. The efficiency terms in this analysis were estimated using a stochastic frontier analysis. This analysis supported the efficiency structure hypothesis. The results found that efficient firms charged lower prices than competitors causing them to capture larger market shares, which lead to increased concentration.

3.2 Data and methodology

In our analysis, we have focused on relationship between structure and performance in conditions of selected manufacturing support service sectors in Slovakia, namely transportation and storage sector and information and communication sector.

Input data for evaluation of market structure were derived from *Statistical Yearbook of the Slovak republic* (2017) and based on the availability of public data following indicators were used for the purpose of evaluation of structure of analyzed sectors: Number of enterprises operating within particular sector (No_enterpr) while enterprises are meant as legal persons producing goods or services. There are included business companies e.g. joint stock companies, co-operatives, limited liability companies, etc. Additionally, we evaluated market structure also according to average size of the firm measured through average number of employees (Size_empl) as well as through average gross output produced by one firm (Size_output).

In our analysis, we evaluated performance through productivity, average earnings and innovation performance. Productivity was measured as gross output per employee (P_output) and value added per employee (P_value_ad). Output represents the value of goods and services, which are the result of the activity of resident units during the accounting period in the territory of the Slovak Republic. Value added is a balancing item and is calculated by a subtraction of intermediate consumption from output of individual institutional sectors or branches.

Further, we analysed development of average gross nominal monthly earnings (Earnings) that consist of basic (tariff) wage set by wage rules including basic components of contracted payments for working overtime, payments for hours not worked, monthly and long-term bonuses paid according to the performance and evaluation criteria, extra payments for working overtime, the night work, work during Saturdays and Sundays, holidays, for environment damaging health, noise, risky and hard work, in-kind wages express in financial terms and other wage in the form of wage advantages whose level and periodicity are set in advance regardless of the situation in an enterprise. Input data for construction of above-mentioned indicators were derived from *Statistical Yearbook of the Slovak republic* (2017).

Additionally, we evaluated also innovation performance based on number of human resources in science and technology (No_HRST) that are defined as persons fulfilling one of the following conditions: successfully completed education at the third level in a Science and Technology (S&T) field of study; not formally qualified as above, but employed in a S&T occupation where the above qualification are normally required. Input data

were drawn from *Yearbook of Science and Technology in the Slovak Republic* (2017).

We conducted our analysis within years 2009–2016 applying correlation analysis. The analysis is performed for each sector on aggregate level separately.

3.3 Results—transportation and storage sector

First, we have conducted our analysis in conditions of the service sector that plays major role in goods manufacturing and completion, namely transportation and storage sector. From the organizational statistics point of view in this sector operates 4.7% of active enterprises in the Slovakia majority of which (84.4%) are purely Slovak companies without foreign capital participation. Almost all of these companies (99.5%) are small or medium enterprises. The transportation and storage sector contributes to the gross output creation by 6.2% and to gross value added creation by 7.03%. The share of the sector on the total employment is 5.9%.

Table 1 presents simple statistics of the variables used in our analysis.

The following Table 2 presents results of correlation analysis, using Pearson and Spearman correlation coefficients.

Table 1. Simple statistics—transportation and storage.

Variable	Mean	Std Dev	Median	Minimum	Maximum
No_enterpr	7264	2233	6947	4397	9918
Size_empl	20.11517	6.21464	19.33974	13.89736	30.26723
Size_output	1.47951	0.27986	1.43647	1.19846	1.87087
P_output	0.07600	0.00961	0.07427	0.06181	0.08833
P_value_ad	0.03169	0.00674	0.03004	0.02354	0.04176
Earnings	819.2875	44.2571	807.5000	768.3000	904.0000
No_HRST	25.01250	4.55488	26.0000	18.30000	29.90000

Source: Own processing.

Table 2. Pearson and Spearman correlation coefficients—transportation and storage.

	No_enterpr	Size_empl	Size_output	P_output	P_value_ad	Earnings	No_HRST
No_enterpr	1	−0.97420***	−0.96880***	0.94309***	0.96113***	0.86565***	0.13220
Size_empl	−1.0000***	1	0.97560***	−0.94075***	−0.93497***	−0.82182**	−0.00780
Size_output	−0.97619***	0.97619***	1	−0.86324***	−0.88734***	−0.76948**	0.06155
P_output	0.90476***	−0.90476***	−0.85714***	1	0.97868***	0.88152***	0.22289
P_value_ad	0.92857***	−0.92857***	−0.90476***	0.90476***	1	0.83249**	0.19006
Earnings	0.97619***	−0.97619***	−0.95238***	0.95238***	0.90476***	1	0.39967
No_HRST	0.23810	−0.23810	−0.16667	0.35714	0.07143	0.26190	1

Note: The asterisks denote the statistical significance of coefficients on a level of 10% (*), 5% (**), and 1% (***), based on p-values. The Spearman's rank correlation coefficients are below the diagonal, while the Pearson's correlation coefficients are above the diagonal.
Source: Own processing.

Table 3.　Simple statistics—information and communication.

Variable	Mean	Std Dev	Median	Minimum	Maximum
No_enterpr	8296	1869	8372	5458	10701
Size_empl	7.07589	1.25280	6.68933	5.95300	9.60205
Size_output	0.68158	0.11967	0.65259	0.56992	0.91418
P_output	0.09637	0.00313	0.09597	0.09235	0.10052
P_value_ad	0.05127	0.00336	0.05079	0.04752	0.05704
Earnings	1608	122.9533	1636	1413	1751
No_HRST	50.65000	7.01997	49.45000	41.5000	61.7000

Source: Own processing.

Table 4.　Pearson and Spearman correlation coefficients—information and communication.

	No_enterpr	Size_empl	Size_output	P_output	P_value_ad	Earnings	No_HRST
No_enterpr	1	−0.94330***	−0.94573***	0.01366	−0.68748*	0.95724***	0.62145
Size_empl	−0.97619***	1	0.98387***	−0.09723	0.50472	−0.91842***	−0.52477
Size_output	−0.92857***	0.90476***	1	0.08136	0.61021	−0.91057***	−0.45440
P_output	0.04762	−0.09524	0.19048	1	0.55204	0.08707	0.44462
P_value_ad	−0.76190**	0.73810**	0.83333**	0.52381	1	−0.56214	−0.23973
Earnings	0.95238***	−0.97619***	−0.88095***	0.21429	−0.64286*	1	0.69430*
No_HRST	0.64286*	−0.61905	−0.47619	0.42857	−0.26190	0.73810	1

Note: The asterisks denote the statistical significance of coefficients on a level of 10% (*), 5% (**), and 1% (***), based on p-values. The Spearman's rank correlation coefficients are below the diagonal, while the Pearson's correlation coefficients are above the diagonal.
Source: Own processing.

Statistically significant strong correlations have been detected between all pairs of variables describing structure of the sector. The direction of relation is negative between number of enterprises active within a sector on one hand and average size of the enterprise on the other hand. With increasing number of the enterprises is the average size of the firm measured by number of employees as well as by gross output lowering. Strong positive correlation is obvious between the two variables measuring average size of the enterprise, which means that for analytical purposes it is irrespective which variable is used to measure the size of the firm. Significant increase of number of enterprises active within this sector was accompanied by increase of performance measured through productivity and earnings. It seems that fragmentation of the sector and increase of competition contributed to better performance and vice versa. However, no relation was recorded in case of changes in market structure and innovation performance.

3.4　Results—information and communication sector

Subsequently, we have conducted our analysis in the second most important sector from the goods manufacturing point of view, namely informa-

tion and communication sector. Within this sector operates 5.1% of the active enterprises in Slovakia, majority of which are small and medium enterprises (99.8%) in purely domestic ownership (84.8%). The information and communication sector contributes to the gross output creation by 3.2% and to gross value added creation by 4.2%. The share of the sector on the total employment is 2.8%.

Table 3 presents simple statistics of the variables used in our analysis.

The following Table 4 presents results of correlation analysis, using Pearson and Spearman correlation coefficients.

Equally, as in the first case, statistically significant strong correlations have been detected between all pairs of variables describing structure of the sector. Regarding relation of structure to the performance most significantly are affected the earnings. Earnings are negatively associated with average size of the enterprise and positively associated with number of enterprises operating within a sector and number of human resources in science and technology.

4　CONCLUSION

The paper presented theoretical background of SCP paradigm, including its basis and critique of

31

traditional concept. Subsequently, we have tested the structure—performance relationship within transportation and storage sector as well as information and communication sector within period 2009–2016.

Our analysis led to ambiguous results. The first mentioned sector recorded strong and statistically significant relationship between structure and performance, namely the change in market structure toward more fragmented led to higher performance from different indicators point of view. In case of the second sector, this conclusion is valid only for the relationship between number of enterprises and the level of earnings. Thus, we can conclude that the structure-performance relationship seems to be sector/industry specific.

ACKNOWLEDGEMENT

The paper presents partial results of the research project VEGA No. 1/0842/17 "The causality links between foreign direct investments and firms' performance" in the frame of the granting program of the Scientific Grant Agency of Ministry of Education, Science, Research and Sport of the Slovak Republic and Slovak Academy of Sciences.

REFERENCES

Bain, J.S. 1951. Relation of profit rate to industry concentration: American manufacturing, 1936–1940. *Quarterly Journal of Economics* 65(3): 293–324.

Bain, J.S. 1959. *Industrial Organization*. New York: Willey.

Bikker, J.A. & Haaf, K. 2002. Competition, concentration and their relationship: An empirical analysis of the banking industry. *Journal of Banking & Finance* 26(11): 2191–2214.

Bobenič Hintošová, A. & Hliboká, L. 2015. The Relationship between industry structure and international competitiveness: evidence from a small open economy. *Journal of applied economic sciences* 10(5): 710–715.

Byeongyong, P.C. & Weiss, M.A. 2005. An Empirical Investigation of market structure, efficiency, and performance in property-liability insurance. *Journal of Risk and Insurance* 72(4): 635–673.

Coughlan, A.T. et al. 2006. *Marketing Channels*. New York: Routledge.

ECSIP, 2014. *Study on the Relation between Industry and Services in terms of Productivity and Value Creation*. Vienna: ECSIP Consortium.

Faulkner, D.O. & Campbell, A. 2003. *The Oxford Handbook of Strategy*; Oxford: Oxford University Press.

Ferguson, P.R. & Ferguson, G.J. 1994. *Industrial Economics*. London: Palgrave.

Ianotta, G. et al. 2007. Ownership structure, risk and performance in the European banking industry. *Journal of Banking & Finance* 31(7): 2127–2149.

Kalirajan, K.P. 1993. On the simultaneity between market concentration and profitability: The case of a small-open developing country. *International Economic Journal* 7(1): 31–48.

Martin, S. 2012. Market structure and market performance. *Review of Industrial Organization* 40(2): 87–108.

Maudos, J. 1998. Market structure and performance in Spanish banking using a direct measure of efficiency. *Applied Financial Economics* 8(2): 191–200.

Miroudot, S. et al. 2013. Trade Policy Implications of Global Value Chains. *OECD Trade Policy Papers No. 161*. Paris: OECD Publishing.

Mitchener, K.J. et al. 2013. Does the structure of banking markets affect economic growth? Evidence from U.S. state banking markets. *Explorations ìì. Economic History* 50(2): 161–178.

Molyneux, P. & Forbes, W. 1995. Market Structure and Performance in European Banking. *Applied Economics* 27(2): 155–159.

Nordås H.K. 2010. Trade in goods and services: Two sides of the same coin? *Economic Modelling* 27(2): 496–506.

Outreville, J.F. 2015. The market structure-performance relationship applied to the Canadian wine industry. *Applied Economics Letters* 22(18): 1486–1492.

Porter, M.E. 1980. *Competitive Strategy*. New York: Free Press.

Scherer, F.M. & Ross, D. 1990. *Industrial Market Structure and Economic Performance*. Boston: Houghton Mifflin.

Setiawan, M. et al. 2013. Structure, conduct and performance: evidence from the Indonesian food and beverages industry. *Empirical Economics* 45(3): 1149–1165.

Shin, D.J. & Kim, B.H.S. 2013. Bank consolidation and competitiveness: Empirical evidence from the Korean banking industry. *Journal of Asian Economics* 24: 41–50.

Statistical Yearbook of the Slovak Republic. 2017. Bratislava: Statistical Office of the Slovak republic.

Yearbook of Science and Technology in the Slovak Republic. 2017. Bratislava: Statistical Office of the Slovak republic.

Ying, C.H. & Tze-Haw, C. 2014. Market structure and competition: Assessment of Malaysian pharmaceutical industry based on the modified structure-conduct-performance paradigm. *International Journal of Organization Innovation* 7: 135–148.

Production Management and Business Development – Mihalčová et al. (Eds)
© 2019 Taylor & Francis Group, London, ISBN 978-1-138-60415-5

DrawDown as method of portfolio risk selection

I. Brezina
Department of Operations Research and Econometrics, Faculty of Economic Informatics,
University of Economics in Bratislava, Bratislava, Slovak Republic

I. Brezina Jr.
Department of Economics, Faculty of Economics, Pan-European University, Bratislava, Slovak Republic

ABSTRACT: On investment market DrawnDown is the maximal percentage decline of capital in portfolio value in selected period. It can be used by risk management of portfolio. It means that it is one from indexes, which can be used by management quality of the portfolio. The value of DrawnDown shows the percentage difference in testing period. It gives investor the information, how successful is the investment strategy. It gives investor the information about the risk of investment too. The value of DrawDown is the risk indicator and the indicator of success of investment. DrawDown is in selected period defined as the difference between maximal value of portfolio and the current value of portfolio. The optimal portfolio selection is in presented model described in discrete conditions. The goal of this optimization is to find the portfolio with maximal average return in selected period.

1 INTRODUCTION

Money Management (MM) is a part of finance market, which developed very quickly. We can characterize it as the set of the rules, which are designed for the management of the tolerable risk measure. This tolerable risk measure is important by portfolio selection of the investment. The portfolio selection of investment is a process of asset allocation. The goal of this asset allocation is to find ideal portfolio, which maximize the asset return, maximize liquidity and minimize the risk of the investment. The well-made portfolio is important for the investor, who would like to be successful on the financial market.

MM as the tool of the investment management is very helpful. It uses different approaches, calculations and analyses, which answer the question, which loss is tolerable by expected risk in selected period on the market and what is the lowest ratio between the profit and the loss, which investor needs to be profitable. One indicator, which is often used in MM, is DrawDown. DrawDown is the indicator of the risk and of the success of investment strategy. On the investment market DrawDown means the highest decline of the capital.

2 DRAWDOWN

The model of DrawDown (DD) portfolio selection is relative new method of the portfolio optimization, which was presented on begin of 21. century by Rockafellar and Uryasev (2000, 2002). They based this method on new portfolio risk approaches, which were presented in 50 s of the past century. Markowitz (1952) and Roy (1952) constructed the Value at Risk indicator, which was the base of new portfolio risk models, for all Conditional Value at Risk (CVaR) model. DD portfolio selection model is the modification of this CVaR model.

Index DD is mostly used by specifying of portfolio risk. It can be considered as the index of the quality of portfolio management. DD is the decline of maximum value of the portfolio to the actual minimum in selected period. DD represents the percentage difference between reached maximum and the actual minimum values of the portfolio in selected period.

Maximum DrawDown (MDD) measures maximal percentage decline in portfolio value in selected period. The period of decline of portfolio value can be selected by MDD. The time, when the portfolio value reaches the same level like before can be selected by MDD too. The value of MDD reflects the change in percentages for higher to lowest value of portfolio during selected period. It is the reason, why MDD value is always in percentages. MDD is the information about the success of selected strategy, about the risk of selected strategy and about the finance, which must be used by selected strategy. If the MDD value is about 40% and more, it indicates, that selected strategy is risky.

3 THE DRAWNDOWN PORTFOLIO OPTIMIZATION

The DrawnDown portfolio optimization was constructed by Chekhlov Uryasev and Zabarankin (2003). The goal of the optimization is to find the optimal portfolio allocation based on DD.

DD portfolio in specified time T is defined as the difference between maximal value of portfolio in previous period and the current value in the time T. If T is the time of assets observation, N is the amount of assets, ω are the weights of N assets and y_t' are cumulated returns in each time periods $(t = 0,1,...T)$, than the value of the portfolio in T can be calculated follows:

$$W(\omega,T) = y_T'\omega \qquad (1)$$

The DD portfolio is than defined (Pfaff 2013):

$$D(\omega,T) = \max\{W(\omega,\tau)\} - W(\omega,T) \qquad (2)$$

We will continue to deal with two indicators: maximal DrawDown (MDD) and average Draw-Down (AvDD). This risk functions can be interpreted by DrawDown portfolio optimization as the inequality of conditions.[1]

The portfolio selection optimization is based on maximal yearly average portfolio return in discrete conditions:

$$R(\omega) = \frac{1}{d.C}y_T'\omega \qquad (3)$$

where d is the amount of periods in time interval [0,T] and MDD and AVDD are limited by the amount of capital (C). We consider, that u is the vector of $(T + 1 \times 1)$ free variables, which present the maximal values of portfolio of wealth. It means, that the maximal rate of portfolio is until the time k limited $1 \leq k \leq T$. In MDD $v1$ is the maximal share on capital. The maximisation of yearly average portfolio return based on MDD conditions is than follows (Pfaff 2013):

$$\max R(\omega,u) = \frac{1}{d.C}y_T'\omega \qquad (4)$$

$$u_k - y_k'\omega \leq v1C,$$
$$u_k \geq y_k'\omega,$$
$$u_k \geq u_{k-1},$$
$$u_0 = 0.$$

---

1. For example: the request MDD should be maximal 100 percent ($v1$) of basic capital (C), $MDD (\omega) \leq v1 C$, where $0 \leq v1 \leq 1$. Analogical $AvDD (\omega) \leq v2 C$ as the linear combination of this two risk functions under conditions $0 \leq v1, v2 \leq 1$.

In the case of portfolio selection optimisation, which is based on AvDD, is first condition of previous model replaced by discrete equivalent of AvDD. This model is than (Pfaff 2013):

$$\max R(\omega,u) = \frac{1}{dC}y_T'\omega, \qquad (5)$$

$$\frac{1}{T}\sum_{k=1}^{T}\left(u_k - y_k'\omega\right) \leq v2C,$$
$$u_k \geq y_k'\omega,$$
$$u_k \geq u_{k-1},$$
$$u_0 = 0.$$

Presented formulations of linear programming models can be extended by more conditions, as for example by budget.

4 EXPERIMENTAL CALCULATIONS

The input data and the development of them in the selected period are form *http://finance.yahoo.com*. We take into account daily values of eight stock indexes in period from 4th January 2010 to 1th March 2014: S&P 500, Russell.3000, DAX, FTSE.100, Nikkei.225, iShares.MSCI.Emerging. Markets, ISHARES.II.PLC.ISHARES.UK.GILTS, GOLD.

The development of the stock indexes is shown on the Figure 1.

The data from the stock market were the input for calculation of MDD and AvDD on the confidence level $(1 - \alpha) = 0,95$. The results of MDD and AvDD calculation are presented on Figure 2.

In Table 1 is the summary of stock indexes values, of risk portfolios (GMV, MDD, AvDD) and of their weights, standard deviation (PMRC), marginal

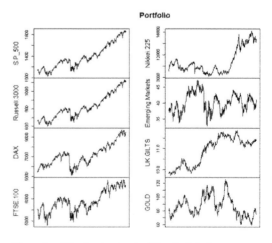

Figure 1. The development of the stock indexes.

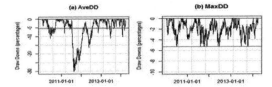

Figure 2. Calculated values of AvDD, MDD.

Table 1. Output of program R.

	GMV	MDD	AvDD
S.P_500			
Weight	7.95	0.00	0.00
PMRC	7.95	0.00	0.00
PMES	7.59	0.00	0.00
Russell.3000			
Weight	0.00	28.80	50.18
PMRC	0.00	57.27	41.88
PMES	0.00	57.33	41.67
DAX			
Weight	6.56	2.60	49.82
PMRC	6.56	0.69	58.12
PMES	6.19	0.53	58.33
FTSE.100			
Weight	9.37	0.00	0.00
PMRC	9.37	0.00	0.00
PMES	9.40	0.00	0.00
Nikkei.225			
Weight	5.28	1.73	0.00
PMRC	5.28	0.42	0.00
PMES	5.01	0.32	0.00
iShares.MSCI Emerging.Markets			
Weight	3.46	7.87	0.00
PMRC	3.46	9.70	0.00
PMES	3.48	9.84	0.00
ISHARES.II.PLC. ISHARES.UK.GILTS			
Weight	66.06	59.01	0.00
PMRC	66.06	31.91	0.00
PMES	67.00	31.97	0.00
GOLD			
Weight	1.32	0.00	0.00
PMRC	1.32	0.00	0.00
PMES	1.33	0.00	0.00
PDR	2.12	1.72	1.40

value of estimator (PMES) and portfolio diversification (PDR) as the output of programme R:

Risk portfolio GMV allocates the investment into seven of eight stocks. ISHARES.II.PLC.

ISHARES. UK.GILTS with 66% is the biggest part of investment. This portfolio has the best value of diversification calculated with GMV method. It is because GMV allocates the portfolio into biggest amount of stocks.

Risk portfolio MDD allocates the investment into five of eight stocks. With about 59% of portfolio is ISHARES.II.PLC.ISHARES.UK.GILTS the best rated stock. Risk portfolio AvDD allocates the investment into two of eight stocks. With a bit more than 50% of investment is Russell.3000 the best rated stock. The rest of this investment less 50% is allocated into DAX.

5 CONCLUSION

Presented DrawDown index as the risk measure and as the measure of investment strategy success is relative new method of portfolio selection optimization. It can be used like the tool by support by the decision making on the finance market. Index DrawDown can be used as the risk management tool; it can be used like the tool of management quality.

Experimental calculations programmed in R language shown the real use of DrawnDown by allocation of disposable finances into the best stocks on the financial market. Help DrawnDown is built the optimal portfolio selection. The Draw-Down portfolio selection model is useful by portfolio management.

REFERENCES

Chekhlov, A. et al. 2003. Drawdown measure in portfolio optimization. *Technical report, ISE Dept.,* University of Florida.

Markowitz, H. 1952. Portfolio selection. *The Journal of Finance* 7(1): 77–91.

Pfaff, B. 2013. Financial Risk Modelling and Porfolio Optimization with R. Chichester: John Wiley & Sons

Rockafellar, R. & Uryasev, T. S. 2000. Optimization of Conditional Value-at-Risk. *The Journal of Risk* 2: 21–42.

Rockafellar, R. T. & Uryasev, S. 2002. Conditional Value-at-Risk for General Loss Distributions, *Journal of Banking and Finance* 26: 1443–1471.

Roy, A. 1952. Safety first and the holding of assets. *Econometrica* 20: 431–449.

http://finance.yahoo.com.

Production Management and Business Development – Mihalčová et al. (Eds)
© 2019 Taylor & Francis Group, London, ISBN 978-1-138-60415-5

Measuring country risk of Slovakia from the economic view

K. Čulková, A. Csikósová & M. Janošková
Technical University of Košice, Košice, Slovak Republic

ABSTRACT: Measuring of country risk presents actual problem, mainly due to the globalization process and debt crises in number of EU countries. Country risk is defined as risk, rising when dealing with exports/imports that have impact on the value of the assets located in that country or the rights on residents therein, arising from changes in the political, economic and social structure of the country. The aim of the contribution is evaluation of economic aspects of country risk in Slovakia, requiring including of factors, explaining current economic situation in the country with possible changes in the future. The main approach to the evaluation is measuring of structural factors, factors of economic policy and foreign debt factors, resulting in total evaluation of country risk in Slovakia not only from the view of country risk, but also business climate. Obtained results must be adapted to uncertainty of economic and financial environment and identification of risk sources and its causes.

1 INTRODUCTION

Presently country risk is very actual idea during evaluation of economic situation of the countries. First reason is process of globalization that is more intensive in last decades, creating new, complex and connected economic, political and social environment (Jensen & Young 2008). The next reason is crisis of state and private debts in European countries. Last but not least is interest of complex net of direct and indirect connections between public sectors, enterprises, households and financial institutions, connected influence of country risk by business and bank risks (Bouchet et al. 2003). The interest to evaluate country risk is cyclical and repeated. For example, in 2002–2007 country risk was not evaluated due to the extensive growth of global economies and almost full absence of any external financial crises (Brown et al. 2015). But during previous period, recording big external financial crises in number of developed economies the country risk was considered, mainly in Asian countries. First indications of importance to measure country risk are connected with oil crisis and collapse of currency system (San-Martín-Albizuri & Rodríguez-Castellanos 2012). Also crises of foreign debt in many countries supported to increase importance of country risk. Importance of country risk resulted in various and different ideas. The main reason of differences is lack of consensus between expert and internal complexity of the risk, mainly due to the various elements, influenced by number of factors. There is therefore necessity to deal with country risk in various levels (Krayenbuehl 1985). Presented contribution provides its measuring at the level of chosen country with aim to find out factors, determining its further development.

2 LITERATURE REVIEW

Though country risk analysis is a well-established field within international business, evidence indicates that established measures of country risk are unreliable predictors of actual volatility. For example, Di Gregorio (2005) proposed an alternative perspective from which to approach country risk by focusing on both the downside and upside elements of country risk, strategies may be devised to harvest upside volatility while containing downside volatility. Rather than being something to always avoid, country risk becomes an opportunity to profit from uncertainty. Measuring of country risk requires to structure possible risks to different groups. Buckley et al. (2018) mentioned group of controllable risk (legally protectable loss) and no controllable risk (e.g. political instability).

Moreover, factors influencing development of country risk must be considered. Country risk is influenced also by public risk, since public finance directly helps supply public services through raising public revenues, and minimizes public risk and ensures fiscal sustainability (Liu & Li 2017). Therefore, the interacting relationships between public risk, public service, public revenue, and fiscal risk should be studied carefully. It is of great significance to get a balance between fiscal, public and country risk. Traditional theories on the role of government and public service provisions are based on public welfare theory and market failure theory. When analyzing market failures, traditional theories urge a role played by the government to address market failures. Next factor, influencing country risk is income level and economic security of the country (Bauer et al. 2008). In this area Doyle (2015) expects increases in income remitted to an economy to result in reduced levels of social welfare transfers at the macro-level. Similarly, sustainability has also been getting attention during country risk evaluation. Sustainability covers social, environmental and economic issues, thus recommending the importance of country risk evaluation (Serai et al. 2015).

Rule of law and political risk may be considered during country risk evaluation as well (Kumari & Sharma 2017). Political risk is defined as the potential for uncertainty and harm to business/economic operations that arise from political (governmental and other) behavior and events (Campisi & Caprioni 2017). To measure its influence to the country risk must include factors such as economic structures, government institutions, policies, and societal characteristics, and are becoming more of a concern to prospective investors in a changing global political economy.

There is necessary to understand also the importance of the major determinants of FDI for country risk development (Kumari & Sharma 2017). Copelovitch & Singer (2017) underlined foreign capital inflows as one of the primary determinants of banking crises in developed countries by arguing that external imbalances are destabilizing only when banks face substantial competition from securities markets in the process of financial intermediation. Abimbola & Oludiran (2018) suggest that the impact of FDI to country risk can be enhanced through financial development under a good environment that has to be provided in the country (Bauer & Zeleňák 2001). Their findings show that countries with high potential market size (GDP per capita), large trade openness and with more business friendly environment (low political risk) attract more FDI.

Evaluation of country risk is necessary nowadays mainly in the developed economies, since it plays an important role in the economic growth for large businesses in the country (Serai et al. 2015). Evaluation of country risk in CEE countries is very important mainly during the crises. In this area Gyódi (2017) made study, suggesting an increase in the importance of macroeconomic fundamentals during the financial crisis. The analysis also supports that sovereign credit ratings and exchange rate risk have a significant impact on government bond spreads. Glova & Dancakova (2018) made study to determine the country risk with respect to the global index and global financial market variables in CEE countries, using multiple linear regression models which is rarely applied in the literature.

3 METHODOLOGY

Risk of any country can be defined as risk, rising during business with certain country or in the frame of the country also through export and import. It measures possible negative influence to the value of assets, existing in the country or rights of residents in the country, resulting from changes in political, economic and social structure of the country (Nath 2008). In the frame of such approach country risk can be divided to different types: economic and financial, political (social risk and legislation risk) and risk of the country in narrow sense (risk of country indebtedness, etc.) (Bekaert et al. 2014).

The research required also determination of factors, influencing country risk. There is number of mutually dependent aspects that influence risk of the country. Relative importance of such factors depends mostly on specific circumstances of any analyzed country and on interested agents (Kosmidou et al. 2008). This is important with regard to the complex and multiple character of the risk type. Factors, connected with economic aspects can be structured to three blocks, as mentioned in Figure 1.

As illustrated by the Figure 1, in most cases these economic factors can be measured by the way of comparable indexes, which helps to provide obtained data would be objective and reliable. Full analysis of economic aspects of country

Structural factors	Economic policy	Indexes of foreign debt
Related to the domestic economy: - GDP development in variation rates. - Climate and geology - Income and distribution per capita. - Cost structure. - Monetary supply development. - Inflation and interest rates. - Development of the financial system.	*Basic instruments:* *fiscal policy, monetary policy and exchange rate policy* - Budgets and fiscal deficit. - Public debt: size, evolution, etc.	- Rate of variation in debt and debt servicing. - Debt composition: instalments, fixed or floating rates, etc. - Indexes: Debt service index: $\dfrac{\text{Servicing of external debt}}{\text{Exports of goods and services}}$
Related to foreign relations and balance of payments: - Level of reserves. - Current and capital account. - Flexibility of payments. - Development of exchange rate and real currency value.	- Use of monetary policy: deficit, inflation controlling, etc. - System of exchange rate.	External-debt-to-export ratio: $\dfrac{\text{Total external debt}}{\text{Exports of goods and services}}$ External-debt-to-GDP ratio: $\dfrac{\text{Total external debt}}{\text{Gross Domestic Product}}$

Figure 1. Economic factors of country risk.

risk demand also including of factors that explain present situation in state economy and how it will be adapted to future changes, influencing ability to pay the debt.

Finally, critical analysis had been made during the research, using most common methods for evaluation of country risk, structured to five categories: statistic techniques, indexes of country risk, methods of classification, mixed processes and methods, considering characteristics of decision maker. Starting with knowledge there is any perfect or irrefutable method, positives and negatives of any measurement system had been regarded.

4 RESULTS OF RISK ASSESSMENT IN SLOVAKIA

The main economic indicators in 2017 are summarized by Table 1, where we see the growth based on internal demand in 2017 remained.

The main driving force will be still permanent consumption of households. It is expected households will make profit from continuing growth of working posts and unemployment decrease. The level of payment will depend on growth lack of qualified working power in automotive sector and IT sector in eastern and middle part of the country. Higher measure of women participation, long term unemployment and migrants do not compensate mentioned lack. Therefore, producers are trying to obtain available work from eastern part of the country, but only with low success due to the low mobility.

Inflation will cause limited repeated appearance, mainly in case gas and electricity prices, regulated by government, would still decrease. Growth of investments is expected after stagnation. Private investments will continue to be managed by foreign direct investments (FDI) in automotive and energetic sector. Construction could remain its present dynamic situation. After a sharp drop due to the gap between two European programs for financing there is expected public investments would be renewed. In spite export, mainly connected automotive industry and tourism, will remain its dynamic position, business will present only weak

contribution to the growth. The reason is also high and important rate of FDI. It will stand till 2018, while their production potential would improve. Overall characteristics of Slovakian economy are given by Figure 2.

There is expected public deficit will still decrease and remain as modest. Such effort will be private and it will depend mainly on incomes increasing. First of all, it could bring benefit from the growth. There is also expected incomes will have benefit from establishing 7% tax from dividend and payment 8% from premium from non-life insurance, increasing of consumption taxes from tobacco and doubling of specific extraordinary tax for big organizations from energetic and telecommunication sector. Special tax 0.2% from banks will remain against any expectation. Finally, there is probable that top of calculation of social provision contributions will be removed. Income tax will be decreased against mentioned from 22% to 21%. As for the expenses, there are expected to be increased slowly in spite of reviving of public investments and further considerable increasing of wages in several sectors.

In this frame burden of public debt will remain as considerable, but under target limited value according pact of stability and growth (60% GDP). In spite

Strengths	Weaknesses
- Membership in Eurozone - Production platform for the European automotive and electronics industry - Satisfactory public and external accounts - Robust financial system dominated by foreign groups	- Small economy dependent on European investments and markets - Heavy concentration of exports on certain sectors: automobiles and consumer electronics - Energy dependence on Russia (gas, oil, uranium) - Regional development inequalities / the east lagging behind - Insufficiency of research and development - Lack of skilled workforce and high long term unemployment

Figure 2. Strengths and weaknesses of Slovakian economy.
Source: Coface 2017.

Table 1. Main economic indicators.

	2014	2015	2016	2017	
% GDP	2.6	3.8	3.5	3.3	
Average inflation per year (%)	−0.1	−0.3	−0.4	1.0	5.4 million Population of inhabitants in 2015
Budget balance (% GDP)	−2.7	−2.7	−2.2	−1.7	
Current account balance (% GDP)	0.1	−1.3	−1.0	−1.3	15.979 GDP per capita in USD in 2015
Public debt (% GDP)	53.6	52.5	53.0	53.0	

of mentioned in accord with debt brake, included to the constitution, the fact it is over 52% creates expenses limitation. The debt is denominated in Euro; therefore, it is not sensible on the currency risk. Health of bank sector, where Austrian and Italian groups dominated with sources, consisting from local deposit to bank, helps to hold lower cost on credits. Comparing of exports and imports in Slovakia from different countries is given by Figure 3.

Current account balance will probably still record small deficit. In spite of the import growth, resulting from growing domestic demand, dynamic sale of automotive and automotive elements, electronic, IT and electric equipment, as well as households' appliances, strong tourism and activity in road transport will hold surplus of business with goods and services. Only half of the sum from interests and dividends repatriation, resulting from strong presence of foreign investors, mainly in automotive industry, will be probably compensated by remittances of Slovakian emigrants. Level of external debt is high. At the end of June in 2016 it presented 87% GDP, of which half was for state and central bank, 20% for non-financial institutions and 15% for banks and in connection with FDI.

Total evaluation of country risk in Slovakia is then given by Figure 4 (Verbenik et al. 2011).

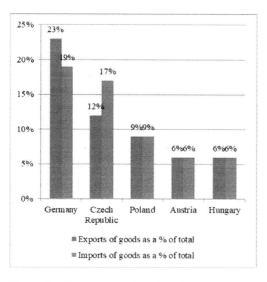

Figure 3. Development of trade exchanges—exports and imports in Slovakia in 2017.
Source: Own processing according Coface 2017.

Country risk – A3
Business climate - A3

Figure 4. COFACE assessment of Slovakia.

5 DISCUSSION

In spite there are several definitions of country risk we can identify risk as risk, raising during credits allocation or securities acquisition with fixed or variable revenue of emitted subjects in the country. It must regard possibility that due to the global reasons and circumstances, debt can be delayed or impossible (Christofides et al. 2016). Regarding factors, influencing country risk, literature provided that number of factors groups were identified, although differences among them are not substantial (Khoury & Zhou 2003). Due to the mentioned, importance of most important factors selection means mainly their ability to identify the risk and in accord with most authors two basic groups of factors had been determined: political and economic factors. But still global effects are more significant to evaluate development of country risk with solving, which demands to deal with debt reduction in the country (Cumby & Pastine 2001).

6 CONCLUSION

The paper has dealt with analysis, centred mostly on the definition and types of country risk; the factors that influence it and the methods most commonly used for assessing it. Due to the characteristics of events, considering during analysis of country risk that are rare and heavy predictable (for example difficulty with foreign debt payment), neither strict quantitative techniques, or using of expert opinions did not provided sufficient results. From this view analysis of country risk can be described as "art supported by science". Instead of attempts—that are made probably in vain—to predict crisis of foreign debts exactly, there is necessary to identify risks sources and its reasons, and to be careful during development of unsustainable economic phenomenon, to consider characteristic of systematic risk in globalized world and to accept uncertainty as basic part of present economic and financial environment.

ACKNOWLEDGEMENT

The article is partial result of research task VEGA No 1/0310/16 and VEGA No. 1/0651/18.

REFERENCES

Abimbola, L.N. & Oludiran, A.S. 2018. Major determinants of foreign direct investment in the west African economic and Monetary region. *Iranian Economic Review*, 22(1): 121–162.

Bekaert, G., Harvey, C.R., Lundblad, C.T. & Siegel, S. (2014). Political risk spreads. *Journal of International Business Studies, 45*(4): 471–493.

Bauer, V., Stavnikovic, M. & Olexova, T. (2008). Safety risk of construction systems during the construction and operation tunnel. In *International Society for Trenchless Technology—26th No-Dig International Conference and Exhibition 2008, No-Dig 2008 MOS-COW2008* (316–321). Moscow; Russian Federation, 3–6 June 2008.

Bauer, V. & Zeleňák, F. 2001. Environmental impacts of mining and processing of gold in Slovak Republic. *Metalurgija, 40*(3): 181–183.

Bouchet, M.H., Clark, E. & Groslambert, B. 2003. *Country risk assessment: A guide to global investment strategy.* Hoboken, HJ: John Wiley.

Brown, C.L., Cavusgil, S.T. & Lord, A.W. 2015. Country-risk measurement and analysis: A new conceptualization and managerial tool. *International Business Review,* 24: 246–265.

Buckley, P.J., Chen, L., Clegg, L.J. & Voss, H. 2018. Risk propensity in the foreign direct investment location decision of emerging multinationals. *Journal of International Business Studies,* 49(2): 153–171.

Campisi, J.M. & Caprioni, E. 2017. Social and political risks: factors affecting FDI in China's mining sector. *Thunderbird International Business Review,* 59(6): 709–724.

Christofides C., Eicher, T.S. & Papageorgiou, C. 2016. Did established Early Warning Signals predict the 2008 crises? *European Economic Review,* 81: 103–114.

COFACE Hanbook 2017. *Country risk 2017. Analysis and Forecasts for 160 countries.* Frande: INCREA.

Copelovitch, M., & Singer D.A. 2017. Tipping the balance: Capital inflows, financial market structure, and baking crises. *Economics and Politics,* 29(3): 179–208.

Cumby, R.E. & Pastine, T. 2001. Emerging market debt: Measuring credit quality and examining relative pricing. *Journal of International Money and Finance,* 20(5): 591–609.

Čulková, K., Csikósová, A. & Janošková, M. 2015. Development of risk payment index in Slovakia comparing with chosen EU countries. *Polish Journal of Management studies,* 12(1): 37–47.

Di Gregorio, D. 2005. Re-thinking country risk: Insights from entrepreneurship theory. *International Business Review,* 14(2): 209–226.

Doyle, D. (2015). Remittances and social spending. *American Political Science Review,* 109(4): 785–802.

Glova, J. & Dancaková, D. 2018. Country equity risk modeling using dynamic capital asset pricing model in selected central and eastern European countries. *Journal of Applied Economic Sciences,* 12(8): 2299–2308.

Gyódi, K. 2017. Determinants of CEE government bond spreads and contagion between 2001–2014. *Acta Oeconomica,* 67(2): 235–256.

International Monetary Fund 2001. *Financial organization and operations of the IMF.* Washington, International Monetary Fund.

Jensen, N.M. & Young, D.J. 2008. A violent future? Political risk insurance markets and violence forecasts. *Journal of Conflict Resolution,* 1: 527–547.

Khoury, J. & Zhou, C. 2003. Country risk: Existing models and new horizons. In A. Mullineux and V. Murinde (Ed.), *Handbook of international banking* (327–365). Northampton, Massachusetts: Edward Elgar Publishing.

Kosmidou, K., Doumpos, M. & Zopounidis, C. 2008. *Country Risk Evaluation: Methods and Applications.* New York: Springer.

Krayenbuehl, T.E. 1985. *Country Risk: Assessment and Monitoring.* Cambridge: Woodhead-Faulkner.

Kumari, R. & Sharma, A.K. 2017. Determinants of foreign direct investment in developing countries: a panel data study. *International Journal of Emerging Markets,* 12(4): 658–682.

Liu, S. & Li, Ch. 2018. Public services evaluation from the perspective of public risk governance. In Ahmad, E., Niu, M., Xiao, K. eds. *Fiscal Underpinnings for Sustainable Development in China: Rebalancing in Guangdong* (53–70). Springer.

Nath, H.K. 2008. Country risk analysis: A survey of the quantitative methods. *Sam Houstan State University Working Paper,* Series 08-04: 1–31.

San-Martín-Albizuri, N. & Rodríguez-Castellanos, A. 2012. Globalisation and the unpredictability of crisis episodes: An empirical analysis of country risk indexes. *Investigaciones Europeas de Dirección y Economía de la Empresa,* 18(2): 148–155.

Serai, M.H., Johl, S.K. & Marimuthu, M. 2015. Conceptual framework of sustainable corporate entrepreneurship. In *2nd International Symposium on Technology Management and Emerging Technologies, ISTMET 2015;* 16 December 2015, Art. No. 7359073, 432–436.

Verbenik, M., Horvath, J. & Gazda, V. 2011. Country risk in the new EU member states: A country beta approach. *International Research Journal of Finance and Economics,* 80: 148–157.

Production Management and Business Development – Mihalčová et al. (Eds)
© 2019 Taylor & Francis Group, London, ISBN 978-1-138-60415-5

Management of earth's mineral resources—lithium's case

J. Dvořáček & R. Sousedíková
Faculty of Mining and Geology, VŠB-Technical University of Ostrava, Ostrava, Czech Republic

Z. Matyášová
Ministry of Finance of the Czech Republic, Prague, Czech Republic

T. Vrátný
ČSAD a.s., Ostrava, Czech Republic

ABSTRACT: Sustainable industrial development cannot be achieved without implementation of mineral safeguarding policies. Profitability of extraction and processing represents a key factor for mineral industry sustained growth and its absence implies need for government intervention, which was the past situation in the Czech Republic in the period, 1945–1989. At the beginning of the nineties of the last century, extraction inefficiency, zero government intervention, and politically oriented decisions resulted in a complete discontinuation of ore mining activities in the Czech Republic. Recently, there has been interest in restoring extraction of residual ore deposits in abandoned mines. This paper considers the issue of lithium deposit of Cínovec. Possible revival of decommissioned ore mines came as a surprise. Technicalities and procedures of the ore mine decommissioning policies implemented in the past will influence future revival efforts and the costs involved, i.e. considerations about profitability of restoring the ore mining activities as such.

1 INTRODUCTION

Human society cannot exist without exploitation of mineral resources. On demand satisfaction of request for minerals can be realized only if sufficient supplies are safeguarded. Supply base consists of (i) domestic extraction, (ii) imports from abroad, (iii) recycling – for example tungsten in alloys, and (iv) substitution – for example natural graphite can be replaced by its synthetic counterpart. A prerequisite of extraction is profitability, i.e. an advantage of ready commodity returns vis-à-vis production costs of the commodity. Another option can be an intervention of government that takes an approach of identifying some minerals as strategic raw materials. If neither of these two factors is in place, mining activities must necessarily be stopped, and the mines abandoned, which was the case of ore mining industries in the Czech Republic.

2 HISTORY OF CZECH LANDS' ORE MINING

The written documents that witness developed ore mining activities in the Czech lands, date back to the beginning of the 13th century. The peak of the historical mining industry development was reached in the first half of the 16th century and was especially related to precious and non-ferrous metal ore mining. In the period, 1945–1989, the Czech ore mining industry development was intense. Specifics of the historical development after WWII, as well as the consequences of the oil and raw material crisis after 73 implied retaining of mining "at all costs". The big breakthrough came in 1990 with the governmental policies of discontinuity of ore mining activities in the country. The market economy comeback after 1989 implied paradigmatic change, which had a dramatic impact on the ore mining inclusive that of uranium.

At the turn of the first half of the nineties of the 20th century, the Czech ore industry activities seemed to cease completely. Nonetheless, the world mineral trade growing trends induced increased demand and related rising of mineral commodity prices. Investors have taken an interest in the matter, and there have been many places in the world where their interest is declared, inclusive the Czech Republic. An example of the situation, perhaps the most notorious, can be served by lithium deposit of the abandoned mine of Cínovec.

3 ORE MINE OF CÍNOVEC

First historical records on the tin deposit of Cínovec date back to 1378. Tin and silver mines active in 1547 are also on record. At the end of the 19th century, tin mining becomes less important as demand for tungsten ores increases. The WWI and WWII periods are marked by war booms.

In the past, a vein-type deposit was exploited. The deposit was opened by drifts and a primary pit was designated as Cínovec I. Mining activities at the locality were terminated in 1978. Apart from the vein-type deposit, there has been a major Sn – W ore deposit in greisen and metamorphosed granitic rocks. In 1961, exploratory boring for the pit was started, and the finished pit was later called Cínovec II. The locality extraction activities commenced in 1980 and were finished in 1990. In 1992, the mining claim of Cínovec was cancelled.

Technicalities of decommissioning the mines of Cínovec were oriented by procedures common to abandonment of vertical openings—shafts and raises in the Czech ore mines. Various variants of three basic modes were employed:

– Complete refill followed by site rehabilitation,
– Placing a reinforced concrete plug at a defined depth and refilling up to the surface level,
– Closure by building a reinforced concrete slab over the shaft opening.

A complete refill of the shaft excludes future possibility of resumption of the mine production. The refill from a certain depth up to the surface was the most common procedure of closing the pits. Considerations of future re-opening were not accounted for. The third mode of closure implies the so called wet conservation, which means that the mine workings are step by step flooded and water runs off on its own or is pumped out of the mine.

The mine localities, Cínovec I and Cínovec II, were connected by the main winding shaft of Cínovec I, the shaft of Cínovec II, and an ore pass. Some vertical openings were already decommissioned in the past. The shafts were refilled by mine waste and separated from horizontal workings by brick walls whose thickness ranged from 45 to 108 cm. An ore pass was also completely refilled and sealed by a steal cover. The wet conservation was used for closing of underground workings. By means of dams, the pit of Cínovec II was flooded up to the highest edit level. The pit and underground workings of Cínovec I is flooded up to the third edit level from where, going through a system of passages, water flows out at the German side of the Ore Mountains.

4   LITHIUM AND LOCALITY OF CÍNOVEC

On Earth, lithium occurs in (i) igneous rocks, (ii) lithium brines, (iii) lithium clays, and (iv) compounds dissolved in sea water (Vikström et al. 2013; Grosjean et al. 2012). It is mostly produced from lithium brines, which production is relatively cheap but the extraction technique is time demanding and it cannot keep step with fast changing demand (Kesler et al. 2012). Lithium production from minerals is less profitable but it is more flexible. Taking into account reserves of lithium identified worldwide, opinions agree that depletion is not imminent in this century (Yaksic & Tilton 2009), or that the reserves will not constitute a limiting factor (Vikström et al. 2013). Recycling, i.e. a process of lithium recovery from decommissioned products has been patented, but the process assumed profitability is too high (Miedema & Moll 2013).

Lithium in both metal and compound form is widely used. The most important fields of application are production of glass, ceramics, batteries, alloys, and lubricant greases. Interest in the so called "green technologies" led to increasing demand, especially as regards production of batteries. The lithium price almost trebled during the first decade of 21st century.

Such demand and price attracted interest of investors and mining companies in this mineral commodity. The attraction of the locality of Cínovec serves an example of the trend.

Cínovec is situated in NW part of the Bohemian Massif, where exploration for useful minerals, namely fluorite, copper, silver, and tin-tungsten ores, has been made in recent years. As regards the historical locality of the mine of Cínovec, the exploration is carried out by a private Czech company, Geomet, which was founded in 2007. Nowadays, it is owned by the Australian joint stock company, European Metals Holding (EMH), whose shares have been floated. Although WEB pages inform that the deposit of Cínovec is Company's 100% ownership (EMH Limited, 23 November 2016), their deposit exploration licence expires on 30 July 2019 (Annual Report 2014). The exploration drills up to the depth of 350 metres evidenced the deposit to be largest in Europe, and, apart from brines, to be the fourth largest reserve of lithium in the world (EMH Limited, 13. December 2016). There are also other minerals present, namely tin and tungsten ores. The lithium-bearing ore is zinnwaldite of metallic content average of 0.2%. Underground extraction is projected inclusive fragmentation. The ore particles suspended in water would be pipe transported to a processing plant next to the mine. Magnetic and gravitational separation would provide for recovering of Sn-W bearing mineral. Lithium mica concentrate is projected to be treated by a metallurgy process to provide for lithium carbonate as final trading commodity. The original project plan was to produce 1.7 million tons of ore per annum. Such extraction volume has never figured in the ore mining history of the Czech Republic. Although the lithium mica based production of lithium carbonate has never been practiced in the world, EMH has announced a successful production of lithium carbonate from zinnwaldite as based on roasting, which should be a simplified version of the well-proven technology that converts spodumene concentrate to lithium carbonate (EHM Limited, 13 December 2016). The spodumene is the most important ore of lithium.

In October 2017, a memorandum of understanding was agreed with EHM. The lithium was made into a political issue of the 2018 election campaign and in March of the same year, the Czech government withdrew from the agreement. The Government of the Czech Republic contracted the state company, DIAMO, and the Czech Geological Survey to provide for auditing of strategic mineral deposits in the country. Nonetheless, EMH can continue in exploration activities and is entitled to apply for mining area allotment and extraction permit.

5 CONCLUSION

It is obvious that decision about recommencing mining activities will depend on economic efficiency of the project initiative, which is mainly determined by market prices and the ore extraction/processing costs. Deactivation of previous decommissioning measures will represent an appreciable cost item. The 'wet' conservation of the historical mine of Cínovec enables a relatively low-cost re-access to the deposit. Nevertheless, practical experience corroborates former theoretical reflections (Dvořáček et al. 2017), namely that:

– Decommissioning of mines without recoverable reserves should prioritize safety and environment protection,
– Closure of mines with residual deposits or hitherto unexploited reserves of other minerals should implement measures that might facilitate future exposing of the deposit.

ACKNOWLEDGEMENT

The authors of this paper would like to express their gratitude to the *Research Fund of Coal and Steel: MERIDA Grant Agreement, No. RFCR-CT-2015-00004*, for its encouragement and financial support.

REFERENCES

Cinovec Lithium Project: Production of Battery Grade Lithium Carbonate from Sodium Sulphate Roast: European Metals Holdings Limited. 13 December 2016 [online]. Cit. [2018-03-11]. Available from: http://www.londonstockexchange.com/exchange/news/market-news/market-news-detail/EMH/13064543.html.

Čada, M. et al. 1978. *Šest set let dolování na Cínovci (Six Years of Mining at Cínovec)*. Teplice: Krajské muzeum v Teplicích (Regional Museum of Teplice).

Dvořáček, J. et al. 2018. The issue of sustainable growth concerning mineral resources. Stochová & Szaryszová (Eds). *New Trends in Process Control and Production Management*. Taylor & Francis Group, London.

European Metals: Annual Report 30 June 2014. ARBN 154 618 989.

Grosjean, C. Et al. 2012. Assessment of world lithium resources and consequences of their geographic distribution on the expected development of the electric vehicle industry. *Renewable and Sustainable Energy Reviews* 16: 1735–1744.

Kesler, S.E. et al. 2012. Global lithium resources: Relative importance of pegmatite, brine and other deposits. *Ore Geology Reviews* 48: 55–69.

Kolektiv autorů 2003. *Rudné a uranové hornictví České republiky (Ore and Uranium Mining in the Czech Republic)*. Ostrava: ANAGRAM.

Lithium Indicated Resource at Cinovec Increased by 420%. European Metals Holdings Limited. 23 November 2016 [online]. Cit. [2018-03-10] Available from: http://www.londonstockexchange.com/exchange/news/market-news/market-news-detail/EMH/13043601.html.

Miedema, J.H. & Moll, M.C. Lithium availability in the EU27 for battery-driven vehicles: The impact of recycling and substitution on the confrontation between supply and demand until 2050. *Resources Policy* 38: 204–2011.

Vikström, H. et al. 2013. Lithium availability and future production outlooks. *Applied Energy* 110: 252–266.

Yaksic, A. & Tilton, J.E. 2009. Using the cumulative availability curve to assess the threat of mineral depletion: The case of lithium. *Resources Policy* 34: 185–194.

Production Management and Business Development – Mihalčová et al. (Eds)
© 2019 Taylor & Francis Group, London, ISBN 978-1-138-60415-5

Economic aspects of Aeronautical Collision Avoidance System operations

M. Džunda, P. Dzurovčin & D. Čekanová
Faculty of Aeronautics, Technical University of Košice, Košice, Slovakia

ABSTRACT: In the presented article we discuss the economic aspects of Airborne Collision Avoidance System (ACAS). We introduce the basic data of the Traffic Alert and Collision Avoidance System (TCAS). We clarify the principle of TCAS. We also summarize the requirements that are placed on the system and analyse the cost of procurement and operation of such systems. We describe the specific systems manufactured by Honeywell that are available on the market. We evaluate these systems in terms of their detection performance, and discuss the cost of procurement, the operation of such systems and their implementation on different types of aircraft.

1 INTRODUCTION

Air transport is one of the most dynamically developing and at the same time the safest type of transport. (Rozenberg 2014) Since collisions in air have mostly fatal consequences, the emphasis on aviation security and also on the economy of air traffic has always had preferences. Every tragedy in the air investigated very thoroughly the cause of the accident and the improvement of the security system. (Sabo 2017) After the collision of airplanes in the air, there have always been voices calling for designing anti-collision systems. In the period free from accidents, interest in anti-collision systems has declined, especially in funding for their development. We have mentioned a few catastrophes from the past that have prompted the development of anti-collision systems. For example, United Airline's Lockheed L049 Super Constellation and Dongles DC-7 crashed in June 1956 over Grand Canyon, DC-7 and Air Force F-100 over Arden, New York. The collision of Lockheed Super Constellation and the DC-8 airplane, flying according to instrument flight rules caused a disaster when approaching Idlewid Airport (now John F. Kennedy Airport) over New York City, also the crash of Boeing 727 of Pacific Southwest Airlines and Cessna 172 over San Diego, which took 135 lives. (EUROCONTROL, 2008) These catastrophes have also resulted in a significant reduction in revenues for the airlines concerned due to the lack of confidence in the quality of the services they provide. (Pavolová 2013).

2 DEVELOPMENTS OF ANTICOLLISION SYSTEMS

In 1981, the Federal Aviation Administration (FAA) decided that the anti-collision systems would be deployed on an aircraft board. At that time, the most well-known Traffic Alert and Collision Avoidance System (TCAS) was improved. The development of this system as a result of the constant increase and demands put on air safety has continued. TCAS has further increased air traffic safety. In the aircraft collision over Cerritos in California, DC-9 collided with Piper Archer. Following this accident, the US Congress approved a resolution according to which aircraft operating in the US airspace must be equipped with an Airborne Collision Avoidance System (ACAS). The collision of Boeing 747 and Ilyushin 76 aircraft near New Delhi in India in 1996 triggered the process of regulations that aircraft flying in other parts of the world should be equipped with ACAS. At the end of the 1980s, ICAO (International Civil Aviation Organization) developed a global operational assessment of TCAS. Its purpose was to determine the performance of TCAS. Version 7.0 of this system is installed on all newly made aircraft. It was also taken over by ICAO as an international standard for flights over Europe and some other countries. The general concept established by ICAO for the anti-collision system is the ACAS (Airborne Collision Avoidance System). (Helfrick, 2004) The amendment to Annex 10 (Volume 4) after its publication in October 2010 introduced provisions that all new ACAS equipment must be in compliance with the new version 7.1 after 1 January 2014. As of 1 January 2017, all ACAS units must conform to this version 7.1. (even those that were installed before January 1, 2014). (EUROCONTROL, 2008) In December 2011, the European Commission published the "Implementing Rule" Regulation, mandating the use of ACAS 2, version 7.1 in European airspace, before the date set out in Annex 10:

- from December 1, 2015 all aircraft currently available with version 7.0.
- from March 1, 2012, all new aircraft with a maximum take-off mass of more than 5700 kg or with a capacity of 19 passengers or more equipped with ACAS 2 version 7.1. (Novak, 2010).

3 THE AIRBORNE COLLISION AVOIDANCE SYSTEM

The Airborne Collision Avoidance System (ACAS) is an aircraft system based on the use of Secondary Radar Response (SSR) signals. (Vagner, 2014) It works independently of ground equipment and provides pilots with information about nearby aircraft that are also equipped with a SSR transponder.

3.1 *ACAS versions*

ACAS I – the system which provides the pilot with information that allows the pilot to visually capture the "aircraft of the threat," but fails to provide the pilot with advice on how to resolve the conflict situation. This means that the pilot is only provided with traffic information TA (Traffic Advisory) (Novak, 2010).

ACAS II – unlike the ACAS I system, provides, in addition to the TA operation, a RA resolution (Resolution Advisory) solution. In case of a violation of the "own aircraft" a protection zone, the system will first inform the crew with the TA information and, if the aircraft is still approaching dangerously, a proposal to resolve the RA conflict is issued. The ACAS II system facilitates and increases safety, especially where vertical separations between aircraft are reduced.

ACAS III – is basically the same as ACAS II. The only difference is that it provides a proposal for conflict resolution, apart from the vertical plane, even in the horizontal plane. As a result of enormous technical difficulties, the development of this system was suspended. (Novak, 2010).

ACAS IV – ACAS IV is the new development stage for ACAS. This will be based on more modern principles and new technologies while meeting the requirements of ACAS III. It will also

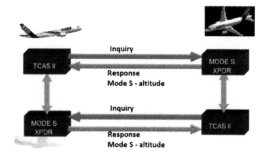

Figure 1. Aircraft communication (Honeywell, 2018).

provide a solution to a conflict in the horizontal plane. Currently, this system is supposed to replace ACAS II.) (Novak, 2010).

3.2 *Aircraft communication in the Traffic Collision Avoidance System*

Airplanes equipped with TCAS communicate with each other via the Mode S data line and, in the event of a conflict, coordinate each other's RAs so that both planes do not choose the same conflict resolution proposal.

4 LATEST TCAS SYSTEMS IN THE AIR TRANSPORT MARKET

Honeywell is a pioneer in the development of TCAS with more than 50 years of experience in designing and support. The SmartTraffic CAS 100 not only implements the necessary safety logic, but also enhances safety in high air traffic density airspace and displays the airspace. Advanced SmartTraffic features also reduce airline operating costs through improved system reliability and software upgrade flexibility by changing the software. This reduces future maintenance costs and enables users to upgrade their systems to the latest ADS-B requirements without changing hardware. The SmartTraffic CAS 100 offers three commercial TCAS models. TPA-100A/B/C are available in 6 MCU configurations and 4 MCU ARINC configurations. TPA-100A – was introduced as a direct replacement for the TPA-81A. In most cases, the TPA-100A may be updated to TPA-100B or TPA-100C with a simple software update. TPA-100B is a replaceable substitute for TPA-81A. The TPA-100B offers the RTCA/DO-300 hybrid tracking function. TPA-100C – has all features like TPA-100B and provides the following optional SmartTraffic™ ADS-B IN features:

- AIRB/VSA – increased view of the situation in the air and visual separation when zoomed in
- SURF – an increased view of the situation at or near the airport
- easy maintenance and access to data

Honeywell is now developing a next-generation TPA100D system that will deliver a higher level of air traffic safety. (Honeywell, 2018).

4.1 Basic CAS data

The passive surveillance – provides visibility of other aircraft over 200 nautical miles by receiving and processing ADS-B squitter information to determine their identity, location, and speed.

Hybrid surveillance – includes algorithms that allow the use of intruder data determined by passive tracking. This provides more insight into the air situation. Honeywell is the only offering TCAS that has hybrid surveillance. Hybrid surveillance uses ADS-B technology.

5 SMARTTRAFFIC CAS 100 OPERATIONAL COSTS

There are various methods that are used to determine economic efficiency. Investment, operational indicators and depreciation costs of systems are most often used. They are usually reported for 10 years duration. Operating costs include depreciation and operating system costs.

Economic efficiency consists of four basic elements:

1. Investment costs – this is the first tool for analyzing the economic efficiency of systems. They are needed to provide anti-collision systems. In addition to these costs, the cost of deploying anti-aircraft systems on an aircraft board is further included.
2. Operating costs – the second tool for analyzing economic efficiency, which represents the costs of technical services and operation of anti-collision systems.
3. Cost savings – is the third tool for economic efficiency that aims to improve the efficiency of the operation. Cost savings are the decommissioning of such anti-collision systems that do not meet the specified requirements. This reduces the costs of technical services and operation of the anti-collision systems.
4. Increasing air traffic efficiency – is the fourth tool for improving economic efficiency. The main goal is to make more efficient use of airspace and create the shortest available flight routes at all phases of flight. This depends on the planning and preparation of the flights, up to the smooth operation of the aircraft service.

The funds used to operate anti-collision systems are used to cover the costs incurred in procurement and operation. We can divide the cost items into the following groups:

Anti-collision system procurement has to meet the requirements for safety, quality, capacity and economy of operation. The main criteria for choosing a new system are its security (safety certificate), price, quality, lifetime, return on investment. Aeronautical technology can be purchased either through direct payment or by leasing. The price of the anti-collusion system includes the price of the technology and the procurement cost.

Depreciation, the result of the use of anti-collision systems is a measure of their attrition. It can either be moral, which arises from the gradual obsolescence of the technique, or physical as a result of its use. Depreciation is carried out over several accounting periods when the cost of acquisition is reduced and reflected in costs. The depreciation principle has to be performed according to Act No. 595/2003 Coll. on Income Taxes as amended and Act No. 431/2002 Coll. on Accounting as amended. The asset may be amortized evenly or expediently.

Maintenance and repair of anti-collision systems is one of the largest cost items. Costs are broken down according to the technology type. Maintenance is carried out by qualified personnel using certified spare parts from specialized companies. Costs incurred for repairs and maintenance must be adequate for the use of the equipment.

Salary and payroll costs have a large share of airline cost. (Šebeščáková, 2013) They consist of salary costs, statutory social insurance, health insurance, other social security and other costs. Salary costs include gross wages and salaries, including non-cash employee benefits.

Honeywell understands the importance of new technologies and their impact on air traffic safety. SmartTraffic CAS 100 was designed to both reducing operating costs and increasing air traffic safety.

Hybrid tracking ADS-B technology enables greater lineage efficiency across the line, reducing fuel consumption and reducing maintenance costs. Future CAS 100 and ADS-B features will be available through software upgrades, reducing future maintenance costs and total aircraft downturns. The SmartTraffic CAS 100 is offered as a whole, reducing the cost of spare parts. SmartTraffic® CAS 100 is available on the following platforms:

Airbus – A320 series (A318, A319, A320, A321), A330, A340 AW-139 Boeing - B737, B777 Dassault F5X Embraer E2 Gulfstream G600 SuperPuma.

TPA-100B and TPA-100 A are the most requested products for 7.1. It has 2 models, 940-0351-001, 6 MCUs for general air transport and 940-0451-001, 4 MCUs for regional and corporate aircraft. (TCAS, 2015).

The price of the new TCAS with the change of version 7.1 ranges from $ 350,000 to $ 360,000 for their two popular TCAS systems. The antennas and the control panel cost another $ 20,000. All commercial aircraft are required to have TCAS, so many users will update the software to meet new standards of change (version 7.1). Software upgrade costs are approximately $ 25,000. No maintenance is planned for these systems. These systems have an average fail-safe operation time of approximately 25,000 flight hours. (TCAS, 2015).

6 CONCLUSION

In this paper, we discuss the economic aspects of the airborne collision avoidance systems. The development of these systems as a result of the constantly increasing demands on air safety continues today. It is clear that aviation disasters have also resulted in a significant reduction in revenues for the airlines concerned due to lack of confidence in the quality of the services provided. As a result, the US Congress has approved a resolution according to which aircraft operating in the US airspace must be equipped with ACAS. Later collisions of aircraft run the process of regulations under which aircraft flying in other parts of the world should be equipped with ACAS. The changes in Annex 10 introduced provisions that all new ACAS devices must be in compliance with the new version 7.1 after January 1, 2014, later, a provision was issued that even those installed before 1 January 2014. In December 2011, the European Commission published the "Implementing Rule" mandating the use of ACAS 2, version 7.1 in European airspace. The cost of purchasing one ACAS 2 system in Honeywell's version 7.1 is about $ 380,000. Although the cost of procurement and operation of airborne countermeasures is relatively significant, the use of such civil aviation systems confirms that these systems have greatly contributed to improving air safety and reducing airline economic costs due to fuel savings and the cost of compensation for passengers.

REFERENCES

EUROCONTROL, 2008. Airborne Collision Avoidance System (ACAS), Available on internet: https://www.eurocontrol.int/sites/default/files/content/documents/nm/safety/ACAS/safety-acas-sire-decision-criteria-for-regulatory-measures-on-tcas-v-7.1-20080725.pdf.

Helfrick, A. 2004. Principles of Avionics. Third Edition. USA: Avionics Communications Inc., 2004. 480 s. ISBN 1-885544-20-0.

Honeywell, Aerospace, Available on internet: https://aerospace.honeywell.com/en/pages/tcas-change-7-1 https://www.eurocontrol.int/sites/default/files/content/documents/nm/safety/ACAS/safety-acas-sire-decision-criteria-for-regulatory-measures-on-tcas-v-7.1-20080725.pdf.

Novák, A. & Kandrera, B. 2010. Modern Surveillance Systems in Air Transport. First edition. Brno: Akademické Nakladatelství CERM, Ltd., 2010. 130 s. ISBN 978-80-7204-699-7.

Pavolová, H. & Tobisová, A. 2013. The model of supplier quality management in a transport company. Nase More. Vol. 60, no. 5–6, pp. 123–126. ISSN 0469-6255.

Rozenberg, R. et al. 2014. Comparison of FSC and LCC and Their Market Share in Aviation. In: International Review of Aerospace Engineering (IREASE). Vol. 7, no. 5 (2014), p. 149–154. ISSN 1973-7459.

Sabo, J. et al. 2017. GNSS approach on small regional non public airports. In: SGEM 2017. Sofia: STEF92 Technology Ltd., 2017 p. 559–564. ISBN 978-619-7408-03-4.

Šebeščáková, I. et al. 2013. The assessment of the contribution of aviation to the national economy. In: eXclusive e-journal. Roč. 1, č. 2, 2013, s. 1–10. ISSN 1339-4509.

TCAS brochure update 2015, Available on internet: https://aerospace.honeywell.com/.

Vagner, J. & Pappová, E. 2014. Comparison of radar simulator for air traffic control. Nase More. Vol. 61, no. 1–2, p. 31–35. ISSN 0469-6255.

Production Management and Business Development – Mihalčová et al. (Eds)
© 2019 Taylor & Francis Group, London, ISBN 978-1-138-60415-5

Data, information and bounded rationality

L. Falát
Department of Macro and Microeconomy, Faculty of Management Science and Informatics,
University of Žilina, Slovak Republic

J. Dubovec
Department of Management Theories, Faculty of Management Science and Informatics,
University of Žilina, Žilina, Slovak Republic

ABSTRACT: The paper deals with effects of behavioral economics on decision-making of a consumer. Authors present the basic differences between neoclassic economics and behavioral economics. They discuss the concepts of bounded rationality and present some consequences of it such as Dunning-Kruger effect, IKEA effect, mental accounting, endowment effect and Allais paradox. They also discuss the role of data in the decision-making process. Finally, authors suggest hypotheses which try to investigate the influence of noise and incomplete information on this decision-making process by an experiment.

1 INTRODUCTION

Many years, economics has been about so-called agents. These agents have almost nothing to do with real ordinary people who are everywhere in the world. The main goal of the economic actor is, according to classical economy, very simple – to maximize needs of the actor, i.e. the needs of people must be satisfied to the maximum. This is usually done using the tool called utility. Utility is subjective feeling of satisfaction resulting from consumption of goods or services. Utility can be categorized as ordinal or cardinal, however, what is more important is the fact that a consumer is able to order goods according to their utility from the consumer's point of view. In addition to this, in case of cardinal approach of utility, the consumer is able to quantify these utilities using the utility function. The utility function is a way for assigning certain number to every possible consumption basket (combination of goods) so that more higher number would be assigned to preferable consumption baskets (Staníková 2015). Using the utility function, total utility resulting from the consumption of certain goods, can be calculated. The total utility is defined as the total satisfaction from consumption of selected goods. It is obvious that the total utility is dependent on the number of consumed goods, their properties, qualities as well as the consumer's preferences. We can also define the marginal utility which is defined as additional utility resulting from the additional consumption of goods or services (In economics, the partial derivatives are used for calculating the marginal utility).

If, for a consumer, the combination of goods has the same utility than some other combination of goods or services, then according to economic theory, the consumer is indifferent among these combinations. The indifferent curve is the set of options (consumption baskets) among which the consumer is indifferent (Staníková 2015). On base of these assumption consumer is able to realize substation of goods (using the marginal utility). Eventually, as the main goal is to maximize consumer's needs, classical economics defines the relation for finding the optimal combination of goods X and Y given the prices of both goods:

$$MU_x/P_x = MU_y/P_y \qquad (1)$$

However, what is equally important are so-called assumptions of stated implications. For making these relations true, some assumptions regarding the human behavior needs to be satisfied. Neoclassical economics has defined some specific aspects of human behavior. One of the most important is so-called optimization of economic actor. This means that a consumer always chooses the best option for him, i.e. the one that maximizes the utility. The economic actor has, according to neoclassical economics, unbiased opinions and beliefs and he has unbounded rationality. This has something to do with another assumption of neoclassical economics which is that the economic actor always has all information needed for decision-making process.

Another assumption, which is related to optimization, is ordering of consumer preferences. Consumer is, therefore always, able to determine correctly which combination of goods or services is far more better than any other. Hence, consumer is able to order their preferences. The ordering of preferences in neoclassical economics is very much dependent on axioms of preferences. According to Staníková (2015) we define these axioms in economic theory:

- Completeness—the order of preferences is complete if consumer is able to order all possible combinations of goods.
- Transitivity—the order of consumer's preferences is transitive if, for every combination of A, B and C the following is true: if consumer prefers A over B and B over C, then he always prefers A over C.
- Dominance—conditional on all else being equal, consumer prefers bigger number of goods over smaller one.

Also, it is important to note that this ordering of preferences is unconditional on time. Another assumption, which is important in neoclassical economics, is self-interest, i.e. the economic actor is selfish. Consumer interested exclusively in himself and he is not interested in public good. Economic actor is characterized by consumer independence as well. The consumer has no problems with self-control, i.e. he always chooses the best option regardless the number of options, current situation, psychological state or social conditions. This also means that emotions do not play any role in decision-making process of the consumer. Also, any other external factors have no role for this decision-making process. Classical economics argue that the economic actor is almost exclusively dependent on the price of the selected goods—using the law of demand: if everything else stays equal and the price of a good increases then quantity demanded decreases and vice versa. Finally, assumption saying the consumer has all relevant information for decision-making also must be met.

2 BOUNDED RATIONALITY

Some economists argue that external factors such as psychic or emotions do play a role in how people make decisions. Adam Smith also argued about over-estimating, risk aversion or self-control problems—these are all situations when the assumptions of neoclassical economics are not valid. Therefore, new area of economics started to be developed. This area is called behavioral economics. Behavioral economics, in contrast with the standard economics, does not suppose ordinary people are rational, it does not suppose these people are economic agents who always, in every situation, make optimal decisions.

Daniel Kahneman and Amos Tversky, Israeli psychologists, worked much on this theory and created the basics of behavioral economics. In this field the term which is connected to the human decision-making process is bounded rationality in contrast 100 percent rationality. On base of multiple experiments Kahneman and Tversky (1974) found out that people use simple rules of thumb to help them make judgments and forecasts. These simple rules are called heuristics—these are some sort of mental shortcuts on base of which people make decisions. Except for this, authors found out that errors in decision-making process (i.e. decisions which are not optimal from the point of utility theory) are not only because of emotions; according to Kahneman and Tversky, people make wrong decisions in some clearly defined situations. However, what is far more important is that these errors in decision-making are not random but they are systematic. It is obvious that random errors in decision-making process would not be a big deal from the neoclassical point of view. However, the fact that these errors in decision-making are systematic and predictable, is a big problem. As Richard Thaler, the Nobel prize winner in 2017, says: "One lesson from my stories is that some things that economic theory says should not matter actually do matter".

Behavioral economics uses findings from many other fields, such as psychology or sociology, to predict decisions of economic actors. Using these findings behavioral economics tries to explain non-optimal decisions of economics actors in real world. This field of economics is very much about systematic biases in decision-making. Therefore, it is obvious that this part of economics does not uses the basic assumption of neoclassic (standard) economics claiming that people are homo economics, i.e. fully rational beings in every situation. Behavioral economics violates the assumption that ordinary people have the same expectations and decisions as the best economists like Smith or Keynes.

Other assumptions, which are removed by behavioral economics is self-control, i.e. the human beings do not always make rational decisions (i.e. by a way that he maximizes the output of the utility function). This related for example to drinking alcohol, obesity or any other regular habits. If the assumption of full rationality was true, then the man would never drink many drinks in the bar, no one would be obese, everyone would eat healthy food, everyone would exercise, everyone would save on retirement exactly what he should, etc. However, unfortunately, that is not true due to the bounded rationality or irrationality of the economic actor. Behavioral economists claim the decision-making is rather conditional on external factors and situations.

As stated above, systematic errors are created in some specifically defined situations. The influence of situation or some factors on decision-making process is called the effect in behavioral economics. Plenty of effects is known to cause errors in optimal decision-making process of the economic actor.

The empirically demonstrated fact that individuals' decisions can be inconsistent with expected utility theory was developed by Maurice Allais (1953). He performed experiments and found out that individuals' decisions can be inconsistent with expected utility theory. This paradox relies in the fact that people do not like risk and prefer certainty and sure option rather than risk. For example, Rubinstein (1988) presents such an explanation of Allais paradox: "Decision maker is asked to choose between a sure chance of $1,000,000 and a l0:89:1 chance of $5,000,000: $1000000: $0." Most people choose the first option. The reason for that is that overvalue the absence of risk compared to any risk. This common preference of the sure lottery is explained by risk aversion which was studied by Kahneman and Tversky.

Endowment effect occurs when people overvalue a good that we own. It is obvious that in that case the objective market value is much lower than the value assigned by owners (Kahneman et al. 1991). It is therefore no surprise that people become relatively reluctant to change the thing for its objective value. "People place a greater value on things once they have established ownership, which is especially true for goods that wouldn't normally be bought or sold on the market, usually items with symbolic, experiential, or emotional significance." The endowment effect is an illustration of the status quo bias and can be explained by loss aversion. (BehavioralEconomics.com).

The effect above is very much connected to so called Ikea effect. This effect is characterized by the increment in valuation of self-made products. In experiments provided by Ariely et al. "participants saw their amateurish creations – of both utilitarian and hedonic products – as similar in value to the creations of experts, and expected others to share their opinions." They also found out that "labor leads to increased valuation only when labor results in successful completion of tasks; thus, when participants built and then destroyed their creations, or failed to complete them, the IKEA effect dissipated".

Another very important concept of behavioral economics is called mental accounting described by Nobel Prize winner Richard Thaler (Thaler 1985). Thaler says "people derive pleasure not just from an object's value, but also the quality of the deal – its transaction utility. In addition, humans often fail to fully consider opportunity costs and are susceptible to the sunk cost fallacy." (BehavioralEconomics.com). According to the theory of mental accounting, people are willing to spend more when they pay with a credit card than cash. The basic assumption of mental accounting is that people treat money differently, depending on factors such as the money's origin and intended use, rather than thinking of it in terms of the "bottom line" as in formal accounting (Thaler 1999).

"An important term underlying the theory is fungibility, the fact that all money is interchangeable and has no labels. In mental accounting, people treat assets as less fungible than they really are." (BehavioralEconomics.com).

Dunning-Kruger effect is a special form of super illusionary effect which claims that people overestimate their abilities in dependence on their real abilities. Authors showed (1999) that the following is true: the less the human can do something, the more he overestimates. And vice-versa, very competent people have tendency to underestimate themselves. Another important fact coming from the finding of Dunning and Kruger is that less competent people do not usually change their opinion after confrontation with reality or other persons (Lacko 2015).

Not surprisingly, people are not only affected by psychologic and emotional factors, they are also influenced by social factors. The concept of sociology to the human behavior and decision-making process has been thoroughly worked out by Robert Cialdini (Cialdini 2006).

Behavioral economics, however, is not just about defining and searching for biases. One of the main goals of this field is to try to remove these errors in decision-making of economic actors, i.e. search for and identify these systematic errors and try to bring people to not making these errors but rather to make optimal decisions or at least better. This was very much worked out by Richard Thaler who was also given the Nobel Prize in 2017.

Thaler, together with Sunstein, defined a subfield of behavioral economics which they called libertarian paternalism. In this subfield economists try to achieve public good. The tool for this noble aim are so-called nudges. Nudges are small pushes forward to optimal decisions. By nudging economists try to set the situation so that people would be "forced" to optimal decision-making process.

In public health, Dan Ariely, another famous behavioral economist, says that if we want to nudge people to preventive medical examination, the examination should be free of charge. He argues that the effect of zero price is a very important effect which significantly biases the decision-making process of the individual. If schools want children to prefer healthy alternatives from high-fat and fried meals, then the choice architecture should be changed – healthy meals should be first options in the menu.

The more effective tax collections can be realized by becoming aware to herring effect. If people get the message that other people act responsibly, then they also tend to do it the same way. The same is true at teenagers and their bad habits such as drinking alcohol or smoking cigarettes. Students who were confronted with the message that most people in their age do not drink alcohol or do not smoke, selected this option in not so many cases.

The effective way how to decrease the consumption of electric energy is as follows – in stating the account of one-year consumption there should be information regarding the consumption of the neighbor. This was acknowledged by experiments in which it decreased the energy consumption very dramatically.

Percentage of vaccinated students can be highly increased by handing out maps to them. Experiment which tested this found out that in that case 28 per cent students visited the vaccination center compared to only 3 per cent who only were present in the lecture.

The concept of nudges is becoming very popular today. Nowadays, there are around 50 nudge units—these are centers which concentrate on using the means of behavioral economics to nudge (push forward) people to right decisions. This concept has been also used by British government in public health.

It is important to note that these concepts of nudges can be also used in the opposite direction – to misuse the systematic biases of people to make money. As Thaler says: "It is easier to make money by catering to consumers biases than trying to correct them." Very often, companies misuses these concepts such as by using Decoy effect, bait or Schwarz paradox. It is therefore so surprise that this system can be easily misused and can lead to manipulation of people. But this is very much denied by the author, Richard Thaler, who challenge to use this for public good.

3 PROBLEM AND HYPOTHESES

Some studies have showed that decision-making process of the economic actor depend on the number of choices which are available in this process. Very often, in case of many options, the consumer is paralyzed by the choice, i.e. he is not able to make fast or right decision. Finally, even though he chooses the best option, he is not satisfied with his choice as much as he would make a choice from small number of options. This is due to the fact that the value of alternative options is very high. This effect is called choice overload and has a lot of do with the paradox of choice (Schwarz 2004).

Also, another interesting fact is that this paralysis of non-effectiveness in decision-making does not have to be caused by only the high number of options is available to the consumer. The noise in data is another important factor which can influence the decision-making process. According to some sources noise comprises 98 per cent of data in the world. The noise data are characterized as data which do not lead to more effective decision-making as they do not contain any useful information or knowledge which is acquired after processing this data. This noisy data, which often come from secondary sources, are reproduced, summarized or modified original news, publications of articles. This data can be interesting, however, what is more important is that their value added from the point of decision-making of the economic actor very often come close to zero.

Besides this, in some cases noisy data have negative effect. It means that this data does not contribute to creating knowledge, the opposite is true. The decision-making with noisy data is very often misleading and worse than if there is no data available. The main idea resulting from this is that not all the data can be a helpful tool in more effective decision-making. It is therefore necessary that this decision-making process would consider only so-called signal data and not the noise. However, the big problem is that the size of noise is rising exponentially in the world.

Let us assume that the economic actor is a human being with bounded rationality in this case, i.e. some other factors also influence his decision-making process which are irrelevant from the point of view of neoclassical economics (such as psychological, emotional, sociological). We therefore decided to investigate if the character of data is significant/influences the decision-making process of the economic actor. Our assumption is that the noise in data influences on the decision-making.

Except for this, the problem of decision-making of the human is that in real world, he does not have all the information relevant for making the right decision. So, we do not have complete information for making the right decision.

It would therefore be interesting to test the fact if the incomplete information influences the decision-making process. Following hypotheses would be interesting to be solved:

1. The complete information is necessary for the right decision (H1).
2. Efficient decision-making can only be realized with complete information, i.e. incomplete information influences on the speed of decision-making process (H2).
3. The noise in data influences on the speed of making information and knowledge from data (H3).

4. The noise in data causes exponential increment of time for creating information from data (H4).

These hypotheses should be tested using experiments. Experiments are the main tool of behavioral economics. If there is the influence of the noise and incomplete information on the decision-making process, it would be good to focus how to use this information in practice. For example, this could be used in decreasing the consumption in supermarket in defining the list of products we need to buy, using smaller supermarkets, defining the goal of the work before working on something, defining the desired output before datamining, etc. In case of high correlation, the investigation how big this influence is and how it is changing with increasing noise would be appropriate.

4 CONCLUSION

Behavioral economics is a field of economics which does not consider assumptions about full rationality of economic subjects. The opposite is true, this field considers factors which neoclassical economics does not – such as psychological, sociological and emotional factors. Using knowledge of psychology behavioral economics tries to explain and deduce human behavior. There are some situations when people do not act right – they make wrong decisions. These situations/factors are called effects – many of these effects have been described. They have one thing in common – people make systematic errors in decision-making. In this paper we described some of them such as Dunning-Kruger effect, Allais paradox, IKEA effect, Schwarz paradox or endowment effect.

Of course, behavioral economics has some critics, too. One of the most common argument of them is that in behavioral economics experiments are performed in laboratories. Critics claim that if you rise stakes, people will understand it and will make right decisions. However, as Richard Thaler says, there is no scientific evidence that as soon as you rise stakes, the decision-making improves. Another argument against behavioral economics is that the aspect of learning. According to critics, in real world people learn over time and in the end people will be good in this decision-making process. However, the problem is that the most important decisions in our lives do not provide sufficient options to learn (marriage, living, etc).

The choice is another important factor which influences the decision-making. As we believe that the character of data also influences the process, we have decided to test this. We defined four hypotheses which will be investigated using experiment. This experiment will consist of two groups of which one will be a control group. We presume that the character of data as well as the noise will show to be significant factors in decision-making process of economics subjects.

ACKNOWLEDGEMENT

This work was supported by the grant of Faculty of Management Science and Informatics, University of Žilina.

REFERENCES

Allais, M. 1953. Le comportement de l'homme rationnel devant le risque: Critique des postulats et axiomes de l'école américaine. Econometrica, 21, 503–46.

Cialdini, R. 2006. Influence. Harper Business; Revised edition, 2006, 336 pages.

Endowment Effect, BehavioralEconomics.com, available online at https://www.behavioraleconomics.com/mini-encyclopedia-of-be/endowment-effect/.

Kahneman, D. et al. 1991. Anomalies: The endowment effect, loss aversion, and status quo bias. Journal of Economic Perspectives, 5(1), 193–206.

Kruger, J. & Dunning, D. 1999. Unskilled and Unaware of It: How Difficulties in Recognizing One's Own Incompetence Lead to Inflated Self-Assessments. Journal of Personality and Social Psychology. American Psychological Association. 77 (6): 1121–1134.

Lacko, D. 2015. Dunning-Krugerův efekt: Proč hlupák zůstává hlupákem. In Psychologon. Brno: Psychologický ústav Filozofické fakulty Masarykovy univerzity, 2015. 9s. ISSN 1805–7160.

Mental Accouting, BehavioralEconomics.com, available at: https://www.behavioraleconomics.com/mini-encyclopedia-of-be/mental-accounting/.

Norton, I.M. 1988. The "IKEA Effect": When Labor Leads to Love, Working Paper, available at http://www.hbs.edu/faculty/Publication%20Files/11-091.pdf.

Rubenstein, A. 1988. Similarity and Decision-Making under Risk (Is there a Utility Theory Resolution to the Allais Paradox?). Journal of Economic Theory. 46. 145–153 (1988).

Schwarz, B. 2004. The Paradox of Choice: Why More Is Less, New York: Harper Collins.

Stanikova, Z. 2015. Úvod do ekonómie, EDIS Žilinská univerzita, 194p.

Thaler, R.H. 1985. Mental accounting and consumer choice. Marketing Science, 4(3), 199–214.

Thaler, R.H. 1999. Mental accounting matters. Journal of Behavioral Decision Making, 12, 183–206.

Tversky, A. & Kahneman, D. 1974. "Judgement Under Uncertainty: Heuristics and Biases." Science 185 (1974): 1124–31.

Production Management and Business Development – Mihalčová et al. (Eds)
© 2019 Taylor & Francis Group, London, ISBN 978-1-138-60415-5

Analysis of the efficiency of airport operations

J. Ferencová

Department of Air Transport, University College of Business, Prague, Czech Republic

ABSTRACT: The aim of the article is an analysis of the efficiency Vienna International Airport operations of handling narrow-body and wide-body aircraft. The analysis is focused on the calculation and comparison of the charges for Boeing 737 and Boeing 747. Description of aircraft focuses on their technical parameters, required ground handling, its partial activities and times for these activities. The calculation is basis for comparison and analysis airport revenues for the receiving of the individual types of aircraft by using the indicators as the duration of ground handling indicates, charges for overall handling, charges for one movement of aircraft and also long-term parking charge, the overall handling and airport charges.

1 INTRODUCTION

Apron capacity can easily become a limiting factor for airside, therefore one of the most important aspects of planning and management of airport operations is to ensure the efficient operation of this area. The objective of analysis of the effectiveness of airport operations by handling narrow-body and wide-body aircraft is to decide which type of aircraft is for the airport more favorable to receive and handle. The analysis is focused on the comparison of the number of planes, the number of handled passengers, airport charges, charges for the overall handling of the aircraft, charges for long-term aircraft parking and also charges for handled passengers, while operating only narrow-body aircraft and subsequently operating wide-body aircraft at a designated airport. Effectiveness calculations are applied to the Vienna International Airport, which has the use of necessary technology and suitable aircraft stands for handling of both compared types of aircraft, namely Boeing 737 as narrow-body and Boeing 747 aircraft as wide-body aircraft.

2 AIRPORT CAPACITY AND PERFORMANCE

Airport capacity is determined by the ability of airport facilities (in cooperation with other services and resources airports) to equip regular rush hour traffic flows in a given period of time at a specified or agreed level of service quality, so according to capacities of the individual parts (runway system, taxiways, aprons, terminal, air traffic control services, terminal maneuvering area TMA, airspace above the airport, airport parking, access roads and transport system city-airport.

2.1 Taxiway capacity

Fully equipped and well-designed system of taxiways should not be a limiting factor for airport capacity. Maximum performance is achieved by taxiway connection to both runway thresholds.

2.2 Runway system capacity

Runway system capacity is limiting factor for the capacity of the airport and an overview of the need for additional airport capacity is obtained by its determination. The parameters influencing this capacity include: layout and the number of the RWYs, the operating mode on the RWY, parameters and structure of operated aircraft, structure and readiness of aircraft crews, training and skills of air traffic controllers, and weather conditions at the airport.

2.3 Apron capacity

Capacity of aircraft stands, mainly their number and nature, may become by small airport area limiting factor for the airside. The amount of required aircrafts stands at the airport for the number of planes in the same period of time mainly depends on the number and type of aircraft that are registered for Gate, on the planned time of use of the stands for each aircraft (turnaround time), which has a direct impact on the number of handled aircraft.

2.4 Capacity of the airspace above airport

Capacity of boundary airspace-airport is influenced by several fields, including the size of TMA, complexity/simplicity of arrival and departure routes, environmental impact and other constraints, the choice of the class of airspace, organization airspace, configuration and airport infrastructure, requirements on navigational aids and terrain around the airport.

2.5 Terminal capacity

This figure is a measure of system throughput (the airport terminal) and should be referred to LoS (Level of Service) that must be offered to passengers in a given situation.

3 NARROW-BODY AIRCRAFT

The classical (narrow-body) aircraft are aircraft with fuselage width of 3–4 meters and with arrangement of 2 to 6 seats side by side along one end

3.1 Boeing 737-100

Boeing 737 is a short to medium twin-jet narrow-body airliner, the best-selling in the history of aviation. Production is concentrated in the factory Boeing Renton Factory in Renton, Washington. Boeing 737 is made in two generations, in the original and the new generation. The generations of the original models are: B737-100, –200, –300, –400, –500; and the new generation models: B737 NG, –600, –700/–700ER, –800, –900/–900ER. Typical turnaround times for the different activities during technical handling of the B737-100 and the subsequent overall duration of the process of ground handling we compute by using Gantt timing diagram (Fig. 1).

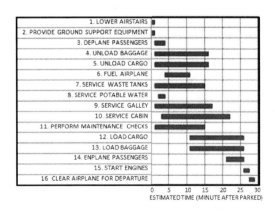

Figure 1. Gantt timing diagram of ground handling of B737-100.

However, the real times may vary, as they depend on the operational procedures, used technique and the conditions at the airport. Total time of aircraft handling on the aircraft stand is 30 minutes.

3.2 Prices for ground handling B737-100 aircraft at Vienna airport

Ground handling of the aircraft B737-100 will be charged according to publicly available document of the Airport Vienna, Airport Charges Regulations, effective from January 1, 2016.

Fee for overall handling and fuelling of the aircraft is charged. Fees for overall aircraft handling is pay use of equipment and facilities used for the provision of services of technical handling. To determine this type of fee is taken as payment basis delivery range of ground handling services and the provision of means of ground handling, calculated according to the type of aircraft stand, where the aircraft is handled and according to the category of aircraft.

The infrastructure charge "fueling" is payable for the use of equipment and facilities used for fueling of the aircraft with fuel and all fluids. This fee basis is the scope of supply of ground handling services performance, in the amount of €3.15/cubic meter.

Fuel tank capacity of B737 is 17 860 liter (17.86 cubic meters), the amount of the fee is calculated as $17.86 \times 3.15 = €56.26$.

4 WIDE-BODY AIRCRAFT

Wide-body aircraft fuselages are wide enough for two specific aisles with 7–10 seats next to each other, allowing them to have a total capacity of up to 850 passengers. The classic fuselage width is 5–6 meters.

Ground handling of aircraft consists of passenger handling, baggage and cargo handling and aircraft handling. Approximate times for these activities and total time (60 minutes) are calculated from the Gantt chart (Fig. 2).

4.1 Boeing 747-400

Boeing 747 with reputed name Jumbo Jet airliner is the most famous. Just like the classic Boeing 737, also B747 are produced in different versions: B747-100, B747 SR B747 SP, –200, –300, –400, B747 Large Cargo Freighter, B747-8.

4.2 Prices for ground handling B747-400 aircraft at Vienna airport

As well as classic aircraft, also wide-body aircraft will be charged for overall handling and fueling of

Table 1. The price list according to the assigned location and type of aircraft.

Infrastructure group	Aircraft types	Position pier	Position apron
5	A318, An148, Avro RJ70/85/100, BAC1-11, Bae ATP, BAe146, 717, 737-100/200/500/600, CRJ900/1000CS100, E170/175/190/195, F28, F70, F100, Il-114, L188 Electra, DC-9 (all types after series 50), Tu-134, Yak-42	€131.33	€95.26

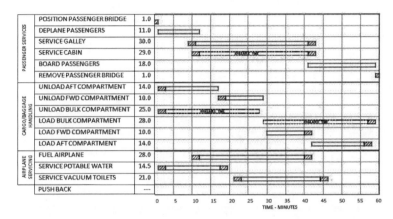

PASSENGER SERVICES	POSITION PASSENGER BRIDGE	1.0
	DEPLANE PASSENGERS	11.0
	SERVICE GALLEY	30.0
	SERVICE CABIN	29.0
	BOARD PASSENGERS	18.0
	REMOVE PASSENGER BRIDGE	1.0
CARGO/BAGGAGE HANDLING	UNLOAD AFT COMPARTMENT	14.0
	UNLOAD FWD COMPARTMENT	10.0
	UNLOAD BULK COMPARTMENT	25.0
	LOAD BULK COMPARTMENT	28.0
	LOAD FWD COMPARTMENT	10.0
	LOAD AFT COMPARTMENT	14.0
AIRPLANE SERVICING	FUEL AIRPLANE	28.0
	SERVICE POTABLE WATER	14.5
	SERVICE VACUUM TOILETS	21.0
	PUSH BACK	---

TIME - MINUTES

Figure 2. Gantt timing diagram of ground handling of B747-400.

Table 2. The price list according to the assigned location and type of aircraft.

Infrastructure group	Aircraft types	Position pier	Position apron
1	A380, A330, A340, A350, An-124, An-22, 747, 777, L5 Galaxy, L1011 Tristar, DC-10,	€432.01	€298.57

Table 3. Comparison of Vienna airport performances.

	2015	VS. 2014
Passengers	22 775 054	+1.3%
Transfer passengers	6 296 386	−3.6%
Local passengers	16 375 638	+3.2%
Flight movements	226 811	−1.7%
MTOW	8 395 038	+2.6%

the aircraft, according to the document Airport Vienna Airport Charges Regulations. Overall handling is in this case charged by aircraft type and allocated aircraft stand.

Capacity of fuel tanks of B747 is 216,840 liters, therefore, so the amount of the fee is calculated: $216.84 \times \text{€} 3.15 = \text{€} 683.05$.

5 VIENNA INTERNATIONAL AIRPORT

Vienna International Airport (German Flughafen Wien-Schwechat, English Vienna International Airport) ranks among the busiest airports in Europe. In 2014 Vienna airport was arrival or departure point for 22.5 million passengers and in 2015 the airport monitored 22 775 054 passengers, which means an increase compared to 2014 by 1.3% (Table 3).

Airport infrastructure consists of:

- RWY 11/29 – 3.500 metres long, 45 metres wide, category IIIb (direction 29)
- RWY 16/34 – 3.600 metres long, 45 metres wide, category IIIb (direction 16)
- 129 parking positions including 42 docking positions on pier stands and 87 on main apron
- Approximately 61 shops and 31 restaurants on the area of 19,000 sq.

5.1 Airport charges on Vienna airport

Airport charges are divided on landing fees and airport tax, according to the division of airport operational activities related to the landing, taxi-ing and aircraft parking, and activities related to passenger handling.

The following charges for Vienna Airport are used from publicly available document Airport Charges Regulations, effective from January 1, 2016.

5.1.1 *Landing fee*
A fee shall be payable for the use of the landing facilities and installations, for the use of aircraft parking positions within the free parking time and for the marshalling in and out of the aircraft.

Basis of assessment and rates for landing fee:

- the MTOW of the aircraft will be rounded up to the next full 1.000 kg (e.g. 4 001 kg = 5 000 kg/5 tons)
- irrespective of the MTOW of the aircraft a mini-mum landing fee for all aircraft will be charged per landing (fixed part of the landing fee), in amount of € 218.23 for passenger flights.

5.1.2 *Passenger service charge*
For the use of the passenger terminal buildings all their facilities and installations by departing pas-sengers and for implementation of environmental measures a charge shall be payable.

Passenger charge After adding the infrastructure charge "passenger" (€ 0.90 per PAX), passenger with reduced mobility charge (€ 0.38 per PAX) is the result charge € 18.43 per passenger.

5.1.3 *Parking charge*
A charge shall be payable for the use by an aircraft of the parking area. The claim of airport operator to that charge shall accrue from the moment the aircraft has been parked or is being moved to the parking position.

After expiration of the free parking period (4 hours) the charge per 24-hour period or part thereof (calculated per actual block to block time) shall be 15% of the applicable landing fee. No parking charge between 22:00 hrs. and 06:00 hrs. The times before 22:00 hrs. and after 06:00, the times before and after this time are added up.

5.1.4 *Infrastructure charge "passenger"*
For the allocation and utilization of infrastructural facilities and installations by an airline respectively its handling agent (airline/supplier of ground handling services) for the supply of passenger-handling services a charge is payable. The charge shall be per departing passenger in amount of € 0.90 per passenger.

5.1.5 *Passenger with reduced mobility charge*
According to article of the EU—Regulation the managing body of an airport is responsible for ensuring the provision of assistance to disabled persons and persons with reduced mobility. For the purpose of funding this assistance a charge on airport users is levied. The charge shall be per departing passenger € 0.38.

5.1.6 *Air navigation charge*
Air navigation charge consists of 2 groups:

a. Approach and Aerodrome Control Charges
For aircraft the charge is calculated according to the formula:
$R = t \times N$, where t – service unit rate € 192, N – weight factor,

$$N = \left(\frac{\sqrt{MTOW}}{50} \right).0,7 \tag{1}$$

b. En-route charges, unit rate € 69.04.

5.1.7 *Noise charge*
Calculation of the noise charge is based on objec-tive individual values of the aircraft, the aircraft operator is required to submit the necessary docu-mentation to the airport operator.

5.2 *Current conditions at the Vienna airport*

The airport has 129 stands available and 126 stands for B737 and 24 for B747, according to the dimen-sions (wingspan and length of the aircraft).

5.2.1 *Indicative airport charges for one movement of the Boeing 737-100*
Approximate calculation of airport charges for air-craft Boeing 737:

– **Landing fee**
Boeing 737-100 with MTOW of 49,940 kg (rounded up to the nearest whole 1000 kg to 50 tons) belongs to the category of aircraft with a MTOW of over 45 tons. Minimum initial fee for landing regardless of the MTOW of aircraft (fixed part of the land-ing fee) is € 218.23.

The variable part per tons over 45 tons: $5 \times € 5.95 = € 29.75$.

Landing fee shall be calculated:

$$Fixed\ part + Variable\ part = € 218.23 + € 29.75 = € 247.98 \tag{2}$$

– **Passenger service charge**
Boeing 737-100 has a capacity of 100 seats, allow-ing for full occupancy and passengers over the age of 2 years. The fee is charged € 17.15 per passenger, so $100 \times € 17.15 = € 1\ 715$.

Infrastructure charge "passenger" ($100 \times € 0.90 = € 90$) and passenger with reduced mobility charge

$(100 \times \text{€ } 0.38 = \text{€ } 38)$ are collected along with the passenger service charge.

The passenger service charge is calculated:

$$\text{€ } 1715 + \text{€ } 90 + \text{€ } 38 = \text{€ } 1843 \qquad (3)$$

– Air navigation charge

Air navigation charge is divided into two parts: Approach and Aerodrome Control Charges $(R = t \times N, R = 192 \times \text{€ } 0.254 = \text{€ } 48.77)$ and En-route charges (unit rate € 69.04).

The calculation of this charge:

Approach and Aerodrome Control Charge +
En-route charges $= \text{€ } 48.77 + \text{€ } 69.04 = \text{€ } 117.81$ (4)

Summary of the airport charges for one movement of the Boeing 737-100.

Airport charges for a Boeing 737-100 without prolonged standing at the airport of Vienna are calculated:

landing fee + passenger service charges +
air navigation charges $= \text{€ } 247.98 + \text{€ } 1\ 843 +$
$\text{€ } 117.81 = 2.208.79 \text{ €}.$ (5)

5.2.2 Indicative airport charges for one movement of the Boeing 747-400

Approximate calculation of airport charges for aircraft Boeing 747:

– Landing fee

Boeing 747-400 with a MTOW of 396 890 kg (397 tons, rounded to the nearest whole 1000 kg) belongs to the category of aircraft with a MTOW of over 45 tons. Minimum initial fee for landing regardless of the MTOW of aircraft (fixed part of the landing fee) is € 218.23 and a variable amount per ton over 45 tons: $352 \times \text{€ } 5.95 = \text{€ } 2\ 094.40$.

The calculation of landing fee:

Fixed part + Variable part $= \text{€ } 218.23 +$
$\text{€ } 2\ 094.40 = \text{€ } 2\ 312.63$ (6)

– Passenger service charge

Boeing 747–400 capacity is 442 seats, counting with full occupancy and passengers over the age of 2 years. The fee is charged € 17.15 per passenger, $(442 \times \text{€ } 17.15 = \text{€} 7\ 580.30)$.

Infrastructure charge "passenger" $(442 \times \text{€ } 0.90 = \text{€ } 397.80)$ and passenger with reduced mobility charge $(442 \times \text{€ } 0.38 = \text{€ } 167.96)$ are collected along with the passenger service charge.

The passenger service charge is calculated:
$\text{€} 7\ 580.30 + \text{€ } 397.80 + \text{€ } 167.96 = \text{€ } 8\ 146.06$

– Air navigation charge

Approach and Aerodrome Control Charges $(R = t \times N, R = \text{€ } 192 \times 23.17 = \text{€ } 4\ 448.64)$ and En-route charges (unit rate € 69.04).

The calculation of this charge:

Approach and Aerodrome Control Charge
+ Enroute charges $= \text{€ } 4\ 448.\ 64 + \text{€ } 69.04 = \text{€ } 4\ 517.68.$

Summary of the airport charges for one movement of the Boeing 747-400.

Airport charges for a Boeing 747-400 without prolonged standing at the airport of Vienna are calculated:

landing fee + passenger service charges +
air navigation charges $= \text{€ } 2\ 312.63 \text{ €} +$
$\text{€ } 8\ 146.06 + \text{€ } 4\ 517.68 = \text{€ } 14\ 976.37$ (7)

6 CALCULATION OF EFFICIENCY

Depending on what the cost is covered by revenue, these revenues are divided into two groups. The first group includes revenues from flight operations (airport fees) and for handling aircraft. The second group includes revenues from non-aeronautical activities, for example commercial activities, financial income.

The calculations focus on airport charges and charges for handling services.

6.1 Calculation

Calculation of efficiency includes two scenarios: complete occupation of aircraft stands by Boeing 737 and then also by Boeing 747.

In both cases, we count on aircraft equipment per unit of time 60 minutes (turnaround time of wide body aircraft Boeing 747) on all available stands, followed by a prolonged parking of the aircraft for 3 days (from the first day 8:00 to the third day 20:00).

6.1.1 Boeing 737-100—airport charges

According to the dimensions of aircraft stands (wingspan and length) we calculated 126 aircrafts stands for Boeing 737 from a total of 129, of which 42 stands are located on the pier apron and 84 stands on the main apron.

Airport charges per aircraft movement of this type are € 2 208.79 and turnaround time of one aircraft is 30 minutes, therefore per unit of time 60 minutes, the airport Vienna is available to handle:

a. 2 aircraft (in case of aircraft located on the pier stand)

b. 4 aircraft (in case of locating on the main apron).

Calculation of airport charges:

a. *2 × 42 × €2 208.79 = € 185 538.36*, the meaning of the individual numbers:
   – **2** – turnaround time of one B737 is 30 minutes, so we are able to handle 2 aircraft of this type on the pier stand in 60 minutes.
   – **42–42** stands on the pier stand, suitable for Boeing 737-100 (according to dimensions).
   – **€ 2 208.79** – airport **charge for one movement** of B737-100.

b. *2 × 84 × € 2 208.79 = € 742 153.44*, the meaning of the numbers:
   – **4** – we are able to park 2 aircraft side by side on one aircraft stand located on main apron, so in 60 minutes we are able to handle 4 aircraft of Boeing 737-100.
   – **84–84** stands with dimensions suitable for Boeing 737-100 available on Vienna airport.
   – **€ 2 208.79** – airport **charge for one movement** of B737-100.

This follows that we can handle 420 narrow-body aircraft in 60 minutes on Vienna airport and the charge is:

$$€ 185 538.36 + € 742 153.44 = € 927 697.80 \qquad (8)$$

6.1.2   Long-term parking of Boeing 737-100
Calculations are performed with aircraft parking time of three days, from the first day 8:00 to the third day 20:00. The first four hours of parking time are free, as well as parking in the time between 22:00 and 6:00, the time before 22:00 and after 6:00 is aggregated. The fee is charged for each 24-hour period plus for any such remaining period, namely 15% of the use of landing fee (in this case it is 15% from € 247.98, which is € 37.20). The plane will be parked together 40 paid hours (two 24-hour periods) and calculate the parking fee in this case will look like this: *2 × 0.15 × € 247.98 = € 74.40 × 126 aircraft = € 9 374.40*, because:

– **2** – two 24-hours periods.
– **0,15–15%** from landing fee the concrete type of aircraft.
– **€ 247.98** – **landing fee** of Boeing 737.
– **126–126 aircraft stands** available for B737 on Vienna airport.

6.1.3   Ground handling of Boeing 737-100
The overall charge for ground handling consists of infrastructure charge "ramp" and infrastructure charge "fuelling".
   Infrastructure charge "ramp"
The charge is payable according to category of aircraft and allocated aircraft stand (main apron/pier position). The calculation for handling on the position pier: *2 × 42 × € 131.33 = € 11 031.72*, where:

– **2–2 aircraft** can be handled in 60 minutes on this type of stand.
– **42–42 aircraft stands** on position pier with dimensions suitable for Boeing 737.
– **€ 131.33** – Infrastructure charge "ramp" for position pier.

The calculation for handling on the main apron: *4 × 84 × € 95.26 = € 32 007.36*, where:

– **4–4 aircraft** can be handled in 60 minutes on this type of stand.
– **84–84 stands** on main apron suitable for Boeing 737.
– **€ 95.26** – infrastructure charge "ramp" for handling on main apron.

The charge for overall handling: charge for handling on position pier + charge for handling on main apron = *€ 11 031.72 + € 32 007.36 = €43 039.08*
   Infrastructure charge "fuelling"
336 aircraft of type Boeing 737-100 are handled on main apron in 60 minutes and 84 aircraft on position pier, so 420 aircraft are fuelled on Vienna airport in 60 minutes.
   The charge for fuelling: *420 × € 56.26 = € 23 629.20*, where the charge for fuelling full tank of one aircraft is € 56.26.
   The charge for ground handling: infrastructure charge "ramp" + infrastructure charge "fuelling" = *€43 039.08 + € 23 629.20 = € 66 668.28*

6.1.4   Boeing 747-400 – airport charges
24 available and suitable stands for aircraft Boeing 747-400 are on Vienna airport, airport charges for one movement of the B747-400 are € 14 976.37 and turnaround time is 60 minutes.
   This follows, that 1 aircraft B747 can be handled in 60 minutes, calculation: *1 × 24 × € 14 976.37 = € 359 432.88*

6.1.5   Long-term parking of Boeing 747-400
Parking time is 3 days period, from the first day 8:00 a.m. to the third (last) day 8:00 p.m., so the aircraft stays on the stand in all 40 payable hours (2 24-hours long periods), calculation of parking charge for the B747-400 is: *2 × 0.15 × € 2 312.63 = € 693.79 × 24 aircraft = € 16 650.94*, because:

– **2** – two 24-hours long periods
– **0.15–15%** from landing fee of the aircraft B747-400
– **€ 2 312.63** – landing fee of B747-400
– **24–24 aircraft** stands suitable for B747-400

6.1.6   Ground handling of Boeing 747-400
As well as by B737-100, the overall charge for handling of B747 also consists of infrastructure charge "ramp" and infrastructure charge "fuelling".

Infrastructure charge "ramp"

The calculation for handling on position pier: $1 \times 9 \times €\ 432.01$, where:

- **1 – 1 aircraft** of this type can be handled on pier stand in 60 minutes
- **9 – 9 aircrafts stands** suitable and available for B747 on Vienna airport
- **€ 432.01** – infrastructure charge "ramp" for handling on position pier

The calculation for handling on main apron: $1 \times 15 \times €\ 298.57 = €\ 4\ 478.55$, where:

- 1–1 aircraft of this type can be handled on main apron stand in 60 minutes.
- 15–15 stands suitable and available for B747-400 on main apron.
- € 298.57 – infrastructure charge "ramp" for handling on main apron

Infrastructure charge "fuelling"

15 aircraft of type Boeing 747-400 are handled on main apron in 60 minutes and 9 aircraft on position pier, so 24 aircraft are fuelled on Vienna airport in 60 minutes.

The charge for fuelling: $24 \times €\ 683.05 = €\ 16\ 393.20$, where the charge for fuelling full tank of one aircraft is € 683.05.

The charge for ground handling: infrastructure charge "ramp" + infrastructure charge "fuelling" $= €\ 8\ 366.64 + €\ 16\ 39.20 = €\ 24\ 759.84$

6.2 Comparison of charges for Boeing 737 and Boeing 747

The individual results of the calculations of income from airport charges, ground handling, as well as long-term aircraft parking are for better clarity shown in the tables.

7 THE RESULTS OF ANALYSIS

In the Table 4, where the incomes of aircraft handling for 1 hour are compared, we can see that incomes of Boeing 737, narrow-body aircraft, handling are notably higher than incomes of Boeing 747 handling.

The situation is the same also by passenger service charges, the number of passenger by receiving Boeing 737 is higher than by Boeing 747, therefore the incomes are also notably higher.

This means that for the airport operator is handling of narrow-body aircraft more favorable.

Notably different is also amount of suitable aircraft stands for individual types of aircraft. This affected capabilities of receiving and handling of number of aircraft in given time period, that's why the big different in income amounts for Boeing 737 and Boeing 747.

Table 4. Comparison of incomes for 1 hour.

		Boeing 737	Boeing 747
Time unit 1 hour:	Airport charges	€927 697.80	€359 432.88
	Charge for ground handling	€66 668.28	€24 759
	Number of handled aircraft	420	24

Table 5. Comparison of incomes for 8 hours.

		Boeing 737	Boeing 747
Time unit 8 hours (1 work shift):	Airport charges	€7 421 582.40	€2 875 463.04
	Charge for ground handling	€533 346.24	€198 078.02
	Number of handled aircraft	3 360	192

Table 6. Comparison of incomes for long-term parking.

	Boeing 737	Boeing 747
Long-term parking charge	€9 374.40	€16 650.94

Table 7. Comparison of incomes for passengers for 1 hour.

		Boeing 737	Boeing 747
Time unit 1 hours	Number of handled passengers	42 000	10 608
	Passenger service charges	€774 060	€195 505.44

Table 8. Comparison of incomes for passengers for 8 hours.

		Boeing 737	Boeing 747
Time unit 8 hours (1 work shift)	Number of handled passengers	336 000	84 864
	Passenger service charges	€6 192 480	€1 564 043.52

Table 8 is focused on comparison of parking charges. Long- term parking of wide-body aircraft brings to airport operator higher incomes than long-term parking of narrow-body aircraft. This follows, that for airport operator is for parking more favorable to receive wide-body aircraft.

7.1 Suggestions and recommendations

As the incomes for handling aircraft of type Boeing 747 are significantly smaller than a Boeing 737, the airport operator can afford outsource this activity, let on the market next provider of handling services, and so to comply with Council Directive 96/67/EC about access to the ground handling market at airports.

In the similar way, the airport operator can act by passenger handling, so let the handling of passengers by airline operating Boeing 747 to other handling providers.

Incomes from long-term parking of Boeing 747 allow to the airport operator to lease the aircraft stands for wide-body aircraft the airport operator and therefore maximize the incomes from this category.

8 CONCLUSION

The article described the efficiency of airport operations by operating the Boeing 737 and Boeing 747, representatives' narrow-body and wide-body aircraft at the Vienna airport.

For the airport is more favorable to receive and handle the narrow-body aircraft Boeing 737, as the comparison of incomes and numbers of aircraft and passengers indicate.

These questions, however, are only partial, because in the article are not used the noise charges and there were only taken the incomes for the airport operator, not the costs of aircraft handling.

The costs of handling would be very different considering the number of handled aircraft of individual types. For handling of 24 Boeing 747 aircraft compared to 420 aircraft handling Boeing 737 it is necessary to have several times less equipment and employees of ground handling.

REFERENCES

Airport charges of Vienna airport. Available at: http://www.viennaairport.com/jart/prj3/va/uploads/data-uploads/Charges%20Regulations%202016.pdf.

Facts about Vienna airport. Available at: http://www.viennaairport.com/en/company/flughafen_wien_ag/fwag_group_facts__figures_.

Ferenc, J. et al. 2011. Ekonomika prevádzky letísk. Košice: TU-LF, 2011. ISBN 978-80-553-0704-6.

International Air Transport Association (IATA) 2017. Airport Handling Manual. 37th Edition.

International Civil Aviation Organization (ICAO). 2010. Tariffs for Airports and Air Navigation Services, 582 p.

International Civil Aviation Organization (ICAO). 2013. Manual on Air Navigation Services Economics, 184 p.

McDonnell Douglas Corporation, Douglas Aircraft Company. 2011. MD-11 Airplane Characteristics for Airport Planning. 190 p. Available at: http://www.boeing.com/assets/pdf/commercial/airports/acaps/dc10.pdf.

Technical parameters and characteristic of Boeing 737. Available at: http://www.boeing.com/assets/pdf/commercial/ airports/acaps/737.pdf.

Technical parameters and characteristic of Boeing 747. Available at: http://www.boeing.com/assets/pdf/commercial/airports/acaps/747_4.pdf.

Production Management and Business Development – Mihalčová et al. (Eds)
© 2019 Taylor & Francis Group, London, ISBN 978-1-138-60415-5

The employee benefits in the manufacturing enterprises

B. Gontkovičová
Faculty of Business Economics with seat in Košice, University of Economics in Bratislava, Košice, Slovak Republic

ABSTRACT: Modern employee remuneration system is no longer just about wages and salaries. The rewards motivate employees, but they do not have to be necessarily based on finance, that's why more and more emphasis is now placed on employee benefits as tools with considerable impact on employee loyalty and performance. This creates platform for discussion about the importance of new forms of employee remuneration. The new trend of various forms of employee benefits appears also in practice of manufacturing enterprises. The aim of this paper is to examine the distribution and structure of employee benefits provided in manufacturing enterprises in Slovak Republic.

1 INTRODUCTION

Employee benefits as form of non-financial rewards can have an even more significant impact on employee satisfaction and motivation than traditional financial rewards. When employees have a job that offers great benefits, they are less likely to leave that job. Many enterprises (employers) associate the benefits with high costs. However, if company loses an employee, loses also money. When an employee leaves, it means for company incurred expense for replacing. For example, cost related with advertising of the vacant job position, training for the new employee which not yet produces. Consequently, it's more economical to give benefits to employees than to have cost with training new ones.

2 EMPLOYEE BENEFITS IN REMUNERATION STRUCTURE

The motivation and employee satisfaction, which lead to an increase in labor productivity, belong among the actual priorities in the field of personnel management. Remuneration is part of the complex personal systems and tools used by the company in the management of human resources. Nowadays, the employee benefits are gaining an increasingly solid position in these systems.

The effective reward strategy defines longer-term intentions in such areas as pay structures, contingent pay, employee benefits, steps to increase engagement and commitment and adopting a total reward approach (Armstrong, 2007).

Financial reward is ranked at the top of employee preferences long term because it enables to fulfil their basic needs of life and money is considered as the sign of triumph and accomplishment. Financial reward enables the human to establish status, rank and authority (Yousaf 2014).

Benefits are programs which an employer uses to supplement the cash compensation that employees receive. These programs are designed to protect the employee and his or her family from financial risks. Some benefits are provided across the board (for all employees), others may be provided for example in relation to the employee function in the company, length of employment, the status of a worker in a company or to its merits (Dědina, Cejthamr, 2005).

From the point of view of the importance degree attached to employee benefits, individual representatives of domestic or foreign professional literature, attribute to provided employee benefits a different role and level of importance. However, all agree that employee benefits play work motivation's role in influencing workplace behavior and performance.

Both, the financial reward in form of salary of wage and also employee benefits play an important role in attracting and retaining employees in the enterprises, because a fair adjustment of the entire scheme of remuneration and employee benefits leads to the increased attractiveness of the enterprises as an employer (Urbancová, Šnýdrová 2017).

Most motivates mutually balanced system that can meet the needs of the employee. Well-chosen benefits make a suitable balance between work and leisure for employees. These are for someone very important and in choosing a job take account of it. Conversely, other employees do not use any of the offered benefits and is essential for them what "money" receive for their work.

Organizations give many and varied reasons for introducing flexible benefits. The principal reasons are as follows (Silverman, Reilly 2016):

- Recruitment and retention needs
- Legislative and social pressures
- Cost-cutting requirements
- Organizational alignment
- Response to mergers and acquisitions
- Pay harmonization
- Generating employee understanding

The retention of top notch talent is getting more and more difficult in the current economic climate because the demand for quality employees greatly exceeds the supply available (Pacific Crest Group 2018).

2.1 Types of employee benefits

Employees' expectations are much higher these days and they want to do things as well as have things. In this way, non-financial recognition schemes provide employees with something tangible that they can remember: a special day out or a great meal can instil much more positive effect than a sum of money paid into a bank account, net of tax and national insurance (Silverman 2004). The employer must well know of their people and their priorities for well setting the remuneration package (Dugasová & Tkáčová 2012). The fact is that up to 56% of employees in Western Europe and 44% of employees in Eastern Europe said their organizations did not support them in achieving a reasonable work-life balance (Hay Group 2013). Employee benefits must focus on your employees' emotional needs not just their financial requirements for them to stay with your firm over the long haul. It is imperative that you give them plenty of reasons to remain loyal to your organization (Pacific Crest Group 2018).

All employee benefits communicate to employees that their work is valued and promote a posi-tive work-life balance. Some of them, such as flexible working hours declare the willingness of enterprise to provide an attractive working environment. Another interferes with company cost and so reduces the living expenses of employees. For example, the use of company car for private purposes may create cost savings in tens to hundreds of euro per month for employee. Similarly, the allowances for pension and life insurance, food beyond the law, transportation reimbursement and above standard medical care have the financial effect for employee. Evenly, the health insurance is the most expensive benefit offered to the employee. Some of the organizations offer pension which is the deferred income collected during the working lives and is returned to the employee after retirement (Yousaf 2014).

One of most common benefit is mobile phone for private purposes. Firstly, paying an expensive cell phone bill sounds like a great benefit that has the effect of increased compensation. On the other hand, it doesn't come without strings attached, since it usually means you are always on call. You feel like you should be taking calls or answering emails 24/7. Most people are better off if they can truly leave work at work (Donald Hatter in Forbes 2018).

3 METHODOLOGY

Methods used in the elaboration of the paper are the most commonly used methods of economic research, and they are based on the aim and structure of the article. These are general methods such as analysis, time comparison, synthesis, induction, deduction and mathematical—statistical methods.

Boxplot provides information about the variability of values in data set through. In its simplest form, the boxplot presents five sample statistics – the minimum, the lower quartile, the median, the upper quartile and the maximum – in a visual display.

The normality of data is a prerequisite for many statistical tests and an underlying assumption in parametric testing. It is tested by Shapiro-Wilk Test. It is more appropriate for small sample sizes (less than 50) and the samples used in research have lesser extent. The test rejects the hypothesis of normality when the p-value is less than or equal to 0.05. The decision for a suitable test (parametric, non-parametric) is determined by besides knowledge of normality also by homogeneity of data. homogeneity of data was verified by Levene's test. If the significance from this test is less than 0.05, then variances are significantly different (homogeneity is rejected) and parametric tests cannot be used. Grubbs' test is using to detect outliers in a univariate data set assumed to come from a normally distributed population.

For analysis and comparison are used data from salary survey provided by Platy.sk. Platy.sk is the

Table 1. Employee benefits.

Education of employees/ Training program	Wedding bonus/ Baby bonus
Home office	Team building
Flexible working time	Beverages in the workplace
Above-standard health care	Additional days of holiday
Discount on dentistry services	Reimbursement of transportation to work
Mobile phone for private purposes	Company contributions to retirement savings
Notebook for personal purposes	Food allowance beyond the law
Company car for private purposes	Contribution for health insurance
Sport and culture vouchers	Company weekend events

author of the salary survey, which has carried out in Slovakia since 2007 and collects information about earnings and employee bonuses in various jobs. Currently, the database has more than 76,000 respondents and presents a salary comparison for about 500 job positions. List of the positions reflects the labor market in Slovakia and is continually updated. It is the biggest salary database in Slovakia. The Platy.sk portal belongs to international network of salary portals Paylab.

4 EMPLOYEE BENEFITS TRENDS IN MANUFACTURING

Growth potential of Slovak economy depends primarily on industrial production, which at the same time creates conditions for the growth of high-tech services, especially in the area of significant growth in the use of information technology in the complex management of enterprises. Implementation of innovation in manufacturing also helps the regions to exploit the opportunities brought about by technological change and modernization of industry (Duľová Spišáková & Stričík 2016).

Manufacturing is the most important component of GDP creation in the Slovak economy. In 2017, 2 458 enterprises with 20 or more employees were in manufacturing. During this period, the average registered number of employees in the sector was 379 929 persons (Ministerstvo hospodárstva SR 2018). In manufacturing, employment rose in the key segments, especially in the automotive industry. Strong employment growth was also recorded in wood processing (Národná banka Slovenska 2017).

As for the relation between wage level in economy as whole and manufacturing sector in Slovakia, according to Statistical Office while the average wage in Slovakia in 2017 was €954, the average wage in manufacturing was €1031. The financial reward is therefore above average. In our analysis we will focus on the providing of employee benefits in manufacturing sector in Slovak economy.

According to Figure 1, the employee benefits become a stable part of reward system. As for manufacturing, while 30% of respondents adduce that they had not any employee benefit in 2010, it is 28% in 2016. These values exceed the average level of employee benefits providing in Slovakia.

4.1 Structure of employee benefits

The time comparison of structure of provided employee benefits in Slovak economy is presented by Figure 2 and Figure 3.

In 2010, education, flexible working hours and free drinks at workplace were the most used benefits in manufacturing and Slovak economy

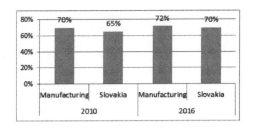

Figure 1. Rate of employee benefits providing (comparison 2010 and 2016).
Source: Own processing according to data from Platy.sk.

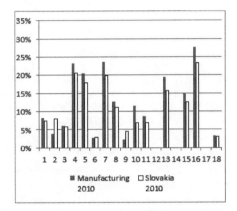

Figure 2. Structure of employee benefits in manufacturing and Slovak economy in 2010.
Source: Own processing according to data from Platy.sk.

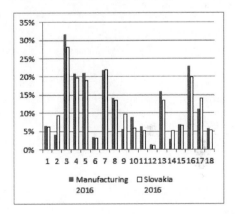

Figure 3. Structure of employee benefits in manufacturing and Slovak economy in 2016.
(Legend: 1 – car also for private use, 2 – extended vacation time, 3 – corporate events, 4 – flexible working hours, 5 – mobile phone for private use, 6 – above-standard medical care, 7 – free drinks, 8 – notebook also for private use, 9 – home office, 10 – transportation reimbursement, 11 – reimbursement of sport or culture activities, 12 – housing allowance, 13 – contributions to supplementary pension savings, 14 – sick day, 15 – food beyond the law, 16 – education, 17 – employee discounts, 18 – extra health insurance).
Source: Own processing according to data from Platy.sk.

as whole. Moreover, a fifth of manufacturing employees used the chance to have mobile phone for private use and receive contributions to supplementary pension savings. However, we do not observe significant differences.

The most change is observed in case of organizing of corporate events in 2016. The corporate events became the most commonly provided employee benefits (32% in manufacturing; 28% in Slovakia). Also, free drinks, flexible working hours and education belong among frequented employee benefits. The employee benefits such as extra health insurance or above-standard medical care are rather rare in Slovakia. It is related with the state funded healthcare system and fact that the healthcare contributions are mandatory. Each employed citizen has to pay contributions to the health insurance company.

However, education reported the decrease. Professionally competent staff is the basis for the success in any kind of business, which requires high-quality training and education (Šimková et al. 2008), more so in the case of manufacturing.

4.2 *Variability and distribution of employee benefits*

Figure 4 provides information about the variability of values in data set through boxplot. The obvious differences are immediately apparent. In both years,

boxplot for manufacturing sector is higher than Slovak average and also has larger variability than compared sample. The positive is that the increasing trend is observed for both samples.

The statistical significance of difference in time is analyzed by paired sample test. Shapiro-Wilk test confirms the normality of data for Slovak economy as whole, but data of manufacturing in 2016 do not have normal distribution. Levene's test confirms the equality of variances and Grubb's test does not confirm the outlier (Table 2).

T test for two paired samples is used for the employee benefits in Slovakia (normal distribution) and Wilcoxon Signed-Rank Test for Paired Samples is used in case of manufacturing. The significance level is 5% for all.

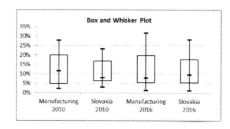

Figure 4. BoxPlots of benefits structure (comparison 2010 and 2016).
Source: Own processing according to data from Platy.sk.

Table 2. Normality, homogeneity and outlier test.

Shapiro-Wilk test			Grubbs' test		
2010					
	Manufacturing	Slovakia		Manufacturing	Slovakia
alpha	0.05	0.05	alpha	0.05	0.05
W	0.9208	0.9224	outlier	0.2768	0.2329
p-value	0.1981	0.1424	G	1.7649	1.8672
			G-crit	2.4090	2.5040
normal	yes	yes	sig	no	no
Levene's tests					
type	means		medians	trimmed	
p-value	0.894438769	0.953715566	0.894438769		
Shapiro-Wilk test			Grubbs' test		
2016					
	Manufacturing	Slovakia		Manufacturing	Slovakia
alpha	0.05	0.05	alpha	0.05	0.05
W	0.8949	0.9172	outlier	0.3160	0.3049
p-value	0.0469	0.1006	G	2.2736	2.0962
			G-crit	2.5040	2.5312
normal	no	yes	sig	no	no
Levene's Tests					
type	means		medians	trimmed	
p-value	0.446000486	0.615882484	0.446000486		

Table 3. Paired sample test results.

Wilcoxon signed-rank test for paired samples			T Test: Two paired samples		
Manufacturing			Slovakia		
	one tail	two tail		one tail	two tail
alpha	0.05		p-value	0.0853	0.1706
mean	85.5		t-crit	1.7396	2.1098
std dev	22.9619		lower		–0.0548
z-score	0.1089		upper		0.0105
effect r	0.0181				
T-crit	47.7310	40.4955			
p-value	0.4567	0.9133			
sig (norm)	no	no	sig	no	no

Table 3 presents the test results of statistical significance of difference in time comparison of employee benefits in Manufacturing and Slovakia.

Based on paired sample test results (p>α) the null hypothesis "The average availability of provided benefits is comparable in both years" is failed to be rejected. Despite the colorful palette of providing benefits, the interannual changes observed in selected economic sectors are not statistically significant.

5 CONCLUSIONS

The aim of the company is to have satisfied and loyal employees which contribute to the objectives and vision of the company. Remuneration is part of the complex personal systems and tools used by the company in the management of human resources. There is not a guaranteed unified model that can be used with the same result in each company.

The paper deals with the question of the employee benefits in manufacturing in Slovakia as sector which is one of most contributors to country GDP. As for financial reward, it is above average in manufacturing. The structure of employee benefits provided in manufacturing was compared with data for Slovak economy as whole and also observed across the time. Employees in manufacturing companies obtain more employee benefits and also in wider structure than Slovak average. Employee benefits such as corporate events, free drinks, flexible working hours, mobile phone for private use and education belong among most used and more than a fifth of employees receive them. As for time comparison, in spite of the obvious differences in absolute term, the statistical significance of the differences was not confirmed.

In the past, remuneration of employees was often narrowed only to the question of wages and salaries. Gradually, the employers in Slovakia are starting to realize the importance and power of employee benefits, evidenced by the fact that more than 70% of employees (in manufacturing, but also in Slovakia overall) use employee benefits.

ACKNOWLEDGEMENT

This paper was supported by the Slovak Scientific Grant Agency as part of the research project VEGA 1/0251/17.

REFERENCES

Armstrong, M. 2007. *A Handbook of Employee Reward Management and Practice*. Kogan Page Publishers.

Dědina, J., Cejthamr, V. 2005. *Management a organizační chování*. Praha, Grada Publishing.

Duľová Spišáková, E. & Stričík, M. 2016. Economic effects of innovation. *Economic development of region with an impact on quality of life: proceedings of the scientific-technical conference*, 20.4.2016, Uzhhorod, pp. 31–39.

Dugasová, B. & Tkáčová, A. 2012. Benefits for employees. *POSTER 2012: 16th International Student Conferenece on Electrical Engineering*. Praha: Czech Technical University in Prague.

Hatter, D. 2018. Paying Cell Phone Bills. *Forbes: 13 Employee Benefits That Don't Actually Work*, 04/05/2018.

Hay Group. 2013. *Developing a Work-Life Culture of Balance*, 2013. [on-line]. http://www.haygroup.com/downloads/ar/ White_Paper_Work_life-Balance.pdf.

Ministerstvo hospodárstva SR. *Priemyselná výroba a jej postavenie v hospodárstve SR* [online]. Odbor priemyselného rozvoja Ministerstva hospodárstva Slovenskej republiky. May 2018. http://www.economy.gov.sk/ uploads/ files/ezNh8 gXF.pdf.

Národná banka Slovenska. 2017. *Report on the Slovak Economy* [on-line]. https://www.nbs.sk/_img/Documents/_ Publikacie/SESR/2017/SESR_1217en.pdf.

Pacific Crest Group 2018. *Employee Benefits Drive Employee Retention*. 2018. [online]. http://www.pcg-services.com/ employee-benefits-drive-employee-retention/.

Platy.sk [on-line]. https://www.platy.sk/.

Silverman, M. 2004. *Non-Financial Recognition. The Most Effective of Rewards?* Institute for Employment Studies.

Silverman, M., Reilly, P. 2016. *How Flexible is Total Reward?* Institute for Employment Studies.

Statistical Office of the Slovak Republic [online]. www.statistics.sk/.

Šimková, H. et al. 2008. Improvement of employees' corporate training in the company Topvar Brewery Inc. *Ekonomie a management*. 11(1):. 53–59.

Urbancová, H., Šnýdrová, M. 2017. Remuneration and employee benefits in organizations in the Czech Republic. *Acta Universitatis Agriculturae Et Silviculturae Mendelianae Brunensis*, 65(1): 357–368.

Yousaf, S. et al. 2014. Impact of Financial and Non Financial Rewards on Employee Motivation. *Middle-East Journal of Scientific Research* 21(10): 1776–1786.

Trends of agrarian trade of the Slovak Republic with third countries

M. Hambálková & A. Vakoš

Department of Marketing and Trade, Faculty of Economics and Management,
Slovak University of Agriculture in Nitra, Nitra, Slovak Republic

ABSTRACT   Slovak agrarian trade was significantly affected by accession of the Slovak Republic to the European Union on May 1st, 2004. This meant to adapt to the conditions of Common Agricultural Policy and Common Trade Policy of the European Union, which are related to the foreign trade of the Slovak Republic with agricultural and food products. These influence its development, increase the agricultural production, sustainability of farming, and support the production of food. The aim of the paper is to evaluate the trends of agrarian trade of the Slovak Republic with third countries that will be achieved by analyzing the development of foreign agrarian trade of the Slovak Republic in the area of commodity and territorial structure. Submitted paper focuses on the Slovak agricultural and food products in the third country markets as well as on the foreign agrarian trade relations between the Slovak Republic and individual international groups.

1 INTRODUCTION

Business is not about winning and losing, it is not a card game.
If people specialize in absolute or comparative advantages, all of them could earn money.
Anonym

Slovak agrarian trade was significantly affected by accession of the Slovak Republic to the European Union on May 1st, 2004. This meant to adapt to the conditions of Common Agricultural Policy and Common Trade Policy of the European Union. Slovakia also created conditions for improving and maintaining trade relations with non-EU countries.

In 2004, the agro-food foreign trade of the Slovak Republic had to adapt to the conditions of the European Union. Each Slovak producer and exporter of agricultural and food products had to re-orientate trade towards the common market. More than 95 percent of domestic agri-food exports went to the EU countries. Concerning the trade with third countries, we face great competition (Matošková & Gálik 2009).

Slovak foreign trade with agro-commodities, according to Hambálková & Récky (2014), has been unfavorable recently. Negative balance is increasing and poses a great threat that affects the competitiveness of domestic products on domestic and foreign markets.

The Slovak Republic had to adapt to the conditions of the Common Agricultural Policy, which has significantly affected our agriculture. In the transformation of the domestic agrarian sector into market conditions, Slovakia has done very well and has made great progress which still needs to be constantly improved. One of the main current aims is to get the Slovak agriculture to about equal level of competitiveness to European agro-sector.

No country in the world can be completely self-sufficient and competitive. There is no such country that has the ability to produce all the necessary products for the economy. Each country should retain Ricard's theory of comparative advantages that the country should focus on producing and exporting those products where it achieves the highest productivity (Rhee 2012).

Foreign agrarian trade builds the relations between the Slovak Republic and individual international groups such as EFTA, CIS, EUROMED, MERCOSUR and GCC.

The European Free Trade Association (EFTA) is an intergovernmental organization set up for the promotion of free trade and economic integration to the benefit of its four Member States. The Association is responsible for the management of:

– The EFTA Convention, which forms the legal basis of the organization and governs free trade relations between the EFTA States.
– EFTA's worldwide network of free trade and partnership agreements.
– The European Economic Area (EEA) Agreement, which enables three of the four EFTA Member States (Iceland, Liechtenstein and Norway) to participate in the EU's Internal Market.

EFTA was founded in 1960 on the premise of free trade as a means of achieving growth and prosperity amongst its Member States as well as promoting closer economic cooperation between the Western European countries. Furthermore, the EFTA countries wished to contribute to the expansion of trade globally (EFTA 2017).

Commonwealth of Independent States (CIS) was created in December 1991. In the adopted Declaration the participants of the Commonwealth declared their interaction on the basis of sovereign equality. At present the CIS unites: Azerbaijan, Armenia, Belarus, Georgia, Kazakhstan, Kyrgyzstan, Moldova, Russia, Tajikistan, Turkmenistan, Uzbekistan and Ukraine. In September 1993 the Heads of the CIS States signed an Agreement on the creation of Economic Union to form common economic space grounded on free movement of goods, services, labor force, capital; to elaborate coordinated monetary, tax, price, customs, external economic policy; to bring together methods of regulating economic activity and create favorable conditions for the development of direct production relations (CIS 2017).

Within the European Neighborhood Policy, the EuroMed transport cooperation builds on the cooperation framework launched in Barcelona in 1995. The Mediterranean members of the EuroMed partnership are: Algeria, Egypt, Israel, Jordan, Lebanon, Libya (since 2012 Libya is an eligible country for EuroMed partnership and has observer status in the UfM), Morocco, Palestine, Syria (cooperation is suspended) and Tunisia. The UfM members include, together with the 28 EU Countries, also the following Mediterranean partners: Albania, Bosnia-Herzegovina, Mauritania, Monaco, Montenegro and Turkey. The key priority of this cooperation is achievement of a safe, sustainable and efficient transport system in the Euro-Mediterranean area (European Commision 2017).

The EU is currently negotiating a trade agreement with the four founding members of MERCOSUR (Argentina, Brazil, Paraguay and Uruguay) as part of the overall negotiation for a bi-regional Association Agreement. Current trade relations between the EU and Mercosur are governed by an inter-regional Framework Cooperation Agreement which entered into force in 1999. In addition, the EU and individual Mercosur countries have bilateral Framework Cooperation Agreements, which also establish a structure for dealing with trade-related matters (European Commission, Mercosur 2017).

Gulf Cooperation Council (GCC) is political and economic alliance of six Middle Eastern countries—Saudi Arabia, Kuwait, the United Arab Emirates, Qatar, Bahrain and Oman. The GCC was established in Riyadh, Saudi Arabia, in May 1981. The purpose of the GCC is to achieve unity among its members based on their common objectives and their similar political and cultural identities (GCC 2017).

2 DATA AND METHODS

Paper was elaborated by using both secondary and primary sources. In order to achieve the aim of the paper, we used the statistical methods, the analytic-synthetic method, the objective method and the comparative method for comparing the territorial and commodity structure. The statistical data of the foreign agrarian trade necessary for the analysis were obtained from the Statistical Office of the Slovak Republic, Ministry of Agriculture and Rural Development of the SR, the EU database, Eurostat and Ministry of Economy of the Slovak Republic. The foreign trade of the Slovak Republic and its statistics were obtained from the data of the EXTRA-STAT and INTRASTAT system. The comparative advantages of SR with agricultural and food products were evaluated by using the revealed comparative advantage index (RCA), see Equation 1 below:

$$RCA = \ln \left[\frac{\left(\frac{x}{m} \right)}{\left(\frac{X}{M} \right)} \right] \qquad (1)$$

where x = export of given commodity; m = import of given commodity; X = total agri-food export of the country; M = total agri-food import of the country.

A comparative advantage is "revealed" if $RCA > 1$.

If $RCA < 1$, the country has a comparative disadvantage in the commodity.

If $RCA = 0$, the country has neither comparative advantage nor comparative disadvantage.

Competitiveness of the Slovak Republic and its agricultural and food products was compared with the world, the EU and third countries. The classification of the commodity structure of foreign agrarian trade of the Slovak Republic was based on description of Harmonized System (HS), used by the Customs statistics of the Slovak Republic as well as by the SITC Rev. 4 (Standard International Trade Classification, Rev. 4).

3 RESULTS AND DISCUSSION

Table 1 shows data on the highest imports and exports of food products of Slovakia with EFTA group in 2016. Among the most exported products belongs HS 1905 Bread, pastry, cakes, biscuits and other bakers' wares (with export value 4604 thousand EUR), followed by HS 1001 Wheat and meslin (with export value 4387 thousand EUR) and HS 1806 Chocolate and other food preparations containing cocoa (amounting to 3646 thousand EUR). From.

the EFTA group, we have imported the most following: HS 0304 Fish fillets and other fish meat (whether or not minced), fresh, chilled or frozen (import volume 3495 thousand EUR), HS 1806 Chocolate and other food preparations containing cocoa (with import value 3300 thousand EUR) HS 2101 Extracts, essences and concentrates, of coffee, tea or maté (with an import volume of 2933 thousand EUR).

Table 2 shows data on the highest imports and exports of food products of Slovakia with CIS in 2016. Among the most exported products belongs HS 0407 Bird's eggs, in shell, fresh, preserved or cooked (export value 10,242 thousand EUR), followed by HS 2106 Food preparations not elsewhere specified or included (with export value 5211 thousand EUR) and HS 2208, Undenatured ethyl alcohol spirits,

Liqueurs and other spirituous beverages (amounting to 3846 thousand EUR). From the CIS group, were as the most important food products imported to Slovakia following: HS 0802 Other nuts, fresh or dried, whether or not shelled or peeled (import volume 7068 thousand EUR), HS 2204 Wine of fresh grapes, grape must (with import value 2057 thousand EUR) and HS 0304 Fish fillets and other fish meat (import volume of 1913 thousand EUR).

In 2016, Export from Slovakia to EUROMED reached volume 36,433 thousand EUR in HS 0102 Live bovine animals, followed by HS 2303 Corn starch export volume 2617 thousand EUR and HS 1104 Cereal grains otherwise worked with export volume 1779 thousand EUR.

As for import from EUROMED to Slovakia, the most important were HS 0805 Citrus fruit, fresh or dried with import volume 5168 thousand EUR, followed by HS 0804 Dates, figs, pineapples, avocados, guavas, mangoes, fresh or dried (import volume 5401 thousand EUR) and HS

Table 1. The largest import and export of agricultural and food products between EFTA group and Slovakia in 2016 (in thousand EUR).

HS	EFTA export	2016	HS	EFTA import	2016
1905	Bread, pastry, cakes, biscuits and other bakers' wares	4604	0304	Fish fillets and other fish meat	3495
1001	Wheat and meslin	4387	1806	Chocolate and other food preparations containing cocoa	3300
1806	Chocolate and other food preparations containing cocoa	3646	2101	Extracts, essences and concentrates, of coffee, tea or maté	2933
0709	Other vegetables, fresh or chilled	1788	2202	Waters, including mineral waters and aerated waters, containing added sugar	2410
1702	Other sugars	1607	2005	Other vegetables prepared or preserved otherwise than by vinegar or acetic acid	2022

Source: Statistical Office of the SR, own processing.

Table 2. The largest import and export of agricultural and food products between CIS and Slovakia in 2016 (in thousand EUR).

HS	CIS export	2016	HS	CIS import	2016
0407	Bird's eggs, in shell, fresh, preserved or cooked	10,242	0802	Other nuts, fresh or dried, whether or not shelled or peeled	7068
2106	Food preparations not elsewhere specified or included	5211	2204	Wine of fresh grapes, grape must	2057
2208	Undenatured ethyl alcohol spirits, liqueurs and other spirituous beverages	3846	0304	Fish fillets and other fish meat	1913
1107	Malt, whether or not roasted	2208	2208	Undenatured ethyl alcohol spirits, liqueurs and other spirituous beverages	1573
1005	Maize (Corn)	2166	1512	Sunflower seed, safflower or cotton seed oil and their fractions	1317

Source: Statistical Office of the SR, own processing.

0802 Nuts, fresh or dried, whether or not shelled or peeled with import volume 2757 thousand EUR (Table 3).

Table 4 shows data on the highest imports and exports of food products of Slovakia with MERCOSUR in 2016. Among the most exported products belongs HS 1806 Chocolate and other food preparations containing cocoa (export value 95 thousand EUR), followed by HS 2106 Food preparations not elsewhere specified or included (with export value 38 thousand EUR) and HS 1905 Bread, pastry, cakes, biscuits and other

Table 3. The largest import and export of agricultural and food products between EUROMED and Slovakia in 2016 (in thousand EUR).

HS	EUROMED export	2016	HS	EUROMED import	2016
0102	Live bovine animals	36,433	0805	Citrus fruit, fresh or dried	5168
2303	Corn starch	2617	0804	Dates, figs, pineapples, avocados, guavas, mangoes, fresh or dried	5401
1104	Cereal grains otherwise worked	1779	0802	Nuts, fresh or dried, whether or not shelled or peeled	2757
2106	Food preparations not elsewhere specified or included	1207	0702	Tomatoes, fresh or chilled	2738
1702	Other sugars	829	0709	Other vegetables, fresh or chilled	2693

Source: Statistical Office of the SR, own processing.

Table 4. The largest import and export of agricultural and food products between MERCOSUR and Slovakia in 2016 (in thousand EUR).

HS	MERCOSUR export	2016	HS	MERCOSUR import	2016
1806	Chocolate and other food preparations containing cocoa	95	0207	Meat, and edible offal, of the poultry of heading	6391
2106	Food preparations not elsewhere specified or included	38	0805	Citrus fruit, fresh or dried	4861
1905	Bread, pastry, cakes, biscuits and other bakers' wares	19	0201	Meat of bovine animals, fresh and chilled	2842
1704	Sugar confectionery (including white chocolate), not containing cocoa	4	1202	Ground-nuts, not roasted or otherwise cooked	2769
2202	Waters, including mineral waters and aerated waters, containing added sugar	3	0210	Meat and edible meat offal, salted, in brine, dried or smoked	2650

Source: Statistical Office of the SR, own processing.

Table 5. The largest import and export of agricultural and food products between GCC and Slovakia in 2016 (in thousand EUR).

HS	GCC export	2016	HS	GCC import	2016
1704	Sugar confectionery (including white chocolate), not containing cocoa	2003	0805	Lac, Natural Gums, Resins, Gum-resins and Balsams	40
2106	Food preparations not elsewhere specified or included	529	2403	Other manufactured tobacco and manufactured tobacco substitutes	9
0207	Meat, and edible offal, of the poultry of heading	101	0902	Tea	7
0106	Other live animals	71	2007	Jams, fruit jellies, marmalades, fruit or nut puree and fruit or nut pastes	1
2201	Waters, including natural or artificial mineral waters and aerated waters, not containing added sugar or other sweetening matter, ice and snow	48	0711	Vegetables provisionally preserved	0.4

Source: Statistical Office of the SR, own processing.

bakers' wares (amounting to 19 thousand EUR). From MERCOSUR were to Slovakia imported as the most important food products following: HS 0207 Meat, and edible offal, of the poultry of heading (import volume 6391 thousand EUR), HS 0805 Citrus fruit, fresh or dried (with import value 4861 thousand EUR) and HS 0201 Meat of bovine animals, fresh and chilled (import volume of 2842 thousand EUR).

In 2016, Export from Slovakia to GCC reached volume 2003 thousand EUR in HS 1704 Sugar confectionery (including white chocolate), not containing cocoa, followed by HS 2106 Food preparations not elsewhere specified or included (export volume 529 thousand EUR) and HS 0207 Meat, and edible offal, of the poultry of heading with export volume 101.

thousand EUR. As for import from GCC to Slovakia, the most important in 2016 were HS 0805 Lac, Natural Gums, Resins, Gum-resins And Balsams (import volume 40 thousand EUR), HS 2403 Other manufactured tobacco and manufactured tobacco substitutes (9 thousand EUR), followed by HS 0902 Tea with 7 thousand EUR (Table 5).

3.1 Competitiveness of selected Slovak agro-food commodities with third country markets by revealed comparative advantage index

Table 6 gives an overview of the most competitive Slovak agro-food commodities in third country markets according the product class (HS Code) by RCA in 2013–2016. The highest comparative advantage was recorded for HS 10 Cereals, HS 11 Milling products, malt and maize, HS 1 Live animals and HS 17 Sugar and confectionery, which had been declining from 2015 onwards. Other competitive products are HS 4 Milk, Eggs and Honey and HS 18 Cocoa and cocoa preparations, which were competitive in the given period (RCA has been higher than 0 since 2013 to 2016). HS 2 Meat and edible offal, HS 19 Baked goods and confectionery, HS 21 Miscellaneous edible preparations and HS 22 Beverages, spirits and vinegar showed a significant decrease in comparative advantage.

4 CONCLUSION

Trade with third countries represents for Slovakia a long-term unfavorable situation where the volume of agricultural and food products is forecasting the volume of exports. Encouraging the export of agri-food commodities to third countries will improve the competitiveness and efficiency of foreign agro-trade. It would be more appropriate to exploit the benefits of the EU's free trade agreements with third countries and to promote bilateral economic co-operation with a special treatment of supply and demand for better market orientation as well as the organization and participation of domestic producers in exhibitions in third country markets. Attention should be also paid to the state protection against the import of agricultural and food products that do not meet EU standards.

Table 6. TOP 10 the most competitive slovak agri-food commodities in third country markets according product class (HS Codes) by RCA in 2013–2016.

HS	Product class	2013	2014	2015	2016
1	Live animals	5.47	V	5.61	1.4
2	Meat and edible offal	5.97	V	3.14	−0.98
4	Milk, Eggs, Honey	2.12	1.91	2.11	0.16
10	Cereals	1.74	2.69	2.65	1.92
11	Milling products, malt and maize	2.62	2.68	3.37	1.52
17	Sugar and confectionery	0.84	1.16	1.46	1.09
18	Cocoa and cocoa preparations	0.92	1.31	1.33	0.16
19	Baked goods and confectionery	0.63	1.11	1.32	−0.46
21	Miscellaneous edible preparations	0.62	0.78	0.93	−0.11
22	Beverages, spirits and vinegar	0.35	0.18	0.14	−0.43

Source: EUROSTAT, own processing.

ACKNOWLEDGEMENT

The paper is part of the research project KEGA 038SPU-4/2016 "Using of new technologies and interdisciplinary associations in consumer studies" conducted at the Department of Marketing and Trade at the Faculty of Economics and Management of the Slovak University of Agriculture in Nitra.

REFERENCES

CIS. [retr. 04–04–2018] Available online at: <http://www.cisstat.com/eng/cis.htm>.
EFTA. [retr. 04–04–2018] Available online at: <http://www.efta.int/about-efta/european-free-trade-association>.
European Commision. [retr. 04–04–2018] Available online at: <https: //ec.europa.eu/transport/themes/international/european_neighbourhood_policy/mediterranean_partnership_en>.

GCC. [retr. 04–04–2018] Available online at: <https://www.britannica.com/topic/Gulf-Cooperation-Council>.

Matošková, D. & Gálik, J. 2009. Selected aspects of the internal and external competitiveness of Slovak agricultural and food products. In: Agricultural Economics.

Récky, R. & Hambálková, M. 2014. Marketingové prísptupy k výrobe, spracovaniu a odbytu olejnín v SR. Nitra: SPU, 2014.

Rhee, Ch. 2012. Principles of International Trade: First step towards globalization, Bloomington: Author House, 2012.

Ružeková, V. et al. 2013. Analýza zahraničného obchodu Slovenskej republiky. Bratislava: EKONÓM, 2013.

Statistical Office of the SR. [retr. 04–04–2018] Available online at: <https://slovak.statistics.sk/wps/portal/ext/>.

Production Management and Business Development – Mihalčová et al. (Eds)
© 2019 Taylor & Francis Group, London, ISBN 978-1-138-60415-5

Corporate sustainability and human resources

Š. Hronová
University of Economics, Prague, Czech Republic

ABSTRACT: Global interconnectedness and turbulent changes force managements to react to unexpected shifts in the external environment as well as to predictable trends such as aging workforce which may significantly influence not only companies' long-term strategies but also their daily operations. Additionally, due to an increasing and thorough monitoring of companies, these are under higher pressure, which might result in their more responsible behavior towards the society and the environment. Nevertheless, some management are motivated intrinsically and apply systematic approach of socially responsible behavior focusing on their workforce as they believe that Human Resources (HR) create an essential condition for corporate sustainability and long-term viability of the business. The main objectives of this treatise are (1) to compile a literature review on the topic of corporate sustainability aimed at HR and (2) to research and assess social responsibility and human capital sustainability and their reporting by companies in the Czech Republic.

1 INTRODUCTION

For companies to remain successful in a modern global context, it is necessary that current and future managements adopt new competencies and skills aimed at flexibility, resilience of organizations and maintaining competitiveness. However, this shall be done with regard to the labor force and their socio-cultural needs. Nowadays, many companies compete for qualified and experienced human resources (HR). App & Büttgen (2016) state that appreciation of employees' work boosts their motivation to remain part of an organization. Such an act is a manifestation of a long-term sustainable approach to human capital.

At present, wise companies are more frequently aiming at the so-called soft concept of human resources management (HRM) and are applying ethical approach to HRM not being focused only on the highest financial performance. Nevertheless, problems may arise "when human and social resources that are desperately needed to implement corporate strategies are not available, or, when highly talented employees and executives suffer from side effects of work...because they are being exploited..." (Ehnert 2011). The importance of corporate sustainability in literature is highlighted, for example, by the following authors: Visser (2017), Engert & Baumgartner (2016), Carrol (1991, 1999), Elkington (1994, 2006), Van Marrewijk (2002, 2003) and others. In the area of corporate sustainability, interconnection with sustainable human resource management practices or the identification of the impact of HRM on the integration of sustainability principles into corporate practice, the works of the following authors are known: Ehnert (2009, 2015), Pfeffer (2010), Ehnert et al. (2012, 2014), Kramar (2014), Mariappanadar (2003, 2014), Cohen et al. (2012), App (2016), Kelana (2016) and others.

There are various media, channels and forms used for communication of companies about their sustainable activities with the internal as well as external public. In addition to the financial field, the non-financial reporting covers the impact of the company's activities on the environment and society. Regular processing and publication of the CSR/sustainability/triple bottom line report or an integrated report offers an answer on how to spread the information. Nevertheless, the most complex solution of communicating economic results as well as the environmental and social impact of corporate activities comes in a form of an integrated report. The sustainability reporting is addressed by a number of authors, for example: Ehnert, Parsa, Roper, Wagner and Muller-Camen (2015), Kaspereit & Lopatta (2016), Ioannou & Serafeim (2017).

2 THEORETICAL BACKGROUND FOR SUSTAINABLE (HRM) APPROACH BASED ON ETHICAL MANAGEMENT

2.1 Ethical principles of corporate governance

Access to a skilled workforce creates an essential condition for ensuring the company's sustainability (Lortie 2016). Managers, however, often have to deal with the contradiction between the economic and social spheres, which can be supported by the paradox theory (Ehnert 2009). These executives, for example, are generally pressed for greater financial performance, leaner operations and higher savings resulting in lower spending on educational policies and social or cultural needs of employees. Concurrently, they are under pressure from the internal and external environment of an organization that emphasizes the social goals which, if fulfilled, lead to a sense of satisfaction among employees and the community. Guerci et al. (2018) claim that involvement of HR professional and management in sustainable HRM leads to increased meaningfulness of their jobs because it offers wider and broader scope going beyond the solely economic focus. This may result in higher job satisfaction and lower turnover.

The way in which corporate staff behaves and communicates in both the external and internal environment is highly dependent on the management and process control systems in the organization. Such a system of corporate governance defines duties and rights of all stakeholders (shareholders, management, statutory bodies, HR and customers. In case of necessary changes within the organization, based on their study, Canterino ct al. (2018) identifies three recurrent manifestations of leadership which are: communicating, envisioning and enabling leadership.

Dimopoulos (2016) highlights the important role of management and the CEO of the company in implementing proactive corporate social responsibility with the adoption of value-creating strategies. In the context of sustainability and ethics, these strategies should build on the capabilities of the company as effectively as possible, and thus ensure the well-being as well as financial success of the organization. However, in order for corporate management to be perceived as ethical, employees must acknowledge management's behavior as morally relevant (Fehr 2015). Denis (2012) points out that management of organizations should be a collective phenomenon. Gollan (2005) in his paper talks about high involvement/ engagement management and its proven impact on higher productivity and efficiency. The organization is therefore a living complex in which mutual respect and esteem should prevail and it is necessary to build its firm foundations to take broad responsibility for its actions (Cohen 2012).

2.2 *Sustainable development, corporate sustainability and CSR*

The terms corporate sustainability, corporate social responsibility (CSR), sustainable development and sustainability are frequently used in corporate communication as mutually interchangeable (Bolis

et al. 2014). Lozano (2012) points out increasing insight and understanding of the terminology by large companies as well as the importance of the role of sustainability in introducing new practices into their business processes. Harmon (2010) according to research among more than three hundred executives draws attention to the alarming fact that HR managers are often not fully involved in the implementation of sustainable business strategies of their companies. The terminology is described below.

The term 'sustainable development' is increasingly used worldwide to mark the way for everything that is good for the society (Cohen et al. 2012). The term appeared in 1987 in the Brundtland report where it was first defined. Five years later, this label was brought to the wider consciousness at Rio de Janeiro Summit. Sustainable development is, according to the 1987 Commission, a development that allows population at the present time to meet their needs, without preventing future generations from meeting their needs. Sustainable development (SD) is often explained by the concept of three pillars of responsibility called Triple Bottom Line (TBL): economic, ecological and social pillars (Elkington, 1994).

Dyllick (2002) derives the term 'corporate sustainability' from the wider concept of sustainable development, with the pillars of sustainability applied to the corporate level. The author points out that the environmental sector should not be preferred to the social one. Rodriguez-Fernandez (2016) in her study recommends that companies invest money in developing policies to strengthen the levels of social behavioral components in order to contribute to global improvement. Linnenluecke (2010) argues that the way to implement the concept of sustainability at the corporate level leads through the adoption of a sustainable corporate culture.

Corporate social responsibility, based on the European Commission's definition from 2011 is the organization's responsibility for its impact on society (COM 2011). Another important definition is found in ISO standard 26000, which defines CSR as the organization's responsibility for the impacts of its decisions and activities on society and the environment. Visser (2011) has been concerned about CSR and sustainability for a long time. In his 2011 book, he introduced the term CSR 2.0 and drew attention to the use of new media in communication and a closer dialogue between the company and its stakeholders. Wuttichindanon (2017) looks for a reason for engaging businesses in reporting on responsible activities if such reporting is optional for them. In looking for answers, he also refers to previous studies, for example, Chiu and Wang (2015), where the authors have come to the same conclusion that corporate visibility and power of shareholders are important determinants of publishing information on responsible and sustainable behavior while economic performance is not.

2.3 Relationship between sustainability, CSR and human resource management

Gond et al. (2011) claim that human resources management plays a key role in supporting CSR, but research in companies has highlighted a fuzzy border between HR and CSR, which prevents the introduction of ethical and accountable management. In his article he argues that the contribution of HR must be explicitly acknowledged in order to further exploit its potential. According to these authors, HR management plays a central role in supporting the CSR concept.

In the context of sustainability and human resource management, De Prins et al. (2014) represent the ROC (Respect–Openness–Continuity) model corresponding to the three pillars of sustainable development showing the link between these two concepts.

2.4 CSR and CSV

In the process of upholding the responsible and sustainable concepts of business activities, another view emerged supplementing the already existing CSR. It was a concept of Creating Shared Value (CSV) by Porter and Kramer (2011) from Harvard Business School. These authors believe that through this approach an enterprise can purposefully link its economic intentions to the interests of society interconnecting corporate activities with the immediate surroundings.

In his later keynote speech, professor Porter at the 2013 Boston Summit presented the company's role in (1) according to CSR as based on compliance with community standards, corporate citizenship and sustainability and (2) according to CSV as an integration of social issues into the process of creating economic value.

3 SUSTAINABILITY AND SOCIAL RESPONSIBILITY IN CORPORATE COMMUNICATION

3.1 Non-financial reporting on social responsibility and sustainability

Due to the increasing pressure on sustainability reporting (Hahn 2013), companies have been gradually responding voluntarily to this situation by disclosing information on the diverse areas of sustainability linked to the company's business (KPMG 2011, 2013). Companies are reporting on their activities for greater transparency and building a wider awareness of their sustainable activities (Sian & Roberts, 2009) mostly in a form of a sustainability/CSR report. Hetze (2016) found that the naming of a document may vary with geographical location: in Europe, the title of the Sustainability Report is preferred while the term CSR Report is rather used in the USA and Asia. Recently, there has been a shift from separate social or environmental reports to a joint/comprehensive TBL report or the so-called integrated report (Hahn 2013). One of the comparative studies among the 250 best companies in the world, according to Forbes, has shown that in organizations focusing on HR reporting, the reports revealed internal employee data rather than those of supply chain employees (Ehnert 2015).

Reports on sustainable and responsible corporate behavior include many different aspects. Above all, they are concerned with ethical and transparent manners of conduct that contribute to fair practices for internal and external stakeholders, healthier and more affluent societies, and the improvement of the current state of the environment. This type of non-financial reporting can be developed according to the guidelines, standards and recommendations of world-renowned institutions.

3.2 Institutions, guidelines and reporting standards

The United Nations (UN) – the United Nations Global Compact, the Organization for Economic Co-operation and Development (OECD) are among the best-known global organizations dealing with sustainability.

Institutions bringing forward guidelines or norms for reporting standards are: Global Reporting Initiative (with their GRI Sustainability Reporting Standards shifting from G4 to GRI Standards in June 2018) or the International Organization for Standardization (ISO) and its ISO 26000 standard. Other reference standards are, for example, SA 8000 issued by the international organization Social Accountability International (SAI) and EMAS developed by the European Commission as a voluntary instrument of environmental management.

4 DEVELOPMENTS IN HRM

4.1 Development of human resources management

Human resources management naturally reflects developments in society and trends in academic disciplines. (De Prins et al. 2014) The objective of human resources management is to provide motivated, qualified and loyal employees. Companies must be aware that development and prosperity will be achieved in particular through their employees.

In practice, strategic principles are used in human resource management, which can be considered antagonistic to certain extent. These are the principles of 'best practice' and 'best fit', whose applications should positively influence the performance of the firm. The first best practice model claims that there are some types of HR activities that will enable a firm to achieve a competitive advantage universally and irrespective of the type of industry (Redman & Wilkinson 2009). The second best-fit model explains that HR strategy must be in line with the organization's strategies, culture, and operational processes. Armstrong (2006) supports the idea of a best-fit model by claiming that different HR strategies are needed to address the specific needs of both the organization and its staff. A successful adaptation of the strategic concept is often important to the company's conditions, so the best fit model seems generally more acceptable.

Authors such as Legge (1995) criticized the hard practices of HRM during the 1990s and supported the soft perspective of the HRM model.

4.2 Strategic Human Resources Management (SHRM)

The first mention of the literature on the strategic human resources management dates back to the 1980s. The question for this period was no longer "*Are HR important?*" but "*How could they be incorporated into strategic management?*" (Lundberg 1983). Strategic management was created in response to radical changes in the external environment; another stimulus was the ever-increasing size of businesses.

The concept of Strategic Human Resources Management (SHRM) can also be seen as a set of management decisions at the highest level. SHRM could also be defined as proactive employee management in a company or an organization.

4.3 Sustainable human resources management

Sustainability in HRM by App and Büttgen (2016) highlights the value of human resources and the importance of employability and long-term employee availability. It is a means of providing a skilled workforce for both the organization's current activities and future activities. The positive feedback of responsible and sustainable access to HR means a greater chance for a company to succeed thanks to these employees.

Cohen (2012) views sustainable HRM as a use of HR tools to support a company's sustainability

strategy and at the same time to create such an HRM system that will contribute to sustainable performance of the company. Sustainable HRM can also be described with the use of the following definition: *"Sustainable HRM is the pattern of planned or emerging human resource strategies and practices intended to enable an organizational goal achievement while simultaneously reproducing the human resource base over a long-lasting calendar time and controlling for self-induced side and feedback effect on the HR systems on the HR base and thus on the company itself"* (Ehnert 2009, De Prins et al. 2014). Kramar (2014) extends the above definition by practices that minimize negative impacts on the environment and the community; emphasizes the importance of executive directors, management, HR professionals and all employees in the process of application of these practices. There are a number of different concepts, but many authors agree on sustainable HRM being an expanded form of SHRM.

5 RESEARCH

5.1 Research sample

In order to analyze the current state of sustainability and HR reporting in the Czech Republic, the 50 most important companies were selected according to CZECH TOP 100 (year 2014). The analysis was based on the following criteria:

1. Whether the company issues a report containing sustainability/HR information in the Czech language.
2. If the firm does not meet point (1), does it report (in the case of transnational companies) in English?
3. If the firm does not meet points (1) and (2), whether it provides information on sustainability and HR at least in its annual report.

Namely, the paper focused on the reporting of the following companies: Škoda Auto a.s., ČEZ a.s., Agrofert Holding a.s., RWE Česká republika a.s., Unipetrol a.s., Foxconn CZ a.s., Energetický a průmyslový holding a.s., ČEPRO a.s., Moravia Steel a.s., ENI Česká republika s.r.o., O2 Czech Republic a.s., BOSH Group ČR, Toyota Peugeor Citroen Automobile Czech s.r.o., AHOLD Czech Republic a.s., ArcelorMittal Ostrava a.s., České dráhy a.s., Siemens s.r.o., Slovnaft Česká republika s.r.o., METROSTAF a.s., MAKRO Cash & Carry ČR s.r.o., Veolia Group Česká republika, GECO a.s., OMW Česká republika s.r.o., Shell Czech Republic a.s., Panasonic AVC Networks Czech s.r.o., T- mobile Czech Republic a.s., MET-ALIMEX a.s., OKD a.s., Pražská energetika a.s., Česká pošta s.p., Porsche Česká republika s.r.o., ČGS HOLDING a.s., Dopravní podnik hl. města Prahy, ŠKODA TRANSPORTATION a.s., MND a.s., ARMEX GROUP s.r.o., EUROVIA CS a.s., Iveco Czech Republic a.s., Ferona a.s., Pražská plynárenská a.s., Automotive lighting s.r.o., ABB s.r.o., AGC Flat Glass Czech a.s., Vodafone Czech Republic a.s., dD´system Czech, IKEA Group Czech Republic a.s., PSG a.s., Lesy České republiky s.p., Plzeňský prazdroj a.s., Alza.cz a.s.

5.2 Reporting standards used

The research probe focused on, first of all, the type of reporting the company uses. It was found that 55% of companies from the sample prepared their non-financial reporting in accordance with the GRI G4. The guidance prepared by General Reporting Initiative provides very thorough explanation of what information to include and how to present the data to stakeholders. 36% of companies made the reports based on their own methodology and 9% offered an integrated form of report. See Figure 1 below.

5.3 HR reporting

In the next step, the author checked for a section consisting of information connected to the company's sustainability, HR, HRM, their training and evaluation and/or other mentions about the organization's labor capital. The results were as can be seen in Figure 2. The pie chart shows that 24% of companies report about their HR in CSR

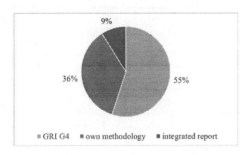

Figure 1. Reporting standards used in sustainability/CSR/integrated reports.

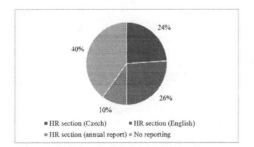

Figure 2. Reporting on HR in a sustainability/CSR/annual report within the given sample.

Table 1. Sectors reporting about sustainability.

Industry	No. of companies	%	Cumulative %
Wholesale, retail	2	4	4%
Automotive	2	4	8%
Coal, petrochemical	3	6	14%
Food, drinks, tobacco	2	4	18%
Electr., machinery, tools	3	6	24%
Energy	3	6	30%
Vehicle, petrol commer	4	8	38%
Transportation, logistics	3	6	44%
Construction	2	4	48%
Metal processing	2	4	52%
Telecommunication	3	6	58%
Other	1	2	60%
TOTAL	30	60	60%
Non-reporting	20	40	40%
TOTAL	50	100	100%

sustainability report in Czech and 26% in English, further 10% has a section about sustainability in HR within their annual report and 40% do not report about this issue at all.

5.4 Reporting according to industries

Table 1 presented below broke down the sustainability reporting according to individual industries. It is visible that among those most involved in this type of reporting are companies from the following sectors: petrol commerce, coal and petrochemical industries, energy and electrical, machinery and tools industries, transport and logistics and telecommunications.

6 DISCUSSION

Global Reporting Initiative guides the companies through the report compilation in a very detailed way, it is probable that firms tend to prefer the G4 standard to other possibilities. Also, it is widely accepted worldwide and it is easier for companies to make a comparative analysis of their activities with operations and results of their competitors in their home country and abroad. The research probe found the fact that two fifth of companies from the given sample did not provide any kind of sustainability/HR information neither on their websites in a form of a sustainability/HR report nor within the annual report.

7 CONCLUSION

One goal of the paper was to compile a detailed literature review. Further, in the research section, the author attempted to analyze the current state of sustainability reporting. Fifty companies were selected from the most important firms from CZECH TOP 100 in 2014. Three criteria were created for the analysis with the aim of identifying whether the company under investigation issues non—financial reports, in what language and if not, whether it informs of its socially responsible behavior at least in annual reports. Close attention was paid to sustainability of HR as the author believes based on a very thorough literature review that experienced and skilled human capital and its well-being ensure long-term sustainability and viability of a business thus contributing to financial profitability of the company in long run.

ACKNOWLEDGEMENT

The paper was prepared under the IP 304026 project called Sustainable Corporate Responsibility at University of Economics, Prague, Czech Republic.

REFERENCES

App, S. & Büttgen, M. 2016. Lasting footprints of the employer brand: can sustainable HRM lead to brand commitment? *Employee Relations*, 38(5): 703–723.

Armstrong, M. 2006. *A Handbook of Human Resource Management Practice*. Kogan Page Publishers.

Canterino, F., Cirella, S. & Shani, A.B. 2018. Leading organizational transformation: An action research study. *Journal of Managerial Psychology,* 33(1): 15–28.

Carroll, A.B. 1991. The pyramid of corporate social responsibility: Toward the moral management of organizational stakeholders. *Business horizons*, 34(4): 39–48.

Carroll, A.B. 1999. Corporate social responsibility: Evolution of a definitional construct. *Business & Society*, 38(3), 268–295.

Chiu, T.K. & Wang, Y.H. 2015. Determinants of social disclosure quality in Taiwan: An application of stakeholder theory. *Journal of Business Ethics*, 129(2): 379–398.

Cohen, E., Taylor, S. & Muller-Camen, M. 2012. *HRM's role in corporate social and environmental sustainability*. Research Report, SHRM. [on-line] www.shrm.org/hr-today/trends-and-forecasting/special-reports-and-expert-views/Documents/Corporate-Social-Environmental-Sustainability.pdf.

Cohen, J.R., Holder-Webb, L.L., Nath, L. & Wood, D. 2012. Corporate Reporting of Nonfinancial Leading Indicators of Economic Performance and Sustainability. *Accounting Horizons*, 26(1): 65–90.

COM 2011. *A renewed EU strategy 2011–14 for Corporate Social Responsibility*. [on-line] www.ec.europa.eu/geninfo/query/resultaction.jsp?QueryText=€%E2%80%9CCSR+is+the+responsibility+of+enterprises+for+their+impacts+on+society%E2%80%9D+COM+2011&query_source=GROWTH&swlang=en&x=0&y=0.

Denis, J.L., Langley, A. & Sergi, V. 2012. Leadership in the Plural. *The Academy of Management Annals*, 6(1): 211–283.

De Prins, P., van Beirendonck, L., De Vos, A. & Segers, J. 2014. Sustainable HRM: Bridging theory and practice through the 'Respect Openness Continuity (ROC)' – model. *Management revue*, 25(4): 263–284.

Dimopoulos, T. & Wagner, H.F. 2016. Corporate Governance and CEO Turnover Decisions. *Swiss Finance Institute Research Paper,* No. 12–16. [on-line] www.ssrn.com/abstract=2040690.

Dyllick, T. & Hockerts, K. 2002. Beyond the business case for corporate sustainability. *Business Strategy and the Environment*, 11(2): 130–141.

Ehnert, I. 2009. *Sustainable Human Resource Management: A conceptual and explanatory analysis) from a paradox perspective. Contributions to management science.* Heidleberg: Springer-Verlag.

Ehnert, I. 2011. Sustainability and HRM: A Model and Suggestions for Future Research. In A. Wilkinson & K. Townsend (Eds.), *The Future of Employment Relations* (pp. 215–237). London: Palgrave Macmillan UK., p. 215.

Ehnert, I., Wes, H. & Zink, K.J. 2012. *Handbook of sustainability and human resource management.* Heidelberg: Springer.

Ehnert, I., Parsa, S., Roper, I., Wagner, M. & Muller-Camen, M. 2014. Sustainability and HRM. In *Sustainability and Human Resource Management* (pp. 3–32). Heidelberg: Springer.

Ehnert, I., Parsa, S., Roper, I., Wagner, M. & Muller-Camen, M. 2016. Reporting on sustainability and HRM: A comparative study of sustainability reporting practices by the world's largest companies. *The International Journal of Human Resource Management*, 27(1): 88–108.

Elkington, J. 1994. Towards the suitable corporation: Win-win-win business strategies for sustainable development. *California management review*, 36: 90–100.

Elkington, J. 2006. Governance for sustainability. *Corporate Governance: An International Review*, 14(6): 522–529.

Engert, S. & Baumgartner, R.J. 2016. Corporate sustainability strategy–bridging the gap between formulation and implementation. *Journal of cleaner production*, 113: 822–834.

European Commission. 2011. *Communication from the Commission to the European Parliament, the Council, the European Economic and Social Committee and the Committee of the Regions.* [on-line] www.ec.europa.eu/ enterprise/ policies/sustainable-business/files/csr/newsr/act_en.pdf.

Fehr, R., Yam, K.C. & Dang, C. 2015. Moralized Leadership: The Construction and Consequences of Ethical Leader Perceptions. *Academy of Management Review*, 40(2): 182–209.

Global Reporting Initiative 2015. G4 – *Global Reporting Guidelines*. [on-line] www.globalreporting.org/resourcelibrary/GRIG4-Part1-Reporting-Principles-and-Standard-Disclosures.pdf.

Gollan, P.J. 2005. High involvement management and human resource sustainability: The challenges and opportunities. *Asia Pacific Journal of Human Resources*, 43(1): 18–33.

Gond, J.P., Igalens, J., Swaen, V. & Akremi, E.A. 2011. The human resources contribution to responsible leadership: An exploration of the CSR-HR interface. *Journal of Business Ethics*, 98(1): 115–132.

Guerci, M., Decramer, A., van Waeyenberg, T. & Aust, I. 2018. Moving Beyond the Link Between HRM and Economic Performance: A Study on the Individual Reactions of HR Managers and Professionals to Sustainable HRM. *Journal of Business Ethics*, 1–18. [on-line] www.link.springer.com/article/10.1007/s10551-018-3879-1#citeas.

Hahn, R. & Kühnen, M. 2013. Determinants of sustainability reporting: a review of results, trends, theory, and opportunities in an expanding field of research. *Journal of Cleaner Production*, 59: 5–21.

Harmon, J., Fairfield, K.D. & Wirtenberg, J. 2010. Missing an opportunity: HR leadership in sustainability. *People and Strategy*, 33(1), 16–21.

Ioannou, I. & Serafeim, G. 2017. The Consequences of Mandatory Corporate Sustainability Reporting (May 1, 2017). *Harvard Business School Research Working Paper No. 11–100*. [on-line] www.ssrn.com/abstract = 1799589.

ISO 26000: *Guidance on Social Responsibility*. [on-line] www.tuv.com/media/india/informationcenter_1/systems/ Corporate_Social_Responsibility.pdf.

Kaspereit, T. & Lopatta, K. 2016. The value relevance of SAM's corporate sustainability ranking and GRI sustainability reporting in the European stock markets. *Business Ethics: A European Review*, 25(1): 1–24.

Kelana, B.W.Y., Mansor, N.N.A. & Sanny, L. 2016. HR sustainability practices instrument comparative analysis in Malaysian SMEs. *Pertanika Journal of Social Sciences & Humanities*, 24: 73–79.

Kramar, R. 2014. Beyond strategic Human Resource Management: Is sustainable Human Resource management the next approach? *The International Journal of Human Resource Management*, 25: 1069–1089.

KPMG. 2011. *KPMG international survey of corporate responsibility reporting*. KPMG: London.

KPMG. 2013. *The KPMG survey of corporate responsibility reporting 2013*. [on-line] www.assets.kpmg.com/content/dam/kpmg/pdf/2015/08/kpmg-survey-of-corporate-responsibility-reporting-2013.pdf. [on-line] www.assets.kpmg.com/xx/en/home/campaigns/2017/10/survey-of-corporate-responsibility-reporting-2017.html.

Legge, K. 1995. *Human Resource Management. Rhetorics and realities*. Basingstoke: Macmillan Press.

Linnenluecke, M.K. & Griffiths, A. 2010. Corporate sustainability and organizational culture. *Journal of world business*, 45(4): 357–366.

Lortie, M., Nadeau, S. & Vezeau, S. 2016. Holistic sustainable development: Floor-layers and micro-enterprises. *Applied Ergonomics*, 57: 8–16.

Lozano, R. 2012. Towards better embedding sustainability into companies' systems: an analysis of voluntary corporate initiatives. *Journal of Cleaner Production*, 25: 14–26.

Lundberg, C. 1983. Managing strategic change: Technical, political and cultural dynamics, by Noel M. Tichy. New York: Wiley, 1983. *Human Resource Management*, 22(3): 322.

Mariappanadar, S. 2014. Stakeholder harm index: A framework to review work intensification from the critical HRM perspective. *Human Resource Management Review*, 24(4): 313–329.

Pfeffer, J. 2010. Building sustainable organizations: The human factor. *Academy of Management Perspectives*, 24(1): 34–45.

Porter, M.E. 2013. *Creating Shared Value as Business Strategy*. Keynote speech at Shared Value Leadership Summit, Boston.

Porter, M.E. & Krammer, M.R. 2011. Creating shared value. *Harvard Business Review*. https://hbr.org/2011/01/the-big-idea-creating-shared-value, accessed on 18th August 2017.

Redman, T. & Wilkinson, A. 2009. *Contemporary human resource management: Text and Cases*. Prentice Hall-Financial Times, Third Edition.

Rodriguez-Fernandez, M. 2016. Social responsibility and financial performance: The role of good corporate governance. *BRQ Business Research Quarterly*, 19(2): 137–151.

Sian, S. & Roberts, C. 2009. UK small owner-managed businesses: accounting and financial reporting needs. *Journal of Small Business and Enterprise Development*, 16(2): 289–305.

Van Marrewijk, M. & Werre, M. 2003. Multiple Levels of Corporate Sustainability. *Journal of Business Ethics*, 44(2), 107–119.

Van Marrewijk, M. 2002. European Corporate Sustainability Framework, *International Journal of Business Performance Measurement*, 44(2–3): 121–132.

Van Marrewijk, M. & Hardjono, T.W. 2003. European Corporate Sustainability Framework for Managing Complexity and Corporate Change, *Journal of Business Ethics*, 44(2–3): 121–132.

Visser, W. 2011. *The age of responsibility: CSR 2.0 and the new DNA of business*. Chicester, UK: John Wiley.

Visser, W. 2017. *The Little Book of Quotations on Sustainable Business*. Kaleidoscope Futures.

Wuttichindanon, S. 2017. Corporate social responsibility disclosure – choices of report and its determinants: Empirical evidence from firms listed on the Stock Exchange of Thailand. *Kasetsart Journal of Social Science*, 38(2): 156–162.

Constraints in making investment decisions in Polish enterprises

K. Chudy-Laskowska & M. Jankowska-Mihułowicz
Faculty of Management, Rzeszow University of Technology, Rzeszow, Poland

ABSTRACT: The purpose of the article and research was to identify the constraints of making investment decisions in Polish enterprises that the managers may encounter. Research findings encompass Polish managers' mainly subjective constrains which were identified by the respondents in the decision-making processes, such as: experience, motivation, time perception, availability of information and knowledge on the decision-making problem, lack of point and interval strategy, level of tasks organization, focus on tasks and on people, faith in success, availability of enterprise resources and also unexpected changes in the environment. The research includes also the importance of the following features of enterprises: innovativeness, implementation of the RFID system, size, range, foreign capital and participation in the cluster. Survey methods such as public opinion poll, and direct questionnaire were employed in the research. Statistical inference was applied during the research. The following non-parametric tests were used: the Mann-Whitney U and the Kruskal-Wallis ANOVA.

1 INTRODUCTION

Investment decisions aim at 'using financial resources to acquire assets, financial assets, and intangible values of fixed assets. It also includes assets acquired to obtain economic benefits, which result from the increase of their value, gaining interest, dividends or other sources including trade deals. [...] constitute the allocation of financial resources, characterized by benefits, outlays, risk and time' (The Encyclopedia of Management 2018).

Investment decisions that aim at enterprise's development consist in increasing its productivity and the possibility to deliver services and their quality. Thanks to investment decisions, also innovations are implemented in the enterprise, therefore manufactured goods are modified in order to improve their competitiveness.

In order for the enterprise to gain and maintain competitive advantage on the market, it is necessary to redefine its strategy and make investment decisions, conductive e.g. to the development of organizational structures, performance areas, markets, innovations, technologies and financing sources. Therefore, it seems important to define the factors, which as subjectively judged by Polish managers, constrain investment decision making.

The purpose of the article was to identify the constraints of making investment decisions in Polish enterprises that the managers may encounter.

Literature review on constraints in making investment decisions was conducted in the theoretical part. In research findings the ranking of choices of 203 managers was presented, regarding the 24 factors that constrain making investment decisions, taking into account the characteristics of enterprises such as: innovativeness, implementation of the RFID system, size, area and range of activity, foreign capital and participation in the cluster.

A research hypothesis was advanced according to which decision makers' perception of constraints varies depending the on characteristics of enterprises' managed by them. Recognizing those constraints constitutes the first step in eliminating them, and thus—in the development of economic entities.

2 LITERATURE REVIEW

It is the configuration of decision maker's psychological conditions, situation and environment that influences which factor turns out to be a constraint. These constraints may be grouped according to the content similarity, pointing out to:

1. Mental preferences of managers e.g. reluctance to act hastily, excessive endeavour to obtain complete information before making a decision, and to carefully consider many options to choose from, perfectionism (Wu et al. 2017),
2. Too strong concentration on tasks or on people (Schaltenbrand et al. 2018),
3. Time perception, e.g. lack of time pressure, failure to follow of interval and point strategies, greater concentration on the past than on the future, lack

of motivation—postponing decisions habitually (Peterson 2007, Downes et al. 2017),

4. Lack of knowledge, information and other enterprise resources (Laskin 2018),
5. Unexpected changes in the environment (Skowronek-Mielczarek & Bojewska 2017).

Both the aforementioned factors and others that constrain making investment decisions are connected to each other, and many authors have accounted for the rationale behind them (Berger 2017, Kahneman 2017, Koźmiński 2013). Many of them were taken into consideration in the research presented below.

The research presented in this article concerns managers who are interested in the development of the telecommunications and RFID (Radio Frequency IDentification) industry (eg FMCG sector, large-area trade, logistics industry). RFID technology provides many innovative business solutions today (Jankowski-Mihułowicz et al. 2016a, 2016b, 2017; Jankowski-Mihułowicz & Węglarski 2016, 2017; Tomaszewski 2016).

3 METHOD OF RESEARCH

The essential aim of this article is to identify cognitive limitations of managers who make investment decisions in Polish enterprises. Selection of the group was purposeful—the research was targeted at people who make investment decisions. Furthermore, in the research a criterion of respondents' availability was adapted—in view of the length of the questionnaire, it was a considerable problem to obtain managers' consent to devote their time and attention to select answers. Among all the distributed questionnaires, only 34% of them were completed and returned. Survey methods such as public opinion poll, and direct questionnaire were employed in the research. The respondents completed 203 anonymous surveys. The research group contacted the respondents during fairs, academic conferences and in enterprises. Furthermore, the respondents downloaded the questionnaire form themselves and having completed it, they sent it to the organizer via e-mail. The research was conducted within the period of 4 months—from 5 November 2014 to 5 February 2015 and was targeted at top and middle-level managers (who make investment decisions), employed in Polish enterprises operating in various lines of business. The questionnaire incorporated questions in the field of macro-environment, competitive environment and enterprise's internal conditions. Moreover, the form contained personal information and an attachment, which constituted an information sheet on the RFID systems.

The majority of the surveyed enterprises was responsible for production – 34%, trade – 28% services – 28%, and 14% conducted mixed business activities.

Taking into account the performance area, one could differentiate the following enterprises among the entities under survey: international (47%), national (15%), regional (18%) and local (19%). Limited liability companies constituted the biggest number of the enterprises under study (47%), 18% of them were joint-stock companies, 10% – general partnerships, 9% – registered partnerships and others. The biggest number of entities was active on the marker for 20 years. Half of the entities was active for less than 15 years and the other half—for longer than 15 years. 25% of the entities was active for less than 8 years and longer than 24 years, 59% of the entities under study had Polish capital, and 41% of them had foreign capital. Merely 10% of entities were members of clusters (IT, Aviation Valley, MPT).

The analysis was conducted by dint of statistical inference, employing the following non-parametric tests: the Mann-Whitney U and the Kruskal-Wallis ANOVA. The research was conducted by dint of the Statistica 10. PL and Excel 10 programs.

Article's interdisciplinary character constitutes its added value, since it combines both decision theory and psychology. Comprehending mentality of managers, who make investment decisions in Polish enterprises is of great importance to potential business stakeholders, especially from outside Poland.

4 RESEARCH RESULTS

Entrepreneurs were supposed to assess 24 factors, which are constraints in making investment decisions in Polish enterprises (on a scale from 0 to 3, where 0 is no impact and 3 is a big impact). For these factors, average ratings have been calculated as shown below:

1. Reluctance to act hastily (2.53),
2. Attachment to the existing state of affairs (2.37),
3. Excessive endeavour to obtain complete information before making a decision, and to carefully consider many options to choose from (perfectionism), (2.37),
4. Failing to follow the point strategy which consists in controlling the actions and attaining one goal at a given moment (2.20),
5. Unexpected changes in the environment (2.18),
6. Inclination to postpone a decision—preoccupation with minor issues instead of key problems (2.17),
7. Too strong concentration on tasks (low agreeableness), (2.14),

8. Lack of financial resources (2.13),
9. Too strong concentration on people (high agreeableness), (2.13),
10. Lack of motivation (postponing decisions habitually), (2.12),
11. Failing to follow the interval strategy which consists in simultaneous implementation of many tasks with various goals (2.12),
12. Lack of human resources (competent staff), (2.07),
13. Lack of pressure of persons (e.g. superiors, recipients, competitors) (2.07),
14. Lack of material resources (2.06),
15. Fear or anxiety about making a decision (decision paralysis), (2.05),
16. Lack of time pressure (acting just before the set date), (2.03),
17. Preference for slow problem solving (2.00),
18. Too low level of organizing (formalizing) activities (1.99),
19. Lack of faith in success, eagerness, willingness towards long-lasting effective work (1.94),
20. Short (temporary) planning horizon (1.93),
21. Lack of information and knowledge (1.91),
22. Too low level of organization of activities (carelessness, chaos), (1.91),
23. Greater concentration on the past than on the future (1.87),
24. Lack of experience (1.82).

The biggest constraint in making investment decisions in Polish enterprises was reluctance to act hastily whereas the least important for the managers surveyed was the lack of experience.

Below, the ranking of managers' choices was presented, regarding the 24 factors that constrain the investment decision-making process, taking into account the characteristics of enterprises such as: innovativeness, implementation of the RFID system, size, area and range of activity, foreign capital and participation in the cluster.

As regards managers from enterprises introducing (62%) and not introducing innovations (38%), the reluctance to act hastily constituted the main constraint in making investment decisions. Among managers from innovative enterprises, attachment to the existing state of affairs ranked second, whereas those avoiding innovations pointed out to excessive endeavour to obtain complete information before making a decision. Differences in the assessment occurred only in the case of too strong concentration on people (probability $p = 0.0198$) – managers ranked it higher in enterprises with low innovativeness.

Both in the case of managers from enterprises that implemented (59%) and did not implement (41%) the RFID system, reluctance to act hastily constituted the biggest constraint in making

investment decisions. As regards the second factor, a group of managers with the implemented RFID system pointed out to the attachment to the existing state of affairs, whereas those who did not implement the system, to the excessive endeavour to obtain complete information before making a decision. It was checked what areas encompassed differences between the two groups of respondents. As shown by the research findings, differences occurred only in terms of too strong concentration on tasks ($p = 0.0464$) – i.e. the factor constitutes the biggest constraint for decision makers from enterprises that did not implement the RFID system yet.

It was also checked if the enterprise size influences the ranking of constraints in investment decision making (Table 1). Reluctance to act hastily was the biggest constraint for respondents from micro- and large enterprises, whereas the attachment to the existing state of affairs—for those from small and middle-sized ones.

The size of an enterprise influenced the assessment of: The reluctance to act hastily ($p = 0.0459$), failing to follow the interval strategy which consists in simultaneous implementation of many tasks with various goals ($p = 0.0379$), too strong concentration on people, ($p = 0.0044$), lack of financial resources ($p = 0.0107$) and lack of material resources. ($p = 0.0011$). Those factors constituted the biggest constraints for managers from micro-, and the smallest for managers from large

Table 1. Ranking of constraints in making investment decisions by company size (only the first three places).

Item	The size of enterprises and the most important factors
Micro-enterprises	
1.	Reluctance to act hastily
2.	Lack of material resources
3.	Too strong concentration on people
Small enterprises	
1.	Attachment to the existing state of affairs
2.	Reluctance to act hastily
3.	Unexpected changes in the environment
Medium-sized enterprises	
1.	Attachment to the existing state of affairs
2.	Point strategy is not applied
3.	Reluctance to act hastily
Large enterprises	
1.	Reluctance to act hastily
2.	Excessive endeavour to obtain complete information
3.	Attachment to the existing state of affairs

Source: Author's own elaboration based on research outcomes.

enterprises. Managers from all types of enterprises indicated reluctance to act hastily as the biggest constraint in making investment decisions. Among service and trade companies, attachment to the existing state of affairs ranked second, whereas managers from manufacturing and mixed-activity companies pointed out the excessive endeavour to obtain complete information (Table 2).

Furthermore it was checked whether there were differences germane to the importance of particular constraints in making investment decisions based on the type of business activity. The test showed that two differences occurred as regards the following factors: lack of experience ($p = 0.0147$) and too low level of organization of activities (carelessness, chaos). Lack of experience constituted the most important constraint for respondents from manufacturing and trading enterprises, and the least important for those running a mixed-activity business. Too low level of organization of tasks turned out the most difficult for investors from small companies, and the lest difficult for companies running a mixed activity business.

Managers from enterprises with local reach pointed out to the attachment to the existing state of affairs as the biggest constraint in making investment decisions. Other managers indicated the reluctance to act hastily (Table 3).

According to the division into the performance area, differences in respondents' choices occurred in the case of two factors, i.e. too low level of organizing (formalizing) activities ($p = 0.0060$) and too strong concentration on people ($p = 0.0327$). Those were perceived the biggest constraints for managers from local enterprises and the smallest for managers from international ones.

Reluctance to act hastily and attachment to the existing state of affairs constituted the biggest constraints for respondents with foreign capital. As regards foreign capital, differences occurred in the case of two factors such as: attachment to the existing state of affairs ($p = 0.0228$) and lack of faith in success ($p = 0.0359$). Both factors constituted a bigger constraint for decision makers from enterprises without foreign capital than for those with one.

The diversification of answers was also checked in terms of cluster affiliation. Reluctance to act hastily constituted a constraint both for those who were and were not cluster members. Among cluster participants, failing to follow the interval strategy which consists in simultaneous implementation of many tasks with various goals was ranked second, whereas among those who are not cluster members, excessive endeavour to obtain complete information before making a decision was ranked as the second factor. Also, the difference in the assessment of factors was checked, and the research showed

Table 2. Ranking of constraints in making investment decisions by area of business activity (only the first three places).

Item	The area of business activity of enterprises and the most important factors
Production enterprises	
1.	Reluctance to act hastily
2.	Excessive endeavour to obtain complete information
3.	Point strategy is not applied
Trade enterprises	
1.	Reluctance to act hastily
2.	Attachment to the existing state of affairs
3.	Too strong concentration on people
Services enterprises	
1.	Reluctance to act hastily
2.	Attachment to the existing state of affairs
3.	Excessive endeavour to obtain complete information
Conducted mixed business activities enterprises	
1.	Reluctance to act hastily
2.	Excessive endeavour to obtain complete information
3.	Attachment to the existing state of affairs

Source: Author's own elaboration based on research outcomes.

Table 3. Ranking of constrains in making investment decisions by business range (only the first three places).

Item	The business range of enterprises and the most important factors
Local enterprises	
1.	Attachment to the existing state of affairs
2.	Reluctance to act hastily
3.	Unexpected changes in the environment
Regional enterprises	
1.	Reluctance to act hastily
2.	Attachment to the existing state of affairs
3.	Excessive endeavour to obtain complete information
National enterprises	
1.	Reluctance to act hastily
2.	Attachment to the existing state of affairs
3.	Inclination to postpone a decision
International enterprises	
1.	Reluctance to act hastily
2.	Excessive endeavour to obtain complete information
3.	Attachment to the existing state of affairs

Source: Author's own elaboration based on research outcomes.

that they occur while assessing the lack of pressure of persons (e.g. superiors, recipients, competitors) (p = 0.0033), and too low level of organizing (formalizing) activities. Those factors constituted bigger constraints for those who did not belong to a cluster, rather than for ones that did.

5 CONCLUSION

Based on the research findings, one may infer that reluctance to act hastily, and attachment to the existing state of affairs constitute primary factors that hamper making investment decisions. Apart from that, one may say that the following aspects of enterprises influenced the ranking:

1. Innovativeness and implementation of the RFID system—excessive endeavour to obtain complete information before making a decision was a constraint for managers who avoided innovations and did not implement the RFID system,
2. Size—managers from micro- and small enterprises pointed out to reluctance to act hastily as the biggest constraint, whereas those from small and medium-sized enterprises to—attachment to the existing state of affairs. It is worth noting that the lack of material resources ranked second among the decision makers from microenterprises,
3. Area of business activity—lack of experience constituted the most important constraint for respondents from manufacturing and trade enterprises and a too low level of organization of activities—for investors from trade companies,
4. Range of activity—managers from enterprises with local reach pointed out to the attachment to the existing state of affairs, whereas those from enterprises with regional, national and international reach indicated the reluctance to act hastily,
5. The foreign capital—attachment to the existing state of affairs and lack of faith in success constituted a bigger constraint for decision makers in enterprises without foreign capital than for enterprises with one,
6. Participation in the cluster—among cluster participants, failing to follow the interval strategy which consists in simultaneous implementation of many tasks with various goals was ranked second, whereas among those who are not cluster members, excessive endeavour to obtain complete information before making a decision was ranked as the second factor.

Enterprises with lower strategic potential struggled with inertia, paucity of information and mate-rial resources, risk (reluctance to act hastily) and low motivation (lack of faith in success). Strong entities pointed out to the following constraints: inertia, long-term planning (no point strategy) and risk. Research hypothesis was confirmed.

ACKNOWLEDGEMENTS

This work was supported in part by the Polish National Centre for Research and Development (NCBR) under Grant No. PBS1/A3/3/2012 titled "Synthesis of autonomous semi-passive transponder dedicated to operation in anticollision dynamic RFID systems".

REFERENCES

Berger, J. 2017. *Invisible Influence: The Hidden Forces that Shape Behavior*. New York, NY: Simon & Schuster Paperbacks.

Downes, P.E. et al. 2017. Motivational mechanisms of self-concordance theory: Goal-specific efficacy and person-organization fit. *Journal of Business and Psychology* 32: 197–215.

Encyclopedia of management (pol.: Encyklopedia zarządzania). 2018. https://mfiles.pl/pl/index.php/Inwestycje.

Jankowski-Mihułowicz, P. et al. 2016a. The Idea of Enhancing Directional Energy Radiation by a Phased Antenna Array in UHF RFID System. *International Journal of Electronics and Telecommunications* 62(2): 115–120.

Jankowski-Mihułowicz, P. et al. 2016b. Development board of the autonomous semi-passive RFID transponder. *Bulletin of The Polish Academy of Sciences Technical Sciences* 64(3): 647–654.

Jankowski-Mihułowicz, P. et al. 2017. Using the phased array antenna to increase geometric size of the interrogation zone in a UHF RFID system. *Archives of Electrical Engineering* 66(4): 761–772.

Jankowski-Mihułowicz, P. & Węglarski, M. 2016. A Method for Measuring the Radiation Pattern of UHF RFID Transponders. *Metrology and Measurement Systems* 23(2): 163–172.

Jankowski-Mihułowicz, P. & Węglarski, M. 2017. Definition, Characteristics and Determining Parameters of Antennas in Terms of Synthesizing the Interrogation Zone in RFID Systems (Chapter 5). In P.C. Crepaldi & T.C. Pimenta (eds), *Radio Frequency Identification*. INTECH, London: 65–119.

Kahneman, D. 2017. *Thinking, fast and slow*. New York, NY: Macmillan Publishers USA.

Koźmiński, A.K. 2013. *Bounded leadership (pol.: Ograniczone przywództwo)*. Warszawa: Wydawnictwo Poltext.

Laskin, A.V. (ed.) 2018. *The Handbook of Financial Communication and Investor Relations*. New York, NY: John Wiley & Sons.

Peterson, R.L. 2007. *Inside the Investor's Brain: The Power of Mind Over Money*. New York, NY: John Wiley & Sons (Part III, Chapter 16).

Schaltenbrand, B. et al. 2018. See What We Want to See? The Effects of Managerial Experience on Corporate Green Investments. *Journal of Business Ethics* 150(4): 1129–1150.

Skowronek-Mielczarek, A. & Bojewska, B. 2017. Innovative behavior of small and medium enterprises in conditions of uncertainty (pol.: Zachowania innowacyjne małych i średnich przedsiębiorstw w warunkach niepewności). *Handel Wewnętrzny* 3(368): 47–59.

Tomaszewski, G. et al. 2016. Inkjet-Printed Flexible RFID Antenna for UHF RFID Transponder. *Materials Science-Poland* 34(4): 760–769.

Wu, T. et al. 2017. Top Management Teams' Characteristics and Strategic Decision-Making: A Mediation of Risk Perceptions and Mental Models. *Sustainability* 9(12, 2265): 1–15.

Production Management and Business Development – Mihalčová et al. (Eds)
© 2019 Taylor & Francis Group, London, ISBN 978-1-138-60415-5

Production planning and production management based on the ERP II system

M. Iskra

Faculty of Business Economics with seat in Košice, University of Economics in Bratislava, Košice, Slovak Republic

ABSTRACT: The common way of reducing production costs is doing it by monitoring and limiting various types of costs e.g. wages, support materials, but production costs can be reduced by improving and optimization of production management e.g. increasing production capacity by production schedules. The paper presents the development of ERP system. It also shows that ERP II system is a great tool for managing the company. There are many complicated statistical and econometric methods implemented in it to make taking operational but also strategic decisions easier.

1 INTRODUCTION

Often, companies try to limit production costs only by reducing typical types of costs, e.g. wages, support materials or external services. However, it should be remembered that increasing production efficiency, and increasing production capacity, can take place through optimized production management, without the need to increase employment and related expenditure. This effect can be obtained by an appropriate system supporting effective use of machines and employees' time. The knowledge of production capacity based on reliable information helps to systematize the production process. The system provides access to current information about the course of the production process, which allows making reliable decisions necessary in the proper functioning of the company. This is particularly important in a situation that requires quick response to unexpected events. The article deals with the subject of automating the processes of arranging production plans, including operations to be carried out and the availability of resources. The proper sequence of production operations leads to more efficient use of machines and employees. Reliable calculation and monitoring of real production capacity is difficult but very important in the business management process.

2 INFORMATION SYSTEMS DEVELOPMENT

2.1 Characteristics of the ERP II system

ERP class systems (Enterprise Resource Planning) create the most advanced group of integrated systems supporting enterprise management. Systems of this class support the management of the entire economic entity and integrate all areas of its activity. They constitute an IT solution that was created as a result of several decades of evolution of management support systems.

Traditional IT systems are focused on statistical analyzes and forecasts based on results, decisions are made as a result of the following: "from what was, it results what will be". A more advanced forecasting formula, known as "requirement planning", follows the principle of "what is, what follows what can happen in the future". The IT system, based on a set of information from today, simulates various scenarios (Handfield & Nichols 2000). There are many various planning processes, the example see Figure 1.

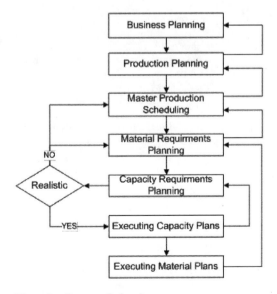

Figure 1. Process of planning.

The ERP platform is considered to be the highest form of an integrated system, including all management functions in the organization—planning, organizing, motivating and controlling.

The key difference between ERP and MRP II is the support of procedures supporting the financial operations of the company, which enables the production process to be captured not only in a quantitative context, but also in value. In addition, the ERP solution includes support for many new processes and areas, such as: human resources management, customer and supplier contacts, procurement, distribution, service, document workflow.

The term ERP II is commonly used to emphasize the importance of Internet technologies that play a key role in it. The opening of ERP systems to the environment has become real due to the XML standard, a universal language that allows the representation of data in a structured manner. Its biggest advantage is the lack of dependence on the platform, thanks to which the process of exchanging data between heterogeneous systems is relatively easy to implement.

2.2 Common functions of ERP II systems

ERP II systems have more often e-commerce solutions implemented such as: B2B (Business-to-Business) and B2C (Business-to-Customer). The B2B platform reduces the costs of handling procurement processes, because the activities related to placing an order and responsibility for its correctness are transferred to the contractor, and data recorded from the B2B file level are on-line in the ERP II system.

Integration with mobile devices is more and more common—dynamic development of information technology and telecommunications enabling the implementation of ERP II systems on mobile platforms, using portable devices PDA class, Smartphone etc.

The use of Business Process Management (BPM)—the implementation of IT tools compliant with the BPM concept allowing modeling of processes taking place inside and outside the organization. The implementation of BPM tools enables flexible adjustment of the system to the specifics of the company's operation.

2.3 Advanced BI solutions

Implementation of Business Intelligence (BI) solutions—use in ERP data warehouse systems, enabling the implementation of the Business Intelligence analytical platform, which gives access to advanced data analysis and exploration tools. BI solutions are increasingly becoming an integral part of the ERP II system, offering a number of tools to expand the analytical capabilities of ERP II systems. Examples include OLAP (OnLine Analytical

Processing), MOLAP (Multidimensional OnLine Analytical Processing), Business Scorecard, and Data Mining.

3 PRODUCTION PLANNING

3.1 MPS Master Production Schedule

A sub-module playing a key role in the MRP-II approach to planning logistic and control of goods flows within an industrial company. MPS contains short and long-term company tasks including production and inventory sales. For each planning position, MPS contains three logistical sub plans:

– plan of demand,
– production plan,
– inventory plan.

Sessions of Generation of the Main Production Schedule are one of the most important sessions in the Master Production Schedule and have modules the following basic tasks (Chojnowski 2010):

– generating a logistics plan consisting of a plan's plan of requirements,
– production and inventory plan for each separate planning position,
– generating planned inter-company collections in multi-branch projects company structure,
– generating planned MPS orders for detailed planning and control of the flow of goods,
– generating coarse material requirements for planning and control "parts" with long lead times,
– generating a coarse demand for production capacity for showing the demand for production capacity in individual bottlenecks groups,
– calculating the critical BOM level for planning positions.

3.2 MRP Material Requirements Planning

Based on the Main Production Schedule and multi-level BOM systems calculate exactly what components are to be made and which parts purchased at a specific point in time. Facilitates consistent planning of goods flow. Generation of optimal material planning for each assortment item covered by the MRP order system, for which the most important is timely and phased delivery of material. Although production capacity is not optimized, the effects of the generated material plan are analyzed taking into account the demand for production capacity.

For data processing systems have several methods:

– Regenerative processing—where it performs for each assortment item full MRP process. The results of previous MRP calculations are not taken into account,

– Net changes—this means that new material needs are calculated only for changed MPS or MRP positions. Changes can occur in forecasts sales, production, purchase or sale orders, material technology statements. "Net changes" require less time than the completely new MRP calculations. One of the reasons for using this method it is possible to carry out a relatively fast simulation of changes.
– Efficiency coefficient: the system multiplies production standards to the plan when generating orders of assortment items of repeatable production work center being a bottleneck by the value of this field. Received as a result of calculations, the production standard makes it possible to generate planned orders. The systems calculate the maximum production standard for the bottleneck working center. This is a production standard expressed as a percentage,
– safe time—is sometimes added to the realization time of the order in order to easing the uncertainty associated with the delivery times of the production order,

Seasonality models: seasonal models are coefficients for each seasonal period. They determine the increase and decrease of the safety margin or expected needs in a given period. Seasonality patterns are the presentation of fluctuations of certain values during the year. They serve as parameters for the forecasting function and advice.

3.3 Forecasting

All forecasting methods are based on real data forecasts, but they use this information in various ways.

The systems use, among others, the following forecasting methods:

– Moving Average: uses to determine the forecast for the upcoming period average demand by a sufficiently large number of past periods (Marz & Warren 2016).
– Exponential equalization: the basic principle of this method is adoption assumptions that numbers from periods closer to the present have

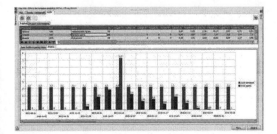

Figure 2. MPS Master Production Schedule—by IMPULS EVO.

more weight than further periods. The older the data, the less weight, are included in the calculation of the forecast (Lee & Sohn 2016).
– Modern methods of Business Intelligence and data mining.
– Machine learning as a part of artificial intelligence—not every task or decision can be made by using algorithm (Szeliga 2017).

4 CONCLUSIONS

The main conclusion is that ERP system is a strategic tool that enable collecting, processing but what is more important it helps making operational and also strategic decisions.

Most of data of any processes in the company are collected automatically, most of documents are making with the support of the system which gives more time for employees to do other crucial work.

Many operational decisions are made by ERP without employees' interaction. Production schedules, orders of materials can be made by the system.

There also are very complicated statistical, econometric methods implemented in ERP systems in order to forecast economic data or make operational or strategic decision. But there are also attempts of using some parts of artificial intelligence—like machine learning.

ERP II system is not only very complicated, but also very expensive. Implementing it is a very difficult and long process but the effect of using it can be very spectacular for the company. It should be noticed that although ERP system is complicated and expensive, it is very easy to use.

REFERENCES

Chojnowski, M. 2010. Ewolucja systemów wspomagających zarządzanie. System ERP II jako wsparcie dla e-biznesu. In *Zeszyty Naukowe Uniwersytetu Szczecińskiego. Ekonomiczne problemy usług*. Nr 58. 2010.
Handfield, R.B. & Nichols, E.L. Jr. 2000. Introduction to Supply Chain Management—Inteligentne systemy informacyjne, In *Computerworld*, nr. 14 (426), 2000.
Lee, H. & Sohn, I. 2016. BigData w przemyśle. Jak wykorzystać analizędanych do optymalizacji kosztów procesów. PWN. Warszawa 2016.
Marz, N. & Warren, J. 2016. Big data. Najlepsze praktyki budowy skalowalnych systemów obsługi danych w czasie rzeczywistym. Helion. Gliwice 2016.
Szeliga, M. 2017, Data science i uczenie maszynowe. ISBN 978-83-01-19232-7. PWN. Warszawa 2017.
Wrycza, S. 2010. *Technologie Informatyka ekonomiczna. Podręcznik akademicki*. Warszawa: PWE. ISBN 978-83-208-1863-5.

Basis for practical financial performance evaluation of enterprises

J. Janičková & A. Lisnik
Catholic University, Ružomberok, Slovak Republic

ABSTRACT: The article deals with two different enterprise and accounting units methodologies of their classification, which are used as a basis for practical financial performance evaluation of enterprises in the process of their management and by assessment of the business environment. The aim of the article is, based on the difference of defined categorization parameters, to determine the average fault divergence, which deforms the performance assessment of enterprises. After determining of preferred method we may provide the financial planning. The source of information is the secondary surveys of the Slovak Business Agency and own business performance survey, according to the parameters of turnover and assets.

1 CURRENT STATE OF KNOWLEDGE

1.1 Business environment

The business environment in the Slovak Republic (SR) has been forming in the transforming economy for almost three decades. The goal of ongoing changes should be to have a more efficient economy (Budaj 2018).

The last decade of business environment development is, besides many other features, characterized by intense electronization, the Internet, the introduction of new technologies, etc. Information technology influences life in all spheres of business and civil life. This situation arises, in particular, from the relatively easy availability of information and communication technologies (Zimermanová 2017).

Business environments can be evaluated through different methodologies, usually a summary of the data according to the selected corporate characteristics. One of the possibilities of an effective assessment of the business environment is to collect data on the financial condition of businesses from publicly available registers. In business, financial managers prefer a practical methodology of retrospective assessment of the financial situation. This process of financial analysis is a part of the fulfilment of the financial management functions of the company. They use, particular ratios or differential, aggregate or partial, indicators, that prepare from the financial statements, because these accounting units have to compile at the end of the accounting period, set up it. In these online interactive processes, they communicate with other stakeholders from the public and private sectors.

1.2 Financial analysis

Financial analysis serves for a comprehensive assessment of the financial situation of the company. It helps to find out, if is the business profitable, what is its capital structure, whether it uses its assets efficiently, whether it is able to repay its liabilities, and so on (Knápková 2013).

Financial decision-making is a succession of steps from identifying a decision-making problem through choosing and evaluating alternatives to a solution after selecting a variant on the basis of the chosen criteria, its implementation and controlling its results. Financial decision-making is subject to the financial management of a business that carries a large number of decisions (Fetisová 2012).

1.3 Classification of enterprises

By the Business Act, an enterprise is a set of tangible and intangible and intangible assets. The enterprise includes things, rights and other property values, that belong to entrepreneurs and serve to operate an enterprise, or because of their nature they serve this purpose.

According to the European Commission Recommendation 2003/361/EC, since 2005, SMEs have been classified into three size categories: micro, small and medium-sized enterprises, the criteria being: number of employees, annual turnover and value of assets. The micro-enterprise has up to 10 employees and the value of both turnover and assets is up to € 2 million. The small business has up to 49 employees and the value of selected financial parameters does not exceed € 10 million. The middle enterprise has up to 249 employees and the turnover and assets limit up to € 50 million (SBA 2018).

Under the conditions of the Slovak Republic, it performs a comprehensive official annual evaluation of the business environment of the Slovak Business Agency, according to 10 principles of the Small Business Act. The latest statistical profiling results are from 2016.

In 2016 small and medium-sized enterprises (SMEs) accounted for 99.9% (557 122) of the total number of business entities (557 758), employed 74.1% of the active labour force, and 52.7% contributed to the creation of added value. Micro enterprises (541 719; 97.1%), small businesses (12 662; 2.3%) and medium-sized enterprises (2 741; 0.5%) predominate in the structure of SMEs. For the first time since 2008 there has been an increase in the total number of natural persons—entrepreneurs. Physical persons accounted for 62.3% of the total number of SMEs (SBA 2018).

1.4 *Classification of accounting units*

Act No. 431/2002 Coll. Of accounting is defined by entities, required to keep accounts, in a simple accounting system or in a system of double-entry accounting, which are referred to as accounting units. The Act in Section 2 introduces a new division of accounting units into three size classes: micro, small, large units.

Three parameters are considered in the three size groups—the total asset value, the net turnover and the average recalculated number of employees of the entity. Entities must meet at least 2 out of 3 terms. When a new entity is created, its owner decides to be included in the size group for the next accounting period separately.

In 2016, in the SBA, according to the analysis for the calculation of the ratios of the financial performance of SMEs, they account for 180 117 accounting units (85.7% of all legal entities) in the system of double-entry accounting. Of this, 165 544 micro (91.9%), 11 638 (6.5%) small, 2 935 (1.6%) large accounting units belong to the search. Interestingly, they are referred to as accounting units, but were classified by SME categorization. It leads to ambiguity in the labelling of businesses and accounting units.

1.5 *Financial performance evaluation methodology*

The results of the financial analysis are used by business managers for internal needs (enterprise management, financial planning, etc.) and for external entities, with whom they cooperate (conclusion of business contracts, loan application in the bank, etc.). Another purpose of using data on the individual financial situation of enterprises is their synthesis for the official statistical evaluation of the business environment. Assessing the financial performance of Slovak SMEs depends on their correct inclusion in two categories.

In the long term, the complex assessment of the business environment is a disadvantage especially for fluctuations in the spectrum of defined

parameters for both categories of categorization. This finding is based on the results achieved in the categorization of SMEs and according to their own decision in the categorization of the accounting units.

In the categorization of entities, only those entities accounting in the double-entry bookkeeping system, are excluded from those, who account in the simple bookkeeping system.

Both categories use 3 levels of and 3 criteria for business differentiation. Criteria and categories are not fundamentally different in the formal designation. Differences are in the content of values for financial indicator limits. For example, an enterprise classified by SME categorization according to the turnover criterion as a micro-enterprise (up to € 2 million) and in the division of accounting units may belong to the group of small entities (more than € 700 thousand). This discrepancy is critical to assessing the financial performance of enterprises in the Slovak Republic and may distort the assessment in each individual enterprise and throughout the business environment. Incorrectly taken data can unjustly improve or damage the financial reputation of businesses, according to the data on websites that offer freely available databases of data on the financial condition of businesses.

According to Table 1, only one parameter—number of employees—is defined formally as well as content. But the financial indicators of turnover and the value of assets are different for assessing financial performance. The difference between the micro and the micro-unit is for the turnover limit of € 1.3 million and for the asset value limit up to € 1.65 million. The difference between values for a small business and for a small accounting unit is for the turnover limit € 9.3–2 mil., for the value of the property up to € 6.5–6 mil. The difference between the values for a medium-sized enterprise and for a large entity is for the turnover limit of € 42 million and for the value of the property up to € 46 million.

Table 1. Common and different traits of MSP and accounting units*.

Category of MSPs (size)	Micro	Small	Medium
Sum of employees	0–9	10–49	50–249
Turnover, Assets (€)	<2 mil.	<10 mil.	<50 mil.
Category of accounting units	Micro	Small	Large
Sum of employees	0–9	11–50	51–more
Turnover (thousand €)	<700	701–8000	>8000
Assets (thousand €)	<350	351–4000	>4000

*by Lukáč, J. – Lisičan, Ľ. 2018. Analysis of financial performance indicators. *Bratislava: SBA*. p. 9.

One of the current possibilities for obtaining information on the financial situation of Slovak companies is a free website created by the Fin-Stat project in 2013. After entering the keyword associated with the business identification to the search engine, a transparent automatic evaluation will be presented through tables and charts, using the value of financial ratios. The data source used by the portal includes all publicly managed and available electronic databases—bulletins, registers (FinStat 2018).

The results of the company's financial analysis should be compared with similar enterprises, especially in the sector. These results, however, are the main starting point for financial planning in the future. The financial plan serves corporate owners and managers as the basic financial instrument of financial policy, but also for meeting corporate goals. For financial planning, financial managers must choose the appropriate method according to Tóthová (2009), who carried out a survey of the preferences of financial planning methods in Slovak companies. The three most used methods were: the revenue share method, the progressive budgeting method, the ratio financial ratios method. The least used methods are the regression method and estimates.

2 SEARCH PROCEDURE

The objective of the survey was to obtain relevant data for the classification of SMEs according to their financial performance in two categories of categorization, to quantify the average deviation of the classification according to two methodologies and to determine the preferred method of financial planning in enterprises.

In 2017, potential respondents—owners, managers or other representatives of SMEs, located in the northeast of the Slovak Republic, were invited to participate in the survey in the number of 300. First, the features of business entities were examined according to three parameters: average number of employees, turnover and property.

The survey involved 203 respondents (68%) who provided relevant data according to the 2015 and 2016 financial statements. Other respondents were unwilling to cooperate on the survey. 69 respondents had to be excluded from the survey because they were not legal entities and charged in the simple bookkeeping system. 6 individuals account in double-entry bookkeeping. This was the first obstacle to exploration and the first inconsistency of methodologies. There were 128 respondents (43%) in the double-entry system. In the evaluation, we ranked enterprises by their size according to all three criteria. However, we didn't

have the criteria for the numbers of employees it's a common feature and was therefore irrelevant. It was focused only on the value of turnover and the property. It had done the proper classification of the accounting units according to the Business Accounting Act. It is detected deviations in both the absolute and relative numbers of enterprises for each year and then the average deviation for the whole period.

Then it has been identified the most preferred method of financial planning that follows the financial analysis process. Respondents rated the most appropriate answer for their.

3 RESULTS, DISCUSSION

In the structure of 128 enterprises, according to financial indicators of value of turnover and assets, in 2015:

a. According to the SME's categorization, 107 micro enterprises (84%), 17 small enterprises (13%) and 4 medium-sized enterprises (3%),
b. According to the accounting criteria of the Accounting Act, 84 micro-units (66%), 36 small units (28%) and 8 large units (6%) were accounted for according to the Accounting Act.

The overall performance of enterprises would change the number of enterprises in each category. The largest decrease in the number of 23 enterprises occurred in the micro-sized enterprise group, a significant increase in the category of small enterprises by 19 and medium enterprises by 4. Overall, if the original SMEs met the categorization criteria accounting for 46 enterprises (36%), which is more than one third, would be among the categories.

Similar results were found in 2016:

a. According to SME categorization, 103 micro enterprises (81%), 23 small enterprises (1%) and 2 medium enterprises (2%),
b. According to the criteria for accounting units under the Accounting act, 87 micro-units (68%), 34 small units (27%) and 7 large units (6%) were required.

The largest drop in the number of 16 enterprises occurred in the micro enterprise group, with a small enterprise group growing by 11 and by medium-sized enterprises by 5. If the original SMEs met the criteria for categorizing of the units, 33 enterprises (26%) would be moved.

The results of survey are shown in next Table 2 and Table 3.

In each year under review, we changed the classification of entities into their categories, as

Table 2. Numerical differences in enterprise and accounting unit categorization in 2015.

2015 year					
SME size	Nr.	Account unit size	Nr.	Difference (sum (%))	Trait
Micro	107	Micro	84	−23 (22)	Decrease
Small	17	Small	36	19 (112)	Increase
Middle	4	Large	8	4 (100)	Increase
Sum	128	Sum	128	0	–

Table 3. Numerical differences in enterprise and accounting unit categorization in 2016.

2016 year					
SME size	Nr.	Account unit size	Nr.	Difference (sum (%))	Trait
Micro	103	Micro	87	−16 (15)	Decrease
Small	23	Small	34	11 (48)	Increase
Middle	2	Large	7	5 (350)	Increase
Sum	128	Sum	128	0	–

opposed to their original classification in the SME categories, according to financial performance indicators—turnover and assets. The change, moving between categories, represents an average of 30% of the total number of businesses. Therefore, it can be assumed that when assessing the financial condition of a business, a natural error must be assumed, and it is necessary to anticipate its effects even in financial planning.

In addition, it was found that the most used methods of financial planning in the surveyed enterprises include: in 47 enterprises (37%) the method of gradual budgeting, in 53 enterprises (41%), financial ratios, in 18 enterprises (14% enterprises (6%) global method. Other methods are also used, but only as complementary.

It manifests, that for better financial management of the enterprise and also for evaluation of the business environment, it will be appropriate to unify the methodology and parameters of categorization of enterprises by size and accounting units. It will be possible to avoid mistakes in the evaluation, but especially in enterprises—in fulfilling managerial functions and business objectives.

REFERENCES

Budaj, P. et al. 2018. Economic aspects of the mining industry in the Slovak Republic. *Acta Montanistica Slovaca*, 23(1): 1–9.

Fetisová, E. et al. 2012. Aktuálne problémy financií malých a stredných podnikov. Bratislava: EKONÓM, 169 p.

FinStat. [2018-03-20]. Retrieved from: https://finstat.sk/o-finstate.

Knápková, A. et al. 2013. Finanční analýza—Komplexní průvodce s příklady. Praha: Grada Publishing, 236 p.

Lukáč, J. & Lisičan, Ľ. 2018. Analýza ukazovateľov finančnej výkonnosti malých a stredných podnikov účtujúcich v sústave podvojného účtovníctva v r. 2016. Bratislava: SBA. p. 9. [2018–04–20] Retrieved from: http://www.sbagency.sk/ sites/default/files/12_analyza_ukazovatelov_financnej_vykonnosti_msp_2016_e.pdf.

MSP v číslach. Bratislava: SBA. [2018-04-14]. Retrieved from: http://www.sbagency.sk/sites/default/files/image/msp_v_cislach_v_roku_2016_final_v_20_10_2017_002.pdf.

Správa o stave malého a stredného podnikania v Slovenskej republike v roku 2016. Bratislava: SBA. [2018–04–14]. Retrieved from: http://www.sbagency.sk/sites/default/files/pictures/sprava_o_stave_msp_v_sr_v_roku_2016.pdf.

Tóthová, A. 2009. Moderné postupy v procese tvorby finančného plánu podniku. Bratislava: Ekonomická univerzita v Bratislave. EKONÓM, 150 p.

Zákon č. 513/1991 Zb. Obchodný zákonník. [2018-03-14] Retrieved from: https://www.noveaspi.sk/products/lawText/1/39560/1/2.

Zákon č. 431/2002 Z. z. o účtovníctve. [2018-03-14] Retrieved from: https://www.noveaspi.sk/products/lawText.

Zalai, K. et al. Finančno-ekonomická analýza podniku. Bratislava: SPRINT. 471 p.

Zimermanová, K. New possibilities for cooperation in theactivities of smes business. *Knowledge for Market Use. Olomouc: Palacký University, Česká republika.* 1179 p.

Production Management and Business Development – Mihalčová et al. (Eds)
© *2019 Taylor & Francis Group, London, ISBN 978-1-138-60415-5*

The concept and methods of staff development in enterprises

M. Jankowska-Mihułowicz
Faculty of Management, Rzeszow University of Technology, Rzeszow, Poland

ABSTRACT: The paper aims to describe the concept and provide an overview of methods of staff development in enterprises that are appropriate in a turbulent environment. The concept of staff development in enterprises proposed herein advocates of an individual and holistic approach to employees that takes notice of maintaining work-life balance. The article accounts for the development of employees, distinguishes learning models ranging from trainings to self-education, as well as points out to stages that are worth taking into consideration while designing the process of staff development. Moreover, the paper presents several methods which constitute useful management tools facilitating adult development. Managers, while applying these methods, aim to support employees in terms of dealing with the complexity of professional and corporate issues, as well as those of private and social nature. Furthermore, the article explains the significance of taking care of staff development in enterprises.

1 INTRODUCTION

Human resources management (HRM or HR) is a notion used in Poland since the 1990s, which is also sometimes referred to as staff management, personnel management, personnel administration or social potential management (Masłyk-Musiał 2000). Human resources management is a model of modern management in terms of organization's personnel function. In this model, human resources constitute the main component of enterprise's assets and simultaneously the source of its competitiveness. Human resources management is a strategic concept, in accordance with which a human resource should be treated subjectively and at the same time optimally used quantitatively and qualitatively in order to fulfill the organization's mission (Kozioł 2000).

One of the research areas of human resources management is staff development, which is governed by the following leitmotif: 'there is a close link between education systems and the education level in a society, and the level of industrial development and competitiveness in a particular country' (Rosłanowska-Plichcińska et al. 1996). J. Jakubowski approached the thought from an individual rather than societal angle, stating that: 'in the knowledge process, i.e. learning, remembering and reminding, tasting, connecting the data and new elements innovatively, one may actively be or ossify, be flexible or fall into patterns, develop or eschew changes. One has to constantly ask, diagnose, and question' (Piasecki 2007).

The aim of this paper is to describe the concept and overview the methods of staff development in an enterprise. The article also covers contemporary conditions governing the performance of enterprises, i.e. turbulent environment and the necessity to holistically perceive employees who find it difficult to fulfill professional, private and social roles and develop in all of these walks of life. In the legal area of management, the paper corresponds mainly to Polish conditions, whereas the social component overlaps with the conditions of Central and Western Europe.

2 THE CONCEPT OF STAFF DEVELOPMENT IN AN ENTERPRISE

Staff development otherwise referred to as employee development, workforce development (Antczak 1999), or personnel development (Piwowar-Sulej 2016). In the broadest sense, it consists in the employee getting a more mature personality. Maturity is positively important for a human in the life spheres—private and professional, and both of these spheres intermingle and mutually condition each other (Jamka & Konarski 2009).

Supporting adult development consists in maintaining their work-life balance, which means juggling professional and family duties with education, social engagement, and leisure (Ramos et al. 2015). Those activities are complementary, not opposite. Such perception enables an individual to understand the multidimensionality of their existence and self-fulfill. Achieving the balance requires cooperation between employers and employees. Rather than striving for perfect harmony, it is more about mitigating a conflict in the said life spheres. It facilitates person's development and enhances their maturity (ten Brummelhuis & van der Lippe 2010, Grant et al. 2013, Gravador & Teng-Calleja 2018, Kossek & Lautsch 2018).

Staff development is defined as activities which have to prepare the employees to 'do their job and hold more responsible positions' (Suchodolski 2010). Contrarily to that, it is also assumed that it constitutes 'a process when employees fill the elements in their potential which are necessary to correctly do their current or planned future tasks' (Piwowar-Sulej 2016).

Employee development is a long and complex process, when employees learn professionalism which is of decisive importance for the organization, since it derives from its needs. Assessment, mastering, and relocating constitute the components of this process (Antczak 1999).

Employee development should take place on all stages of their professional career. According to D. Super, those stages encompass: growth, studying and discovering, opening, stagnation and regress. They should occur in harmony with natural processes that a human is subject to (Suchodolski 2010).

In the process of supporting adult development it is advisable to move from trainings to self-learning. In this sequence, the following learning models were enumerated (Rosłanowska-Plichcińska et al. 1996):

1. internal trainings for employees in the enterprise,
2. trainings for employees conducted by academic teachers,
3. professional training programs conducted in training centers,
4. training programs organized by higher education institutions,
5. curricula with education modules (internships) conducted by enterprises,
6. education (evening studies, distance learning),
7. self-learning (so called self-directed learning).

Self-learning does not mean that a manager or trainer left the employee on their own, but that an employee is supported throughout the self-controlled development in the company: advisory, coaching, mentoring, e-learning or internal and external trainings (Antczak 1999).

On the one hand, it is believed that teams fail because they lack trainings (Blanchard 2016), but on the other hand, 'enterprises notice the fact that the current array of trainings does not suffice to main original competence in the future and increase the competitive advantage. They notice the contradiction between current needs of adjusting to present market requirements, and the necessity to invest in an employee who is a strategic

asset in the long-term perspective. [...] Enterprises look for new solutions in this area' (Rosłanowska-Plichcińska et al. 1996). Enterprises may address both of these problems by a self-developed training offer, on the grounds that only those who develop faster than others win this competitive battle on the market. Furthermore, the key success factor is the intellectual leadership, i.e. the ability to create knowledge an master the skills (Rosłanowska-Plichcińska et al. 1996), ergo the key competence set.

While modeling the process of staff development, the following stages need to be considered (Nowacka-Sahin 2007):

1. strategic analysis aiming at learning the sector and then developing a diversified training offer,
2. intensive and active promotion of the training offer,
3. defining the training features and needs of a particular group of employees; at the organizational, task and individual (Danilewicz 2014) level,
4. establishing the goal, plan and budget of a training, and recruitment of trainers; particularly desired features: competence, expert knowledge, openness, flexibility, communication skills, good manners (Aniszewska et al. 2001),
5. designing the training process—selection of methods and techniques corresponding to the demand and training opportunities and compatible with trainers' abilities,
6. integration and motivation of trainees,
7. measuring trainees' knowledge and skills at the beginning of the training,
8. conducting the training,
9. measuring trainees' knowledge and skills at the end of the training,
10. of the trainees (Doughty 2007),
11. trainees' feedback; example methods are questionnaire an follow-up (Buchen 2011),
12. improving the training process and content based on feedback,
13. repeating points 1–13.

Experts highlight the fact that 'the selection of training and education methods, as well as the forms of informing should encompass local conditions' (Aniszewska et al. 2001), therefore e.g. culture (traditions, habits), age diversity, the unemployment rate, employment structure).

Research findings show that the main reason for the lack of interest in personal trainings in Poland was the fact the training offer was not adjusted to enterprises' needs, and secondly, the offer was not attractive (Bącal 2007). Nowadays, it is not only the effectiveness but also the impressiveness (Godlewska-Werner 2007) of trainings that is emphasized, therefore the importance of well-prepared trainers and the use of multimedia (text, pictures, sound, motion, music, and speech), (Chaber 2007). The aim of impressiveness is to gain and maintain the attention of training participants.

3 METHODS OF STAFF DEVELOPMENT

Based on literature review, one may point out to the following methods of staff development (Armstrong & Taylor 2016):

1. **learning in the workplace** e.g.: instructing, assigning specialist tasks, commissioning tasks, action learning (solving real problems), cooperation projects etc.; **promotion** – vertical (managerial authority) or horizontal (expanding expert qualifications); **relocation of employees** e.g.: rotation, restructuring; **group learning** e.g.: trainings (systematic, just-in-time, bite-sized or outdoor), moderations (with discussion, case study, and role playing), learning from others—sharing experience (conversation), SIS (steal ideas shamelessly); **self-directed learning** supported by action learning, advisory, and guidance, coaching (Syrek-Kosowska 2015), (e.g.: life coaching, performance coaching, team coaching), (Kauffman et al. 2015), mentoring, as well as standardized personal development in accordance with a self-defined learning program, discussed in the form of a learning contract with a supervisor or advisor responsible for the management of developing managerial skills; gamification and enterprise gamification (Jiménez Arenas 2018),
2. **learning outside the workplace** e.g. professional internships (work placements) trainings, lectures, conferences, seminars, symposia, sharing experience, programmed learning, group case studies, trainings in terms of role-playing, group dynamics, team working, organizational skills, interpersonal trainings, creative workshops, learning by doing, studying, consulting, case studies analysis, benchmarking etc.; **distance learning** e.g. correspondence courses, radio, TV, video and computer courses, knowledge pills, e-learning e.g. synchronic, non-synchronic, individual (self-learning) and blended learning,
3. **blended learning** – simultaneous application of many learning methods (e.g. in the workplace and outside it; individual and group).

One needs to remember that staff development also takes place and is supported by maintaining the work-life balance, which means taking care of employees' well-being. The concept encompasses recognizing their individuality, various needs (ensuing e.g. from age, lifecycle stage, the length of their professional career, the level of development etc.), rewarding for achievements, and caring about them, as well as creating a satisfying working environment, stress management, work-life balance, responding to sexual harassment and threatening (Armstrong & Taylor 2016), individual support, collective benefits for employees, and providing more flexibility in terms of e.g.: working hours, calculating working hours on an annual basis, proving an opportunity to work part-time, days off and breaks in professional life without losing the position. Collective benefits for employees encompass subsidized meals in company's canteen, sport and social clubs, psychological advice, company's cars, get-togethers, holidays for kids and adults, self-arranged holidays, vouchers, childcare services i.e. creating and maintaining company's nursery schools, children clubs, and kindergartens. Employees may also use (e.g. medical) group insurance.

4 CONCLUSION

S. Rao—who lectures at universities such as: Columbia University, The London School of Economics and Political Science, University of California, Berkeley and Northwestern University (in Kellogg School of Management), and is also the author of bestsellers such as: *Are You Ready to Succeed* and *Happiness at Work* – once said: 'I don't believe in the idea that a human being has a professional and a private life. I think we have one life. I don't believe people who say: 'I'm getting divorced, my children don't recognize me, my own dog bit me yesterday, even my lover has a lover, but I'm doing great at work'. It doesn't work like that. Your life is integrated, it is a whole which works or not' (Lankosz 2012). In consonance with that, the concept of staff development in an enterprise proposed in this paper postulates an individual and holistic approach to an employee. In the article, several methods considered useful tools in adult development were presented. They constitute a useful interdisciplinary collection which may be applied by managers. Nevertheless, the application of these methods requires knowledge, skills, efforts, engagement and financial resources. Research findings in the field of management show that taking care of staff development in an enterprise is a valuable investment providing positive feedback not only in companies (profits), but in all areas of employees' activity—good is favoured, that is what humanists hope for.

REFERENCES

Aniszewska, G. et al. 2001. *Sposoby edukacji, informowania i szkoleń*. Wrocław: Biuro Koordynacji Projektu Banku Światowego.

Antczak, Z. 1999. Rozwój pracowników. In T. Listwan (ed.), *Zarządzanie kadrami. Podstawy teoretyczne i ćwiczenia*. 122–127. Wrocław: Wydawnictwo Akademii Ekonomicznej im. Oskara Langego we Wrocławiu.

Armstrong, M. & Taylor, S. 2016. *Zarządzanie zasobami ludzkimi*. Warszawa: Wolters Kluwer.

Bącal, J. 2007. Perspektywy rozwoju zarządzania zasobami ludzkimi w małych i średnich przedsiębiorstwach w Polsce. In O. Konieczny & R. Schmidtke (eds), *Inwestycja w kadry. Perspektywa instytucji szkoleniowych*: 44–66. Katowice: Polska Agencja Rozwoju Przedsiębiorczości.

Blanchard, K. 2016. *Przywództwo wyższego stopnia*. Warszawa: Wydawnictwo Naukowe PWN.

Buchen, I.H. 2011. *Partnerski HR. Nowe normy efektywnej rekrutacji, pracy i szkolenia kadry pracowniczej*. Warszawa: Oficyna a Wolters Kluwer business.

Chaber, A. 2007. E-learning i nowe media szkoleniowe. In O. Konieczny & R. Schmidtke (eds), *Inwestycja w kadry. Perspektywa instytucji szkoleniowych*: 177–194. Katowice: Polska Agencja Rozwoju Przedsiębiorczości.

Danilewicz, D. 2014. Organizacja procesu rozwoju kompetencji. In M. Juchnowicz (ed.), *Zarządzanie kapitałem ludzkim. Procesy—narzędzia—aplikacje*: 288–315. Warszawa: Polskie Wydawnictwo Ekonomiczne.

Doughty, D. 2007. Certyfikat w dziedzinie zarządzania i rozwoju zasobów ludzkich—model dla sektora małej i średniej przedsiębiorczości w Polsce. In O. Konieczny & R. Schmidtke (eds), *Inwestycja w kadry. Perspektywa instytucji szkoleniowych*: 215–226. Katowice: Polska Agencja Rozwoju Przedsiębiorczości.

Godlewska-Werner, D. 2007. Dobre szkolenie—efektowne i efektywne In O. Konieczny & R. Schmidtke (eds), *Inwestycja w kadry. Perspektywa instytucji szkoleniowych*: 159–175. Katowice: Polska Agencja Rozwoju Przedsiębiorczości.

Grant, C.A. et al. 2013. An exploration of the psychological factors affecting remote e-worker's job effectiveness, well-being and work-life balance. *Employee Relations* 35(5): 527–546.

Gravador, L.N. & Teng-Calleja, M. 2018. Work-life balance crafting behaviors: an empirical study. *Personnel Review* 47(4): 786–804.

Holliday, M. 2006. *Coaching, mentoring i zarządzanie: jak rozwiązywać problemy i budować zespół*. Gliwice: Wydawnictwo Helion.

Http://nf.pl, 2018.

Huflejt-Łukasik, M. et al. 2015. Co powinien wiedzieć i potrafić profesjonalny coach: jak wybierać coachów do organizacji? In D. Czarkowska (ed.), *Business coaching jako dźwignia rozwoju przedsiębiorczości*: 67–87. Warszawa: Wydawnictwo Poltext.

Jamka, B. & Konarski, S. (eds) 2009. *Zarządzanie zasobami ludzkimi a zdolności adaptacyjne przedsiębiorstw. Trudne obszary*: 118. Warszawa: Szkoła Główna Handlowa w Warszawie.

Jiménez Arenas, S. 2018. *Podstawy modelu grywalizacji* [in:] http://grywalizacja24.pl/podstawy-modelu-grywalizacji/.

Kauffman, C. et al. 2015. Coaching oparty na psychologii pozytywnej. In D. Czarkowska (ed.), *Business coaching jako dźwignia rozwoju przedsiębiorczości*: 249–263. Warszawa: Wydawnictwo Poltext.

Kossek, E.E. & Lautsch, B.A. 2018. Work-life flexibility for whom? Occupational status and work-life inequality in upper, middle, and lower level jobs. *Academy of Management Annals* 12(1): 1–4.

Kozioł, L. 2000. *Zarządzanie zasobami ludzkimi w firmie*. Wydawnictwo Biblioteczka Pracownicza, Warszawa.

Lankosz, M. 2012. Srikumar Rao: Macie już rzeczy, które miały was uszczęśliwić. Dlaczego więc nie jesteście szczęśliwi? *Wysokie obcasy*, 18 October 2012. In http://www.wysokieobcasy.pl/wysokie-obcasy/51,96856,12696594.html?i = 0.

Łasiński, G. 2007. *Rozwiązywanie problemów w organizacji. Moderacje w praktyce*. Warszawa: Polskie Wydawnictwo Ekonomiczne.

Masłyk-Musiał, E. 2000. *Strategiczne zarządzanie zasobami ludzkimi*. Warszawa: Oficyna Wydawnicza Politechniki Warszawskiej.

Migoń, A. 2015. Mentoring jako skuteczne narzędzie wsparcia dla początkujących przedsiębiorców. In D. Czarkowska (ed.), *Business coaching jako dźwignia rozwoju przedsiębiorczości*: 265–279. Warszawa: Wydawnictwo Poltext.

Nowacka-Sahin, M. 2007. Identyfikacja potrzeb szkoleniowych. In O. Konieczny & R. Schmidtke (eds), *Inwestycja w kadry. Perspektywa instytucji szkoleniowych*: 139–157. Katowice: Polska Agencja Rozwoju Przedsiębiorczości.

Piasecki, P. 2007. Idea Lifelong Learning. In O. Konieczny & R. Schmidtke (eds), *Inwestycja w kadry. Perspektywa instytucji szkoleniowych*: 87–116. Katowice: Polska Agencja Rozwoju Przedsiębiorczości.

Piwowar-Sulej, K. 2016. *Zarządzanie ludźmi w organizacjach zorientowanych na projekty*. Warszawa: Wydawnictwo Difin.

Piasecki, P. 2007. Idea Lifelong Learning. In O. Konieczny & R. Schmidtke (eds), *Inwestycja w kadry. Perspektywa instytucji szkoleniowych*: 107–117. Katowice: Polska Agencja Rozwoju Przedsiębiorczości.

Piwowar-Sulej, K. 2016. *Zarządzanie ludźmi w organizacjach zorientowanych na projekty*. Warszawa: Wydawnictwo Difin.

Ramos, R. et al. 2015. Busy yet socially engaged: volunteering, work-life balance, and health in the working population. *Journal of Occupational and Environmental Medicine* 57(2): 164–172.

Rosłanowska-Plichcińska, K. & Zespół Euromanagement. 1996. *Inwestowanie w pracownika. Koncepcje i praktyka zachodnich przedsiębiorstw i uniwersytetów*. Warszawa: Wydawnictwo Poltext.

Suchodolski, A. 2010. Rozwój i zarządzanie karierą pracowników. In T. Listwan (ed.), *Zarządzanie kadrami. Podstawy teoretyczne i ćwiczenia*: 211–234. Warszawa: Wydawnictwo C.H. Beck.

Syrek-Kosowska, A. 2015. Coaching kadry zarządzającej wobec rosnącej złożoności biznesu. In D. Czarkowska, *Business coaching jako dźwignia rozwoju przedsiębiorczości*: 105–128. Warszawa: Wydawnictwo Poltext.

ten Brummelhuis, L.L. & van der Lippe, T. 2010. Effective work-life balance support for various household structures. *Human Resource Management* 49(2): 173–193.

Production Management and Business Development – Mihalčová et al. (Eds)
© 2019 Taylor & Francis Group, London, ISBN 978-1-138-60415-5

Startup support in Slovakia and European Union

M. Janošková, K. Čulková & D. Hrehová
Technical University of Košice, Košice, Slovak Republic

ABSTRACT: In present complex and dynamic business environment there is specific space for innovation and startups as modern phenomena of the business. But in theory and practice there are various opinions to this form of business that show to the objective reasons why mainly startups obtain presently such considerable support to make a business. Contribution shows difference of startups perception in various countries, difference not only in its definition, opinion of experts, but also in quantified indicators, as well as difference for example from small enterprises. Startups demands due to their innovativeness, progressiveness and high risk, financial and non-financial support. Except of traditional sources and way of financing we show in the contribution also new forms of financial support from various sources, while comparing financing through capital investment in Slovakia and other EU countries.

1 INTRODUCTION

In present dynamic business environment special place belong to innovation and startups as modern phenomena of business. In spite in any modern economy startups are main drive of innovation, in Slovakia there is still very few of them. Similarly, as SMEs, also existing startups must in such turbulent environment develop permanently the effort to hold and protect them. Startups do not have fear to risk in spite of still new sources of values finding for client and determining impacts to their business.

SMEs present inseparable part of developed market economy, due to their contribution to the flexibility of market mechanism, potential of competition environment and innovation activities. Development of SMEs is defined as one of the priorities of economic development in Slovakia. Important factor in this process is creation of proper business environment, which assumes simplification and clarification of legislative, decreasing of administrative and tax burden, strengthening of support infrastructure and improving of access to the capital as basic or supplementary source of financing.

SMEs present stabilized element of any developed economy. A positive means also the fact that SMEs can adapt to the changing business trends and actual economic situation more flexibly than big corporations. From long term view they have the most substantial importance mainly in economically less developed regions, in which they do not act as big enterprises and transnational corporations. In such areas SMEs present essential majority for working posts and present local capital.

SMEs and startups support is one of the most important themes of European Union. Among basic strategic documents belong European Chart for SMEs from 2000, Law of SMEs from 2008 (Small Business Act) and its actualization in 2011, Strategy Europe 2020 and Action Plan for business 2020.

2 LITERATURE REVIEW

Startups are presently the trend, which address mainly young people, attracting them by expectation to achieve the success and the profit rapidly. Encouragement is also presented successes, achieving by some new startups in the world.

Definition of startups is presently not unique, it depends many times from the view of its creator, and therefore, we recommend several basic views. One of the most favorable startup business from Silicon Valley, Steve Blank (2010), defines startup as *"temporary arrangement, created for finding of repeated and graded business model."* According Gromova (2013) main product of startup is single company, which risen, its business aim with its working team, which is not only the main creator, but also guarantee of created aim realization. The other definition is given by Eric Ries (2010), pupil of Steve Blank, according whom startup is *"human institution, created with aim to bring new product or service in conditions of extreme uncertainty."* Paul Graham (2012), British programmer and co-founder of American accelerator YCombinator, defines startup as *"company, orientated to the rapid growth. The company is startup not only because it was newly raised. For the startup there is not decisive to work exclusively in IT area, but there is important it would be financed by risk capital. Single considerable think is its rapid growth."*

Other opinions to startups show the reasons, why startups obtain presently in business such considerable support. For example, special access to startup had been risen in Israel, which in spite of not disposing of any natural sources, succeeded mainly by principle of startup business to create bigger number of new, rapidly growing enterprises in comparing with Japan, China, South Korea, Canada or Great Britain. Israel businessmen were forced to overcome negative conditions, limited sources, permanent war conflicts and connected high measure of uncertainty, which resulted in single combination of innovativeness and business success.

Conception of startup support and development of startup eco-system in Slovakia (2013) defines startups as *"business initiatives with high growth and innovative potential that can start and support in long term intelligent and inclusive economic growth and by this way to attract also foreign investments."*

Every startup begins with original idea that runs through its single development from business model to the way of fully valuable company. Mostly start-ups are compared with micro enterprises or small enterprises, but there are some differences. According Sobeková Majková (2017) the differences are mostly as follows:

- Startup is orientated more to the world markets; traditional small enterprises are orientated rather to domestic market. According mentioned startup business is more ambitious, but also riskier. Their business model has not yet been tested at the market, and there is not certain if the market would accept them.
- Startups have business idea based on innovation, which presents their main competition advantage. Other beginning enterprises have not to have innovation as main reason for their rising.
- Due to the internet founders and employees of startup can make their job anywhere in the world, but it is not possible in traditional small enterprises.
- From the view of financing traditionally risen enterprises are rather family business and external financing is not so often. Startups on the other hand are looking for investors with aim to obtain finances for further development of product, its growth and entrance to foreign market.
- Traditionally risen enterprises are growing slowly, but by rather regular trend. Startups grow differently, which means at the beginning they have many time the loss, lately they record intensive and rapid growth.

- The way of startups to success at the market is different from common small enterprise. Startup, which comes to the market with unknown innovation must regard that such prototype, which is developed, have not to be successful and the business will terminate.

Great idea is only the beginning of business activity of startup; its further development is unique, individual process, also due to the conditions, in which it exists. Startups bring innovation and vitality to the economy, as well as new products and services, which can find very easily its space at the market, new processes and techniques, and startups contribute to the rising of new working posts, supporting development of knowledge economy, connecting science, research and innovation with business work, increasing economy competitiveness, etc.

3 SUPPORT OF STARTUP BUSINESS

Similarly, as other type of business, also startups have certain measure of risk. There is number of proves about successful, or less successful businesses. Experiences prove that also in countries with more knowledge of startups only approximately 10% of startups succeeded to hold on the market from long term view considerably and real expectation can be filled only by 1% of startups. In spite of mentioned there is necessary to give attention to their support and further development. Without support number of business ideas would not be successful.

The best evidence about efficiency and success of this new trend of business are for example Google, Skype, Twitter or Facebook (Blank 2013). Although unfavorable one's mention that majority of the project finish with any success, on the other hand some of startups change due to their innovation characteristic of sectors, whole economy or they create new markets. But support of this segment in majority of EU member states does not belong among political priorities, since they have commonly only low share on working posts creation. Presently technological companies in spite of high contribution to economy create also less working posts in comparing with industrial giants, created in 20th Century.

Startups that are successful to achieve success on whole-world markets and influence the production of segments significantly are also in Europe. As an example we can mention Slovakian company ESET, or Estonian Skype. But in comparing with USA number of startups that are successful in growing, is considerably lower. In spite this rate is described rather to more qualitative business environment and lower dedication to business, while view to the successful startup centers of Europe, as for example London, Berlin or Paris prove that also Europe has qualitative business projects.

One of the reasons for failure of startups is their financing, problems of Slovakian startups and SMEs can be solved by improving of their access to financing. Free movement of capital in the frame of project of common European market is given by Roman Agreements from 1957, as one of the four basic freedoms of integration project that resulted lately in EU rising. In spite of capital markets development and deepening of common market integration, capital markets in EU remain fragmented to national level of member states. Due to the mentioned level of investments in EU after 2010 is circulating under common values in past, problem of insufficient depth and fragmentation of European capital markets became key theme of European Commission. Such appeals are not new, in case Europe wants presently to startup its economic growth again, it demands urgent solutions.

Due to the innovativeness, progressiveness, and also high risk of startups, they demand financial as well as non-financial support. Except of government and its institutions also other subjects are participating at the mentioned. Such subjects are not only supporters of good ideas and new trends, but also they present direct interest. They use meanwhile various forms of financial and non-financial support.

Except of traditional sources and ways of financing of SMEs business, also startup business use new, less known forms of financing, where belong mainly Business Angels, Venture capital funds, Private equity, Crowdfunding etc. For startup financing there are recommended more new forms through risk investment that are adapted to the capital demand and development of business in various period of their development. In beginning period of business common source of financing are own saving of businessman and investments—Family, Friends, Fools, which do not expect commonly any revenues. In this case beginning startups are looking also for local institutional sources that are provided by incubators and accelerators. In further period also individual investors enter to the financing, for example Business angels. Following is period of startup development, when further business development demands higher volume of investments, provided by Venture capital, or Private equity funds.

In the frame of contribution, we analyze previous development of such investments in Slovakia in comparing with EU countries during 2013–2016 according available sources from Invest Europe.

3.1 Business angels investments in Europe

Insufficient volume of Business angels' investments in economy has negative impact to the share of startups projects that survive initial period of

business (Sudek 2006). The results of mentioned is low number of startups in lately periods of development, where risk capital is more easily available. Investment to Business Angels in Europe during 2013–2016 is given by Table 1. Average volume of individual Business Angels investments in European countries is in 2016 at the level 166,000 EUR, which is similar as in 2013, although in 2015 it was 184,000 EUR, presenting decrease by 10%. According EBAN (2017) average investment per one company increased by 13% to 22,500 EUR (from 10,000 to 500,000 EUR). Total volume of available Business Angels investments achieved in European economy 6.1 bln EUR (The European Trade Association for Business Angels, in SBA 2016).

Development of Business Angels investments according individual EU countries in 2013–2016 (first 10 ranks) is illustrated by Table 2. The first rank with considerable lead has Great Britain with 98 mils. EUR in 2016, which is by 48% more in comparing with second Spain. Slovakia recorded in 2016 2.1 mil. EUR on 21 mentioned projects (EBAN 2017).

3.2 Risk capital (Venture Capital)

Access to risk capital in Europe is still rather weak. According data from Invest Europe (2017) volume

Table 1. Average business angels investments in Europe in 2013–2016.

	2013	2014	2015	2016
Average investment/ enterprise	165,000	174,000	184,000	166,000
Average investment/ BA	20,400	20,000	19,990	22,500

Table 2. Business angels investment in the European countries in 2013–2016.

Rank	Country	BA	Investments	Sum of BA investments (mil. EUR)			
				2013	2014	2015	2016
1.	Great Britain	8000	800	84.4	87.0	96.0	98.0
2.	Spain	2800	488	57.6	52.6	55.0	66.0
3.	Finland	566	400	26.4	34.5	36.5	53.0
4.	Germany	2020	206	35.1	37.0	44.0	51.0
5.	Turkey	1400	314	14.7	22.4	31.0	47.0
6.	France	4500	415	41.1	38.0	42.0	42.7
7.	Russia	170	148	41.8	30.0	29.2	34.2
8.	Denmark	225	250	11.8	20.0	23.0	22.8
9.	Sweden	813	97	19.4	20.6	21.8	22.4
10.	Austria	334	36	2.9	15.0	16.3	22.0
29.	Slovakia	85	21	–	1.3	1.8	2.1

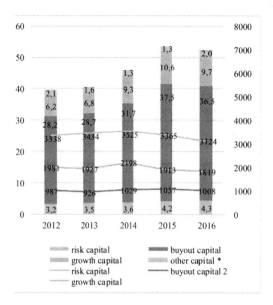

Figure 1. Development of capital investment of startups in Europe.

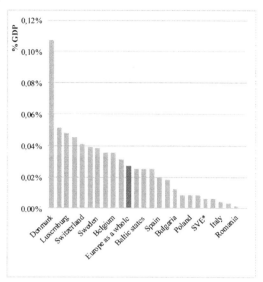

Figure 2. Investment of risk capital as percentage share on European countries in 2016.

of available risk capital investments was for example in 2015 only 0.025% of GDP in European Union, which presents 4.2 bln EUR. It means only 7.8% sources from total available investments of capital financing. In 2016 the volume was 4.3 bln EUR, presenting 8.2% share on GDP for totally 3124 enterprises. Development of investments volume through capital investing in Europe between 2012–2016 is illustrated by Figure 1.

Persistent problem is also for example differences in risk capital investments between individual EU member states. In economies with developed capital market (western and northern Europe) the investments presents higher percentage share on GDP in comparing with south and middle Europe.

Available volume of Venture Capital recorded in 2015 in Europe total growth by 5%. Also investments to startups development increased, when most rapid growth recorded investment to initial capital, mainly by 18%. Slovakian market with Venture capital in comparing with other European countries is rather marginal, but according data from Invest Europe (2017) it records growth in last years. In 2015 19 startups obtained such type of financing with total volume 8.9 bln EUR, presenting 0.0115% GDP (SBA, 2016). Volume of risk capital investments as share on GDP in individual European countries in 2016 is given by Figure 2.

3.3 Private equity

Volume of PE financing of startups in Europe in 2009 decreased by half, which means to 0.20% GDP against 2008 from 0.43% GDP. From 2012

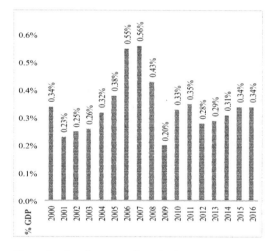

Figure 3. Development of total Private equity volume in Europe as a share on GDP.

it grows again, in 2016 it recorded 0.345% GDP. Development of total volume of PE investments in European countries as share on GDP in 2000–2016 is illustrated by Figure 3. According Invest Europe (2017) available volume of investments presented in 2016 47.7 bln EUR, which presents yet 14% growth against 2014, mainly 0.34% share on GDP. Volume of PE investments in Slovakia recorded in 2016 volume 0.02% GDP.

According Invest Europe (2017) total volume of capital, invested to European companies in 2016 remained stable in comparing with 2015 at level 52.5 bln EUR. Number of companies that obtained investments decreased by 8%, which means 5899, from which 83% presents SMEs and startups. More than third of total sum, invested to European companies presented transboundary investments. Risk capital investments increased in 2016 (in comparing with 2015) by 2% to 4.3 bln EUR. 3124 companies obtained the investment, which presents decreasing by 7%. The most investments had been to ICT sector (communication, computer technique and electronic), it is yet at 44% of total risk capital investment, further investments went to sector of biotechnology and health care (27%), consumer goods and services (9%), etc.

Invest Europe (2017) mentions statistics of market by data clustering according portfolio companies' placement. At European level it means investments to European companies without regard to placement of private investment

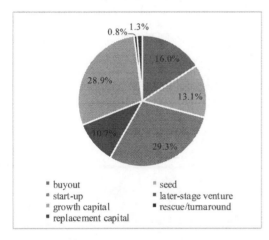

Figure 4. Percentage share of companies' number in Europe according type of financing.

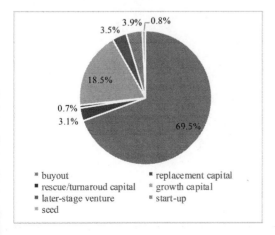

Figure 5. Percentage share of invested sum according type of financing.

companies. Figure 4 illustrates percentage rate of number of companies according type of financing in 2016, when startups financing presenting yet 29.3%.

Figure 5 illustrates percentage rate of invested sum according type of financing. According mentioned source the volume of risk capital in 2016 presented 4.3 bln EUR for 3124 companies, from which 3.9% belong to startups.

4 CONCLUSION

Business presents part of effective running of market economy, it presents factor that creates market economy. In Slovakia there is one of main goals to achieve level of developed European countries as shortly as possible, when business development plays irreplaceable importance. Single business is drive power of changes, measure of economy development, and tool for adaptation to main world trend. Startups presents perspective form of business, as business initiators with high growing and innovative potential that due to the newness and originality of ideas and products present possibility to bring high value added for the client and support economic growth.

Practice showed that any business, in spite based on application of verified business models, is connected with certain risk rate, while business activities in startups, orientated to new and innovative solutions are connected with high risk. Also due to the mentioned support of new trends of business, including startups, is therefore very important. It should be not only interest of businessmen and their clients, but also interest of whole society and country, as well as whole EU.

One of the possibilities to finance Slovakian startups is also transnational capital, coming from EU countries. There are acting several important domestic institutional investors (funds, organizations, accelerators, and professional investors), providing risk capital for Slovakian SMEs and startups. Majority of available sources is given by private equity, some enterprises combine private means with financial sources from EU. In Slovakia provider of capital investments presents also National holding fund in administration of Slovak Business Agency that operates with public sources, it has legal form of interest association of legal persons, which are members of Ministry of Economy SR, Association of Businessmen in Slovakia and Slovakian trade union.

ACKNOWLEDGEMENT

The article is partial result of research task KEGA No. 031TUKE-4/2016 and VEGA No. 1/0651/18.

REFERENCES

Blank, S. 2010. What's A Startup? First Principles. [on-line] www.steveblank.com/2010/01/25/whats-a-startup-first-principles/.

Blank, S. 2013. The 6 types of startups. In *Steve Blank blog* [on-line] www.blogs.wsj.com/accelerators/2013/06/24/steve-blank-the-6-types-of-startups-2/.

CEEDTECH. 2015. An Inside Look at the Slovakian Startup Ecosystem. [on-line] www.ceedtech.eu/blog/an-inside-look-at-theslovakian-startup-ecosystem.

Čulková, K., Csikósová, A. & Janošková, M. 2015. Development of established and cancelled companies in Slovakia. *Journal of Applied Economic Sciences*, 10(5): 644–653.

EBAN. 2017. EBAN Statistics Compendium. European Early Stage Market Statistics. [on-line] www.eban.org/wp-content/uploads/2017/11/Statistics-Compendium-2016-Final-Version.pdf.

European Commission. Europe 2020 strategy. [on-line] www.ec.europa.eu/info/business-economy-euro/economic-and-fiscal-policy-coordination/eu-economic-governance-monitoring-prevention-correction/european-semester/framework/europe-2020-strategy_en.

Graham, P. 2012. Startup=Growth? What to start a startup? [on-line] www.paulgraham.com/growth.html.

Gromov, G. (2013). From the Gold Mines of El Dorado to the—Golden Startups of Silicon Valley. [on-line] www.silicon-valley-history.com/.

Ingenium Slovakia. 2013. Koncepcia pre podporu startupov a rozvoj startupového ekosystému v SR. [on-line] www.rokovania.sk/File.aspx/ViewDocumentHtml/.

Invest Europe. 2017. 2016 Private European Equity Activity. [on-line] www.investeurope.eu/media/651727/invest-europe-2016-european-private-equity-activity-final.pdf.

Papula, J., Papulová, E., Papula. J. & Papulová, Z. 2017. *Podnikanie a manažment, Korene, podstata, súvislosti a trendy.* Praha: Wolters Kluwer.

Ries, E. 2010. *Startup Lessons Learned.* [on-line] www.startuplessonslearned.com/2010/06/what-is-startup.html.

Slovak Business Agency. 2016. Analýza prístupu MSP, vrátane startupov, k možnostiam financovania v kontexte podpory vytvorenia jednotného kapitálového trhu v rámci Európskej únie. [on-line] www.sbagency.sk/sites/default/files/analyza_mspstartupy_financovanie_jednotny_trh-final.pdf.

Slovak Business Agency. Stratégia Európa 2020 – Akčný plán pre podnikanie 2020. [on-line] www.sbagency.sk/strategia-europa-2020-akcny-plan-pre-podnikanie-2020.

Sobeková Majková, M. 2017. V čom sa startup líši od bežnej firmy? [on-line] www.podnikajte.sk/start-podnikania/c/3132/category/pravneformy/article/startup-bezna-firma.xhtml.

Sudek, R. 2006. Angel investment criteria. *Journal of Small Business Strategy*, 17(2): 89–104.

Zákon o malých a stredných podnikoch (Small Business Act for Europe). [on-line] www.ec.europa.eu/growth/smes/business-friendly-environment/small-business-act_sk.

Production Management and Business Development – Mihalčová et al. (Eds)
© *2019 Taylor & Francis Group, London, ISBN 978-1-138-60415-5*

Learning management systems

J. Kádárová & J. Kobulnický

Faculty of Mechanical Engineering, Technical University of Košice, Košice, Slovak Republic

ABSTRACT: The paper deals with the latest trends in Learning Management Systems (LMS), so in applications that resolve the administration and organization of learning within the e-learning. These systems contain a variety of tools for communication and management of studies and also made available to students with learning materials. Moreover, the article outlines a brief history of these systems from the 20's of the last century, the efficiency and profitability of their use for students and staff in moving these applications in the world of e-learning technology. Part of the article is a list of the most widely used learning management systems in the world and our Technical University of Kosice, compared with other universities in Slovakia.

1 INTRODUCTION

We live in an epoch of constant changes, in the implementation of new ideas and conceptions, but also the roles through which we try to move ourselves and society forward. Multilateral effects of technological progress are reflected in various sectors, including of the education sector. This fact cannot be denied, because information and communication technologies currently represent a worldwide extraordinary motive force of structural changes. Beside of reduction of expenses also own organizing of workflow of the pedagogical employee is changing. Wider application of new technologies in the learning process puts higher demands on the qualifications, on the structure formation of new learning documents and other forms of communication (Lepiš 2006).

Nowadays we are from all sides flooded with phenomenon such as e-business, e-marketing, e-publishing, e-learning, e-government, etc. The letter "e" in this case reflects the processing of electronic information and their distribution through electronic communications networks. Technical development cannot be stopped, and gradually becomes a basic pillar also during the creation of new forms of education (Lepiš 2006).

The technological base of the electronic education is learning management system (LMS). LMS is an application for administration and organization of teaching within the e-learning. These systems generally integrate a variety of online tools for communication and management of the study (bulletin board, forum, chatting, records etc.) and also made available to students education materials or content of education by on-line or even off-line.

There are a wide spectrum of LMS applications—from the simple through a variety academic LMS up to wide-ranging commercial applications.

2 LMS CHARACTERISTICS

Learning management systems (LMS seem like a new concept, but its development goes back to the twenties of the last century. They were not the cloud-based software as we know them today. The history of LMS was evolutionary and closely linked with the development of digital technologies and the Internet. Each milestone in the history of LMS is described as evolutional, advanced in knowledge transfer and independent learning. Some of the most important historical milestones LMS shows Table 1.

With technologies that are rapidly ongoing also ideas for new features and LMS utility are constantly growing. LMS functions depend on the specific requirements. For example, the LMS solution, which is successful in university, does not mean that it will be successful for large organizations. But, among the key features that should contain every LMS system, belong:

- Reports and statistics, which teacher/instructor should see—details about time, accesses to course, activity and results with the possibility of exporting in various formats, with the possibility of printing or sending by mail.
- Automated evaluation of courses or tests is very helpful for instructors/teachers for a large number of evaluations.
- Virtual classrooms allow users to access from the Internet 24/7.

Table 1.   Historical milestones of LMS. Source: ProProfs (2013).

Year	Historical milestones of LMS
1924	Dr. Sidney L. Pressey, psychology professor invented a relatively simple machine, which is regarded for the first teaching machine. It was a mechanical intelligent machine with tests of multiple choice answers. The machine gave to the user questions and user get instant feedback of the correct answer.
1929	M. E. LaZerte invented "problem cylinder", a mechanical device that does not allow only answer questions but also to control them.
1956	Engineers Gordon Pask & Robin McKinnon-Wood invented SAKI—first customizable teaching system. This keyboard device was able to learn typing and was able to teach himself.
1960	University of Illinois created a revolutionary computer-aided learning system named PLATO. The system includes instructors and creators who produce teaching material. The system is able to simultaneously educate thousands of students, each of which has a dedicated access to study materials.
1983	With nativity of the Internet in 1982, MIT launched an 8-year research "Project Athena" to survey the possibility of on-line education on thousands of computers.
1990	SoftArc presented FirstClass on the Macintosh platform, which is declared as the first Learning Management System. The United Kingdom's Open University used from FirstClass to provide on-line training across Europe.
1997	Courseinfo developed the Interactive Learning Network, which is the first LMS that uses relational database MySQL. In this year the company has developed and a year later released a software product on-line courseware application named Blackboard.
2002	In this year was released open-source LMS Moodle for internal network.
2004	It was released a set of standards—SCORM 2004 for teaching technologies that are the base of many current LMS.
2008	It was released Eucalyptus as the first open-source, AWS API compatible interface for deploying of private clouds. This allows for LMS system to run entirely online, without having to be installed on a personal computer or internal network.
2012	Up to the present day, the most modern LMS hosted in the cloud, companies are dispensed from the burden of installing and maintaining in-house systems.

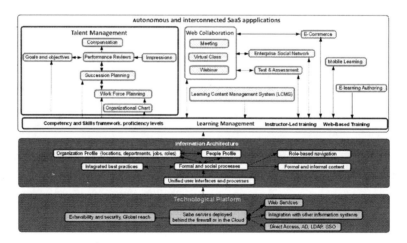

Figure 1.   LMS Architecture. Source: Artifact Software (2012).

- Social education promoting sharing thoughts, ideas and creativity through LMS community modules, chatting areas or social networks.
- Management of users consists in setting user's roles (admin, teacher and student) creation of their profiles, the possibility to export and import.

- Different templates include assessment tests, options timeout setting, compulsory questions, difficultness and many others.
- On-line Content Management System allows to you easily upload learning material in various forms, such as articles, PDF files, presentations, videos, images, audio files, etc.

- The communication tool, which includes a help-desk, sending messages, chatting, discussion forum and also automated notification system about courses. These allow students to communicate with the teacher or other classmates.
- Multilingualism with the availability of basic world languages.
- Integration of e-commerce, which includes setting of prices, shopping cart, various alternatives for realization of payments, storage and invoice system, dashboard sales and marketing support.
- Responsive design that allows compatibility with tablets and smartphones.

SABA, one of LMS providers concisely illustrated the interconnections of the individual components of the LMS that ensuring the proper functioning of the system, which is also shown in Figure 1.

3 LEARNING MANAGEMENT SYSTEMS TRENDS AND ITS FUTURE DIRECTIONS

Together with rapidly changing e-learning industry LMS trends are also changing because they belong to them, see Table 2.

4 RESEARCH WITHIN AREA OF THE USE OF LMS

On the base of a research of Capterra Inc. (2014), which provides services within area of selection the

Table 2. Learning management systems trends.

Learning Management Systems trends
Gamification (education based games) – under this term it means, interactive "games" aimed at development and education. Gamification gives corporate training to a brand-new level by facilitating the involvement of students in the learning process, reducing the stress associated with learning and enhances longer retention of information in memory. LMS providers should provide the possibility of Gamification into LMS solutions. Together with the possibility of Tin Can would be possible to monitor gaming, aimed to the record of the experiences of the student.
mLearning (Mobile Learning) in the present time places emphasis on creating of native applications. HTML5 is a key player in the implementation of mobile features. Using of mobile devices, in accordance with recent surveys, is in preference of desktop computers, and even it is already in the foreground, which also means that growth of different educational applications, which will become part of the "informal education" of students. mLearning is also one of the possibilities for integration of social media into the learning process, which for many people become the main forum for the sharing of new ideas and knowledge.
Social learning creates a better environment for LMS supports education, facilitates communication and allows sharing.
MOOCs (massive open online courses) provide access to education for millions of people simultaneously and around the world in the form of online open courses. They are used by elite Universities Harvard, MIT and Georgetown, and it means that this trend there will continue to evolve.
Tin Can API as a new standard for learning technologies allows collecting a wide range of student's data. We can track and measure results, and compares data about productivity and evaluates performance of learners with the possibility to store their information on education.
Cloud-based LMS are hosted on the Internet and they are accessible after logging on site of service provider. It is a powerful tool that can move the educational system through reducing of expenses and enhancing accessibility.
Talent Management is a critical function for the successful development of the organization and it was found that it is also a valuable tool for LMS. Many companies already have begun to integrate TM and LMS. TM identifies the strengths and weaknesses of employees, and in conjunction with the appropriate LMS it is possible these gaps in knowledge train and improve through new courses and learning materials, which are specific to the needs of students.
Talent Management is a critical function for the successful development of the organization and it was found that it is also a valuable tool for LMS. Many companies already have begun to integrate TM and LMS. TM identifies the strengths and weaknesses of employees, and in conjunction with the appropriate LMS it is possible these gaps in knowledge train and improve through new courses and learning materials, which are specific to the needs of students.
Personal Learning Environment (PLE) in LMS records the increasing demand. It helps students to manage their learning with opportunities to adapt their own learning environment and to store and organize training materials and interaction with other channels such as blogs, wikis, RSS channels and social networks.
Scenario-Based Learning has the possibility to create e-learning courses that are engaging for students, giving them the means for increasing an efficiency and overall knowledge base. It enables students to gain skills for future use and is based on real life experience or situational simulation, achieving truly effective e-learning.
Just-In-Time Learning is a solution providing training for employees, just when and where they need it. Their task is to use the Internet to scan tutorials and other tools to provide information to solve their problems, specific tasks or for rapid updating their skills. LMS shall be mobile and flexible, to be compatible with JIT learning.

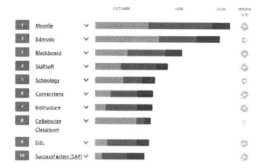

Figure 2.   The 10 Top LMS. Source: Capterra Inc. (2014).

Table 3.   Moodle statistics. Source: Moodle (2014).

Characteristics	Values
Registered sites	53,452
Countries	228
Courses	7,479,202
Users	69,193,714
Enrolments	145,533,763
Forum posts	136,488,626
Resources	68,013,731
Quiz questions	273,291,562

Table 4.   Usage of the most widely used LMS at Slovak Universities.

Name of Faculty/University	Number of the registered users
Faculty of Chemical and Food Technology STU	>5500
Faculty of Social and Economic Sciences Comenius University	>1200
6 Faculties of Matej Bel University	>6500
Faculty of Aeronautics TUKE	>700
Faculty of Electrical Engineering and Informatics TUKE	>80

appropriate LMS software, in the Figure 2 shows the ranking of the best. This list was created on the base of measuring by combining of the total number of customers, active users and presentations on social networks.

Survey companies Expertus Inc. and Training Industry Inc. showed that LMS systems are most frequently used in technologic companies with representation of 19%. They use them also in education, banking and finance, healthcare and business advice to the percentage representation of 8–9%.

Today the open source Moodle belongs among the most popular LMS. It is deployed in many educational institutions, from secondary school to university. The official website of solutions Moodle presents that it has an user base of 53,452 registered and verified websites in 228 countries, serving 69 million users and offer more than 7 million courses, see Table 3.

The worldwide success of Moodle software solutions was gradually transferred also to Central Europe and thus to Slovakia. LMS Moodle belongs at Slovak schools among the most common elective alternative, where according to the official website moodle.org is registered 168 certified e-learning portals. The main advantage is the possibility of free distribution, which substantially reduces the costs of e-learning portals for schools. However expansion of e-learning in most cases covers only the minimum number of faculties at Universities and the degree of its using in the educational process is very variable. E-learning tools are most frequently utilities, which are used within the Slovak education environment for sharing of educational materials and syllabi for individual learnings. The degree of usage tools for communication, transmission of seminar papers, testing and creating of collective work among different schools is varied.

The highest degree of quality and quantity of used e-learning tools achieves Faculty of Chemi-

cal and Food Technologies at Slovak Technical University in Bratislava with more than 5500 users and the Faculty of Social and Economic Sciences at Comenius University with 1200 users. Both portals present a high degree of coverage of the individual educational courses and subjects and they use a wide range of e-learning tools such as sharing of documents, transfer of seminar papers, testing, communication through forums and chatting, logging to the test and also tools for collective elaboration of the submission or the creation of dictionary entries.

E-learning portal of the Matej Bel University also has a high degree of coverage of study fields and learnings. All the Faculties belonging to the University are represented at the portal. Overall we can say that website has more than 6500 users.

Technical University of Kosice is consisting of nine faculties and only two of them used LMS Moodle, namely Faculty of Electrical Engineering and Informatics and in greater measure the Faculty of Aeronautics.

5   CONCLUSION

E-learning himself is very interesting and perspective area and its possibilities are endless. Day by day there are new technologies that can be in the course of time used also for e-learning as evidenced by the before mentioned trends and future directions of the key e-learning tool in LMS education. Education is an area that will always have its importance because people need to constantly acquire new knowledge, which is why it pays to invest in it.

ACKNOWLEDGEMENTS

This contribution is the result of the projects implementation: Project VEGA 1/0741/16 Controlling innovation of the industrial companies for the sustaining and improving their competitiveness.

This contribution is the result of the projects implementation: Project KEGA 026TUKE-4/2017 Implementation of innovative educational approaches and tools to enhance the development of the core competencies graduate study program Industrial Engineering.

REFERENCES

Antošová, M., Csikósová, A. & Mihalčová, B. 2014. Professional Education of Employees Provided through Tax School. *Procedia – Social and Behavioral Sciences,* 116: 1626–1630.

Artifact Software. 2012. *Features and benefits of an LMS.*

Barrish, J. 2014. *Top Learning Management System Software Products.* Capterra Inc.

Cimermanová, I. 2014. Creating social climate in a virtual learning environment. In: *E-learning and language teaching in an academic environment.* Prešov: Prešovská univerzita.

Csikosová, A., Teplická, K. & Seňová, A. 2012. Communication and Humanization of University Education Through E-Learning. *Procedia – Social and Behavioral Sciences,* 46: 2978–2982.

Dzedik, V. & Ezrakhovich, A. 2018. Analysis of quality management systems with the use of machine learning methods. *Quality – Access to Success,* 19 (164): 40–42.

Expertus Inc. & Training Industry Inc. 2010. *The Current and Future State of Learning Management Systems.*

Ghazal, S., et al. 2018. Acceptance and satisfaction of learning management system enabled blended learning based on a modified DeLone-McLean information system success model. *International Journal of Information Technology Project Management,* 9 (3): 52–71.

Graf, S. & Kinshuk. J. 2007. Providing adaptive courses in learning management systems with respect to learning styles. In T. Bastiaens, & S. Carliner (Eds.), *Proceedings of World Conference on E-Learning in Corporate, Government, Healthcare, and higher Education.* AACE.

Hrehová, D. & Teplická, K. 2016. Harmonization of skills and needs of the global labour market. In *International Multidisciplinary Scientific GeoConference: Ecology, Economics, Education and Legislation, SGEM.* Albena; Bulgaria. 30 June 2016.

Kádárová, J. & Turisová, R 2011. eLearning at universities and in corporate education. *Geopolitics of Ukraine: history and contemporaneity,* 6: 406–418.

Kádárová, J. et al. 2014. Education in Industrial Engineering in Slovakia. *Procedia – Social and Behavioral Sciences,* 143: 157–162.

Kádárová, J. et al. 2014. Holistic system thinking as an educational tool using key indicators. Procedia – Social and Behavioral Sciences, 143: 180–184.

Lepiš, F. 2006. E-learning – tomorrow's communication. In: *Inovácie v edukácii technických odborných predmetov.* Prešov: Prešovská univerzita.

Medved, J.P. 2014. *Top 7 Trends in LMS for 2014.* Capterra Inc.

Moodle. 2014. *Moodle Statistics.*

Pappas, Ch. 2014. *Top Learning Management System Trends for 2014.* eLearning Industry.

ProProfs. 2013. *History of learning management systems.*

Turisová, R. & Kádárová, J. 2011. Financing of Slovak universities. *Geopolitics of Ukraine: history and contemporaneity,* 6: 251–261.

Production Management and Business Development – Mihalčová et al. (Eds)
© 2019 Taylor & Francis Group, London, ISBN 978-1-138-60415-5

Factors retaining R&D employees in high technology enterprises

K.E. Kamińska
Ateneum-University in Gdansk, Gdańsk, Poland

ABSTRACT: In modern economy, the high technology sector is the most important contributor to its development. In high-tech enterprises, knowledge as a resource plays a special role, affects the company innovation potential, and thus is a key factor for the company success. Knowledge is closely related to employees, therefore employees involved in creating innovations play a key role in high-tech enterprises, such employees are very valuable for the company and their loss is very costly. The article presents the results of research on the importance of individual factors of attractiveness of high-tech enterprises for R&D employees.

1 INTRODUCTION

At the turn of the 1970s and 1980s, Toffler (1980) announced the coming of a new era. In his concept of the "three waves" he presented the stages of socio-civilization development. The main feature of the changes taking place is the change in the method of value creation. The third wave is the era of knowledge and information, it is a period that is based on intellectual work, not on the strength of muscles, therefore the most important resource becomes knowledge. Tobin (1996) defines knowledge as the sum of information and action or applications. The essence of knowledge lies in its use, not in gathering information, the same in knowledge what counts is how users use information resources (Szaban 2003). Contemporary economy is a knowledge-based economy, its main driving force is knowledge and innovation. Therefore, the source of successes lies not in the allocation of rare resources but in the creation of new knowledge that gives ideas, the implementation of which increases the value of management effects. The main products of knowledge are innovations and competences. Knowledge is difficult to measure and estimate, for this reason the study of economic growth focuses on more tangible manifestations of its use such as innovation (OECD 1999).

2 THE ESSENTIAL OF HIGH TECHNOLOGY ENTERPRISES

A high technology sector plays a special role in the knowledge-based economy, which contributes the most to its development. This sector is one of the basic determinants of modernity and competitiveness of the economy. The ability to effectively grow is determined by technical progress, which originates from the high technology sector and results from the intensity of research and development activities. Frascati Manual emphasizes that research and development activities are based on creative and systematic work undertaken to increase knowledge resources and to use them to create new applications (OECD 2015).

The concept of high technology sector is difficult to define because modern technologies often refer to various traditionally understood industries. The high technology sector can be defined as functioning at the interface between science and industry, it is based on the processing of research results in industry. It is characterized by high education intensity, high level of innovation, rapid diffusion of innovation and close scientific and technical cooperation. This sector requires large capital expenditures and carries a high investment risk. Enterprises in this sector are intensively engaged in research and development, effectively use knowledge, create inventions and innovations as well as technologically advanced goods, thus contributing to the increase of efficiency of the entire economy.

The term "innovation" is widely understood as the implementation of a new or significantly improved product or process, a new marketing or organizational method. Guided by this definition as an innovative enterprise, one can include a very large group of companies undertaking development activities with varying intensity. Oslo Manual defines an innovative company as one that has implemented at least one innovation over a three-year period (OECD 2005). The activities of these enterprises may consist in introducing solutions applied elsewhere or improving products offered without conducting original research or development works. On the other hand, a high-tech enterprise systematically introduces innovations resulting from continuous research and development works. A high technology enterprise is one for which innovations are the subject of basic activity, leading to an increase in the level of modernity and strengthening the competitive position. A feature that distinguishes high-tech companies from other companies is the fact that it is a place of effective cooperation of knowledge and technology. Zakrzewska-Bielawska (2011) emphasizes that high-tech enterprises should be a source of new knowledge, inventions and innovations, thus they should conduct systematic, active research and development activities on their own and be open to cooperation with the environment, creating various types of network connections and clusters with other organizations, operate at the interface of economy and science in the industry recognized as high technology and/or produce products classified as high technology and to use modern information technology in a wide range. A high technology enterprise is an innovative, knowledge-based and learning company with a significant share of R&D employees in the total number of employees and the demand for highly qualified personnel.

3 THE IMPORTANCE OF R&D EMPLOYEES IN HIGH TECHNOLOGY ENTERPRISES

Employees are increasingly recognized as the most valuable component of an enterprise, especially employees participating in knowledge processes, creating innovations, employees of R&D departments. In a knowledge-based economy, knowledge workers employed in enterprises are perceived as human capital, which has a definite value and is a source of future income for both an employee and an enterprise (Król & Ludwiczyński 2006). The benefits of investing in human capital through education and training are greater than those achieved through investment in material resources (Schultz 1961). It is the most difficult to imitate resource of the organization. The company is not its owner and can only lease it, which is why leaving the company will mean the loss of certain skills, experiences and informal connections that he had (Sopińska 2010). The change in the strategic approach to resources and the treatment of human capital as a source of competitive advantage have contributed to the increased interest in recruiting and retaining people with the highest potential. Demographic changes, globalization and the transformation of the economy into a knowledge-based economy resulted in enterprises noticing shortages in the number of specialists and starting to compete for them (Beechler & Woodward 2009). Thus, the con-

cept of the "war for talents" was created, and the approach developed according to which the most valuable employees are perceived as talents for the organization (Michaels et al. 2001). Regardless of the nomenclature, such a special group of employees, such as research and development employees, requires proper management (Lewis & Hackman 2006), which will enable their effective utilization and retention in the enterprise. Skilled workers are a source of innovative ideas, the same main feature of an innovative company is that it gives great interest to talented people and puts a lot of attention and effort into their possession (Leavy 2005).

The effective use of other organizational resources depends on the quality of human resources (Walkowiak 2007). Skilled workers who are able to implement innovative processes represent a specific, very valuable and difficult to copy set of competences, which include not only technical competence, knowledge and experience, but also knowledge of the organization and the principles of its operation and the ability to effectively cooperate with colleagues, communication and sharing the knowledge. The process of shaping the full competency profile of a R&D employee is time-consuming. The uniqueness of projects carried out by high-tech enterprises means that these enterprises do not have the possibility to recruit a fully competent employee from the labor market, but shape such employees through participation in projects and training.

An employee may leave the company at the initiative of the employer or employee. The employee decides to leave the company usually when the tasks performed do not give him satisfaction or receive a more attractive employment offer (Sidor-Rządkowska 2010). Staff turnover is a natural phenomenon in the enterprise. As positive aspects of the turnover one can point out, among other things, the influx of new ideas and other experiences, while the negative aspects of turnover include: costs of employee leaving, employment and training, and loss of valuable knowledge and experience for research and development employees. A high employment turnover rate may raise concerns when it is higher than in competing companies, when there is insufficient number of properly qualified people on the labor market, new employees should be trained, and when departing employees take with them knowledge that can be very useful for a competitive company (Taylor 2006). Therefore, turnover brings negative effects for the enterprise, especially when it is in the group of the most valuable employees, ie R&D employees. Recognizing the causes of unwanted turnover gives you the opportunity to develop actions aimed at retaining the desired employees in the company.

Employees leaving the enterprise on their own will is underestimated. Many managers think that replacing a leaving employee will not cause any difficulties. On the other hand, in times of crisis, usually company leave employees, whose high qualifications allow them always to find a job. The more difficult the situation on the labor market, the higher is the quality of employees leaving (Sidor-Rządkowska 2010). It happens that all or a significant part of the knowledge that the company has at its disposal is found in several key employees. Leaving the company by one of them, regardless of the reason, causes the loss of priceless capital and the creation of a gap. Often, this knowledge becomes the possession of competition, which may further weaken the position of the company on the market, especially during bad economic times. Therefore, first of all it is necessary to identify and evaluate the competences available to the company. Then, introduce activities aimed at retaining the most valuable employees to counteract the negative effects of employees leaving the workplace.

4 THE ATTRACTIVENESS OF HIGH-TECH ENTERPRISES FOR R&D EMPLOYEES

The aim of the study was to determine the importance of individual factors in retaining employees of research and development departments in high technology enterprises. In order to achieve the goal, the attractiveness factors of high technology enterprises have been distinguished, they concern various areas of the company's functioning, thus enabling a comprehensive approach to the issue, including:

– job specifics,
– professional development opportunities,
– workplace equipment,
– remuneration system,
– terms and conditions of employment,
– organizational culture,
– relationships with co-workers.

The study was conducted in enterprises that represent the characteristics of a high technology company and have a research and development department. To exclude the influence of external factors on the attractiveness of high-tech companies, the research was carried out in Poland in one province with a high share of high technology companies—the Pomeranian.

As part of empirical research, a case study method was adopted what enabled deeper and comprehensive analysis of individual companies. As information sources, company documents, questionnaire surveys, interviews and direct observation were used.

The results of the conducted research show that the importance of individual factors of attractiveness of high technology enterprises for research and development employees is diversified. The research allowed to determine which of the examined list of factors have a significant impact on the retention of research and development employees in high technology enterprises. The factors that make the high technology company the most attractive place of work for research and development employees, and retain them, are:

– professional development opportunities,
– job specifics.

While, the factors that have an average impact on the employees' decision regarding the choice of place of work:

– terms and conditions of employment,
– remuneration system,
– relations with co-workers.

The factors that do not affect the decision about where to work, and at the same time do not retain employees in the current workplace are:

– organizational culture,
– workplace equipment.

Research and development employees are characterized by a specific set of expectations in relation to the employer, Michaels et al (2001) present studies conducted among managers who showed that the hierarchy of factors affecting their decision regarding the choice of place of work is different.

The opportunity to gain new experience, knowledge and skills through participation in pioneer, innovative projects is an element that strongly encourages R&D employees to work in a given company. Very important in deciding on where to work is also the specificity of work, it means research and development of innovative products, Jemielniak (2007) presents similar results, based on research conducted in Poland and the USA.

It would seem, according to the common belief, that the employees of research and development departments, especially the IT industry, are independent people who do not like commitments. At the same time, the research carried out shows that it is very important for them to feel secure employment (this is confirmed by the Jemielniak study 2008). The above research shows that R&D employees are encouraged to work in high technology enterprises with stable employment combined with flexible working hours (Jemielniak 2009). An important factor in making a decision about a workplace is a remuneration system offering additional material benefits and appreciating the individual achievements of employees. An atmosphere at work conducive to the implementation of tasks and built-in and tested relationships with colleagues based on trust largely retain an employee in the enterprise (this is confirmed by the Jemielniak study 2008).

Cheng et al (2010) reached similar conclusions, pointing out that more effective impact on the professional satisfaction of research and development employees is based on effective work on innovations than conflicts arising in relations between employees.

Research has shown that depending on the situation on the labour market and in the enterprise, medium-importance factors can go to a group of key factors. If the employee does not see the possibility of obtaining a higher remuneration, this factor becomes invalid, while at the same time the probability of obtaining higher remuneration increases, the significance of this factor may increase, thus it may become the key to making a decision about the choice of a workplace. In a situation when a company offering higher remuneration appeared on the market, research and development employees transferred to the competition, despite the fact that the new job did not offer more attractive development opportunities. An employee with the option of professional development and a higher remuneration, with a similar level of tension associated with not meeting these needs, will most likely choose a job that offers more opportunities for professional development than the one offering higher remuneration. However, if the need to obtain a higher remuneration is stronger, it will become more important. It is estimated that in Poland the amount of remuneration is still not reaching a satisfactory level, therefore, raising the amount of remuneration will increase the satisfaction with work, which may encourage employees to stay in the company. It can be stated that in Poland salary can be included into motivators, not for hygiene factors (Herzberg 1968). Research conducted in Germany in 2008 shows that the importance of remuneration was much lower. It follows from this that due to the different economic situation in different countries, and even in different regions, the importance of remuneration as a factor encouraging to work may be different.

The research shows that research and development employees expect rewarding their own achievements individually. Work in the research and development department is mainly based on teamwork. Working in a team, employees share ideas and solve problems together. As the benefits obtained from teamwork by the organization, one should indicate, among others, increasing the company's innovativeness and focusing greater knowledge, skills and experience. The employees, on the other hand, are provided the broadly understood support at work and are mobilized to act. That is why it is so important to motivate team members properly to support the synergy effect and increase motivation to work rather than stimulate competition. The company should develop a motivating system aimed at strengthening team behavior by rewarding individual employees for individual contributions to the team's work. In this case, it is necessary to reward the commitment, loyalty and creativity of employees. The importance of teamwork in an enterprise can not be overestimated. Individual bonus systems focus employees' attention on maximizing individual efficiency, indicate the most valuable employees in the team, while group bonus systems favor close team integration and focus employees on maximizing group efficiency. Expecting premiums for employee's individual performance can not be considered desirable. Such actions can deepen rivalry between colleagues, thereby destroying teamwork.

The values presented by the company, even if they are shared by employees, do not affect employees' decision about employment in a given place of work. The equipment of the workplace, despite the fact that it is modern, does not matter to the research and development employee in the selection of the employer. Probably because the high level of equipment is considered obvious.

All companies participating in this study declare that research and development employees are "the most valuable group of employees", "without which it would not be possible for the company to function" and "their leaving would be a big loss for the company." In addition, in interviews, all interviewees replied that the period of shaping the full competence profile of a research and development employee in a given enterprise is about three years, at the same time it is not easy to replace outgoing research and development employees with new employees. The reason may be shortages of employees with appropriate competences on the labor market and time-consuming process of full preparation of new employees for the implementation of tasks. Research shows that working in a research and development department requires competence from various areas, not only technical but also soft skills. The research has shown that the development of research and development worker competence takes place through participation in innovative projects. Due to the uniqueness of innovative projects, it can be stated that the development process of research and development employees lasts throughout their entire career, with individual components of competences being developed to a different extent, and experience and education complement each other. Managers participating in the study pointed out that in the period of shaping the full competence profile, research and development employees will get to know the organization, team members, work rules and their tasks. Therefore, the loss of such valuable employees may not only be difficult to replace but also very expensive.

5 CONCLUSIONS

Research and development employees employed in high-tech enterprises constitute a specific group of employees with similar expectations towards the employer, for whom professional development is the highest value. Awareness of the importance of individual factors of the attractiveness of high-tech enterprises affects the company's ability to retain R&D employees. Having a group of valuable employees not only enables the company to function efficiently, but also determines the company's competitive position. Enterprises that systematically carry out research and development works, develop interesting and innovative projects and provide stable working conditions to employees, competitive remuneration and an atmosphere conducive to cooperation can effectively retain research and development employees in the enterprise.

Depending on the market situation, the emergence of new competition and other factors on which the company has no influence, the level of R&D employees turnover in the company may change. Thus, the importance of individual factors can change, and the factor that has a medium impact on the employee's decision about work can become a key factor in deciding on leaving work. High technology enterprises shaping individual factors may affect the turnover of research and development employees. Thus, they can more effectively retain the most valuable employees.

REFERENCES

Beechler, S. & Woodward, I.C. 2009. The global "war for talent". *Journal of International Management* 15: 273–285.

Cheng, C-F. et al. 2010. Exploring the impact of innovation strategy on R&D employees' job satisfaction: A mathematical model and empirical research. *Technovation* 30: 459–470.

Herzberg, F. 1968. One more time: How do you motivate employees?. *Harvard Business Review* January-February.

Jemielniak, D. 2007. Managers as lazy, stupid careerists?: Contestation and stereotypes among software engineers. *Journal of Organizational Change Management* 20(4): 491–508.

Jemielniak, D. 2008. *Praca oparta na wiedzy. Praca w przedsiębiorstwach wiedzy na przykładzie organizacji high-tech*. Warszawa: Wydawnictwo Akademickie i Profesjonalne.

Jemielniak, D. 2009. Time as symbolic currency in knowledge work. *Information and Organization* 19: 277–293.

Król, H. & Ludwiczyński, A. 2006. *Zarządzanie zasobami ludzkimi. Tworzenie kapitału ludzkiego organizacji*. Warszawa: Wydawnictwo Naukowe PWN.

Leavy, B. 2005. A leader's guide to creating an innovation culture. *Strategy & Leadership* 33(4): 38.

Lewis, R.E. & Heckman, R.J. 2006. Talent management: A critical review. *Human Resource Management Review* 16(2): 139–154.

Michaels, E., et al. 2001. *The War for Talent*. Boston: Harvard Business School Press.

OECD. 1999. *The Future of the Global Economy. Towards a Long Boom?* Paris: OECD.

OECD. 2005. *Oslo Manual. Guidelines for Collecting and Interpreting Innovation Data*, Third Edition. Paris: OECD/European Communities.

OECD. 2015. *Frascati Manual 2015. Guidelines for Collecting and Reporting Data on Research and Experimental Development*. Paris: OECD Publishing.

Schultz, T.W. 1961. Investment in Human Capital. *The American Economic Review* 51(1): 1–17.

Sidor-Rządkowska, M. 2010. *Zwolnienia pracowników a polityka personalna firmy*. Warszawa: Wolters Kluwer Polska.

Sopińska, A. 2010. *Wiedza jako strategiczny zasób przedsiębiorstwa. Analiza i pomiar kapitału intelektualnego przedsiębiorstwa*. Warszawa: Oficyna Wydawnicza SGH w Warszawie.

Szaban, J. 2003. *Miękkie zarządzanie. Ze współczesnych problemów zarządzania ludźmi*. Warszawa: Wydawnictwo Wyższej Szkoły Przedsiębiorczości i Zarządzania im. Leona Koźmińskiego.

Taylor, S. 2006. *Płynność zatrudnienia. Jak zatrzymać pracowników w firmie*. Kraków: Oficyna Ekonomiczna.

Tobin, D.R. 1996. *Transformational Learning: Renewing Your Company Through Knowledge and Skills*. New York: Wiley.

Toffler, A. 1980. *The Third Wave*. New York: Morrow.

Walkowiak, R. 2007. *Zarządzanie zasobami ludzkimi. Kompetencje, nowe trendy, efektywność*. Toruń: Dom Organizatora.

Zakrzewska-Bielawska, A. 2011. *Relacje między strategią a strukturą organizacyjną w przedsiębiorstwach sektora wysokich technologii*, Łódź: Politechnika Łódzka.

Production Management and Business Development – Mihalčová et al. (Eds)
© 2019 Taylor & Francis Group, London, ISBN 978-1-138-60415-5

Performance management—discussion to key performance indicators

J. Klučka & A. Kelíšek
Faculty of Security Engineering, University of Žilina, Žilina, Slovak Republic

ABSTRACT: Business Performance Management (BPM) is a powerful approach to manage, monitor and to secure sustainability of an enterprise. BPM has different aspects relevant for managerial activities in an enterprise. Problems can be classified in following phases of BPM implementation process: identification of performance measures—Key Performance Indicators (KPIs), their implementation and data link with relevant processes, regular implementation of results into managerial activities and system hierarchy of BPM in a company. The authors contribute on research project of the Austrian-Slovak scientific and technical cooperation in the field of business performance of small and medium-sized enterprises in both countries. In the initial phase of the project, it was necessary to identify preferences and problem areas of small and medium-sized enterprises through a questionnaire. At present, 150 respondents are processed in the database. Outputs from the questionnaire (soft data) that suggest interesting findings of researchers will be discussed in the article.

1 INTRODUCTION

Performance management can be seen as a part of managerial activities within a company. The results are implemented in organizational strategy, planning and reporting. It provides feedback to decision makers to assist them in improving performance and to key stakeholders (Barbuio 2017). Business performance management is defined in many sources (Sandt 2005), (Garengo et al. 2005), (Key 2014).

Performance management is an assessment of an employee, process, equipment or other factor to reflect progress toward predetermined objectives of a company. Applying performance management in a company, its owners, executive management can identify profitable and non-profitable activities. The performance management is thus focused on the past—assessment of achieved results but awareness of the past leads to adoption and modification of a strategy that focuses on the future while historic overview is covered in (Sandt 2005).

Business performance management (BPM) is a powerful tool to monitor effectiveness and sustainability of an enterprise.

BPM is being developing. At the beginning the stress was put on the financial ratios therefore called "Financial analysis". It covers financial figures with implicit statement "after all everything is based on financial results of a company". Constrains of this approach are focused only on financial data and on the past. To overcome a narrow focus was/is implemented Balanced Scorecard that adds to financial measures also dimensions like internal processes, customers and learning & growth.

2 PERFORMANCE MANAGEMENT AND PERFORMANCE INDICATORS

Any managerial decision is based on data and the right decision is in relation to defined business objectives. Performance management provides data concerning achievement of objectives.

The reasons for monitoring/measuring business performance are expressed in (Pidd 2012):

– If you don't measure results, you can't tell success from failure.
– If you can't see success, you can't reward it.
– If you can't reward success, you're probably rewarding failure.
– If you can't see success, you can't learn from it.
– If you can't recognize failure, you can't correct it.
– If you can demonstrate results, you can win public support.

Briefly, if one cannot measure it also cannot manage. Therefore this approach creates more questions that must be solved in practice—in application of BPM in an enterprise.

The problem of BPM can be classified:

– according to specific problems relating to different aspects of BPM, see literature (Garengo et al. 2005),
– according to type of business, see literature (Hudson 2001),
– according to stages related to BPM implementation, see literature (Barbiu 2017), (Arlen 2017), Parmenter 2015a), (Parmenter 2015b),
– according to the field BPM is applied in an enterprise, see literature (Pidd 2012).

The list of problems related to BPM can be classified (see also Fig. 1):

1. Identification of key processes in an enterprise— a key process is any operation, that is related to strategic key objectives formulated in an enterprise strategy; performance of key processes guarantees long term sustainability of an enterprise,
2. For each key process identify input, output and description of the process and its relation to enterprise objectives declared in a strategy plan of an enterprise,
3. Allocate key performance indicators (KPIs) to each key process; summarize KPIs in a company—they should monitor current and future perspectives of a company/specified process; the level of KPI must be within pre-define tolerance (lower and upper limit of output); hence it can be derived the current status of a process/company,
4. Identify within an organization data sources and responsible persons for monitoring and transformation of data to managerial processes—the formal aspect of managerial communication has to be incorporated into clear responsibilities and competencies,
5. Define formal structure of managers that will be responsible for implementation of recommendations based on performed KPIs; create the unique system of BPM that will be implemented within an enterprise; identified KPIs will be part of the complex BPM in an company.

The paper deals with the above mention problem (see point 3.) There are different approaches to

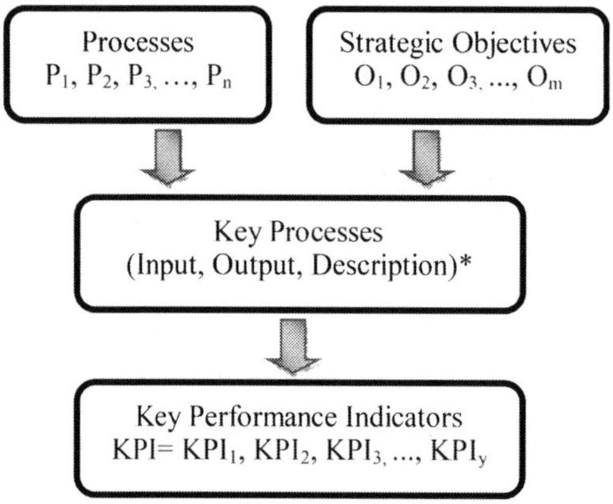

KPI identification. Globerson (1985) provides list of criteria KPIs must fulfil:

– Performance criteria must take possible the comparison of organizations which are in the same business.
– The purpose of each performance criterion must be clear.
– Data collection and methods of calculating the performance criterion must be clearly defined.
– Ratio-based performance criteria are preferred to absolute number.
– Performance criteria should be under control of evaluated organizational unit.
– Performance criteria should be selected through discussions with the people involved (customers, employees, managers).
– Objective performance criteria are preferable to subjective ones.

Maskell (1989) presents seven principles of performance measurement system design:

– The measures should be directly related to the firm's manufacturing strategy;
– Non-financial measures should be adopted;
– It should be recognized that measures vary between locations—one measure is not suitable for all departments or sites;
– It should be acknowledged that measures change as circumstances do;
– The measures should be simple and easy to use;
– The measures should provide fast feedback; and
– The measures should be designed so they simulate continuous improvement rather than simply monitor.

The problem of KPIs identification is complex because of the fact that KPIs in an enterprise should cover all relevant fields/activities and also all hierarchical levels. Due to it variety of different KPIs will be implemented in a company (see also Neely, Platts 2005).

Figure 1.   Scheme of KPIs identification.
Source: Authors.
*Note – matrix presentation (organizational unit e.g. production, marketing…, organizational level e.g. strategic, tactic, operative).

3   OBJECTIVES AND METHODOLOGY

The content of the paper is inspired by discussions and consultations with a head of a software developer in the Slovak republic.

The software developer creates and sells product targeted to small and medium sized enterprises (SME) with objective to monitor, improve performance management of a company.

Objectives of the paper can be described as:

– Why and how to measure a business performance?
– Performance indicators—how many, logic, characteristics and relations to managerial decisions

– Problems in identification of performance measures; this rather complex problem is limited to various aspects of key performance indicators (KPIs).

4 DATA AND RESULTS

Based on the research (performed in March-November 2017) and as emerged from the discussion with a representative of software developer was identified:

– Representatives from SME responsible for business performance are hardly able to define KPIs for their company; in fact they have problems to formulate the strategy of a company.
– There is no distinction between PIs and KPIs; even there is a problem to identify key activities, results that cover and satisfy long-term sustainable growth of a company.
– In majority the KPIs are oriented backward, on the past.
– KPIs with the highest frequency were dealing with sales and effectiveness of sales representatives,
– Depth and breadth of KPIs is based on ad-hoc approach without any consistent methodology.
– Implemented variety of KPIs creates non consistent set of ratios/figures,
– KPIs depend also on the status of a company: subsidiaries have specific needs, usually derived from a headquarter directives,
– KPIs are enormously different because of branches/sectors a company is providing/producing its core activities.

During January–April 2018 was conducted research concerning the broader scope dealing with BPM. Totally 150 SMEs were interviewed. Questionnaires were filled in via paper or internet. The total amount of questions was 20; in the paper we discuss set of selected questions and answers relevant to the subject of the paper.

The statistical sample of enterprises covered 51% SMEs with 1–9 employees and 30% SMEs with 10–49 employees. 72% of contacted enterprises declared yearly turnover less than 2 million €.

Questions dealing with KPIs directly or indirectly will be further analysed. To the question "Dealing with business performance management" 49% declared regularly, 25% non-regularly and 25% not at all.

To the question reflecting the time point when an enterprise started performing BPM—from total 101 answers within time period 2010–2016 – was 42% of enterprises. The rest 58% was within 2000–2009.

To the question dealing with specific factors for BPM as the most relevant were listed: financial, operating, financial structure and solvency, marketing and macroeconomic measures.

Answers to the question, concerning regularity of discussion to performance management results was: regularly – 59%, non-regularly – 35% and not at all – 6%.

Evaluation of business performance is performed by each head of department within objective of her/his department—answer to this question was yes = 49%, no = 51%.

5 DISCUSSION

The number of enterprises dealing with BPM was surprisingly high. We clarify this due to the structure of the sample—relative high percentage of enterprises with BPM (30%). Also macroeconomic measures and their monitoring seem surprising.

The impact of BPM to applied management and managerial decisions is based on the answer relatively high. It can be understood that entrepreneurs understand the priority of BPM and therefor 59% of participants practice regularly discussion to analysed results. Hence can be questionable applied measures and their fulfillment—this can be seen as the role of executive management in an enterprise. From the context the last question presents relative high level in BPM in interviewed companies. In about 50% they have BPM organized according to branches/unites; as opposite can be deduced that there is one unique system that measure performance of a company as a complex system.

In literature there are different approaches to KPIs. We see as the fundamental: whether the performance measure reflects key success factors and relations to strategy. Strategy is seen as relevant base for long term sustainability and future development of a company.

The number of implemented KPIs was also discussed. The proposal between 4–10 indicators can be applied but as the most important must be seen not the number but the relevance to managerial decision. KPIs without this relation are useless. The matrix presentation and compatibility within organizational levels must be approved.

The vital role in implementation of performance management stands on qualified staff. Staff also communicate within or outside a company and deliver results and makes proposals (as interpretation of results) is soaring performance of a company.

6 CONCLUSION

The results from the paper can be summarized:

– There is a lack of know-how in identification of performance indicators (SMEs in the Slovak republic),
– SMEs in the Slovak republic that apply software in business performance do not create consist-

ent and strategy related indicators; solutions are based on ad-hoc approach,
- KPIs and their application depend on staff; results are derived from the ability and willingness to incorporate them into managerial decisions.

Business performance management is relatively new approach that is applied in SMEs in the Slovak republic. The further development can be expected in SMEs despite the fact that this field is not formulated to regulatory agencies; this decision is solely based on the owners and executive management.

ACKNOWLEDGEMENTS

This work was supported by the Slovak Research and Development Agency under the contract No. SK-AT-2017-0003.

REFERENCES

Arlen, Ch. 2017. *KPIs in Service.* Service Performance, 2017, available at: http://www.serviceperformance.com/articles-2012/KPIs_in_Service.pdf.

Barbuio, F. 2017. *Performance Measurement: A Practical Guide to KPIs and Benchmarking in Public Broadcaster.*, Commonwealth Broadcasting Association, 2017. Available at: https://publicmediaalliance.org/wpcontent/uploads/2014/12/PerformanceMeasurementAPracticalGuide.pdf.

Garengo, P. et al. 2005. Performance measurement systems in SMEs: A review for a research agenda. *International Journal of Management Reviews*, 7(1): 25–47. DOI: 10.1111/j.1468-2370.2005.00105.x.

Globerson, S. 1985. Issues in developing a performance criteria system for an organization. *International Journal of Production research*, 23(4): 639–46.

Hudson, M. et al. 2001. Theory and practice in SMR performance measurement systems. *International Journal of Operations and Production Management*, 21(8): pp. 1096–1115, MCB University Press, ISSN 0144-3577.

Key Performance Indicators. 2014. *Developing Meaningful KPIs*. Intrafocus. 2014, available at: https://www.intrafocus.com/wp-content/uploads/2014/09/Developing-Meaningful-Key-Performance-Indicators-V7.pdf.

Kucharčiková, A. et al. 2011. *Efektivní výroba*, Computer Press, Brno, ISBN 978-80-251-2524-3.

Marr, B. 2010. *How to design Key Performance Indicators, Management Case Study.* The Advanced Performance Institute, 2010 available at: www.ap-institute.com.

Maskell, B.H. 1989. Performance measures of world class manufacturing, *Management Accounting*. May, pp. 32–3. – Seven principles of performance measurement system design. Available at: https://www.emeraldinsight.com/doi/abs/10.1108/01443570510633639.

Neely A. & Platts, K. 2005. Performance measurement system design: A literature review and research agenda. *International Journal of Operations and Production Management*, December 2005, DOI: 10.1108/01443570510633639

Parmenter, D. 2015a. "Winning" KPIs in SMEs. *Finance and Management. ICAEW*. Available at: http://kpi.davidparmenter.com/wp-content/uploads/sites/6/2017/02/Parmenter-Winning-KPIs-for-SMEs.pdf.

Parmenter, D. 2015b. *Key Performance Indicators.* Wiley, New Jersey, ISBN 978-1-118-92510-2.

Pidd, M. 2012. *Measuring the Performance of Public Services*, Cambridge University Press, Cambridge, 2012, ISBN 978-1-107-00465-8.

Price Waterhouse Coopers. 2007. *Guide to key performance indicators.* Available at: https://www.pwc.com/gx/en/audit-services/corporate-reporting/assets/pdfs/uk_kpi_guide.pdf.

Sandt, J. (2005). Performance Measurement. Übersicht über Forschungsentwicklung und –stand, in: *Zeitschrift für Controlling und Management* – ZfCM, 49. Jg. (2005), Heft 6, S. 30–48.

Production Management and Business Development – Mihalčová et al. (Eds)
© *2019 Taylor & Francis Group, London, ISBN 978-1-138-60415-5*

Analysis of the CSR reports from pharmaceutical companies in Poland

H. Kruk
Gdynia Maritime University, Gdynia, Poland

ABSTRACT: Many enterprises perform voluntary activities in the field of Corporate Social Responsibility (CSR). These initiatives include ethical behaviour, philanthropic activities, pro-environmental and social actions. CSR is an important element of a corporate strategy as it contributes to building a positive image of a company and attracts the customers. CSR actions improve welfare of the society, but also enhance competitiveness and market position of the enterprise. Both employers and employees are involved in CSR initiatives. For this reason and due to the diversification of such actions, CSR reporting practices are not unified. The article contains an analysis of CSR actions taken by selected pharmaceutical companies in Poland in the years 2015–2016. Activities can be divided into the following groups: programs beneficial to employees, actions for cooperating entities and customers, environmental actions, initiatives supporting local societies and philanthropy. The analysis is based on CSR reports and additional data from websites.

1 INTRODUCTION

1.1 *Corporate social responsibility—theoretical approach*

Corporate Social Responsibility refers to all voluntary actions of enterprises, exceeding legal obligations, connecting economical purposes with social and environmental ones (Jamali & Mirshak 2007; Żemigała 2007). According to a new definition of the European Commission, CSR is "the responsibility of enterprises for their impact on society". The main purposes are: magnification of shared value creation (for the enterprise itself, stakeholders and the entire society), identification as well as prevention and minimisation of negative impacts brought about business activities (COM(2011)681).

A.B. Carroll (2015) mentions two basic areas of CSR: society protection and improvement of its welfare. The first is strictly related to such initiatives like environmental care, lack of discrimination or production of safe goods. The latter concerns activities for local societies, including philanthropy and cooperation with community.

According to the principles of UN Global Compact initiative, there are four main CSR spheres: environment, human rights, labour conditions and anti-corruption (Runhaar & Lafferty 2009). A. Dahlsrund, having analysed CSR definitions, identified five basic areas, namely: social, economic, stakeholders, environmental and voluntariness (Jankalova 2016).

The most important components of CSR are: environmental care, human rights, labour standards, fair business practices, consumer protection, anti-corruption actions, good practices and initiatives for communities and societies. Rarely are mentioned such components like: innovations, development as well as science and technology (Wuttichindanon 2017).

The concept of the social responsible business was included into the strategy "Europe 2020" as well (Antošová & Csikósova 2014, Antošová & Csikósova 2015).

1.2 *CSR and sustainable development*

Many researchers find CSR and the idea of sustainable development similar (i.e. Amini & Bienstock 2014, Baumgartner & Rauter 2017, Jankalova 2016, Kruk 2015).

According to the first definition used in the so-called Brundtland Report, it is "development that meets the needs of the present without compromising the ability of future generations to meet their own needs" (WCED 1987). There are three fundamental dimensions (pillars) of sustainable development: social, ecological and environmental ones.

J. Elkington introduced the idea of "three bottom lines": economic prosperity (profits), environmental quality (planet) and social equity (people) and subsequently linked them with the sustainability (Carroll 2015).

CSR actions, in fact, result from the implementation of sustainable development rules into business practices. They are directly related to sustainable production.

Considering similarities between the concept of sustainability and CSR components, the latter ones may be assigned to three dimensions of the sustainable development.

1.3 *CSR and financial performance of enterprises*

CSR is, on the other hand, perceived not as altruistic initiatives of the enterprises but rather as a business strategy intended to provide benefits (Akdoğanet et al. 2016).

There are direct and indirect relations between CSR actions and financial performance of enterprises. Such linkage was proven by many researchers. CSR initiatives allow to improve enterprise's reputation, reduce costs, attract new customers and qualified workforce as well as help enterprises to strengthen their competitive advantage (i.e. Carroll 2015, García-Madariaga & Rodríguez-Rivera 2017, Rodriguez-Fernandez 2016).

However, a new problem appears: has CSR activity exchanged into yet another element of business strategy? And how may one separate voluntary actions of a socially responsible business from the actions leading to improve competitiveness and relationships with customers and suppliers?

Many enterprises produce CSR reports in order to demonstrate their responsibility towards internal and external stakeholders and meet their expectations, to build positive corporate image (reputation), to prove legitimacy, to include CSR into broader business strategy or to gain long-term profits by cost and risk reduction (Bonsón & Bednárová 2015, Carroll & Shabana 2010).

According to the research conducted by L.S. Mahoney, L. Thorne, L. Cecil and W. LaGore (2013), enterprises publishing CSR reports may be divided into two groups: the first one uses reports to draw attention to their voluntary activities (involvement in CSR) while the second group prepares reports to pretend to be the "good" ones (putting themselves in a good light) even if the enterprises do not have significant social and environmental achievements (the so-called greenwashing explanation).

2 RESEARCH METHOD AND RESULTS

2.1 *Research method*

The analysis encompasses the CSR reports obtained from the pharmaceutical concerns producing medications in Poland or having their research and development centres here. If a firm operates within the global market, only entities providing separate information for Polish branch have been chosen. The reports referred to the years 2015 and 2016 or were published jointly for these two years. The reports were available for the following entities: Adamed Group, Polpharma Group and Roche Polska (together with Roche Diagnostics Polska). The analysis was completed by the feedback on the socially responsible actions in Anpharm (Servier group production site) and Sanofi Group published on the company's webpages, in a general report "Raport odpowiedzialny biznes w Polsce" (Report: "Responsible business in Poland 2016") and on the website of Forum Odpowiedzialnego Biznesu (Responsible Business Forum) (www.odpowiedzialnybiznes.pl).

Pharmaceutical companies were chosen for the analysis due to the sector's specificity: on the one hand, on a par with other enterprises, pharmaceutical firms aim towards profit maximisation, on the other hand, they offer special goods—medicaments. Such products are subjects to permanent clinical, legal and ethical controls. Moreover, promotion of prescription medicines does not target final receivers (patients) but doctors (Możejko-Pastewka 2006).

Measures adopted by pharmaceutical companies were divided into the following groups: environmental, social and charity (for communities and philanthropy), economic (for clients, suppliers and other stakeholders) and employees-oriented (including all the aforementioned dimensions).

2.2 *CSR actions improving environmental quality*

Initiatives related to the environment (also referred to as as the so-called "silent stakeholder"—without voting rights and ability to express an opinion— or even primary stakeholder) concern diminishing negative environmental impact (Lulewicz-Sas & Godlewska 2015). Activities like reduction of water, energy and raw material consumption, minimising emissions of pollutants and wastes volume (as a result of waste segregation and recycling), more efficient use of natural resources, reduction of environmental fines and improvement of ecological consciousness may be listed here (Bonsón & Bednárová 2015, Lulewicz-Sas & Godlewska 2015, Malik 2015, Miska et al 2018).

All pharmaceutical companies mentioned such results of their actions like: reduction of energy consumption, waste amounts (as a result of recycling and segregation) and greenhouse gases (including CO_2) as well as air pollution. Four concerns (80%) replaced some old cars with the new, more ecological ones, three firms encouraged their workers to use public transport and one, Roche Polska, promoted the use of alternative transport media (bicycles). One company (Adamed Group) pointed at the limitation of business trips by using tele- and videoconferences, while another entity

(Polpharma Group) encouraged employees to link business travels (car-pooling). Three firms (60%) informed that the actions taken contributed to the limitation of water use and reduced sewage volumes. Two concerns listed less stationery use among other pro-environmental effects of their initiatives. Four companies reported that they had the environmental management systems complied with ISO 14001 standard, while another one (Anpharm) had ISO 50001 certificate (energy management system). Some concerns also declared other actions. For instance, Polpharma Group reported the exchange of substances used in the production process into safer ones and the limitation of solvents usage. That company also bought semi-products from local suppliers and thereby decreases pollutant emissions during transport (let alone supporting local business). Roche Polska bought 50% of energy from renewable energy sources.

2.3 Social dimension of CSR actions

In case of a social dimension of CSR initiatives, the following activities may be distinguished: actions for local communities, including creating or maintaining job places and local sourcing, supporting arts, culture, sport events and communal projects, grants for schools and universities, health initiatives, cooperation with local authorities, donating non-profit organisation and other charity actions, (Öberseder et al 2013, Kadłubek 2015).

All the pharmaceutical companies analysed encouraged volunteering, organised or took part in numerous charity actions and social campaigns of various kinds, supported chosen institutions or organisations (hospices, orphanages, community centres, foundations and others), which included investment and building renovation. Moreover, all of them educated children and the youth (various subject matters). All concerns also introduced apprenticeship programmes, internships, workshops for schoolchildren, tertiary students and (or) doctoral students (including scholarship programs). Three companies reported that they were providing programmes against social exclusion and to create equal opportunities. Also, three concerns had educational activities for adults (classes, workshops, often for selected groups, i.e. teachers and elderly people). Furthermore, the entities informed about other actions. Roche Polska was a culture and art sponsor (museums, cultural events etc.) and, together with the Adam Mickiewicz University in Poznan conducted post-graduate IT course. Adamed Group in cooperation with Kozminski University established post-graduate course "Supply chain management". Sanofi Group organised activities to promote healthy diet or created the so-called "Green Warsaw map". Another company,

Polpharma Group, organised the Open Day every year, when inhabitants of Starogard Gdanski and local residents had possibility to visit the factory.

2.4 Economic oriented towards CSR actions

Such CSR activities are addressed to external stakeholders like: suppliers, customers and other business partners. Enterprises (including pharmaceutical concerns) pay special attention to these groups of recipients. Economic dimension of CSR actions includes: risk and uncertainty reduction, treating customers in a fair way, providing information, safe and high-quality products, maximation of shareholders' wealth, reduction of information asymmetry, fair corporate governance, cooperation with local suppliers, careful selection of suppliers, timely payments, leading business actions in compliance with law, business ethics' promotion (Bonsón & Bednárová 2015, Carroll & Shabana 2010, Malik 2015, Miska et al 2018, Öberseder et al 2013).

The above-mentioned actions may be divided into three groups: for patients, for physicians (M.D.) and pharmacists as well as for other stakeholders (suppliers, investors etc.).

All pharmaceutical companies informed about developed activities intended for patients' organisation and individuals, especially these providing up-to-date information. Each of them conducted communication campaigns about selected diseases, their prevention, provided trainings, other education initiatives and published informative materials for patients (brochures, guidebooks and others, like patients daily diaries). Three concerns offered free consultations, precautionary examinations or diagnostics. Enterprises take advantage of various methods of contact: by telephone (helplines), webpages (usually separated internet websites for particular diseases), educational portals, blogs or use social media (Facebook or Twitter). Two entities (Polpharma and Adamed), reported preparation of special information (medicine package leaflets) for the visually impaired and the blind, while one (Polpharma) had software application for patients.

The second important stakeholders' group are physicians and pharmacists. Each company had educational and communication activities (conferences, workshops, training programmes) for the customer groups. Polpharma Group and Adamed Group prepared computer software applications for them. Additionally, Polpharma published textbook for MD students and doctors in 2015.

All stakeholders (patients and doctors) might also report about adverse drug reactions.

Four pharmaceutical companies informed about their Codes of Ethics implementation and the application as well as about Compliance policy, one: the Code of Transparency. Moreover, four concerns reported about the implementation of anti-corruption policy, two (Polpharma Group, Roche Polska): about ethical relationships with suppliers and educational actions for that group of stakeholders. Roche Polska declared that while concluding cooperation agreements, it considers the suppliers' ethical conduct. Adamed Group provided assistance for new business start-ups.

All pharmaceutical concerns remained the holders of GMP (Good Manufacturing Practice) certificates.

2.5 CSR actions for employees

Social responsibility initiatives for employees may be ascribed to the above-mentioned action groups as well. In case of the social dimension, all activities targeting workers, durable employment and supporting employee volunteering are included. Activities concerning economic dimensions of CSR may refer to staff training, ensuring safety of work, mentoring programme, wages increase, welfare improvement, non-discrimination, attracting new, skilled employees. Pro-environmental actions include the enhancement of ecological awareness and endorsement of activities to minimise negative environmental impact (Bonsón & Bednárová 2015, Malik 2015, Öberseder et al 2013). Such CSR actions were usually distinguished in reports, therefore initiatives for employees—internal stakeholders also was examined separately.

Each pharmaceutical company was helpful in possible career planning, in professional development, provided training, courses or subsidised external courses. Sanofi Group not only had its own mentoring programme, but, together with Orange Polska, implemented cross-mentoring as well. All pharmaceutical concerns had initiatives for employee's health and safety at work. Three firms conducted trainings to built ecological consciousness of the staff. Polpharma Goup and Roche Polska announced that they awarded employees notifying pro-environmental projects. Four companies reported that they supported non-work hobbies, especially in case of sport activities and provided health benefits packages for workers and their families. Three concerns implemented innovative ideas and improvements introduced by employees. Also, three firms informed about their anti-discrimination programmes (supporting staff diversity). Polpharma Group and Roche Polska informed about fair and transparent wage policy. Furthermore, Polpharma reported that all its staff members were engaged under employment contracts. Adamed Gorup and Roche Polska had facilitating work arrangements and additional assistance for young parents. Moreover, Roche Polska had pension scheme for employees and employee share purchase plan as well, while Polpharma Polska also supported retired ex-workers.

All companies also supported employee volunteering (in various areas). Adamed Group also supported employees' honourable blood donors club.

3 CONCLUSIONS

Based on the analysis carried out, the following conclusions may be reached. CSR activities of pharmaceutical companies were mainly focused on internal stakeholders (staff) as well as external ones, particularly patients, doctors and pharmacists. A wide offer dedicated to employees resulted in a very good opinion about firms as employers (i.e. Roche Polska received the Top Employer Poland and the Top Employer Europe certificates in 2015 and 2016, Polpharma took the first place in Poland's Most Attractive Employers test in 2015 and 2016, in 2015 Adamed Group was awarded the title of the Solid Employer of the Year and the Solid Employer of the Pharmaceutical Industry). In general, in case of actions supporting external stakeholders, considerably more actions had social dimension than the environmental one. Each company has different drug specialisation but all of them offer many initiatives addressed to patients or doctors. However, in this case it is difficult to distinguish between CSR actions and pure marketing strategies. Environmentally friendly actions were much more unified and usually involved energy and water consumption diminishing, reduction in pollution and CO_2 emissions or waste segregation and recycling.

Results of the analysis are not entirely comparable because each concern published the data in the report or on the webpage in a different format. Also, the extent of information provided varied. For these reasons, information provided by one concern was not included by the other one.

REFERENCES

30 lat społecznej odpowiedzialności Grupy Adamed. Raport otwarcia 2015. 2016, https://adamed.com.pl (01.03.2018).

Akdoğan, A.A. et al. 2016. A strategic influence of corporate social responsibility on meaningful work and organizational identification, via perceptions of ethical leadership. Procedia – Social and Behavioral Sciences 235: 259–268.

Amini M. & Bienstock, C.C. 2014. Corporate sustainability: an integrative definition and framework to evaluate corporate practice and guide academic research. Journal of Cleaner Production 76: 12–19.

Antošová, M. & Csikósova, A. 2014. Social behavior of companies in Slovakia and their support by European Union. *Procedia – Social and Behavioral Sciences* 109: 307–311.

Antošová, M. & Csikósova, A. 2015. Influence of European Union policy to corporate social responsibility. *Procedia Economics and Finance* 23: 733–737.

Baumgartner R.J. & Rauter, R. 2017. Strategic perspectives of corporate sustainability management to develop a sustainable organization. *Journal of Cleaner Production* 140: 81–92.

Bonsón, E. & Bednárová, M. 2015. CSR reporting practices of Eurozone companies. *Revista de Contabilidad – Spanish Accounting Review* 18: 182–193.

[COM(2011) 681] European Commission, 2011. *Communication from the Commission to the European Parliament, the Council, the European Economic and Social Committee and the Committee of the Regions. A renewed EU strategy 2011–2014 for Corporate Social Responsibility.* Brussels.

Carroll, A.B. & Shabana, K.M. 2010. The business case for corporate social responsibility: A review of concepts, research and practice. *International Journal of Management Review* 12(1): 85–105.

Carroll, A.B. 2015. Corporate social responsibility: The centerpiece of competing and complementary frameworks. *Organizational Dynamics* 44: 87–96.

García-Madariaga, J. & Rodríguez-Rivera, F. 2017. Corporate social responsibility, customer satisfaction, corporate reputation nad firm's market value: Evidence from the automobile industry. *Spanish Journal of Marketing – ESIC*: 21: 39–53.

Jamali, D. & Mirshak, R. 2007. Corporate Social Responsibility (CSR): theory and practice in a developing country context. *Journal of Business Ethics* 72(3): 243–262.

Jankalova, M. 2016. Approaches to the evaluation of corporate social responsibility. *Procedia Economics and Finance* 39: 580–587.

Kadłubek, M. 2015. The essence of corporate social responsibility and the performance of selected company. *Procedia – Social and Behavioral Sciences* 213: 509–515.

Kruk, H. 2015. Corporate Social Responsibility (CSR) – links between sustainability and other related concepts of CSR. In L. Lešková (ed.), *Zasvätení a poslaní pre sociálne služby a odkaz bl. Sáry Salkaházi. Zborník z medzinárodnej vedeckej konferencie, 9. ročník,* Košice: Katolícka Univerzita v Ružomberku, Teologická fakulta Košice.

Lulewicz-Sas, A. & Godlewska, J. 2015. Assessment of environmental issues of corporate social responsibility by enterprises in Poland – results of empirical research. *Procedia – Social and Behavioral Sciences* 213: 533–538.

Mahoney, L.S. et al. 2013. A research note on standalone corporate social responsibility reports: Signaling or greenwashing? *Critical Perspectives on accounting* 24: 350–359.

Malik, M. 2015. Value-enhancing capabilities of CSR: A brief review of contemporary Literature. *Journal of Business Ethics*: 127: 419–438.

Miska, C. et al. 2018. Culture's effects on corporate sustainability practices: A multi-domain and multi-level view. *Journal of World Business* 53: 264–279.

Możejko-Pastewka, B. 2006. Promocja produktów leczniczych – zagadnienia etyki w branży farmaceutycznej. *Problemy zarządzania* 2: 186–195.

Öberseder, M. et al. 2013. CSR practices and consumer perceptions. *Journal of Business Research* 66: 1839–1851.

Raport odpowiedzialny biznes w Polsce. Dobre praktyki. 2017. Warszawa: Forum Odpowiedzialnego Biznesu.

Raport społecznej odpowiedzialności Grupy Adamed 2016. 2017, https://adamed.com.pl (01.03.2018).

Raport społecznej odpowiedzialności Grupy Polpharma 2015–2016. 2017, https://www.polpharma.pl/ (01.03.2018).

Roche Polska i Roche Diagnostics Polska – zaangażowanie społeczne. Raport 2016. 2017. Warszawa: Roche Polska Sp. z o.o., Roche Diagnostics Polska Sp. z o.o.

Rodriguez-Fernandez, M. 2016. *Social responsibility and financial performance: The role of good corporate governance.* BRQ Business Research Quaterly 19: 137–151.

Runhaar, H. & Lafferty, H. 2009. Governing Corporate Social Responsibility: an assessment of the contribution of the UN Global Compact to CSR strategies in the telecommunications industry. *Journal of Business Ethics* 84(4): 479–495.

Społeczne zaangażowanie Roche Polska. Raport 2015. 2016. Warszawa: Roche Polska Sp. z o.o..

WCED – World Commission on Environment and Development: 1987. *Our common future.* Oxford: Oxford University Press.

Wuttichindanon, S. 2017. Corporate social responsibility disclosure – choices of reports and its determinants: Empirical evidence from firms listed on the Stock Exchange of Thailand. *Kasetsart Journal of Social Sciences* 38: 156–162.

Żemigała, M. 2007. *Społeczna odpowiedzialność przedsiębiorstwa.* Kraków: Oficyna a Wolters Kluwer business.

Production Management and Business Development – Mihalčová et al. (Eds)
© 2019 Taylor & Francis Group, London, ISBN 978-1-138-60415-5

Sport and healthy lifestyle support as a part of CSR

V. Kunz
University of Finance and Administration, Prague, Czech Republic

ABSTRACT: In recent years, Corporate Social Responsibility (CSR) has become the focus of the academic sphere, a number of international organizations, the European Union and businesses themselves. CSR is considered to be a modern business concept that expresses the company's focus on long-term goals; it interferes with all areas of corporate activities. CSR strategy is often linked to the focus of economic activity of business entities. Primarily, the paper focuses on businesses that try to promote sport and healthy lifestyles through their CSR programs prepared not only for their employees but also for the surrounding communities. It also responds to critical voices warning of the fact that for a number of companies, for example from socially sensitive sectors or food business, it is rather about investment into improving public relations or balancing negative publicity.

1 CSR AND SPORT

In recent years, corporate social responsibility (CSR) has become the focus of the academic sphere, a number of international organizations, the European Union and businesses themselves (Antošová & Csikósová 2016, Janošková & Palaščáková 2018). Around the globe, there are an increasing number of companies that are starting to implement their CSR activities focused on sport strategically in the context of their CSR policies (Aguinis & Glavas 2012, Levermore & Moore 2015).

Various experts (Giulianotti 2015, Levermore 2010, Walters & Tacon 2010) believe that an increased interest in CSR in sports is also affected by the very strong ties between CSR and sports. Sports events attract audience at local, regional as well as global level, which provides an excellent opportunity to appeal to the general public with urgent social problems. In addition, it is also the place where a very strong affective connection between sports organizations and their fans is established, which can benefit not only partner corporations supporting the sports organizations, but also the local community. This high level of loyalty and identification of fans with the club as well as the significant influence of sports organizations towards local communities can be effectively utilized in their involvement in CSR activities or in enhancing community integration and overall development (Kolyperas et al. 2015).

Smith & Westerbeek (2007), who addressed the possibilities for using sports as an appropriate channel for CSR, identified key aspects of specific features in sports which predestine the sporting field for becoming an appropriate stage to implement socially responsible activities, and not only from the point of view of their potential influence on the actual impact of CSR activities. At the same time, they can also have a rather significant influence on the nature and scope of cooperation with other partner organizations (including businesses) in CSR projects). These unique features include, in particular, the interest in sports by mass media, the attractiveness of sports for youth, their positive health impact or the ability of sports to appeal to various cultures and act as an important unifying factor.

Businesses that decide to include sports and movement activities in their CSR programmes can also take advantage of the attributes in sports or, as the case may be, these attributes can bring them a wide range of potential benefits, whether in the form of improved corporate image and reputation through reinforced local relations, more efficient facilitation of the community investment programme via a well-established infrastructure, or reinforced corporate culture and loyalty of their staff (Bason & Anagnostpoulos 2015).

2 SPORTS SPONSORHISP AND CSR – IS THERE A CONNECTION?

Most definitions describe sponsorship as a reciprocal business relation between the sponsor and the sponsored entity. Under that relation, the sponsor provides (most often) financial or, as appropriate, material or other form of support in return for a certain consideration. The most common is to associate the sponsor's name with a major event or activity, which can support marketing communications and brand of the sponsoring organization very effectively. Numerous experts (Plewa et al. 2016) emphasize with increased intensity that, in order to achieve their communication objectives, businesses should be using "softer" means of their integrated marketing communication rather than the relatively aggressive conventional communication means which were frequently used in the past.

Sponsorship can constitute one of these suitable alternatives because it is perceived as less commercially aggressive and it produces less scepticism among the general consumer public, in particular where it focuses on the community area or uses volunteer programmes, for instance. Sport provides unique opportunities for sponsors by attracting a mass audience to the local, regional and global scene, and—at the same time—it generates strong emotional responses. In global terms, sports have gradually and unambiguously become the primary field of sponsorship, nowadays attracting nearly three-fourths of sponsorship expenditure incurred by businesses worldwide, i.e. over USD 50 billion (Kunz 2018).

While sponsorship of international and nationwide events as well as leading sports teams usually does not suggest the sponsors' interest in the local communities, supporting regional or local sports events by businesses is much more likely to be perceived as an integral part of their CSR policies (Bayle 2015). And it is this community sports foundation that may appeal to the representatives of the business sphere who strive to win favour with the local public or, as appropriate, endeavour to demonstrate to be an integral part of the local communities and contribute to their development. When considering sports sponsorship as a CSR policy instrument for a business, it is thus very important to bear in mind that the efficiency of the sponsorship or of the corporation's CSR, as the case may be, is strongly affected by the nature of the sports event (Plewa & Quester 2011).

3 BUSINESSES PROMOTING HEALTHY LIFESTYLE

In addition to the traditional sports sponsorship, which has become a conventional field of engagement by businesses in the support of sports and movement activities, the number of other business CSR initiatives to support active and healthy lifestyle not only among staff, but also within the local communities has been increasing rather significantly in the past years both globally and in the Czech Republic. This often corresponds to the strategic notion of CSR strategies in businesses, as it is the case with Vodafone for example: its main mission in the CSR field is now to achieve a healthy lifestyle among young people, particularly by encouraging the development of their movement and sports activities.

CSR initiative by ČEZ, called "Orange Playgrounds", can be used as an illustrative example of a movement support programme in the Czech Republic. Through its ČEZ Foundation, which was established as early as in 2002 as one of the first corporate foundations in the Czech Republic, the energy group strives to help city districts or municipalities with the financing of construction and reconstruction of outdoor children playgrounds and sports fields. Since 2003, the Orange Playground grant programme has supported the development of over four hundred outdoor playgrounds which have various forms. Children playgrounds, sports fields and multifunctional grounds in the vicinity of kindergartens and primary schools were the most frequently constructed form, but there is an increasing trend to construct also areas with power training elements for youth, adults or senior citizens, including the so-called work-out fields (Kunz 2018).

In addition, it is also rather often to see businesses in the food industry, for instance, that focus their CSR practice on emphasizing healthy lifestyle across their CSR programmes, whether in the form of educational programmes, initiatives encouraging healthy nutrition or various sports events, targeting mostly children and youth. Nestle, for example, has been running the Nestlé Healthy Kids global programme to promote healthy lifestyle since 2009, with participation of nearly 8 million children in more than 80 countries. The programme is aimed at motivating primary school pupils aged 9–12 years to embrace correct eating habits and encouraging their interest in movement activities as part of a balanced and healthy lifestyle. In 2015, the programme was also launched in the Czech Republic, with 50 thousand children participating in the awareness training in the meantime, also under the auspices of the Ministry of Education, Youth and Sports of the Czech Republic.

The Danone Group also pays major attention in their CSR policy to activities supporting sports and healthy lifestyle, focusing primarily on children and youth age groups. Since 2000, for example, it regularly hosts the Danone Nations Cup, an international soccer tournament for children between 10 and 12 years of age. Every year, more than 2.5 million of children from over 34,000 schools and 11,000 clubs from across the globe participate in this largest tournament in the world for this age category (Kunz 2018).

4 SPORT SUPPORT BY COMPANIES FROM SENSITIVE INDUSTRIES

The impact of trade on the world of sport has never been greater than at present, which raises pressure on the behaviour of sports organizations that in a number of cases have gradually transformed from their exclusive focus on sporting activities to typical commercial companies. Influential external actors in the sporting environment have their own pragmatic interest in sporting success, be it glory, prestige or higher financial income. Sponsors and the media are exerting direct and indirect pressure not only on sports organizations but also on athletes themselves, including the impact on their goals, motives or behaviour.

Sport and the sporting industry are an integral part and the mirror of contemporary postmodern society. Just as it is, the sport world is similarly complex and contradictory. Thus, in addition to the previously mentioned wide range of social benefits, a variety of negative side-effects may be associated with sport, which may also be affected by the irresponsible behaviour of professional athletes, sports organizations or other stakeholders (eg. spectators, sports officials, sponsors, etc.).

In connection with the promotion of sport, the growing involvement of companies from socially sensitive sectors is critically accentuated whether it is a gambling operator, a producer of alcoholic beverages or a companies offering "junk food" (Blumrodt et al. 2010).

Given that this type of sponsorship is very frequently used in highly watched media broadcasts of sports, it gains considerable attention from a wide audience including the riskiest population groups (gamblers, alcoholics or youth). Many research studies show that quite short exposures to brands in connection with sport can bring about a relatively high level of brand awareness.

Given their worldwide popularity and audience, sports make it possible for sponsorship to not only promote brands towards the general public, but also enhance the legitimacy of certain products which are often part of the portfolios of businesses operating in the so-called socially sensitive industries. Lamont et al. (2011) indicate that producers of alcoholic beverages and tobacco products have become the most important sponsors in the sporting world ever.

In particular, increasingly more attention is drawn to the inconsistency in using sports, which should represent health and active lifestyle, in conjunction with the promotion of these brands. In addition, it is reminded that, for example, the integration of gambling with top sport empowers the idea that it is an acceptable form of entertainment or a harmless addition to watching sports.

In recent years, a number of sensitive businesses have stepped up their product promotion through sports sponsorship. Logos or products of businesses operating in socially sensitive industries appear not only on the players' jerseys and outfits or at the sports stadiums themselves to increase their visibility during television broadcasting as much as possible, but also during commercial breaks in sporting broadcasts.

According to some experts (Lamont et al. 2011), the risky behavior of risk groups can potentially be promoted, which can lead not only to public health deterioration but also to other pathological phenomena and problems, whether it is crime, debt traps or disruption of family relationships.

Even though in the current world of sport sponsorship is one of the key sources of income for sporting organizations (ranging from the lowest sports competitions to the highest levels of professional sport), regulators, sponsors and sports organizations themselves should not only remember the potential social consequences of supporting harmful products through sports sponsorship, but also be aware of the increasing negative public response towards issues of not keeping up with ethical standards. A number of critics (Plewa et al. 2016) are also increasingly appealing to sports organizations to curb sponsorship deals with companies offering these potentially harmful products in the future.

5 RESEARCH

The actual research focused on analysing the main partners of Czech professional soccer, which has been—together ice-hockey—among the two most popular collective sports in the Czech Republic in the long term, enjoying the greatest interest of fans, media as well as sponsors. The goal of the research was to identify the main lines of business from which major sponsors of Czech professional soccer stem from, on one hand, and to reveal the role and representation of businesses from the so-called socially sensitive industries within the sponsorship of this sport in the Czech Republic, on the other hand. In addition, a survey was conducted among 550 respondents above 18 years of age to find out which sponsors are linked to Czech soccer in the participants' minds.

The structure by industry of the main partners was analysed for all the sixteen teams in the domestic top soccer league in the 2017/2018 season, followed by an analysis of the situation in this field in relation to the Czech national soccer team and the HET soccer league and, where appropriate, the Czech cup. Information about the main partners was obtained from the official websites of the different clubs, as well as from the website of the Football Association of the Czech Republic. The survey was conducted using an electronic questionnaire that was posted at vyplň.cz website at the beginning of February 2018.

The actual analysis by industry of the clubs' main partners in the top soccer league in the Czech Republic for the 2017/2018 season showed that businesses in the following four lines of business were represented the most among the 128 general and chief sponsors of the clubs:

- Operating of betting and lottery games – 5 clubs in total supported by four betting businesses, such as Sazka Bet (Sparta Prague), Synot Tip (Slovácko).
- Manufacture and sale of sports equipment – 5 businesses in this field have partnerships with 8 clubs, e.g. Adidas (Olomouc), Puma (Teplice), Umbro (Slavia), Nike (Brno), Lion Sport (Bohemians).
- Production of beer and alcoholic beverages – 4 clubs in total supported by five businesses in this industry, such as Gambrinus (Olomouc), Pivovary Lobkowicz (Slavia), Bílinská Kyselka (Teplice), Pepsi (Jablonec).
- Insurance—we were able to find partners from this field in 4 clubs, e.g. E-pojištění (Karviná), ČPP (Jablonec), Generali (Sparta).

Businesses that have their registered office or operate their branches in the same region as the clubs also often acted as the leading partners of Czech soccer clubs (for instance AGC – FK Teplice, Preciosa – Liberec, Škoda Auto – Mladá Boleslav, Lukrom – Zlín, Sigma Group Olomouc, Doosan Škoda Power – Plzeň).

In addition, most major partners in the entire Czech soccer domain (national team, soccer league and cup) are engaged in similar lines of business as their club partners, whether we look at corporations running betting and lottery offices (Tipsport, Fortuna), beer and beverage producers (Plzeňský Prazdroj – Gambrinus, Pepsi), telecommunication companies (T-Mobile) or manufacturers of sport clothes (Puma). Other major partners of Czech soccer include also car dealers (AAA Auto), operators of gas station networks (MOL Czech Republic) or manufacturers of paints or garage doors (HET, Hörmann).

Table 1 below captures the main sponsors of Czech football from socially sensitive sectors in the Czech Republic.

The results of the survey showed that the respondents very often make links between the sponsorship in Czech soccer with the sponsors from socially sensitive industries (as regards brands, Plzeňský Prazdroj and Fortuna were the

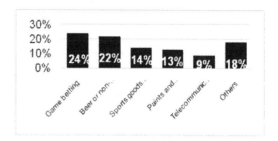

Figure 1. Which sponsors do you associate with Czech football?

most frequently indicated by the respondents), as shown in the following diagram.

6 CONCLUSION

Support for sports and a healthy lifestyle is being increasingly integrated in the marketing strategies and CSR programmes of businesses in the world as well as in the Czech Republic, towards both their own staff and the local communities. Although one can see a growing number of new CSR activities in this domain, sports sponsorship remains the primary sphere of their interest here.

Given their worldwide popularity and audience, sports make it possible for sponsorship to not only promote brands towards the general public, but also enhance the legitimacy of certain products. In connection with the rising global expenditure incurred by businesses for sporting sponsorship (including support for the Olympic movement), the increasingly large engagement of businesses from socially sensitive industries, which rank among the tops sponsors of sports, is being pointed out with strong criticism.

The article brings not only topical, but also rather complex findings (including the issue of representation of businesses from socially sensitive industries) as regards the sponsorship situation in professional soccer, which has been one of the most popular collective sports in the Czech Republic in the long term.

The results of research in the most popular collective sport in the Czech Republic showed a very strong representation of companies from the so-called socially sensitive sectors (especially betting operators and breweries) not only among sponsors of individual clubs, but also representations and leagues. Similarly, the research among the public has shown that Czech football is often associated with the support of businesses in these areas.

At the same time, the survey results showed a very strong representation of businesses from the so-called socially sensitive industries (particularly operators of gambling and breweries). In the

Table 1. Sponsors of football from socially sensitive sectors (CR).

Area	Clubs	Representation, league, cup
Sport betting operations	5 – e.g. Sazka Bet (Sparta), Synot Tip (Slovácko)	2 – Tipsport, Fortuna
Beer production	2 – e.g. Gambrinus (Olomouc) Pivovar Lobkowicz (Slávia)	1 – Plzeňský Prazdroj

current sports world, although funding from sponsors is one of the key sources of income for sporting organizations, from the lowest levels of sports competitions to the highest ranks of professional sports, the regulators, sponsors as well as the sporting organizations themselves should bear in mind the potential social consequences of supporting harmful products through sports sponsorship.

The results achieved may provide a valuable reflection on how approach to sponsors should be shaped in the future, not only for selected clubs, but also for managing executive sports authorities that are likely to come under even more pressure in the future from the stakeholders and the general public in relation to compliance with the ethics. The research findings can also be useful in the future decision-making of government officials on possible further legislative restrictions in this field.

ACKNOWLEDGEMENT

The result was generated using the institutional support for long-term policy development of research organization at the University of Finance and Administration.

REFERENCES

Aguinis, H. & Glavas, A. 2012. What we know and don't know about corporate social responsibility: a review and research agenda. *Journal of Management*, 38(4): 932–968.

Antošová, M. & Csikósová, A. 2016. Corporate social responsibility in small and medium enterprises in Slovakia. *Actual Problems of Economics*, 175(1): 217–224.

Bason, T. & Anagnostpoulos, C. 2015. Corporate Social Responsibility through Sport: A Longitudinal Study of the FTSE100 Companies. *Sport, Business and Management: An International Journal*, 5(3): 218–241.

Bayle, E. 2015. Olympic Social Responsibility: A Challenge for the Future. *Sport in Society*, 19(6): 752–766.

Blumrodt, J., Desbordes, M. & Bodin, D. 2010. The sport entertainment industry and corporate social responsibility. *Journal of Management & Organization*, 14(6): 514–529.

Giulianotti, R. 2015. Corporate social responsibility in sport: critical issues and future possibilities. *Corporate Governance*, 15(2): 243–248.

Janošková, M. & Palaščáková, D. 2018. Corporate Social Responsibility as a strategic goal in business: A case study. In Ch. R. Baker (Eds.), *Corporate Social Responsibility (CSR): Practices, Issues and Global Perspectives* (109–144). New York: Nova Science Publishers.

Kolyperas, D., Morrow, S. & Sparks, L. 2015. Developing CSR in Professional Football Clubs: Drivers and Phases. *Corporate Governance*, 15(2): 177–195.

Kunz, V. 2018. *Sportovní marketing. CSR a sponzoring.* Praha: Grada Publishing.

Lamont, M., Hing, N. & Gainsbury, S. 2011. Gambling on Sport Sponsorship: A Conceptual Framework for Research and Regulatory Review. *Sport Management Review*, 14(3): 246–257.

Levermore, R. & Moore, N. 2015. The need to apply new theories to Sport CSR. *Corporate Governance*, 15(2): 249–253.

Levermore, R. 2010. CSR for Development Through Sport: Examining its Potential and Limitations. *Third World Quarterly*, 31(2): 223–241.

Plewa, C. & Quester, P. 2011. Sponsorship and CSR: is There a Link? A Conceptual Framework. *International Journal of Sports Marketing and Sponsorship*, 12(4): 22–38.

Plewa, C., Carrillat, F.A., Mazodier, M. & Quester, P.G. 2016. Which sport sponsorships most impact sponsor CSR image? *European Journal of Marketing*, 50(5/6): 796–815.

Smith, A. & Westerbeek, H. 2007. Sport as a vehicle for developing corporate social responsibility. *Journal of Corporate Citizenship*, 25(7): 43–54.

Walters, G. & Tacon, R. 2010. Corporate Social Responsibility in Sport: Stakeholder Management in the UK Football Industry. *Journal of Management and Organization*, 16(4): 566–586.

Production Management and Business Development – Mihalčová et al. (Eds)
© *2019 Taylor & Francis Group, London, ISBN 978-1-138-60415-5*

The position of aviation startups on the European innovation market

D. Liptáková, E. Jenčová & Z. Šusterová
Faculty of Aeronautics, Technical University of Košice, Košice, Slovak Republic

ABSTRACT: The word "startup" has become a synonym for the start of a successful business in the Slovak environment. The vision of triumph is fed by stories of successful startups from abroad as well as Slovakia, which should serve as motivation. In fact, startup is a risk investment that can lead to extraordinary profits, but at the same time end with the liquidation of the business and the disappointment of the parties involved. The startup environment is therefore the subject of intense research. The article describes the term startup and its basic characteristics. The main focus is put on the startups presented by Pioneers Festival in Vienna, an international gathering of startups, investors and executives. The composition of startups in the years 2015 to 2017 has been analyzed. Startups with aviation background are described more closely and their position in the Gartner Hype Cycle is analyzed.

1 INTRODUCTION

In previous years the trend is showing of growing numbers of startup events and growth of communities in larger cities of Slovakia. The word "startup" has become a synonym for the start of a successful business. This idea is mainly supported by success stories of startups from abroad, but also from Slovakia, which should serve as motivation. In fact, startup is a risky investment that can lead to extraordinary profits, but at the same time end with the liquidation of the business and the disappointment of the parties involved. The startup environment is therefore the subject of intense research, the goal of which is to define the very concept of startup, and also to describe the conditions for its creation and success, resp. failure.

A common feature of aviation and startups is the speed of growth and scalability. Startups are usually created as "garage companies" that want to become a new Microsoft. Aviation has shifted from the earliest years of the Wright Brothers and other pioneers in the course of one century to a convenient mean of global mass transport for passengers and cargo. Most startups start with an idea and a small team of enthusiastic collaborators who are looking for sources of financing their product during its preparation for the market. In opposite, development in the field of aviation requires whole teams of experts and a large amount of capital. That's why it's interesting to watch the aviation startups and find out how they deal with this challenge.

2 THE AIM OF THE RESEARCH, MATERIALS AND METHODS

2.1 *Aim of the research*

The aim of the proposed paper is to analyze the composition of startups at the annual event Pioneers Festival in Vienna in the years 2015 to 2017. A closer look will be paid to startups from the field of aviation. The article will analyze their business ideas and compare them with the Gartner Hype Cycle.

2.2 *Origin of the data*

The data for this article come directly from the Pioneers Festival organizers as one of the authors of this article is co-organizer of the festival.

As the festival is attended every year by up to 500 startups, this article will analyze the composition of teams chosen by organizing committee and considered as the most promising. These were presented to the public as Top50 in 2015 and 2017 and Top70 in 2016. This means the data is analyzed from 170 contestants.

3 THE LIFE AND SUPPORT FOR STARTUPS

3.1 *Definition of the term startup*

Startups involve risk and it is a question for applied psychology whether this risk factor is contributing to the popularity of the startups. They openly declare their instability, uncertainty, but also innovation and growth, attracting a certain group of people looking for challenges. Outdated definitions speak of startups as culture, mentality to innovate and bring solutions to problems or market deficiencies. The Slovak Business Agency (SBA 2015) describes the key aspects of the startup as product, innovation and uncertainty that it must face. The novelty of a product or service distinguishes startup from classic companies. Classic firms are trying to maintain and protect themselves, instead of uncovering new sources of value for the customer and seeing the impact of their business on them.

Companies that duplicates an existing business plans cannot be considered as startups or cannot brings an alternative product or service to an existing market. Robehmed (2013) believes that companies that are on the market for more than 3 years will usually cease to be a startup. They can be redeemed by a larger company, have more than one office, have substantial sales, have more than 80 employees, more than 5 people in the board of directors, or the original founders sell their shares. In the current dynamic market environment, it is difficult to give accurate figures. It is simpler to define that a company is no longer a startup if it cannot grow dynamically, or when employees replace uncertainty and risk for the atmosphere of stability.

The startup creators' usual practice is to create a team of people which will be able to execute the business idea (Gopalkrishnan 2017), or in reversed order, based on the knowledge and experience of the team members they develop a possible startup concept (Conti et al. 2013). Consequently, they focus on developing a sustainable business model, product development, and search for sponsors and investors to help the emerging company to place their product in the market with the help of financial support, as well as using their own distribution channels or contacts (Davola et al. 2003).

Technological startups, in particular, are always at the center of the interest of various funds and companies, because they present a chance for a high return on investment. For example, aside from the latest development, the company Uber raised from its formation in 2009 to 2014 $2.5 billion and its estimated value in 2014 was $40 billion (Raymundo 2014). For this reason, various forms of support are created for startup founders. Incubators and accelerators are usually physical spaces to which startup companies have moved their offices and work on their project. At the same time, they receive financial, legal, commercial or marketing support. The simplest form of assistance are various meetings and competitions where startups present themselves. They receive valuable feedback and such events are a great place for networking and linking to sponsors, mentors and other startups, which is extremely important in order to higher the chances of funding (Hochberg et al.

2007). An example of local support is the Eastcubator Startup Center which operates in Košice to provide individuals and teams with space for work and meetings. Its members are also organizing an annual Startup Weekend competition and different MeetUps and seminars.

3.2 *Pioneers festival*

The Pioneers Festival is a large format meeting of emerging businesses with investors, media, executive directors, entrepreneurs. One of the world's events is held each year in Vienna in May. The number of participants is limited to 2500 pioneers, that is new technology developers who can present themselves and look for support. Selected companies and startups receive the opportunity to introduce themselves on stage in front of the whole assembly, where they compete for a special prize. In order to make their presentation interesting, the organizers give these selected participants the opportunity to have online sessions and personal mentoring with experienced entrepreneurs on site who will advise them on how to capture the attention of audience and sell their idea in the shortest time.

3.3 *Composition of startups*

Strong startup communities, incubators and accelerators often organize various meetings and competitions to support regional startup scene. The Pioneers event, nevertheless, is of great significance because of the large number of participants. Situation of the event in Vienna is also useful as the city has an advantageous location in central Europe with good connectivity and entrepreneurial background. Due to these and other factors the festival is of great importance and is also popular. Startups from many countries take part in the festival, some travelling great distances. The composition of startups on the Pioneers festival in the years 2015 to 2017 depending on the country of origin is presented in Figure 1. About three quarters of the Top startups were from Europe. It is more appropriate to say that their companies were founded in Europe. Almost 50% of startups came from German speaking countries such as Austria, Germany or Switzerland. Some startups were founded in the United States of America. But there were also startups from Brazil or Chile. Teams from the American continent made 11% of the contestants. Identically 5% of the teams came from Middle East (Israel) and Asia (Malaysia, Japan etc.). A few startups have their location in Australia and Africa.

By looking at the composition of startups considering the final user of their products, a wide variety of usage can be seen (Fig. 2). Most of the companies focused on provision of solutions to businesses (Business to Business, B2B). There

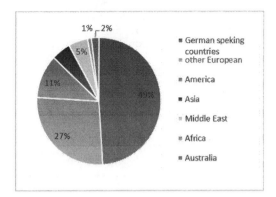

Figure 1. Composition of Top startups at the Pioneers festival 2015–2017 considering their country of origin. Source: Own processing.

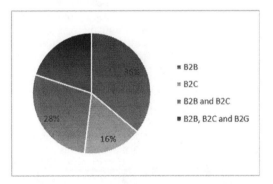

Figure 2. Composition of Top startups at the Pioneers festival 2015–2017 considering the user of the product. Source: Own processing.

were also products that could be applied by private as well as by business clients (Business to Client, B2C and B2B solutions). Over the three years it is recorded a growth of startups who offer their solutions to be used in public administration by law enforcement or local government (Business to Government, B2G). The trend is so apparent that the term GovTech came into use. It is a neologism, a compound word from the words "government" and "technology". It was created just like popular terms such as "FinTech", "BioTech" or "AgTech". The latter is also receiving growing attention.

3.4 Aviation and aerospace startups

During the years 2015 to 2017 there were several startups with technology deriving from aviation and aerospace. More could be seen during the festival events in exhibition stands. But for the Top50 (or Top70) only 5 were chosen. Among them startups with names: Dronamics, Olaeris, Skypicker, SpaceVR and Airmada.

The Bulgarian team of Dronamics has focused on developing advanced unmanned, optimized heavy and long-haul aircraft. Their drones should be used commercially, or in special missions. Dronamics became the winner of the Pioneers Challenge for the best-presented project and received a premium prize of €100,000.

The company Olaeris developed an autonomous unmanned aircraft for use by public forces such as fire crews or police forces. With the help of the sensors, their device is able to come to the point of interference and the attached camera allows the situation to be monitored. The device can also be operated manually. A strategic deployment of drones in the agglomeration for rapid intervention is envisaged.

Skypicker is a service that offers search for the cheapest flights, combining low cost and classic carriers to receive the lowest bid.

SpaceVR is a virtual reality platform that offers its users the possibility to experience space travel in immersive virtual reality. It uses 360-degree cameras feeding footage from low earth orbit.

Airmada is yet another project focused on drones and UAV (Unmanned Aerial Vehicles). They created a concept of stations capable of planning and controlling the UAV flights, thus removing the necessity of having a UAV operator on site. The stations also track UAV health indicators, swaps, charge batteries and upload live data feed from the drone's sensors to the client's IT software.

During the exhibition phase of Pioneers, two more startups from the field of aviation and aerospace caught out attention. The company Accion Systems has developed ion pulse motors to compensate satellite positioning on a 200 kg track. The advantage of their product is to have small size auxiliary thrusters with new type of fuel and the potential to be produced in a mass scale.

Hexo + is a mobile device application that enables the user to control an unmanned airplane with a camera from the ground. Control instructions include "tracking from a height" or "360-degree flight" and so on. The role of this system is to allow the user to shoot spectacular aerial shots of their activities.

When looking at the different companies and their focus, it is clearly possible to see the trend of creation and work with UAV systems for different purposes, from carrying heavy loads, deployment for the defense and protection of the population to amusement of individuals.

4 TRENDS IN TECHNOLOGY DEVELOPMENT

Every year the US Gartner analytical group publishes an analysis of nascent technologies across sectors in the form of the Gartner Hype Cycle. The curve showing the expectations of new technologies over time has 5 sections in which emerging technologies are placed, based on their potential and the way they are used. The assigned icons to individual innovations indicate the estimated time when the technology reaches the last level of the curve. This information can then be used to create a business strategy, it can direct the research and development departments, entrepreneurs, or start-ups looking for new ideas. Similar analyses are created by Gartner for individual market sectors.

4.1 Segments of the Gartner Hype Cycle

The first segment calls Gartner, 2015 Innovation Trigger. It features new technology concepts that gain publicity. Often no product is available or the commercial use of the technology itself is not confirmed.

Some companies respond to the public appeal and use this new technology. First successes as well as failures are created. Technology achieves the Peak of Inflated Expectations. As sustainable successes do not occur, innovation goes into the Trough of Disillusionment. Technology companies will be successful only if they can modify the product to such an extent as to get early adopters.

The next phase that technology can go through is the Slope of Enlightenment. Products created with the new technology are starting to penetrate the market, companies create new adapted generations, or new pilot products are created. Technology has proven its usability. At this stage, conservative companies might be still reluctant to use it.

Plateau of Productivity is the final level assigned by Gartner's analytical group to new technologies. At this stage, the applicability of technology at the wider market is clearly visible and its general application is beginning to take place (Dedehayir & Steinert 2016).

4.2 Aviation innovations in the Gartner Hype Cycle

Looking at the Gartner Hype Cycle, the curve analysing new technologies doesn't show innovations directly related to the aviation. The reason may be that no breakthrough technology has emerged on the market recently. There are rather minor innovations and improvements to existing tools. Even the quadcopters and other types of unmanned aircraft that enjoy a wave of enthusiasm from the public are actually a decades-old concept. However, a closer look at the Gartner Hype Cycle indicates the direction in which the development of these devices should be taken in order to create new profitable opportunities in the future.

In 2010, the "mobile robots" technology emerged for the first time, and Gartner assumed that the mainstream adoption would not be less than ten years away. In 2012, Gartner cut the expected adoption of mobile robots to 5–10 years, and also introduced a new technology of "autonomous vehicles" with the same expected adoption time. In 2015, Gartner placed the autonomous vehicles at the top of the curve, into the second phase, and renamed the mobile robots to "smart robots".

The solutions of the teams who participated in the Pioneers festival in 2015 to 2017 with the concept of using drones were compatible with Gartner's predictions. Three solutions from Top startups presented unmanned aircraft capable of autonomous movement without manual intervention by the operator. The product portfolio of Olaeris contained a smart robot solution. Their proposal assumes that the network of drones deployed in the agglomeration would operate without operator intervention, and the drones would be able to mutually interchange locations and replace themselves in the need of recharging at the site during an operational flight.

5 CONCLUSION

In its relatively short history, the aviation has undergone many transformations. This is thanks to many pioneers in their fields who were able to come up with solutions that oftentimes could not be engaged at the time of their creation due to different technological limitations. The drafts had to wait for many years until experts returned to them and put them into practice. Nowadays there is little left for inventors who dream of creating disturbing technology. They rather innovate existing concepts to bring as much savings or increased efficiency as possible. However, with proper market analysis of current and especially future consumer needs there is a possibility to identify new means how to alter existing technologies into new products.

Evidence that approach can bring results are the winners of Pioneers Challenge contest 2015 team Dronamics. They presented a cargo drone in a way that promised its commercial use. Dronamics is a startup, that means a young venture focused on fast growth offering itself as a risky investment with a high return potential. In today's marketplace, they apparently do not have a great chance of success, because many countries are worried about drones as a possible security risk, as well as threats to people and property both on land and in the air. However, a steadily growing number of similar projects and an increasing amount of invested resources will eventually put pressure on lawmakers, and in the course of a few years, the market environment may change completely.

REFERENCES

Conti, A. et al. 2013. Patents as Signals for Startup Financing. In: *The Journal of Industrial Economics*, 09/2013, Volume 61, Issue 3.

Davola, A. et al. 2003. Venture capital financing and the growth of startup firms. In: *Journal of Business Venturing*, 2003, Volume 18, Issue 6.

Dedehayir, O. & Steinert, M. 2016. The hype cycle model: A review and future directions. In: *Technological Forecasting and Social Change*, 07/2016, Volume 108.

Gartner 2018. *Research Methodologies: Gartner Hype Cycle* [online]. [cit. 20–02–2018]. Available at: http://www.gartner.com/technology/research/methodologies/hype-cycle.jsp.

Gopalkrishnan, S.S. 2017. The Role of Humor in Startup Success: The Mediating Role of Team Performance. In: *Journal of Organizational Psychology*, 09/2017, Volume 17, Issue 3.

Hochberg, Y. et al. 2007. Whom You Know Matters: Venture Capital Networks and Investment Performance. In: *The Journal of Finance*, 02/2007, Volume 62, Issue 1.

Raymundo, O. 2014. *The 15 most valuable startups in the world* [online]. Available at: https://www.inc.com/oscar-raymundo/most-valuable-startups-in-the-world.html.

Robehmed, N. 2013. *What is a startup?* [online]. Available at: https://www.forbes.com/sites/natalierobehmed/2013/12/16/what-is-a-startup/#420eb40f4044.

SBA 2015. *Startupy – nápady, ktoré menia svet*. Slovak Business Agency Available at: http://www.sbagency.sk/startupy-napady-ktore-menia-svet#.Vhj68fmqqko.

Production Management and Business Development – Mihalčová et al. (Eds)
© *2019 Taylor & Francis Group, London, ISBN 978-1-138-60415-5*

Economic crime in Slovakia

J. Lukáč, M. Freňáková & O. Kmeťová
Faculty of Business Economics with seat in Košice, University of Economics in Bratislava, Košice, Slovak Republic

ABSTRACT: Economic crime can be classified as one of the most important areas of crime based on the damage it causes. In practice, we encounter crimes such as embezzlement, fraud, currency and tax related criminal offences, criminal offences in the area of Value Added Tax (VAT) and other criminal offences that we place in a group of economic crimes. The most widespread crime in this area is the unlawful claim for refund of remission of VAT, which is reflected in the reduction of the tax base of the entrepreneur by execution a fictitious transaction and issuing a fictitious invoice. The aim of this paper is to approach the different types of economic crime in Slovakia in years 2016 and 2017.

1 INTRODUCTION

Economic crime can be classified as one of the most important areas of crime based on the damage it causes. In practice, we encounter crimes such as embezzlement, fraud, currency related criminal offences (forgery, fraudulent alteration and illicit manufacturing of money and securities) and tax related criminal offences (tax evasion, failure to pay tax), criminal offences in the area of value added tax (VAT) and other criminal offences that we place in a group of economic crimes. The most widespread crime in this area is the unlawful claim for refund of remission of VAT (Kmeťová et al. 2017), which is reflected in the reduction of the tax base of the entrepreneur by execution a fictitious transaction and issuing a fictitious invoice.

Several authors have dealt with the issue of specific economic crimes. Marjit et al. (2017) have investigated tax loopholes that allow firms to exploit borderline cases between legal tax avoidance and illegal tax evasion. Tax loopholes may serve as a separating mechanism that helps governments maximize revenues and curb corruption. Dobrovič et al. (2017) have pointed out the tax system and activity of tax authorities at carrying out a control activity and as well as the activity of its bodies in order to eliminate tax evasions and tax frauds for a sustainable development of state economy, have paid attention to tax systems and have dealt with tax frauds and have provided the proposals for the possibilities to combat against tax frauds and tax evasions more effectively.

The aim of this paper is to approach the different types of economic crime in Slovakia in years 2016 and 2017.

2 DEFINITION OF ECONOMIC CRIME AND ECONOMIC CRIMINAL OFFENCES

Under economic crime we mean, mainly, unlawful actions which (Chmelník et al. 2005):

- Regardless of the perpetrator's status, these unlawful actions fulfill the facts of one of the criminal offences listed in the relevant chapter of a special part of the Criminal Code.
- Fulfilled the facts of another criminal offence if the perpetrator and also the injured party are involved in the commission of a criminal offense in the position of business entities and criminal activity is related to their business.
- Fulfilled the facts of another criminal offence if it has occurred in relations based on commercial or labor law at the employer's expense, or on the basis of another legal relationship relating to the economy, economics or finance.
- Fulfill the facts of the criminal offences committed by public officials and criminal offences relating to bribery if they have been committed by a representative of the public administration in the exercise of its authority in relation to the performance of economic tasks of general interest or such proceedings were against that representative.
- International documents include them to economic crime.

The part two of the Criminal Code (Act No. 300/2005 Coll.) defines the classification of criminal offences, where economic criminal offences include: abusing participation in economic competition; unlawful business activity; unlawful trading in foreign currency and providing foreign-exchange services; illegal alcohol production; breach of regulations governing imports and exports of goods; breach of regulations governing the handling of controlled goods and technologies; endangering foreign exchange trade; distortion of data in financial and commercial records; damaging financial interests of the European Communities; endangering trade, bank, postal, telecommunication and tax secrets; insider trading; deceitful practices in public procurement and public auction; harm cause to a consumer; forgery, fraudulent alteration and illicit manufacturing of money and securities; uttering counterfeit, fraudulently altered and illicitly manufactured money and securities; manufacturing and possession of instruments for counterfeiting and forgery; endangering circulation of domestic currency; forgery, fraudulent alteration and illicit manufacturing of duty stamps, postage stamps, stickers and postmarks; forgery and fraudulent alteration of control technical measures for labeling goods; tax and insurance evasion; failure to pay tax and insurance; failure to pay tax; breach of regulations governing state technical measures for labeling goods; infringing trademark, registered appellation of origin and trade name rights; infringing industrial property rights; infringement of copyright.

Economic crime also goes against the economic order and its functioning. However, economic crime cannot be limited only to economic criminal offences in the sense of the specific part of the Criminal Code. The fundamental differences between property crime and economic crime, according to police statistics, are also reflected in the severity of the damage caused. Significant differences can also be found in the characteristics of perpetrators (Novotný et al. 2004).

Economic crime is a specific type of crime. It causes economic damage to the state and damage to natural and legal persons. We can include to economic crime these criminal offences: embezzlement, fraud, unlawful acquisition of payment card, harm cause to a consumer, passive bribery, but also criminal offences as endangering the environment or poaching (Hurbánková 2017).

The Appendix of Recommendation No. R (81) 12 of the Committee of Ministers to member states on economic crime contains the list of economic offences. The offences referred to in the recommendation are the following:

1. Cartel offences.
2. Fraudulent practices and abuse of economic situation by multinational companies.
3. Fraudulent procurement or abuse of state or international organizations' grants.
4. Computer crime.

5. Bogus firms.
6. Faking of company balance sheets and bookkeeping offences.
7. Fraud concerning economic situation and corporate capital of companies.
8. Violation by a company of standards of security and health concerning employees.
9. Fraud to the detriment of creditors.
10. Consumer fraud.
11. Unfair competition and misleading advertising.
12. Fiscal offences and evasion of social costs by enterprises.
13. Customs offences.
14. Offences concerning money and currency regulations.
15. Stock exchange and bank offences.
16. Offences against the environment.

The term economic criminal offence may be understood in the broadest and most legal sense as all legal and illegal practices on the basis of which the persons responsible for business entities, in particular their owners, managers, proxies and other persons empowered to represent the business entity, cause damage to: people, nature, state, society, science, culture, or other entities in order to achieve, increase or secure their profits.

3 ECONOMIC CRIME IN SLOVAKIA

In the next section we will analyze the information about economic crime in Slovakia in years 2016 and 2017. Analyzed data on economic crime are available on the website of the Ministry of the Interior of the Slovak Republic.

From the map of economic criminal offences in Slovakia (Fig. 1) we can see the situation in economic crime in Slovakia at the end of 2017. The more bright colored districts show a lower number of cases of economic crime, on the contrary, the dark colored districts show a high number of economic criminal offences. The lowest number of criminal offences in the area of economic crime was recorded in the districts of Revúca, Svidník, Stropkov, Stará Ľubovňa, Kežmarok and Bánovce nad Bebravou. The highest number of economic crimes was dealt with by the District Directorates of the Police Force in Bratislava II. and III., Žilina, Trnava, Trenčín, Košice, Prešov and Michalovce. The clarity of criminal offences is 7108 cases out of a total 14460.

Table 1 provides an overview of the crimes committed in Slovakia in years 2016 and 2017 through data on prosecuted and investigated persons, data on minors and juveniles perpetrators and data on the impact of alcohol and drugs in economic crime. On the basis of the analyzed data, we find out that the total number of prosecuted and investigated

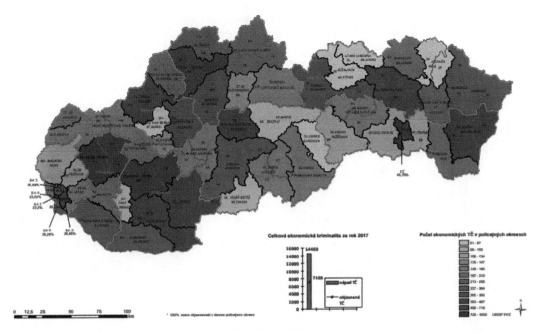

Figure 1. Map of economic criminal offences in Slovakia in 2017.
Source: The Ministry of the Interior of the Slovak Republic (2018).

Table 1. Data on prosecuted and investigated persons in Slovakia in years 2016 and 2017.

Type of crime	Persons in total		Number of minors		Number of juveniles		Impact of alcohol		Impact of drugs	
	2016	2017	2016	2017	2016	2017	2016	2017	2016	2017
Economic crime in total	8069	8184	28	28	110	91	32	60	1	2
Tax Evasion	3776	4139	x	x	2	x	4	3	x	x
Theft	33	25	x	x	x	x	x	x	x	x
Endangering Currency	48	42	x	x	1	3	1	x	x	x
Endangering Foreign Exchange Trade	x	x	x	x	x	x	x	x	x	x
Corruption	115	154	x	x	x	2	1	3	x	x
Embezzlement	528	492	x	x	2	1	1	3	x	x
Fraud	1218	1135	x	x	12	5	2	12	x	x
Infringement of Copyright	20	25	x	x	2	x	x	x	x	x

x – not available.
Source: Own processing based on statistics of the Ministry of the Interior of the Slovak Republic.

persons increased year-on-year by 115, which represents an increase of 1.43%. It is clear from Table 1 that the most economic criminal offences in Slovakia in both years 2016 and 2017 were perpetrated in the area of tax evasion and fraud. But while the number of persons prosecuted and investigated in the area of tax evasion has increased (an increase by 363 persons, representing 9.61%), the number of prosecuted and investigated persons in the area of fraud has decreased (a decrease by 83 persons, representing 6.81%). We state that the impact of

alcohol and drugs in economic crime in Slovakia in years 2016 and 2017 has been negligible.

Table 2 provides an overview of the economic criminal offences committed in Slovakia in years 2016 and 2017 and describes detected criminal offences, their clarity and damage caused as a result of these offences expressed in thousand euros. On the basis of the analyzed data, we find out that the total damage caused by economic criminal offences in Slovakia in 2017 was 1,425,195 thousand euros, which is an increase of 1,122,029 thousand euros

145

Table 2. Data on economic criminal offences in Slovakia in years 2016 and 2017.

Type of crime	Detected criminal offences		Clarified criminal offences		Damage caused in thousand EUR		Addition clarified	
	2016	2017	2016	2017	2016	2017	2016	2017
Economic crime in total	14895	14460	6994	7018	303166	1425195	1591	1500
Unfair Competition, Infringement of Copyright	68	61	23	18	208	283	16	15
Usury (§ 235)	2	2	1	1	x	x	x	x
Unlawful Business Activity (§ 251)	47	28	17	17	350	969	6	2
Concealment of a Thing (§ 236)	25	24	9	7	15	40	3	2
Harm Cause to a Consumer (§ 269)	3	x	x	x	x	x	x	1
Breach of Regulations Governing Imports and Exports of Goods—Smuggling (§ 254)	3	4	1	1	680	x	1	x
Distortion of Data in Financial and Commercial Records (§ 259)	83	74	28	27	1959	1121671	15	11
Breach of Trust by Maladministration of Estates of Another (§ 237)	77	79	15	18	11550	55662	17	17
Theft (§ 212) except Theft of Consignment	35	32	29	22	186	567	4	x
Unlawful Enjoyment of a Thing of Another (§ 215)	4	3	2	1	22	1	x	x
Harm Done to a Thing of Another (§ 245)	18	28	6	8	50	102	x	x
Endangering Currency (§§ 270–273)	1361	1459	33	49	70	55	7	4
Tax and Fees Evasion (§§ 276–279)	5585	5734	3721	4082	133801	111714	646	644
Abuse of Power by a Public Official (§ 326)	15	20	7	8	367	411	4	3
Passive Bribery (§ 328)	49	78	20	38	x	x	7	9
Harm Done to a Creditor (§ 239)	193	143	33	22	18859	7893	47	29
Counterfeiting and Altering a Public Instrument (§ 352)	214	223	139	148	49	279	6	9
Forgery and Fraudulent Alteration of Control Technical Measures for Labeling Goods (§ 275)	x	x	x	x	x	x	1	x
Endangering Health due to Decayed Foodstuffs and Other Items (§ 168)	2	x	1	x	x	x	x	x
Illegal Alcohol Production (§ 253)	8	6	6	3	x	x	x	1
Unlawful Enjoyment of a Motor Vehicle of Another (§ 216)	72	48	43	33	1321	306	3	7
Breach of Mailing Secrets (§ 196)	2	2	2	2	x	x	x	x
Embezzlement (§ 213)	706	622	426	422	14410	15474	124	110
Deceitful Practices in Public Procurement and Public Auction (§ 266)	16	15	1	2	419	189	3	1
Breach of Regulations Governing the Handling of Controlled Goods and Technologies (§§ 255, 256, 257)	1	1	x	1	x	x	x	x
Insider Trading (§ 265)	4	3	x	2	5	625	1	x
Illegal Gambling and Wagers (§ 229)	2	x	1	x	x	x	x	x
Fraud (§ 221)	2312	2264	874	837	74314	62351	380	325
Unlawful Manufacturing and Enjoyment of Payment Means, Electronic Money or Other Payment Card (§ 219)	1713	1541	424	435	1341	885	81	96
Legalization of the Proceeds of Crime (§ 233)	115	117	12	16	2567	17598	7	8
Stealing Postal Items	2	1	x	1	2	1	x	x
Stealing Consignment Shipped by Road	2	1	1	1	2	90	x	x
Harm Done to and Abuse of an Information Carrier (§ 247)	32	54	x	x	46	139	x	1
Poaching (§ 310)	284	263	179	165	167	125	4	4
Endangering and Damaging the Environment (§ 300)	13	14	1	2	79	24	2	x
Abuse of Property (§ 248)	3	1	x	x	x	x	x	1
Endangering Economy Secrets	5	3	2	1	x	10	x	x
Active Bribery (§§ 332, 333, 336/2)	57	90	40	59	x	x	6	4
Failure to Pay Wages and Redundancy Payment (§ 214)	260	221	89	96	616	616	25	27

(*Continued*)

Table 2. (*Continued*).

Type of crime	Detected criminal offences		Clarified criminal offences		Damage caused in thousand EUR		Addition clarified	
	2016	2017	2016	2017	2016	2017	2016	2017
Failure to Fulfill the Reporting Obligation	1	2	x	1	x	x	x	x
Sharing (§ 231, 232)	16	11	10	10	x	x	1	2
Credit Fraud (§ 222)	690	499	507	357	10072	9769	119	95
Subsidy Fraud (§ 225)	123	75	80	53	3400	609	14	17
Insurance Fraud (§ 223)	67	26	44	12	417	425	8	5
Unjust Enrichment (§ 226)	26	33	11	3	143	346	1	2
Fraudulent and Induced Bankruptcy (§§ 227, 228)	7	4	1	x	166	727	x	x
Falsification and Fraudulent Alteration of Motor Vehicle Identification Numbers (§ 220)	58	37	6	4	95	37	x	1
Crashes and Breakdowns of the Operation other than Traffic Accidents	12	10	3	x	13	6	1	x
Unauthorized Handling of Waste (§ 302)	198	221	10	16	4291	2316	2	6
Breach of Water and Air Protection Regulations (§ 303)	7	5	x	x	x	26	x	x
Unlawful Manufacturing and Enjoyment of Payment Means, Electronic Money or Other Payment Card (§ 219)	28	38	9	16	10	34	x	2
Damaging Financial Interests of the EC (§ 261)	50	43	31	14	6068	7112	16	16
Breach of Plant and Animal Species Protection Regulations (§ 305)	213	181	96	77	15010	5581	13	23
Illicit Manufacturing and Possession of Nuclear Materials (§ 298)	4	1	x	x	4	x	x	x
Other economic criminal offences	2	11	x	x	1	42	x	x

x – not available.
Source: own processing based on statistics of the Ministry of the Interior of the Slovak Republic.

compared to 2016, which represents an increase of 370.10%. It is clear from Table 2 that this increase was due to a significant increase in damage caused in the area of Distortion of Data in Financial and Commercial Records (§ 259). The damage caused by this type of crime in Slovakia in 2017 amounted to 1,121,671 thousand euros, which is an increase of 1,119,712 thousand euros compared to 2016. A large part of the damage in Slovakia was caused in both years by economic criminal offences in the area of Tax and Fees Evasion (§§ 276–279) and Fraud (§ 221).

4 CONCLUSION

A well-motivated and qualified state administration, tax optimization, a comprehensible and stable tax system, well-functioning markets, a business environment and a functioning democracy and justice in the country are essential for a successful fight against economic crime, the main activity of which is to detect the fight against tax fraud.

According to the Global Economic Crime Survey 2016 (Pwc 2017), economic crime is still a serious problem affecting companies in the world. In Slovakia, more than a third (34%) of respondents met with one or more cases of economic crime in 2016. The incidence of economic crime is comparable to the average for Central and Eastern Europe (33%) and the global average (36%).

REFERENCES

Act No. 300/2005 Coll. of 20 May 2005 Criminal Code.
Chmelík, J. et al. 2005. *Úvod do hospodářské kriminality.* Plzeň: Aleš Čeněk.
Dobrovič, J. et al. 2017. Sustainable development activities aimed at combating tax evasion in Slovakia. In *Journal of Security and Sustainability Issues*, 6(4): 761–772.
Hurbánková, Ľ. 2017. Analýza trestných činov na Slovensku. In *Ekonomika a informatika: vedecký časopis FHI EU v Bratislave a SSHI*. Bratislava: Ekonomická univerzita v Bratislave, 2017, 15(2): 36–44.
Kmeťová, O. et al. 2017. Fiscal interest of the state and respecting the rights and legitimate interests of the taxable entities in case of refund of excess remission of value added tax. In *Investment management and financial innovations: international research journal. –* Ukraine: Business Perspectives, 14(2): 207–217.

Marjit, S. et al. 2017. Tax Evasion, Corruption and Tax Loopholes. In *German Economic Review*, 18(3): 283–301.

Ministry of the Interior of the Slovak Republic. 2018. Retrieved from: https://www.minv.sk/.

Novotný, O. et al. 2004. *Kriminologie.* Praha: ASPI Publishing.

Pwc. 2017. *Globálny prieskum hospodárskej kriminality 2016.* [online]. 2017 [cit. 2018–03–10]. Retrieved from: https://www.pwc.com/sk/sk/forenzne-sluzby/assets/gecs-slovensko-2016.pdf.

Recommendation No. R (81) 12 of the Committee of Ministers to member states on economic crime. 1981. Retrieved from: https://rm.coe.int/CoERMPublic-CommonSearchServices/DisplayDCTMContent?documentId=09000016806cb4f0.

Production Management and Business Development – Mihalčová et al. (Eds)
© 2019 Taylor & Francis Group, London, ISBN 978-1-138-60415-5

Sustainable CSR. The case of physically disabled employees

M. Maciaszczyk & M. Rzemieniak
Lublin University of Technology, Lublin, Poland

ABSTRACT: Modern times can be characterized by dynamical changes, globalization and growing interest of business surroundings in ethics of the functioning of companies. Therefore, a financial profit can no longer be the only goal of the company but rather an aspiration to reach the sustainable development should be the key objective. The article is focused on explanation of the essence of Corporate Social Responsibility (CSR) as well as on the phenomenon of disability and the situation of disabled employees on job market. In the article research approach leaning against preliminary research of the writing and empirical examinations were considered. The ethnographic interviews were carried out among people with disabilities and entrepreneurs running a business in Lublin. The results showed that the level of awareness of the concept of CSR among employers is still inadequate. In the paper the importance of as well as the set of recommendations for business were given.

1 INTRODUCTION

1.1 Disability as a global phenomenon

The increasing number of people that face disability is very often perceived as an extremely challenging and a problematic issue in various aspects of everyday existence, both in social and economic dimensions. Health is an extensive phenomenon containing physical health, emotional well-being and a social cohesion of a human unit (Stokols 2001). That approach can be referred to as a social model because it perceives human health from the broader perspective and challenges all the market participants to look not only at the signs of disease, illness and impairment, but also to examine the individual's overall quality of life and subjective level of well-being (Kirenko 2006, Odette et al. 2003). So the main stress is put on providing necessary services in order to minimize all the barriers to full participation in all aspects of everyday life (Aitchison 2003, Shaw & Coles 2003). Therefore the dilemma of disability is revised and defined as an inadequate support services to the specific needs of disabled people. Architectural, sensory, cognitive and economic barriers and the strong tendency for people to generalize and be discriminatory against people with impairments are also crucial in the described model (Shelton & Tucker 2005). However, disability is a multifaceted reality and is not only about using wheelchair, though such an image is created in contemporary media (Fulcher 2016).

People with different types of disabilities represent the large percent of the working age population all around the globe. Even though, due to a lack of comprehensiveness and unified data worldwide, it is not possible to rate the exact number of disabled people, it has been estimated that there are 600 million to 859 million people with different types and levels of disabilities (van Horn 2002). According to Eurostat data the indicator for disabled between 16 and 64 in European countries reaches the average level of to 15.7%. It is important to notice however, that this number is fluctuating from about 6% in Romania or Italy, 20% in Denmark, Slovenia, Sweden, Czech Republic or Portugal, up to 27.2% in United Kingdom and 32.2% in Finland (Eurostat 2006).

In modern societies the biggest problem can constitute a direct contact of healthy members of society with disabled persons, since sometimes they are burdened with stereotypes. There is also the peculiar approach based on sympathy, mercy, arrogance or ordinary inability to cooperate with the disabled person. Such an inability of healthy persons can result from the fact that the view of the individual with given impairment is scarcity. Handicapped persons should become immune to an ineptitude or even curiosity of individuals untouched with the illness. Most often disabled persons don't need, and what's more, don't wish the special treatment which would outreach their abilities of dealing with different situations.

Undoubtedly the person living in a wheelchair needs the driveway to the building, the lift or a wider passage. This form of assistance is most often sufficient, since these individuals are undergoing difficult and laborious process of rehabilitation in order to be able to freely live in society and not to ask strangers for help in any problematic situation (Łagowska & Cebula 2016).

Disability can lead to a number of results that touch not only the person himself, but also the closest environment. One of the other measurable effects of disability internationally is the destabilization of a budget, both on the national and family level.

However appropriate research and recognition of the phenomenon and its consequences could facilitate designing business and social operations that would help disabled people become knowledgeable participants in the society and the market rather than marginalized and underestimated incidental users (Maciaszczyk & Maciaszczyk 2014). The answer to those problems can be a Corporate Social Responsibility—the concept, according to which enterprises at the stage of building the strategy up are taking public interests and the environmental protection into account, as well as relations with all sorts groups of stakeholders, including disabled consumers and workers.

1.2 *Corporate social responsibility*

Although in recent years corporate social responsibility has been a topic of grooving management and academic interest (Nejati & Ghasemi 2012, Visser & Tolhurst 2010, Dobers 2009, Dahlsrud 2008, McWilliams et al. 2006, de Bakker et al. 2005), there is still no one exact and cohesive definition (Wood 2010, Scherer & Palazzo 2007, Van Marrewijk 2003) which results in empirical studies difficulties (Orlitzky et al. 2011, Lozano 2008).

Corporate Social Responsibility, also known under the names of CSR, corporate sustainability, conscience, corporate sustainable business, corporate citizenship or responsible business (Wood 1991) is a type of a concept that has been treated as voluntary corporate decisions at the level of individual organizations (Sheehy 2015). In its simplest type CSR is a company's responsibility towards its environment and the whole society. In other words CSR focuses on involving the enterprise in pro-ecological and pro-social activities, ethical and responsible functioning in contacts with stakeholders as well as on discovering and including shifting social expectations into the strategy of the management and monitoring the influence of such a strategy on the competitiveness of the company on the market (Kuraszko & Rok 2007). Both researchers and entrepreneurs deeply trust that a pure economic profit should not be the only base for the evaluation of market measures of any corporation, because companies are no expected to be conventional participants to the global economy, but to harmonize and balance activities and manage the interests of stakeholders (Jamali et al. 2008, Shahin & Zairi 2007). And even though the concept of CSR is within the area of interest for many market participants and companies are disclosing CSR information more often (Archel et al. 2008, Adams 2004), it is vastly doubtful whether the current CSR reports can satisfy the increasing demand for accountability (Milne & Gray 2007).

Corporate social responsibility may include different types of initiatives (Kotler & Lee 2008) like corporate philanthropy and charity, community volunteering, socially-responsible business practices, cause promotions and advocacy campaigns, cause-related marketing and corporate social marketing focusing on behavior or attitude change campaigns.

1.3 *Corporate social responsibility + disability*

The contemporary market makes up many challenges for enterprises. Among others there are such aspects as aging of humankind and the increase in the number of people with disabilities. The answer to such dilemmas may become the idea of Corporate Social Responsibility, especially the area related to disabilities often referred to as CSR+D or CSR-D where "D" stands for disability (Leoński 2017). The CSR-D definition prepared by ONCE Foundation in *Guide on Corporate Social Responsibility and Disability*, envisions the general enclosure of the disability issue in the different activities of companies' CSR strategy, considering people with disabilities among its stakeholders, both internal and external. However it is important to notice that such an approach to people with disabilities means that they should be treated equally, considering both equal rights and equal duties.

The CSR-D policy aims to mainstream the disability issue in the political and corporate CSR agendas and postulates the introduction of operations focused on enhancing social inclusion and employment of people with disabilities in Europe, contributing at the same time to the development of responsible competitiveness of the enterprise. It is extremely important that the strategy developed is of a long-term character and not an incidental event in the activity of the company.

2 CSR IN THE WORKPLACE

2.1 *The meaning of employment of individuals with disabilities*

Relevant European Union and international legal acts prohibit employment discrimination against individuals based on disability. It is also required to actively recruit, employ, train and promote qualified individuals with disabilities. In reality, however, both the unemployment rate of working age disabled individuals and the rate of working age disabled individuals that are not in the labor force remain significantly higher than for those without disabilities. And despite the technological development that have helped to make it achievable for people with disabilities to apply for and perform almost any job and although the situation in Poland is getting better, the considerable disproportion in the unemployment rate of individuals with and without disabilities continues to persist.

The aspect of employment is crucial as the low level of employment among people with disabilities is the foremost factor in the economic and social disparities they experience (Schur et al. 2005). Employment not only increases financial resources, but helps fully integrate people with disabilities with mainstream society throughout growing their independence, extending their social networks, building their sense of efficacy and usefulness resulting from filling an appreciated social role (Maciaszczyk 2014, Schur 2002).

2.2 The awareness level of CSR concept significance

In attempt to discover the level of CRS concept awareness among entrepreneurs running businesses in the region of Lubelskie province well as among people with disabilities an ethnographic interview was conducted. In contrast to traditional interviews where the interviewer sets the agenda, ethnographic interviews let the interviewee select the important information to share in order to provide a description of their experiences (Westby et al. 2003). That allowed to assess the current situation regarding inclusion of the disability dimension in the CSR strategy of companies.

General findings reveal that there is still a gap between theoretical knowledge of CSR-D concept and its realization. In support of social stability the companies, in cooperation with executive authorities and civil society organizations, design projects considered to address the problems of socially vulnerable population groups, like disabled.

Managers asked about a code of ethics or any document emphasizing non-discrimination of people with disabilities stated that there is no such document in their company, although they try to good practices. All of the interlocutors stated that they know that there are state laws prohibiting discrimination based on disability but at the same time they admitted that are slightly afraid of hiring people with disabilities as they are perceived as troublesome and restitutionary. Additionally at the same time there's a stereotype among healthy members of the society that disability recipients don't want to work. In realty, only a small number of social security beneficiaries admitted that they are afraid of losing their disability allowance and a vast majority stated that their desire to socialize through work has never vanished.

2.3 Why CSR-D?

Many ask themselves what to implement CSR in the area of disability for? There are a few important reasons. First of all, demographic changes activate societal transformations in the age and health structure of people which means that individuals with disabilities can appear in our environment at any time. Companies are key market actors whose activities can impact positive changes in the area of social inclusion of disabled through work. Employing disabled persons has a positive impact on the social inner and outer environment of the company.

Focusing on opportunities and not limitations of people with disabilities can change the way they are perceived among company staff. Companies then need employees who, thanks to their personal experiences, expectations and assets, can contribute to creating competitive offer and making the venture successful. Developing a product meeting the needs of a vast group of people means increasing the market of consumers and people facing different disabilities stand for an immense segment of consumers potentially interested in goods or services provided to the market.

3 CONCLUSIONS

Socially responsible enterprises in Poland often tend to forget that disability is a fundamental element that can constitute CSR policies. Entrepreneurs more often choose other, more popular CSR practices while the CSR-D concept is still trying to reach a high attention. It should be underscored that contemporary organizations must cope with market changes.

Interviews with entrepreneurs, experiences of people with disabilities and analysis of CSR reports prepared annually by companies (csrplusd.eu/cathegory/csrd/) prove that companies concentrate primarily on activities considered as classic CSR, underestimating the equality of disabled persons while looking for and hiring employees.

It is crucial to improve the staff's disability awareness as solid knowledge of disability may become a perfect basis for corporate social responsibility programme and support company's CSR strategy. To all intents and purposes in every single local environment there are individuals with disabilities. It is also very common that our partners, co-workers or employees experience invisible disabilities which, despite the fact that are concealed, do influence their existence and work.

CSR is still too recurrently mistaken for philanthropy. This is predominantly observable when attempts are made to include the aspects of disability in company's CSR activities. The phenomenon is a legacy of the earlier approach to persons with disabilities treated only as passive recipients of social security assistance and not active employees fully involved in the company's operations and being able to generate its significant profits. Such an approach to the matter and treating disability and philanthropy identically makes entrepreneurs more eager to pay for the needy rather than to employ them and actively engage in the process of creating market value of the company.

CSR can bring long-term profits rather than immediate material gains. Therefore, introducing tolerance and understanding and managing diversity in the workplace is simply investing in the enterprises' most valuable asset—people.

REFERENCES

Adams, C.A. Year. The ethical, social and environmental reporting- performance portrayal gap, *Accounting, Auditing & Accountability Journal*, 17(5): 731–757.

Aitchison, C. 2003. From Leisure and Disability to Disability Leisure: Developing Data, Definitions and Discourses. *Disability and Society*, 18(7): 955–969.

Archel, P. 2008. The organizational and operational boundaries of triple bottom line reporting: A survey, *Environmental Management*, 41(1): 106–117.

Dahlsrud, A. 2008. How corporate social responsibility is defined: An analysis of 37 definitions, *Corporate Social Responsibility and Environmental Management*, 15(1): 1–13.

de Bakker, F. G. A. et al. 2005. A bibliometric analysis of 30 years of research and theory on corporate social responsibility and corporate social performance, *Business and Society Review*, 44(3): 283–317.

Dobers, P. 2009. Corporate social responsibility: Management and methods, *Corporate Social Responsibility and Environmental Management*, 16(4): 185–191.

Fulcher, G. 2015. *Disabling policies?: A comparative approach to education policy and disability.* London, New York: Routledge.

Guide on Corporate Social Responsibility and Disability, http://rsed.fundaciononce.es/en/index.html, 2018-04-13.

http://csrplusd.eu/category/csrd/; 2018-05-01.

Jamali, D. et al.2008, Corporate governance and corporate social responsibility synergies and interrelationships. *Corporate Governance: An International Review*, 16: 443–459.

Kirenko, J. 2006. *Jakość życia w niepełnosprawności (in): Palak, Z., (Eds.): Jakość życia osób niepełnosprawnych i nieprzystosowanych społecznie.* Lublin: Wydawnictwo UMCS.

Kotler, P. & Lee, N. 2008. *Corporate social responsibility: Doing the most good for your company and your cause,* Wiley & Sons.

Kuraszko I. & Rok B. 2007. Społeczna odpowiedzialność biznesu i ekonomia społeczna. "Ekonomia Społeczna. Teksty", nr 7, 2007, s. 5–7.

Łagowska-Cebula, M. 2016. Problemy osób niepełnosprawnych. *Repozytorium Uniwersytetu Rzeszowskiego. Problemy Społeczno-kulturowe*: 48–81.

Leoński, W. 2017. Społeczna odpowiedzialność biznesu w obszarze niepełnosprawności (CSR+D), *Zeszyty Naukowe. Organizacja i Zarządzanie/Politechnika Śląska*: 253–262.

Lozano, J. M. 2008. CSR or RSC? (beyond the Humpty Dumpty syndrome), *Society and Business Review*, 3(3): 191–206.

Maciaszczyk, M. & Maciaszczyk, P. 2014. *Determinants of buying process of disabled consumers. in: Dzuričková, J., Gontkovičová, B. (eds.) Zborník recenzovaných príspevkov z 2. ročníka medzinárodnej vedeckej konferencie Marketing manažment, obchod a sociálne aspekty podnikania,* Koszyce: Podnikovohospodáska fakulta so sídlom v Košiciach, Ekonomická univerzita v Bratislave: 132–136.

Maciaszczyk, M. 2014. *Zachowania konsumenckie osób niepełnosprawnych ruchowo: raport z badań,* Lublin: Politechnika Lubelska.

McWilliams, A. et al.2006. Introduction: Corporate social responsibility: Strategic implications. *Journal of Management Studies*, 26(1): 1–18.

Milne, M. J. & Gray, R.2007. Future prospects for corporate sustainability reporting. *Sustainability accounting and accountability*, 1: 184–207.

Monachino, M. S. & Moreira, P. 2014. Corporate social responsibility and health promotion debate: An international review on the potential role of corporations. *International Journal of Healthcare Management*, 7 (1), p. 53.

Nejati, M. & Ghasemi, S. 2012. Corporate social responsibility in Iran from the perspective of employees. *Social Responsibility Journal*, 8(4): 578–588.

Odette, F. et al.2003. Barriers to Wellness Activities for Canadian Women with Disabilities, *Health Care for Women International*, 24: 125–134.

Orlitzky, M. et al. 2011. Strategic corporate social responsibility and environmental sustainability, *Business & Society*, 50(1): 6–27.

Scherer, A. G. & Palazzo, G. 2007. Toward a political conception of corporate responsibility: Business and society seen from a Habermasian perspective, *Academy of Management Review*, 32(4): 1096–1120.

Schur, L. 2002. The difference a job makes: The effects of employment among people with disabilities, Journal of Economic Issues, 36: 339–348.

Schur, L. et al.2005. Corporate culture and the employment of persons with disabilities. *Behavioral sciences and the law*, 23(1): 3–20.

Shahin, A. &Zairi, M. 2007. Corporate governance as a critical element for driving excellence in corporate social responsibility. *International Journal of Quality and Reliability Management*, 24: 753–770.

Shaw, G. & Coles, T. 2004. Disability, Holiday Making and the Tourism Industry in the UK: a preliminary survey, *Tourism Management*, 25(3): 397–404.

Sheehy, B. 2015. Defining CSR: Problems and Solutions, *Journal of Business Ethics*, 131(3): 625–648. doi:10.1007/s10551-014-2281-x.

Shelton, E.J. & Tucker, H. 2005. Tourism and Disability: Issues Beyond Access. *Tourism Review International*, 8(3): 211–219.

Stokols, D. 2001. *Creating Health-Promotive Environments: Implications for Theory and Research.* in: Jammer, M.S., Stokols, D., (Eds.), *Promoting Human Wellness: News frontiers for Research, Practice and Policy.* Berkeley, CA, University of California Press.

Van Horn, L. 2002. *Travellers with Disabilities: Market Size and Trends,* http://ncpedp.org/access/isu-travel.html, viewed on 30th of October 2017.

Van Marrewijk, M. 2003. Concepts and definitions of CSR and corporate sustainability: Between agency and communion, *Journal of Business Ethics*, 44(2–3): 95–105.

Visser, W. & Tolhurst, N. 2010. *The World Guide to CSR*, London: Routledge.

Westby, C. et al. 2003. Asking the right questions in the right ways: Strategies for ethnographic interviewing. *The ASHA Leader*, 8(8): 4–5.

Wood, D. J. 1991. Corporate Social Performance Revisited, *The Academy of Management Review*, 16(4): 691–718. doi:10.2307/258977.

Wood, D. J. 2010. Measuring corporate social performance: A review, *International Journal of Management Reviews*, 12(1): 50–84.

Production Management and Business Development – Mihalčová et al. (Eds)
© *2019 Taylor & Francis Group, London, ISBN 978-1-138-60415-5*

Innovative activity in Poland

P. Marzec & G. Krawczyk
The John Paul II Catholic University of Lublin, Poland

ABSTRACT: The article discusses innovative activity in Poland based on selected measures, namely: the average share of innovative enterprises in the total number of enterprises, expenditures on innovative activity in enterprises in relation to GDP and per one professionally active person, expenditures on innovative activity in enterprises in relation to gross fixed capital formation, expenditures on innovative activity in enterprises from the services and industrial sectors, expenditures on innovative activity in enterprises according to sources of financing of innovative activity—services and industrial enterprises, innovative industrial enterprises by size classes in total, categorised in terms of introduced innovations and by ownership sectors in total. Quantitative data from public statistics indicate the existence of a significant innovation potential among a small group of companies dealing with innovations (about 16.1% of companies identified in the public statistics in 2016). In the coming years, we can expect further development of the innovative potential.

1 INTRODUCTION

In recent decades, a huge increase in the importance of innovation in economic processes has been observed. What is important, this process concerns many spheres of life, influencing not only the dynamics of development but also the perception of future social and economic trends (Prystrom 2012). Such advanced processes taking place in the modern world economy as globalization, economic and social integration, regionalization or development of economy based on knowledge and information have not taken place so far. Over the last few decades, they have led to an increase in the importance of such economic categories as: innovations, innovativeness. Innovation, which has accompanied humanity since the beginning of time, determines the strength and speed of the development of civilization. Nowadays, however, the sphere of innovativeness has become an exceptionally specific area of adjustment of the functioning of companies and the country to the rapidly changing market conditions and environment in the world economy (Wosiek 2017). J.A. Schumpeter is the author of the theory of economic growth and business cycle induced by breakthrough innovations. It is the so-called Schumpeter's economy that originates from it. Schumpeter's position on this range of innovations, which is now described as classic, related to the following five cases (Schumpeter 1960, quoted from: Grzybowska 2013):

– introduction of new products with which the consumers have not dealt so far into the production

– introduction of a new production method which has not yet been tested in the industry concerned
– opening of a new market
– use of new raw materials or semi-finished products (including the acquisition of a new source of supply for raw materials or semi-finished products)
– introduction of a new industrial organization (e.g. creation of a monopoly or its abolition)

Innovativeness is one of the most important economic issues from both a theoretical and a political perspective. Many governments are taking action to transform the country into a knowledge-based economy, where innovation is a key driver of economic development. In countries such as Poland, which are not leaders in the international technological race, but whose distance from the leaders is not very long, the key to the transformation to a knowledge-based economy is not only the ability to innovate, but also the ability to absorb innovations developed abroad (Truskolaski 2013).

Innovativeness is one of the important factors in the growth of the competitiveness of enterprises. The specificity of innovation means that there is no universal indicator to measure it at macroeconomic level. In practice, there are many measures used to determine the level of innovativeness (Ambroziak 2017). This article attempts to assess the innovative activity in Poland. A low level of innovativeness of the Polish economy was assumed as a research problem. The analysis used Local Data Bank maintained by the Central Statistical Office and available on its websites at www.stat.gov.pl.

2 INNOVATIVENESS IN POLAND

When analysing the average share of innovative enterprises in the total number of enterprises, we observe, until 2011, a decrease from 22.5% to 13.8% in year 2012, then we observe a slight increase and a decrease. In 2016, an increase to the level of 16.1% is observed (Fig. 1).

When analyzing expenditures on innovative activity in enterprises in relation to GDP, we can observe a decrease in this indicator in the examined period 2007–2013 from 2.38% to 1.99% in 2013. Since 2013, observed is a rebound and an increase in this indicator. In 2015, it reaches 2.43% (Fig. 2).

When analyzing expenditures on innovative activity in enterprises per one professionally active person, we can observe an increase in the examined indicator from the minimum value of PLN 1506 in 2007 per one person. In 2015, the indicator reaches the maximum value of PLN 2515 per person. In 2016, the indicator slightly decreases to PLN 2260 per person (Fig. 3).

When analyzing expenditures on innovative activity in enterprises in relation to gross fixed capital formation, we can observe a decrease in the indicator over the examined period. In 2007, it was 12,24% and in 2014, it was only 11.08 (Fig. 4).

Total expenditures on innovative activity in enterprises from the service sector in 2016 amounted to PLN 10 billion 700 million. This included expenditures on research and development in the amount of over PLN 4 billion. Total capital expenditure on fixed assets amounted to PLN 2.6 billion. Total capital expenditures on fixed assets (machinery and technical equipment) amounted to PLN 2 billion. The purchase of software amounted to almost PLN 1 billion. The marketing associated with the

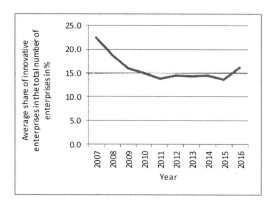

Figure 1. Average share of innovative enterprises in the total number of enterprises.
Source: Own study based on CSO (GUS) data.

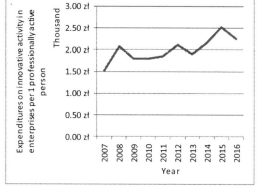

Figure 3. Expenditures on innovative activity in enterprises per 1 professionally active person.
Source: Own study based on CSO (GUS) data.

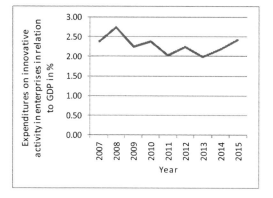

Figure 2. Expenditures on innovative activity in enterprises in relation to GDP.
Source: Own study based on CSO (GUS) data.

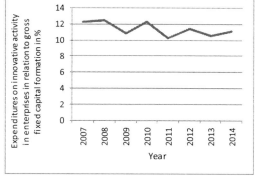

Figure 4. Expenditures on innovative activity in enterprises in relation to gross fixed capital formation.
Source: Own study based on CSO (GUS) data.

introduction of new or substantially improved products was PLN 600 million. Capital expenditures on fixed assets—buildings and premises, civil engineering objects and land amounted to PLN 600 million. The purchase of knowledge from external sources was PLN 500 million. Capital expenditures on fixed assets—imported machinery and technical equipment amounted to PLN 500 million (Fig. 5).

Total expenditures on innovative activity in industrial enterprises in 2016 amounted to PLN 28 billion. These included expenditures on research and development amounting to PLN 5 billion. Total capital expenditure on fixed assets amounted to PLN 21 billion. Total capital expenditure on fixed assets (machinery and technical equipment) amounted to PLN 14 billion. The purchase of software amounted to PLN 500 million. The marketing associated with the introduction of new or substantially improved products was PLN 400 million. Capital expenditures on fixed assets—buildings and premises, civil engineering

objects and land amounted to PLN 7 billion. The purchase of knowledge from external sources was PLN 150 million. Capital expenditures on fixed assets—imported machinery and technical equipment amounted to PLN 5 billion (Fig. 6).

When analyzing expenditures on innovative activity in enterprises according to the sources of financing of innovative activity in enterprises from the service sector, it was found that the total amount of the funds was almost PLN 11 billion. Own resources amounted to PLN 9.5 billion. The budget was PLN 170 million. Resources from abroad amounted to PLN 300 million. Bank debts amounted to PLN 450 million (Fig. 7).

When analyzing expenditures on innovative activity in enterprises according to the sources of financing of innovative activity in industrial enterprises, it was found that the total resources amounted to almost PLN 28 billion. Own resources

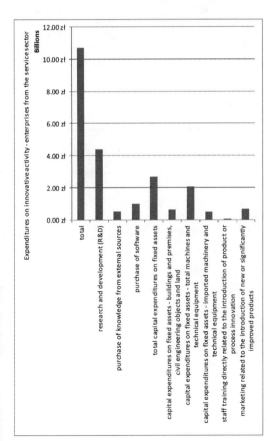

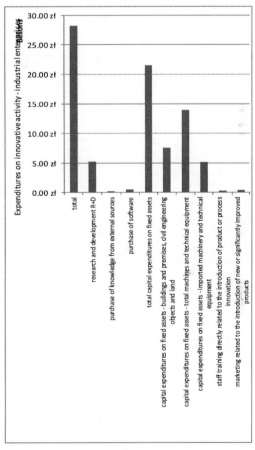

Figure 5. Expenditures on innovative activity—enterprises in the service sector.
Source: Own study based on CSO (GUS) data.

Figure 6. Expenditures on innovative activity—industrial companies.
Source: Own study based on CSO (GUS) data.

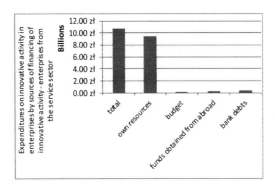

Figure 7. Expenditures on innovative activity in enterprises according to the sources of financing of innovative activity—enterprises from the service sector.
Source: Own study based on CSO (GUS) data.

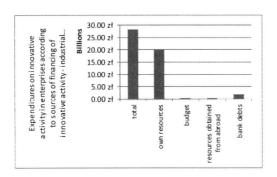

Figure 8. Expenditures on innovative activity in enterprises according to the sources of financing of innovative activity—industrial enterprises.
Source: Own study based on CSO (GUS) data.

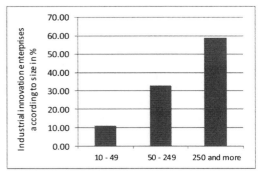

Figure 9. Industrial innovation enterprises according to size.
Source: Own study based on CSO (GUS) data.

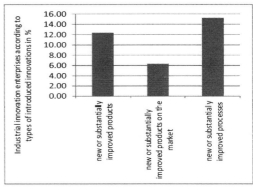

Figure 10. Industrial innovation enterprises according to types of introduced innovations.
Source: Own study based on CSO (GUS) data.

amounted to PLN 20 billion. The budget was PLN 500 million. Resources from abroad amounted to PLN 500 million. Bank debts amounted to PLN 2 billion (Fig. 8).

Then analyzing innovative enterprises taking into account their size as measured by the number of employees, it was found that most of them, i.e. 58%, were enterprises with more than 250 employees. There are 32% of enterprises employing from 50 to 250 people. 10% are enterprises employing from 10–49 people (Fig. 9).

Innovation is the implementation of a new or substantially improved product (manufacture or service) or process, a new organizational method or a new marketing method in business practice, the organization of a workplace or relations with the environment. Products, processes as well as organizational and marketing methods do not have to be novel for the market in which the enterprise operates, but they have to be novel for the enterprise itself at least. The products, processes

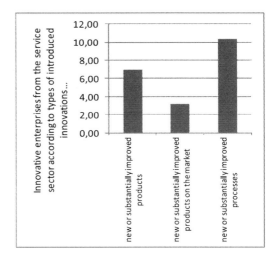

Figure 11. Innovative enterprises from the service sector according to the type of introduced innovations.
Source: Own study based on CSO (GUS) data.

158

and methods do not have to be developed by the enterprise itself, they can be developed by another enterprise or by a unit of a different nature (e.g. research and development institute, research and development center, university, etc.). When analyzing innovative enterprises according to the types of introduced innovations, most of them are new or substantially improved processes (15.23%). New or substantially improved products account for 12.40%. New or substantially improved products for the market are 6.26% (Fig. 10).

When analyzing innovative enterprises according to the types of introduced innovations, most of them are new or substantially improved processes (10.40%). There are 6.91% of new or substantially improved products. There are 3.14% of new or substantially improved products on the market (Fig. 11).

3 SUMMARY

The article presents situations in the field of innovativeness in Poland. Recent years have brought changeable trends in the numbers describing the situation in this area. In conclusion, a number of issues need to be pointed out:

- When analyzing the average share of innovative enterprises in the total number of enterprises, we observe a downward trend until 2011
- When analyzing expenditures on innovative activity in enterprises in relation to GDP, we observe a downward trend of the analyzed indicator
- When analyzing expenditures on innovative activity in enterprises per one professionally active person, we observe an upward trend of the analyzed indicator
- When analyzing expenditures on innovative activity in enterprises in relation to gross fixed capital formation, we observe a downward trend of the analyzed indicator
- Total expenditures on innovative activity in enterprises from the service sector in 2016 amounted to PLN 10 billion 700 million
- Total expenditures on innovative activity in industrial enterprises in 2016 amounted to PLN 28 billion

- When analyzing expenditures on innovative activity in enterprises according to sources of financing of innovative activity in enterprises from the service sector, it was found that own resources amounted to PLN 9.5 billion, the budget was PLN 170 million, the resources from abroad amounted to PLN 300 million, bank debts amounted to PLN 450 million.
- When analyzing expenditures on innovative activity in enterprises according to sources of financing of innovative activity in industrial enterprises, it was found that own funds amounted to PLN 20 billion, budget funds amounted to PLN 500 million, resources from abroad amounted to PLN 500 million, bank debts amounted to PLN 2 billion.
- When analyzing innovative enterprises taking into account their size measured by the number of employed, it was found that most of them, i.e. 58%, are enterprises employing over 250 people.
- When analyzing innovative enterprises according to the types of introduced innovations, most of them are new or substantially improved processes.

REFERENCES

Ambroziak Ł.A., 2017. Pozycja konkurencyjna nowych państw członkowskich UE w handlu towarami zaawansowanymi technologicznie. *Ekonomista* 5/2017: 506–526.

Grzybowska B., 2013. Wiedza i innowacje jako współczesne czynniki wzrostu gospodarczego, *Ekonomista* 4/2013: 521–532.

Prystrom J., 2012. Narodowy system innowacji jako czynnik rozwoju gospodarczego na przykładzie Szwecji, *Ekonomista* 4/2012: 499–513.

Truskolaski S., 2013. Działalność innowacyjna inwestorów zagranicznych i przedsiębiorstw polskich, *Ekonomista* 4/2013: 533–552.

Wosiek R., 2017. Konferencja naukowa: "Innowacyjność i konkurencyjność międzynarodowa. Nowe wyzwania dla przedsiębiorstw i państwa" (Szkoła Główna Handlowa w Warszawie, 17 października 2016 r.), *Ekonomista* 5/2017: 601–607.

Production Management and Business Development – Mihalčová et al. (Eds)
© 2019 Taylor & Francis Group, London, ISBN 978-1-138-60415-5

Information processing by computer-based simulators

S. Mildeová

University of Finance and Administration, Prague, Czech Republic

ABSTRACT: The current environment of business enterprises hints at the changing conditions in the market and growing customer demand. The computer science field reacts to the new requirements for information and knowledge support by developing new information technologies. The aim of this paper is to show computer business simulators as useful software tools that enable enterprises to benefit from the large amount of available information. The author will use examples from Czech enterprises for specific cases of applications of computer business simulators, based on System Dynamics Modeling. There is some evidence showing that these software tools are being used to optimize existing solutions as well as to search for new ones in different fields and for a variety of issues. Application of computer business simulators will be illustrated for issues ranging from developing an effective and measurable strategy, uncovering hidden resources, and project management to predictions of risks and unintended consequences.

1 INTRODUCTION

The developed world is undergoing constant changes with regards to market conditions, evolving technology, and growing customer demand, as well as, sales management and sales communication and their tools. Adequate and timely response to this change requires relevant information. Companies today have an incredible amount of diverse information at their disposal. Information in itself is no longer a competitive advantage for the company, however. In order to gain or maintain a competitive advantage, the company has to be able to use the variety of information to its advantage and to expand the company's knowledge portfolio (Lasi 2014), (Havlicek & Roubal 2014).

One way of information processing is to work with information in the modeling and subsequent simulation experimentation. Experimenting makes sense in areas where it would otherwise be unrealistic or very costly. This is the case for decision-making at higher management levels. Using simulation experimentation, management can anticipate the consequences of their decisions and optimize decision-making outcomes. If an interactive simulation interface is created above the simulation model, the manager has a handy software tool to uncover hidden resources, explore the implications of the intended changes, anticipate risks and unintended consequences.

The aim of the paper is to discuss business simulators. That this is a useful software tool for information processing is demonstrated through cases of application of computer business simulators in the practice of Czech enterprises. The author bases

their analysis on System Dynamics, whose modeling tools are suitable for information support of decision-making processes at higher levels of management. The methods used are research activity, analysis of publicly accessible information about companies and a controlled interview with the representative of one of the supplier companies.

2 COMPUTER-BASED SIMULATORS

2.1 *System dynamics modeling*

The trend towards Digital Information Economy is associated with innovations in the field of information and communication technologies driven by professionals from the field (Pavlicek et al. 2011). An innovative way of information processing for organizations is Business Intelligence. An integral part of Business Intelligence is computer modeling. Fiser (2012) states that thousands of formal models are transformed into computer programs daily.

This article is based on System Dynamics, or more precisely, Business Dynamics. Business Dynamics explains how System Dynamics can be successfully applied to solve business and organizational problems (Sterman 2000).

Systems dynamics was originally developed by Jay W. Forrester (Forrester 1961) to help in the managerial decision-making process. It deals with the behavior of systems as they change in time. This includes defining the elements of the system and marking their mutual relationships to understand the behavior of the system within the process of time. Systems dynamics methodology, and its tools, help to find causal relationships, delays and feedback loops often leading to a different behavior of the system than was originally desired. Model building is at the core of System Dynamics. The basic building blocks of System Dynamics models are Stock and Flow diagrams (SFD) (Fig. 1).

System Dynamics modelling (mainly its feedback principles) is similar to the concepts of cybernetics and model-based cybernetically grounded management (Schwaninger 2015). Compared to the agent-based simulation, which is also a frequent computer modeling method (Vojtko & Heskova 2010), System Dynamics models are a continuous simulation as is shown in Figure 2.

System Dynamics is used not only in the field of information processing by organizations, it is a completely universal method (Iandolo 2018). For example, in the Czech Republic it is applied in the field of medicine (Bob et al. 2009). System Dynamics is also useful in education for training specialists (Krejci et al. 2011) or it is used to make education more effective (Svirakova 2017).

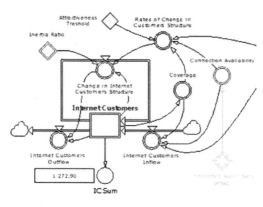

Figure 1.   Stock and Flow diagram. (Source: Author).

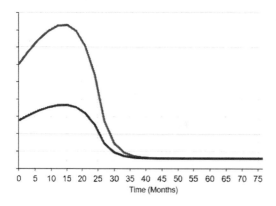

Figure 2.   Simulation result. (Source: Author).

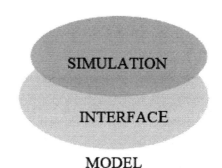

Figure 3.   Structure of the simulator. (Source: Author according to Hirsch 2006).

2.2   *Business simulator*

For routine use of the model, its transformation to business simulator is suitable. We could recognize a simulator as a useful tool for reflecting real systems behavior for estimations of a future development. However, a widely used, fixed definition of a simulator probably does not exist, and it is changing due to simulator development. Certainly, business simulators came out of flight simulators that are still widely used (Socha et al. 2017).

A business simulator consists of three parts (Hirsch 2006). The model is a core structure with all equations defined. (It is stock-and-flow diagram in our case). The interface represents a layer between user and model. There are usually inputs, outputs, help indices, etc. that should help an user to control the model. The simulation environment is everything else that is needed for successful work (printed materials, techniques for using the simulator—teamwork, coaching, etc.) (Fig. 3).

Interactive interface allows for easy control of the simulation over time, it is possible to quickly verify the planned changes and their impact on the business operation and to study the influence of varying environment. We must realize that the user-friendly interface programmed above the model corresponds to today's concept of Business Intelligence rather than just the model itself. According to Mosko (2015), multimedia is already a standard.

3   RESULTS OF A SURVEY CONDUCTED IN CZECH COMPANIES

3.1   *Survey*

In this section, the author will present the results of computer business simulator search, based on

System Dynamics Modeling, in the practice of Czech enterprises. The starting point is a survey conducted by Smutny (2014), where the importance of using the internet for marketing purposes is demonstrated in the environment of Czech companies. In the survey, two key companies have been found to develop Business simulators based on System Dynamics. The first firm is Proverbs, and historically, it was the first in the Czech Republic to do such business. The other firm, called Solvica, is a typical startup. The following cases are based on the practice of this company (Solvica 2018). The reason is that Solvica is cooperating with leading Czech suppliers of enterprise information systems. This is important for information processing, or rather, integration of business simulator in the enterprise ICT applications and systems.

3.2 *Business simulators in Czech companies*

The first illustration of Business simulator is within project management in the field of information and communication technologies. A specific area of project management are ICT projects. All major interventions in information and communication technologies take the form of projects. A business simulator is a product which is useful and it makes it easier for people to work in this rapidly evolving environment of modern technology. Software development requires more than a few clever programmers today. Complex teams of architects, technicians, analysts and testers work on more complex ICT projects. Additionally, we must consider deadlines getting shorter and increasing demands of customers. Using a dynamic simulation, the project manager quickly and easily detects how busy the teams will be over time and how many will be needed in each project phase. It is a powerful way to assign team members work in situations where a company receives tens or hundreds of requests each week and/or accumulates unprocessed ticketing in the helpdesk system. A simulator is an application that reliably assigns work to team members as a project manager would. According to the requirements for a particular task it selects the most suitable worker who is able to solve it and who, on the basis of the actual workload, will be able to complete it as the first one. Work capacity of individual team members is monitored on a panel that updates with each change. Here they can see if they can meet all the required deadlines, at the same time. So, the simulator enables constant control over the results of the work.

The second use of the business simulator is demonstrated the area which every business must face—creating budgets. Budget preparation is often necessary to spend a lot of time collecting documents from various sources before management finishes successfully. The simulation software solution reduces the time needed to create a budget by up to 40%. When creating a budget, more complex calculations, which are necessary for production, are needed. Using a clear user interface can minimize errors in calculations. The simulator will streamline budgeting and achieve standardization of the plan across departments or plants. Therefore, each individual budget can be compared to one another. Subsequently, the final results can be presented clearly and attractively thanks to the visualization that the simulator allows. A business simulator will help keep every deadline.

An interesting illustration of a business simulator assumes that sometimes production is higher, sometimes lower. The manufacturing sector reflects this, and it must face staff shortages. In addition to seasonal fluctuations, there are fluctuations due to buyers. Additionally, once the company produces for more customers, the order cycles overlap and the situation becomes easily disordered. Managing human resources in a manufacturing company is a demanding task. This means increasing the number of employees only when it is necessary and at the same time saving the costs associated with redundancy in a weaker period. By taking advantage of the dynamic simulation, the company can estimate the changes in production environment and predict its future development.

The last area that has been selected to illustrate Business Simulator options is hospital management. Demand for health care is steadily rising and with it the financial cost of health services, while resources remain limited. The investigated simulator makes it possible to handle work with resources, personnel and medical technology and materials. The acquired insight can provide support for any critical decision taken by the hospital; for example, when it comes to reducing the number of staff, failing an important device, or increasing the capacity of bed care. Simulation calculations have shown how to efficiently use expensive devices, reduce the number of workers needed, and even prevent full waiting rooms. By modifying selected factors, management can quickly and easily check how changes are reflected in the operation of the hospital or its divisions. It is able to verify the most appropriate way of expanding the hospital, what impact the construction of a new department will have, and whether time is not being wasted due to the inappropriate layout of the space. Management can then verify their plans and designs before investing in building modifications. This helps to prevent subsequent changes, which are often costly and time consuming, avoiding unnecessary costs and complications.

An important issue for hospital facilities is the ongoing struggle with a shortage of qualified staff related to labor market disparities (Potuzakova & Mildeova 2015). The reasons for the systemic character of the healthcare organizations include a variety of workplace features and the need for highly skilled workers. This prolongs and raises the costs of recruitment and training. The created business simulator allows the HR department to make changes before the operations of individual departments are compromised. Through the integration of the personnel information system in the simulation model, it is possible to design and implement the most suitable personnel solution and, in addition, to anticipate the development of the situation in the future (Solvica 2018).

4 DISCUSSION

Published research in the area that the paper discusses focuses on application of the various System Dynamics models. These are for example the simulation of farmers' behavior (Kolackova et al. 2017), auditing of information systems (Mildeova et al. 2013), (Dalihod 2014), Dynamic modelling of national healthcare system (Jankuj & Voracek 2015) or the airport efficiency modeling (Letavkova et al. 2013). Mostly, there was no interface above the model, so it was not considered a simulator.

Also, none of the authors investigated the issue in the environment of supplier companies, which is where the contribution of this paper can be found. The researched supplier companies Proverbs and Solvica are Small and Medium Enterprises (SMEs). According to Belas et al (2014) or (Hajduova 2015), SMEs play an important role in the economy of any country, but their business activities are confronted with a number of business risks. For startups such as Solvica, some of whose products have been described in the paper, these risks are often associated with foreign capital.

The combination of research and the application level of corporate practice is in line with the Europe 2020 strategy. It is worth mentioning that the Czech Republic is not lagging in comparison with other countries, as stated by Dulova Spisakova et al. (2017). Therefore, the author's next exploration within the Europe 2020 Contexts will probably focus on: 1. comparison of the offers of Solvica, Proverbs, or other companies, 2. an analysis of the profitability and sustainability of companies offering BS, 3. a view from the side of customer needs, 4. an investigation of companies' awareness and knowledge of these tools.

5 CONCLUSION

The topic of the paper was business simulators. The author within the practice of Czech enterprises searched and analysed specific cases of applications of computer business simulators, based on System Dynamics Modeling. In the survey, two suppliers have been found who use System Dynamics to develop Business simulators.

The survey shows that dynamic simulation helps both private companies and the public sector. As far as business is concerned, we have shown that the simulator is a product that will help both manufacturing and non-production companies improve quality for their customers. Solvica, whose products the article has highlighted, states (Solvica 2018) that for designs made with the support of dynamic simulation, it is possible to save up to 25% of costs, reduce the time needed by up to 50%, check the assumptions in a fraction of time otherwise needed and with zero risk.

Research has shown that solutions are being custom prepared for companies and so they can allow for the specifics of both the client and the sector. For example, project management in ICT companies is now directly linked to the question of how to increase the efficiency of project management and the success of new projects. The answer to this question is to make the right changes from the beginning; however, this is not an easy task. A business simulator is a way for a computer company not to pay unnecessary overtime but to promote work efficiency instead. It is a powerful way to assign team members work. This can help the project manager to avoid problems such as cost overruns, failure to meet deadlines or costly extras. A business simulator will help keep every deadline during budget preparation, as well. Budget preparation is a complex process that requires a lot of effort, and it is typical for every business. Errors are not avoidable and most will be reflected here. Using business simulations can minimize errors in calculations, plans can be made easily and with clear overview.

Another illustration of business simulator related to the manufacturing sector. Today, a rapid response to increase in demand is essential here. In addition to seasonal fluctuations, there are fluctuations due to buyers who confirm orders only a short time in advance. Manufacturing companies often have to rely on agency workers to manage the increase in workload. To handle fluctuations in demand effectively and keep up with competitors, the company should have as many employees as is needed at any given time. With business simulator, the most appropriate staffing arrangement can be found while maintaining or even reducing payroll costs and with the guarantee of covering all customer requirements. Based on order prediction, the ideal ratio is set between permanent staff and external agency staff. Finally, the reader saw that business simulator is an effective ICT tool for hospital management, i.e. a nonprofit organization. The simulation helps to cope with the increasing pressure to increase the efficiency of hospital facilities, raising not only the quality of care, but also satisfaction at the workplace. With a dynamic business plan, the optimal solution for delivering high-quality services while respecting the budget can be found.

We have proven that whether a company is looking for a better HR strategy, wants to increase the efficiency of management and success of new projects, or increase efficiency in production, a business simulator is a useful tool to boost business and find the best solution. Thanks to the simulation, or more specifically, using a computer model that is the core of a simulator, issues can be identified and solved more quickly. Obtained insight supported by objective analysis can be used to optimize existing solutions as well as to search for new and testing risky scenarios. With dynamic simulation, it is possible to respond appropriately and in a timely manner to changes to support the company's strategic goals for sustainable development and lasting competitiveness.

ACKNOWLEDGMENTS

The paper is a result of an institutional research project no. 7429/2018/08 "Analysis of ICT startups" supported by University of Finance and Administration, Prague.

REFERENCES

Belas, J., Habanik, J., Cipovova, E. & Novak, P. 2014. Actual trends in business risks for small and medium enterprises. Case studies from the Czech Republic and Slovakia. *Ikonomicheski Izsledvania*, 23(4): 159–181.

Bob, P., Susta, M., Chladek, J., Glaslova, K. & Palus, M. 2009. Chaos in schizophrenia associations, reality or metaphor? *International Journal of Psychophysiology*, 73(3): 179–185.

Breckova, P., Mares, D. & Lansky, J. 2015. Prosperity and Stability of SME Segment by Industry in the Czech Republic. In Loster, T. & Pavelka, T. (eds.), *The 9th International Days of Statistics and Economics* (220–230), Prague: VSE.

Dalihod, M. 2014. Communication Audit Conclusions of IT Processes through Instruments of System Thinking. *Acta Informatica Pragensia*, 3(3): 251–258, DOI: 10.18267/j.aip.52.

Dulova Spisakova, E., Mura, L., Gontkovicova, B. & Hajduova, Z. 2017. R&D in the context of europe 2020 in selected countries. *Economic Computation and Economic Cybernetics Studies and Research*, 51(4): 243–261.

Fiser. J. 2012. Will we think in programming languages? *Acta Informatica Pragensia*, 1(1): 1–21. DOI: 10.18267/j.aip.12779.

Forrester, J.W. 1961. *Industrial Dynamics*. Portland: Productivity Press.

Hajduova, Z., Lacko, R., Mildeova, S. & Stricik, M. 2015. Case study in the field of innovation in selected companies in Slovak Republic. *Analele Stiintifice ale Universitatii Al I Cuza din Iasi—Sectiunea Stiinte Economice* [online], 62(1): 103–119. DOI: 10.1515/aicue-2015-0008.

Havlicek, K. & Roubal, O. 2014. Sales management and sales communication of SMEs. *European Research Studies Journal*,16(4): 29–42.

Hirsch, G. 2006. Designing Simulation-Based Learning Environments: Helping People Understand Complex System, In: *International Conference of the System Dynamics Society*, New York: University at Albany (1–48).

Iandolo, F., Barile, S., Armenia, S. & Carrubbo, L. 2018. A system dynamics perspective on a viable systems approach definition for sustainable value. *Sustainability Science*, 1–19, DOI: org/10.1007/s11625-018-0565-2., in press.

Jankuj, M. & Voracek, J. 2015. Dynamic modelling of national healthcare system. *Measuring Business Excellence*, 19(3): 76–89.

Kolackova, G., Krejci, I. & Ticha, I. 2017. Dynamics of the small farmers' behaviour—scenario simulations. *Agricultural Economics (Czech Republic)*, 63(3): 103–120.

Krejci, I., Kvasnicka, R. & Domeova, L. 2011. Introducing system dynamics at CULS Prague. *Journal on Efficiency and Responsibility in Education and Science*, 4(4): 187–196.

Lasi, H., Kemper, H.G., Fettke, P., Feld, T. & Hoffmann, M. 2014. Industry 4.0. *Business & Information Systems Engineering*, 4(6): 239–242.

Letavkova, D., Matuskova, S. & Neustupa, Z. System dynamics simulations for airport efficiency. 2013. In *International Multidisciplinary Scientific GeoConference Surveying Geology and Mining Ecology Management, SGEM*, 1: 241–248. Albena: SGEM, DOI: 10.5593/SGEM2013/BB2.V1/S07.0327145092.

Mildeova, S., Dalihod, M. & Kral, M. 2013. System Thinking in Informatics. In: *CONFENIS – 2013. 7th International Conference on Research and Practical Issues of Enterprise Information Systems*. Linz: Trauner Verlag (290–298).

Mosko, J., Lokoc, J., Grosup, T., Skopal, T. & Lansky, J. 2015. MLES: Multilayer exploration structure for multimedia exploration. *Communications in Computer and Information Science*, 539: 135–144.

Pavlicek, A., Sigmund, T., Oskrdal, V. & Hubacek, J. 2011. A comparison of national ICT metrics, indicators and models in successful ICT driven economies. In Kaluza, J. et al. (eds.), *9th International Conference on Strategic Management and its Support by Information Systems* (125–133). Ostrava: TU Ostrava.

Potuzakova, Z. & Mildeova, S. 2015. Analysis of causes and consequences of the youth unemployment in the EU]. Politická ekonomie, 63(7): 877–894. DOI:10.18267/j.polek.1043.

Schwaninger, M. 2015. Model-based Management: A Cybernetic Concept. *Systems Research and Behavioral Science*, 32(6): pp. 564–578.

Smutny, Z. 2014. The use of social media for marketing purposes by Czech companies doing business in the environment of services on the internet: A national survey. In Doucek, Chroust, G. & Oskrdal, V. (eds.), *22nd Interdisciplinary Information Management Talks* (145–151), Linz: Johannes Kepler Universitat Linz.

Socha, V., Socha L., Hanakova, L. & Vlcek, S. 2017. The use efficiency of flight simulators for pilots training In Stofova L. & Szaryszova, P. (eds.), *New Trends in Process Control and Production Management: Proceedings of the International Conference on Marketing Management, Trade, Financial and Social Aspects of Business (MTS 2017)*, London: CRC Press/Balkema.

Solvica. 2018. Retrieved from //http://www.solvica.cz/.

Sterman, J.D. 2000. *Business Dynamics. Systems Thinking and Modeling for a Complex World.* Boston: Irwin/McGraw-Hill.

Svirakova, E. 2017. Using systems thinking as an efficient tool for teaching transfer of creative innovations. *Turkish Online Journal of Educational Technology*, December Special Issue INTE: 786–796.

Vojtko, V. & Heskova, M. 2010. Analysing retailing opportunities and threats using agent-based simulation. In Soliman, KS (ed.), *Proceedings of the 14th IBIMA Conference on Knowledge Management and Innovation in Advancing Economies, IBIMA 2010*, 4: 2514–2523. Istanbul: IBIMA.

Production Management and Business Development – Mihalčová et al. (Eds)
© 2019 Taylor & Francis Group, London, ISBN 978-1-138-60415-5

Social counselling to families in Slovakia

A. Novotná, V. Révayová & A. Žilová
Department of Social Work, Faculty of Pedagogy, Catholic University, Ružomberok, Slovakia

ABSTRACT: The paper is devoted to the conditions and availability of social counselling to families in Slovakia as part of the social development of human capital and support to families in various stressful situations. The authors briefly define the theoretical backgrounds of the subject, especially the family's strenuous situations, goals, functions, and the role of social counseling. They also offer the results of empirical research on the availability and focus of social counseling to families within the state, self-governing and private sector provided in Slovakia. Quantitative research strategy was implemented.

1 INTRODUCTION

The family undergoes some changes and stressful situations that may be associated with its developmental stages, the workforce of family members, and their personal orientation or preferences. In these situations, the family encounters everyday problems that may, in certain circumstances, be long-term, or the family is not able to solve these situations by themselves anymore. Social counseling is one of the options to find solutions to these situations and, at the same time, to eliminate the possible negative consequences. In this context, we understand social counseling for families as one of the tools to develop human capital.

2 SOCIAL COUNSELLING AS A WAY TO DEVELOP AND MAINTAIN SOCIAL CAPITAL

The development of social capital is an essential part of management, particularly process management in enterprises. In family life, the family faces the above-mentioned problems resulting from:

1. life-cycle of the family- birth of a child, joint housing, marriage, death of a family member, elderly person in the family,
2. the so-called "fate" such as a disease or disability of a family member and other natural, socio-economic changes (natural disasters, changes in the social system that the family can not adapt to, technological changes or changes of the location of production, etc.) that have an impact on life and family functions.
3. personal or social features or stereotypes of the family or its members – no parenting skills, the bad financial management, the low resilience of

individuals or family in general, or as the result of other changes, weak working habits and discipline that are transmitted within the family to other members.

The social system offers many opportunities to develop social capital, for example, education, further education – within the framework of schools, out-of-school and corporate trainings and it will not be discussed in this paper. In the paper, we focus on the social counselling to develop and maintain social capital in the above-mentioned situations. Social counselling helps individuals and families to mobilize or develop their own strengths and competencies while facing the strenuous situations. Unlike social work, which has currently a more donor character, social counselling is based on the principle "help to self-help" Social counselling does not reduce the ability of the family to resolve their problems by its own, but empower them, orientate the family, and develop their abilities and options. Social counselling is the suitable way to develop and care of the social potential in enterprises as it develops and supports the functional elements of the family rather than creating the "social client" in the sense of helpless families and individuals not trying to solve their situation but waiting for the solution or means for the solution from outside.

The social counselling should be the first instance of solving family problems, although if family's strengths are being exhausting. The social counselling prevents the family from the invalidism or from the disability to work. However, three preconditions need to be fulfilled. Firstly, employees and managers of enterprises need to be aware of this option of support and development. The second precondition is the sufficient quality of the provided social counselling, which is discussed on another professional platform. The third condition is the availability of social counselling, which was the subject of our research conducted in Slovakia and the results are presented in this paper.

3 SOCIAL COUNSELLING AND FAMILY

3.1 *History of the social counselling*

The counselling itself was in the form of an inexpert "advising" in the whole history of mankind part of the communication and social life of the people At the turn of the 19th and 20th centuries, counselling began to be used as a method in some professions. Social counselling was basically linked to two categories of situations: the first was to address people's problems who were incapable to engage to the work process for various reasons (sickness, disability, etc.) and with all the consequences of this phenomenon for individuals, family and society. The second category was the prevention of problems and the consequence of these problems within the social counselling. This category was essential in the emergence of social counseling as a profession in the industrialization period, namely the effort of employers to support their employees in solving their personal or family problems, which were not explicitly relevant to the work performance, in the sense of "satisfied workforce, is a powerful workforce".

3.2 *Social counselling and its institutional provision*

Act no. 485/2013 amending Act no. 448/2008 on social services, defines social counselling as "professional activity aimed at assisting a person in an unfavorable social situation. Social counselling is done at the level of basic social counselling and specialized social counselling."

Strieženec (1996, p. 157) states that "social counselling is based on help, support, development, optimal empowerment of the individual and better orientation in life". This simplicity of definition is focused on the nature of social counselling. Gabura (2013) looks at the goal of social counselling in a more specific way and points out that "it is necessary to find a consensus between clients and the social environment in which they live, more acceptable status positions of clients within an existing social structure. Social counseling is, therefore, a tool that helps a person to make decisions, act in a way that is meaningful, constructive, and socially useful. It enables to fulfil the social needs of people who often feel threatened, isolated, misunderstood, confused, frustrated or lost in the world."

Social counselling is provided to the family at the level of basic and specialized counselling (Legal Act No. 448/2008). Given the nature and extent of the problem, the provision of social counselling, depending on its level, is provided by social counselling subjects such as:

- the state and its organizations (Office of Social Affairs and Family, Social Insurance Agency)
- public providers (regions, municipalities and cities) and institutions and facilities established by them
- non-public providers (non-governmental organizations, associations, associations, etc.) and organizations.

3.3 *Family and the strenuous life situations*

Family is the basic unit of a society. If we are to perceive the family, it is necessary to provide it with adequate help when it deals with various situational problems. Problems can arise in different areas of family life, role of mothers, fathers, child education, shared leisure time, interpersonal relationships, family communication, family member's disease, impact of the mass media on the family. If a problem arises in any of these areas of family life, a stressful situation may arise, and the family may not be able to get through it by their own means. Social counseling is a relevant starting point in solving the family's strenuous situation. Authors such as Tokarova et al. (2007) consider family counseling as a qualitatively different way of looking at people's problems by focusing their attention to interaction between people in the context of significant interpersonal relationships. Its effort is to systematically solve all problems of the family community and its individual members. Strenuous family situations are as follows: dysfunction of the family, problems relevant to the upbringing of the children, socio-economic problems, family incompleteness, divorce, death, various addictions, health problems or disability of a family member, violence, marginal groups, unemployment, sociopathological phenomenon etc.

4 SOCIAL COUNSELLING FOR THE FAMILIES IN THE SLOVAK REPUBLIC– RESEARCH RESULTS

4.1 *Methodology of the research*

The authors of the article made their own research in years 2015–2016, the results of which are further presented. The research problem was descriptive and defined as the availability, conditions and areas of providing social counseling to families in Slovakia. The object of the research was facilities providing social counselling in the state, self—governing and private sector regions of the Slovak Republic.

The subject of the research was family aimed social counselling in particular counseling facilities focused on families 'stressful situations such as family members' unemployment, family dysfunction, failure of the upbringing of the children, socio-economic problems, the elderly, the process of adoption and alternative family care, people with disabilities, pre- divorce, divorce and post-divorce problems, family torture and abuse, family reunification, penitentiary and post-penitentiary care.

The main objective of the research was to find out the availability and conditions of providing social counseling in various types of social counseling to families in the Slovak Republic.

The research was done in all of the social facilities which are entitled to provide social counselling according the Legal Act No. 448/2008 on Social Services.

In particular, research was done in a low-threshold day center, an integration center, a community center, a, a shelter, a halfway house, facility for temporary care of children and a low-threshold day center for children and a family, a subsidized housing facility, elderly house, home of social services, specialized equipment, day-care center, center for the social rehabilitation, day center and the center of the support for independent housing. Regarding to the investigation of family situations as addiction to alcohol and other narcotics, as well as the process of adoption and alternative custody and family violence, we addressed also resocialization centers, children's homes, crisis centers and the Office of Labor, Social Affairs and Family. We had sent the question blank to all of the facilities from the base file. We administered a total of 1085 questionnaires electronically; a return rate was 11%, which means 121 returned questionnaires. The selection file consisted of 121 social facilities, using a stratified selection that allowed us to map all of Slovakia. We have chosen a quantitative research strategy to capture the complexity of the problem.

The selected methodological research tools, that we used, were: the analytical method of relevant literature and available information, secondary research analysis of available statistical and information data on social facilities providing social counseling. The proprietary research tool was an electronic, combined, own-origin questionnaire. At the stage of statistical and analytical processing of empirical data, we used quantitative analysis methods to evaluate acquired data. Data were evaluated using the IBM® SPSS 22 statistical program. Based on statistical analysis, we have interpreted the obtained results using mathematical and statistical methods, logical methods In the descriptive statistics, we relied on the use measure of central tendency. We used the median, modus,

arithmetic mean at the central level. When testing for correlations and differences, we used a non-parametric Kruskal-Wallis H test, Chi-square test, and Spearman's correlation coefficient.

4.2 *Research results*

The perceptual share of the facilities according to the regions was as follows: The Košice Region (28.1%), the Prešov Region (15.7%), the Banska Bystrica Region (13.2%), the Trenčín Region (12.4%), the Bratislava Region (2.5%). In the process of defining the research sample, we were interested in social facilities which provide, besides other social services, also social counselling. The largest share of responses was in the category other. In the other social facilities, the largest representation was the facility for the elderly (18), the Labor Office for Social Affairs and Family (18), the Social Services Home (16), the specialized facility (11), the Day-Care Center (9), the community center (7), nursing facility (4). Less-frequented social facilities were shelter, center for social rehabilitation, early intervention service, emergency housing facility, resocialization center, halfway houses, crisis center, a low-threshold day center for children and families, children house, houses of refuges.

Research shows that the social facilities are mostly framed by the private sector where the most common providers are nonprofit organizations and civic associations. Social facilities belonging to the self-government sector are, according to research findings, mostly provided by a municipality/city. For easy access to social counselling services, regional branches were established, mostly managed by the state and the private sector.

According to our findings, social counselling to the family is simultaneously provided to the family and to the individual family member itself. Only a minimum of facilities (11) provides social counselling to only one family member.

Families are most often applying to social facilities dealing with a socio-economic problem, or if the member of the family is disabled or elderly is in the family. Other problematic situations in families, which are leading to social counselling are the loneliness of the elderly in the house, the acute psychiatric problem of the family member, the assistance services to the elderly, the homelessness, the immediate placement of the senior in the facility, the infirm elderly in the family, the execution, the family loans, the material need of the family, information about various social subsidies, and applying procedures, returning a child to a biological family, returning to life having lived before the falling into the disability, illiteracy, non sui juris individuals, people suffering by psychological disturbances and people without documents. nursing services, child-trafficking, lonely mothers with children in material need, palliative care to the patient and his/her family, provision of social counselling and community status, problematic learning outcomes related to learning disabilities, attention disorders, custody issues, client representation, sexual orientation issues, families with oncological patients, families that no longer manage the psychiatric illness of the household member, loss of housing, inheritance issues, truancy, integration of mentally ill people.

In the partial research focused on the frequency of providing basic social counselling in individual problem areas in families, we found out that basic social counselling is most often provided to people with disabilities and to their families, family with the elderly and families with socio-economic problems. Other common areas of concern where basic social counselling is provided include unemployment of family members, dysfunctional families, abuse families, families after the loss of one family member, families not managing the upbringing of children, addicted individuals and their families.

In the partial field of research focused on the frequency of specialized social counselling in particular problem areas in families, results show that specialized social counselling is most often provided to seniors in families, people with disabilities and their families, families with socio-economic problems, unemployed family members. Other areas include families failing to up bring children, dysfunctional families, and abuse in families.

The least frequent problematic areas within basic and specialized social counselling are the families after the loss of one family member, divorce and post-divorce issues, the process of adoption and the substitute custody, addicted individuals and their families, the post-penitentiary care of a family member. This may indicate the low interest of clients to solve these problems, but also the reduced interest in dealing with these issues by social counselling providers.

The statistically significant difference in coverage of the strenuous areas of the family by basic social counselling in the state, self-government and non-government sector is in these areas:

- in dysfunctional families where, basic social counselling is mainly provided in the private and self-governing sector
- for families, failing to up-bring children, where the basic social counselling is mainly provided in the self-government sector
- for families with socio-economic problems where basic social counselling is mainly provided in the self-government sector
- for families in the process of substitute custody, where basic social counselling is provided to the largest extent by the state sector,

- for families with disabled family members, where basic social counselling is mostly provided by the private sector,
- for divorcing families and families dealing with post-divorce issues, where basic social counselling is mostly provided by the state sector,
- for families dealing with abuse where basic social counselling is mostly provided by the self-government sector,
- for families with an unemployed member, where basic social counselling is mainly provided by the self-governing sector,
- for families in post-penitentiary care, where basic social counselling is mostly provided by the self-government sector.

There is no statistically significant difference in coverage of basic social counselling for families with the elderly – mostly provided by the private sector, for families with an addicted member, where the social counselling is mainly provided by the self-government sector and to the surviving family members basic social counselling private sector.

In providing specialized social counselling, we have found the statistically significant differences in the provision of specialized social counselling in individual strenuous situations:

- in dysfunctional families where specialized social counselling is mostly provided by the state sector,
- in families who do not manage to up bring children, where specialized social counselling is mostly provided by the state sector,
- in families with socio-economic problems, where specialized social counselling is mostly provided by the state sector,
- in families in the process of adoption and substitute custody, where specialized social counselling is mostly provided by the state sector,
- in families dealing with divorce and post-divorce issues, where specialized social counselling is mostly provided by the state sector.
- in families dealing with abuse where specialized social counselling is provided to the largest extent by the state sector,
- in families with an unemployed member, where specialized social counselling is provided mainly by the state sector,
- in families with an addicted member, where specialized social counselling is mostly provided by the state sector,
- in the post-penitentiary care of a family member, where the specialized social counselling is provided mainly by the state sector.

Research results show that there is no statistically significant difference in the provision of specialized counselling among the state, self-government and the private sector for people with disabilities and their families, families with the elderly and families after the loss. When it comes to people with disabilities and their families, then the specialized social counselling is mostly provided by the private sector. In the case of families with the elderly and families after the loss, the specialized social counselling is provided mostly by the private sector.

By researching problems faced by families applying for the social counselling regarding the sector of provision, we have verified results by using the Kruskal Wallis Test. The statistically significant differences were found in following strenuous situations: dysfunctional families, families failing to bring children, families with socio-economic problems, issues of foster custody, families dealing with divorce and post-divorce issues, families dealing with abuse, and families with unemployed members. Families dealing with the above-mentioned problems are turning mostly to the state sector facilities.

The availability of social counselling for families provided by particular sectors was detected by using the Chi-square test. Based on the results, we can state that the number of branches of state social facilities exceeds the number of private facilities and facilities of the municipalities and its self-government competencies.

5 CONCLUSION

In recent years, we can observe the gradual development of social counselling in Slovakia, particularly in the theoretical field. In the executive area, development can be seen mainly thanks to the Legal Act No. 448/2008 on Social Services and its amendments, which anchored the social counselling into the legislation of the Slovak Republic and in the Mydlíková's *"Standards of Quality of Social Counseling"* The concept of providing social counselling currently has a broad scope. Looking at the current family, we can see its instability, especially facing one of the above-mentioned strenuous situations, that's why we see social counselling as one of the primary options to help the family.

At the same time, we can say that social facilities providing social counselling in particular sectors need to be strengthened especially in the state and self-government sectors. Developments and changes in social counselling for families are inevitably related to the cooperation and interest of all stakeholders in creating conditions that would encourage the provision of social counselling to families within regions – in the state, self-government and the private sector. The interest and support are also needed from the employ-

ers, respectively the management of enterprises because the family's problems affect the disposable human capital of the enterprise.

REFERENCES

Gabura, J. 2012. Teória rodiny a proces práce s rodinou. Bratislava: IRIS, 2012. 318 p.

Gabura, J. 2013. Teória a proces sociálneho poradenstva. Bratislava: IRIS, 2013. 65 s. ISBN 978-80-89238-92-7.

Hrozenská, M. a kol. 2008. Sociálna práca so staršími ľuďmi a jej teoreticko-praktické východiská. Martin: Osveta, 181 p.

Kozubík, M. et al. 2013. Poradenstvo v sociálnych službách. Nitra: Fakulta sociálnych vied a zdravotníctva UKF, 209 p.

Levická, J. & Balogová, B. 2010. Sociálna práca s pozostalými. In *Sociální práce/Sociálna práca: Sociální práce s umírajícimi.* 2010(2): 96–101.

Markovič, D. 2015. Kariérové poradenstvo v prostredí vysokých škôl na Slovensku. Ružomberok: Verbum, 126 p.

Matulník, J. 2012. Oslabenie rodiny v súčasnosti na Slovensku. In *Mosty k rodine,* 3(1): 6–7.

Mojtová, M. 2014. Sociálna práca v paliatívnej a hospicovej starostlivosti. Bratislava: SAP-Slovak Academic Press, 120 p.

Mydlíková, E. a kol. 2005. Štandardy kvality sociálneho poradenstva. Bratislava: AD, 100 p.

Mydlikova, E. et al. 2007. "Vyložme si karty na stôl!" Bratislava: Asociácia supervízorov a sociálnych poradcov, 56 p.

Odbor sociálnych vecí. 2009. Optimalizácia a zefektívnenie siete poradenských služieb. [online]. Available at: http://web.vucke.sk/files/socialne_veci/koncepcne_materialy/projekt_optimalizacia.pdf.

Pavelová, Ľ. 2007. Vybrané kapitoly z poradenstva pre sociálnych pracovníkov. Bratislava: VSZaSP sv. Alžbety, 96 p.

Repková, K. 2011. Verejní a neverejní poskytovatelia sociálnych služieb na Slovensku – analýza Centrálneho registra poskytovateľov. Bratislava: Inštitút pre výskum práce a rodiny, 35 p.

Schavel, M. & Oláh, M. 2008. Sociálne poradenstvo a komunikácia. Bratislava: VŠZaSP sv. Alžbety, 62 p.

Strieženec, Š. 1996. Slovník sociálneho pracovníka. Trnava: AD, 255 p.

Vitkovičová, K. et al. 2007. Sociálne poradenstvo ako nástroj riešenia hmotnej núdze a sociálnej núdze. In *Sociálna práca. Kapitoly z dejín, teórie a metodiky sociálnej práce.* (ed. Tokárová a kol.) Prešov: ACENT PRINT, pp. 529–533.

Zákon NR SR č. 448/2008 Z. z. o sociálnych službách a o zmene a doplnení zákona č. 455/1991 Zb. o živnostenskom podnikaní (živnostenský zákon) v znení neskorších predpisov v znení neskorších predpisov.

Zákon NR SR č. 485/2013 Z. z., ktorým sa mení a dopĺňa zákon č. 448/2008 Z. z. o sociálnych službách.

Žilová, A. 2007. Prínosy poradenstva pre nezamestnaných. In *Sociálna práca. Kapitoly z dejín, teórie a metodiky sociálnej práce* (ed. Tokárová a kol.) Prešov: ACENT PRINT, pp. 524–528.

Production Management and Business Development – Mihalčová et al. (Eds)
© 2019 Taylor & Francis Group, London, ISBN 978-1-138-60415-5

Participation of the Armed Forces in crisis management

M. Ostrowska & S. Mazur
Krakowska Akademia im. Andrzeja Frycza Modrzewskiego, Kraków, Poland

ABSTRACT: Effective protection in crisis requires a smooth operation and effective cooperation of all authorities, state institutions that are responsible for maintaining the proper state of security and those that are properly prepared to carry out tasks in the field of fighting a crisis. There are elements that directly support the defense system such the Police, the State Fire Service, the Border Guard, specialized rescue units and the Armed Forces of the Republic of Poland. The Armed Forces of the Republic of Poland have unprecedented hardware and organizational resources for such situations. An appropriate use of armed forces for supporting of civil institutions is the basic element of the entire national security system. In this article, we discuss the way that Army does and may provide support in a situation when other forces are unable to meet the tasks and sometimes they are not even able to carry them.

1 INTRODUCTION

Management is also very common system for organizing society. It contains elements of planning, assessment of current conditions and the ability to collect, analyse and process information in order to improve quality in a specific sphere (Sienkiewicz et al. 2010). Management has many of its definitions. Very often it is defined in a specific context because we can talk about managing in the private environment (e.g. managing your own time, abilities etc.) as well as in public environment (e.g. management of resources in the enterprise, risk management, system management connected with a specific area) (Charette et al. 2004). This is a very broad term and therefore allows for the inclusion of numerous issues in its scope.

Crisis management is an indispensable element of national security. It plays a very important role in solving all problems related to security, counteracting and preparing for threats that may occur. It consists in maintaining and restoring the situation in stable mode. Crisis management is characterized by intentional action, which is carried out by government bodies at all levels of country organization and employs specialized organizations, guards and inspections, as well as engaging society (Sienkiewicz et al. 2010).

The purpose of the article is to present the possibilities of using the Polish Armed Forces in the process of crisis management.

2 CRISIS MANAGEMENT

According to Rogozińska & Mikrut, "crisis" can be understood as a situation in which there is a threat to the basic values, interests and objectives of institutions, as well as social groups. The concept of crisis also includes situations in which the rights and freedoms of citizens, their lives and property are at stake. It should also be added that, as a rule, the crisis is an event occurring in a large area and lasting for a long time (Rogozińska & Mikrut 2010). The reasons for this may be external (e.g. military operations, economic phenomena), as well as internal (e.g. catastrophes, strikes). In turn, to determine whether an event has the characteristics of a crisis, the above cited author uses a term such as the severity of the crisis. This concept was closely related to the concept of "crisis", because thanks to it one can characterize a potential crisis in terms of time and scale. "The weight of the crisis is a derivative of two sizes: the scale (size) of the threat and the time that will elapse from the moment a signal about the possibility of an event to its occurrence. This evaluation can change in a very wide range" (Rogozińska & Mikrut 2010).

Nowadays, the crisis is often equated with the crisis, wrongly, because it is untrue, as explained by E. Nowak, while distinguishing three factors thanks to which we can differentiate between crisis and crisis situation. The first factor is that the crisis is part of a crisis situation, the second factor is that all crises are crisis situations, but not in every crisis situation there is an element of the crisis. The third factor, that the author means, is the difference between crisis and crisis situation. Now of emergence when crisis occurs, it does not have to cause violations of the essence of the organization, but it is a challenge for the subjective state of the normality of organization functioning.

Crisis management is the activity of public administration bodies, which is an element of national security management. It consists of preventing crisis situations, preparing the responsible bodies to take control over them by means of planned actions, reacting in the event of emergencies, removing their consequences and restoring resources and critical infrastructure (Nowak 2007).

Sienkiewicz & Górny (2011). define crisis management as a "decision-making process aimed to choose a rational strategy against real actions and/or potential crisis situations. It is a way of managing specific system resources, ensuring the return to the normal state from the state of crisis or maintaining this state, despite the occurrence of symptoms of a crisis situation" (Act of 2 April 2007 on Crisis Management).

Crisis management is characterized by the principles by which statutory tasks are effectively implemented. These principles are such:

1. The principle of the territorial primacy—means that the basis for action of the authorities is the territorial division of the state.
2. Principle of one-man management—decision-making powers belong to one-person bodies, the decision is made on one-person basis and is responsible for them.
3. The principle of responsibility of public authorities in crisis situations assumes the competence and responsibility in the field of making decisions.
4. The principle of fusion—giving the authorities of the administrative authorities a general authority guaranteeing the fulfillment of the responsibilities imposed on them.
5. The principle of universality—crisis management is organized by public authorities in cooperation with existing specialized institutions and organizations and the society; in addition, the public administration body may define the obligation of a material or personal service.
6. The principle of hazard categorization—the division of threats into groups by type and size, as well as the allocation of organizational and financial legal solutions.

The crisis management process consists of two periods. The first of these is the stabilization period; it includes the prevention and preparation phases, i.e. the precrisis action. This period is the entirety of organizational activities that are undertaken at all levels of power, preparation and implementation of investments to prevent the emergence of potential threats, as well as the development and implementation of operational procedures. The second period is the implementation, which includes the reaction and recovery phases (Żebrowski 2012).

3 ORGANIZATIONAL STRUCTURE OF THE POLISH ARMED FORCES

The organizational structure of the Armed Forces is hierarchical. The head of the Armed Forces in time of peace is the President of the Republic of Poland, who performs the tasks with the help of the Ministry of National Defence.

The Chief of General Staff, who has the General Command of the Armed Forces, which is the combined command responsible for commanding the military units of the RSZ during peace and crisis, and the remaining units after the division of Operational Command units during the war, manages the Armed Forces. Its structure includes command and staff as well as Inspectorates: Land Forces, Navy, Air Forces, Special Forces, as well as Types of Military and Training. They are the main tools in the hands of the General Commander in carrying out tasks in their areas. The Ministry of Interior and Administration will be responsible for the Inspectorate of Information Systems and the Inspectorate of Support for the Armed Forces and divisions, flotillas, wings, independent brigades as well as training centres. Sub-units of support and security measures have become subordinate to the Tactical Unions. DG RSZ also plays a leading role in the training process of troops discharged for participation in stabilization operations, crisis response and humanitarian operations (www.mon. gor.pl).

The organizational structure also includes the Operational Command of the Armed Forces Types is the main command body responsible for the operational command of the Armed Forces, transferred to its subordination in accordance with the decision of the Minister of National Defense. He is responsible for planning and commanding troops and assigned non-military elements in combined, peace, rescue, humanitarian operations and activities aimed at preventing acts of terrorism or removing their consequences, as well as forces allocated to support government and self-government administration in the event of non-military crises.

Additionally, in the structure we have the Command of Territorial Defence Forces responsible for planning, organizing and conducting training of sub-ordinate military units and organizational unions, planning and organizing mobilization and operational development and use of WOT, preparation of WOT forces and resources for combat operations. Military Gendarmerie is a separate and specialized service that is part of the Armed Forces of the Republic of Poland. In the Armed Forces of the Republic of Poland and in the presence of soldiers, he carries out tasks planned for the Police. The Military Police operate based on the Act of August 24, 2001 on the Military Police and military law enforcement bodies, which defines the scope of activities and organization, as well as the rights and duties of soldiers of the Military Police.

Soldiers of the Military Police can take an active part in combating natural disasters, extraordinary environmental threats and liquidate their effects, and actively participate in search, rescue and humanitarian operations aimed at protecting life and health and property, and perform other tasks specified in separate regulations.

According to the amended Act on the universal defence duty, art. 3 par. 3 we have the following types of Armed Forces:

1. Land Forces;
2. Air Forces;
3. Navy;
4. Special Forces;
5. Military of Territorial Defence.

4 NORMATIVE ACTS

In accordance with the provisions of the Constitution of the Republic of Poland, the Polish Armed Forces serve to protect the independence and indivisibility of its territory and ensure the security and inviolability of its borders.

In the State Security Strategy, the Polish Armed Forces are the basic, specialized element of the state defence system and the main—apart from diplomacy —instrument for the implementation of the State Security Strategy. They perform tasks resulting from both crisis response plans and state defence.

According to the content of the Strategy, the task of the state's policy and defense system is to counteract political and military threats, including primarily defending the territory of Poland against possible armed aggression and ensuring the inviolability of borders, protecting state organs and public institutions and ensuring its survival in a crisis and conflict (Paździor & Szmulik 2012).

Tasks of the Polish Armed Forces are recorded, among others in the Constitution of the Republic of Poland, according to which the Armed Forces of the Republic of Poland serve to protect the independence of the state and the indivisibility of its territory and ensure the security and inviolability of its borders, in addition, the Armed Forces of the Republic of Poland participate in stabilization and preventive tasks. During peace, it is a crisis response task.

The Armed Forces of the Republic of Poland perform tasks in the field of crisis response based on:

– the Act of November 21, 1967 on the Universal Defense of the Republic of Poland (Journal of Laws No. 241, item 2416, as amended),

– the Act of April 26, 2007 on Crisis Management (Journal of Laws of May 21, 2007),
– the Act of 18 April 2002 on the State of Natural Disaster (Journal of Laws No. 62, item 558, as amended),
– the Act of 21 June 2002 on the state of emergency (Journal of Laws No. 113, item 985, as amended),
– the Act of 6 April 1990 on the Police (Journal of Laws No. 7 item 58, as amended),
– the Act of 24 August 1991 on the State Fire Service (Journal of Laws 1991 No. 88 item 40),
– the Act of 25 July 2001 on State Emergency Medical Services (Journal of Laws No. 113 item 1207).

National security strategy Art. 75 presents the tasks of the Armed Forces:

– monitoring and protection of air space and support for the protection of the state border on land and sea;
– conducting reconnaissance and intelligence activities;
– monitoring of radioactive, chemical and biological contamination on the territory of the country;
– cleaning the area of explosives and dangerous objects of military origin;
– conducting search and rescue operations;
– assistance to state authorities, public administration and the public in responding to threats (crisis situations) and elimination of their consequences.

In this last task, the formations of the National Reserve Forces should play a special role, separated if necessary for use by voivodes.

Article 119 states that "reforms require the functioning of the National Reserve Forces, which should become compact, enabling real reinforcement and complement of operational capabilities both for the needs of local response in crisis situations and in the conditions of their use for actions in defense of the country. This change should be combined with a wider reform of the preparation of mobilization reserves and the construction of a universal territorial security system."

4.1 Constitution of the Republic of Poland of April 2, 1997

The Art 228 specifies that "in situations of particular danger, if ordinary constitutional measures are insufficient, an appropriate extraordinary state may be introduced: martial law, state of emergency or a state of natural disaster." Art. 229 says that "In the event of an external threat to the state, armed attack on the territory of the Republic of Poland or when the international agreement requires a joint defence against aggression, the President of the Republic may, at the request of the Council of Ministers, enter martial law in part or on the whole territory of the state". However, in art. 232 "In order to prevent the consequences of natural disasters or technical failures bearing the features of a natural disaster and to remove them, the Council of Ministers may introduce for a specified time, not longer than 30 days, a state of natural disaster on a part or the entire territory of the state. Prolongation of this state may take place with the consent of the Sejm."

4.2 *Act of November 21, 1967 on general defence duty Polish Republic*

The Art. 3.1states the "Armed Forces of the Republic of Poland", hereinafter referred to as the "Armed Forces", are guarding the sovereignty and independence of the Polish Nation and its security and peace. In the same article of paragraph 2 the army's tasks are specified in detail "The Armed Forces may also take part in combating natural disasters and their consequences, counter-terrorism and property protection, search and rescue or protection of human health and life, cleaning up areas of explosive and dangerous materials of military origin and their neutralization as well as in the implementation of tasks in the field of crisis management."

4.3 *Act of April 26, 2007 on crisis management*

According to Art. 25. 1. "If in a crisis situation the use of other forces and resources is impossible or may prove insufficient, unless other regulations provide otherwise, the Minister of State may, at the request of the voivode, transfer to his disposal subunits or divisions of the Polish Armed Forces hereinafter called "Branches of the Armed Forces", along with directing them to perform tasks in the field of crisis management."

This Act sets out the rules for the participation of the Armed Forces in crisis situations. Art. 13 points 2 presents the tasks of crisis response centres and they read as follows:

– 24-hour on-call service to ensure the flow of information on needs of crisis management;
– co-operation with administrative crisis management centers the public;
– the control over the functioning of detection and alarm systems and early warning of the population;
– co-operation with entities conducting search and rescue operations and humanitarian;
– study of regular on-call duty as part of defence readiness of states.

4.4 *Act on the state of natural disaster*

In art. 18. it was noted that "during the state of natural disaster, if the use of other forces and means is impossible or insufficient, the Minister of National Defence may hand over to the voivode at the disposal of the natural disaster, subunits or divisions of the Polish Armed Forces, with their referral to perform tasks related to the prevention or removal of natural disasters."

4.5 *The State of Emergency Act*

The art. 11 p. 1states: "during the state of emergency, the President of the Republic of Poland may, at the request of the Prime Minister, decide on the use of branches and subunits of the Armed Forces of the Republic of Poland to restore the normal functioning of the state if the forces and means used so far have been exhausted", point 2 details "The use of branches and subunits of the Armed Forces of the Republic of Poland, referred to in paragraph 1, may not jeopardize their ability to carry out tasks resulting from the Constitution of the Republic of Poland and ratified international agreements."

4.6 *Police Act*

Art. 18 points 4 specifies "the threat of a terrorist offense or its accomplishment in relation to objects of special importance for the security or defense of the state, or that may result in danger to human life—if the use of police units and subunits is insufficient, to help police units and subunits may branches and subunits of the Armed Forces of the Republic of Poland, hereinafter referred to as "Armed Forces", may be used. Pts. 3 "Use of the Armed Forces in the cases referred to in paragraph 1 shall be based on the decision of the President of the Republic of Poland issued upon the request of the Prime Minister. "Pts. 5" cases of urgent decision to grant assistance referred to in paragraph 1 and 4, shall be taken by the Minister of National Defence, at the request of the minister competent for internal affairs, specifying the scope and form of assistance, notifying the President of the Republic of Poland and the Prime Minister immediately thereof.

4.7 *Act on the State Fire Service*

Military Fire Protection (WOP) is a body performing in the cells and organizational units' subordinate to the Minister of National Defence or over-seeing the tasks of the State Fire Service, as well as other tasks resulting from the specificity of the Armed Forces operation:

– organizes and conducts rescue operations during the fight against fires and the elimination of other local threats, in cells and organizational units subordinate to or supervised by the Minister of National Defence;

– provides assistance to the State Fire Service in carrying out rescue operations, and performs auxiliary rescue operations during natural disasters and other local threats to other emergency services, outside the cells and organizational units subordinate to or supervised by the Minister of National Defence;

– identifies fire risks and other local hazards in cells or organizational units subordinate to or supervised by the Minister of National Defence;

4.8 *Act on State Emergency Medical Services*

Article 24 paragraph 4 specifies Inclusion into the system as medical rescue teams of air search and rescue groups subordinate to the Minister of National Defense is made by way of an agreement between the minister competent for health and the Minister of National Defence.

Use of the ISP in a crisis situation According to the Act on Crisis Management, if in a crisis situation the use of other forces and resources is impossible or may prove insufficient, unless other regulations provide otherwise, the Minister of National Defense, at the request of the Governor, may transfer to his disposal subunits or divisions of the Armed Forces Of the Republic of Poland, hereinafter referred to as 'the Armed Forces' departments, together with their referral to carry out tasks in the field of crisis management. Armed forces departments may participate in the implementation of tasks in the field of crisis management, according to their specialist preparation, in accordance with the voivodship emergency response plan. The tasks in question include:

1. complicity in risk monitoring;
2. performing tasks related to the assessment of the effects of phenomena occurring in the area of occurrence of threats;
3. performing search and rescue tasks;
4. evacuating the injured population and property;
5. performing tasks aimed at preparing the conditions for temporarily detaining the evacuated population in designated places;
6. complicity in the protection of property left in occurrence of threats;
7. isolating the area of occurrence of hazards or the location of the rescue operation;
8. performing security, rescue and evacuation works at endangered construction objects and monuments;
9. carrying out works requiring the use of specialized technical equipment or explosives

being in the resources of the Armed Forces of the Republic of Poland;

10. removal of hazardous materials and their disposal, using the forces and resources provided by the Armed Forces of the Republic of Poland;
11. elimination of chemical contamination and contamination and biological infections;
12. removal of radioactive contamination;
13. performing tasks related to the repair and reconstruction of technical infrastructure; complicity in ensuring the pass ability of transport routes;
14. providing medical assistance and performing sanitary and hygienic tasks and antiepidemic;
15. performance of tasks included in the provincial crisis response plan.

Crisis threats usually appear suddenly, unexpectedly and have a violent course. In order to provide quick assistance from the army in crisis situations, the liaison element in the Provincial Crisis Management Centres are the heads of Provincial Military Staffs; who are part of the Provincial Staffs of Crisis Management.

The introduction of branches and subunits for emergency action can take place in three ways:

The basic procedure—the voivode requests the Minister of National Defense to allocate forces and resources to support civil entities involved in the crisis. The voivode during the formulation of the application may consult the competent regional military administration body in the given region. Order procedure—directing forces and funds allocated from the Polish Armed Forces based on the decision of the Minister of National Defense or the order of the head of the General Staff of the Polish Army. The basis for a decision is the motion of the Minister of the Interior or the provisions of the Plan of Armed Forces' use in crises.

Alarm activation—it is used during the rapid development of a local crisis. In special cases, the commander of a military unit makes a decision on joining the action and then reports the situation to the immediate superior.

5 CONCLUSION

The basic function of the state is to ensure the security of its citizens. Therefore, it is necessary to undertake legal and organizational undertakings aimed at preventing and minimizing the effects of any threats. Threats caused by the forces of nature and human activity in certain circumstances may be a source of crisis situations. Actions taken in their face often diverge from routine actions taken by enforcement entities of the national security system.

Crisis situations of a non-military nature occur in the area of each state. Organizing quick and effective protection in such situations requires joint actions of several state authorities. Elements that support non-military defense system include: Police, State Fire Service, Border Guard, Emergency Medical Services and Armed Forces.

In order to make the most of the potential available to the military organization, it became necessary to implement the relevant legal regulations. The use of branches and subunits of the Armed Forces of the Republic of Poland in the situation of non-military threats is applied only and exclusively, when the use of other forces and resources is impossible or may not be sufficient to solve the crisis situation. In this context, the provisions of the law on extraordinary states and the act on crisis management are particularly important.

In 2002–2011, the rules for the participation of the Armed Forces in combating non-military threats were established. From the composition of the Armed Forces, forces and measures adequate to the threat were separated and maintained in the required standards of combat readiness.

REFERENCES

Act of 18 April 2002 on the state of natural disaster (Journal of Laws No. 62, item 558, as amended).

Act of 2 April 2007 on Crisis Management (Journal of Laws of 2007, No. 89, item 590 as amended).

Act of 26 April 2007 on crisis management (Journal of Laws of 21 May 2007).

Act of 26 April 2007 on crisis management (Journal of Laws of 21 May 2007).

Act of 6 April 1990 on the Police (Journal of Laws No. 7 item 58, as amended).

Act of April 26, 2007 on crisis management (Journal of Laws of 2007, No. 89, item 590.).

Act of July 25, 2001 on State Medical Rescue (Journal of Laws No. 113, item 1207).

Constitution of the Republic of Poland of April 6 1997 r. Dz. U. z 1997 r. nr 78, poz. 216.

Cylkowski, J. 2015, *Use and use of the Polish Armed Forces in crisis management* In. Security culture. Science – Practice – Reflections 20, 2015, pp. 111. http://wop.wp.mil.pl/pl/31.html.

Kuśmierek Z. 2014, *Participation of the army in crisis situations* In. Scientific Journals of the State Higher Vocational School, Legnica, pp. 19.

National Security Strategy of the Republic of Poland, Warsaw 2014.

Nowak, E., 2007, *Crisis management in non-military threat situations*, National Defense University, Warsaw, pp. 38.

Paździor, M. & Szmulik, B. (ed.) 2012, *Public security institutions,* C.H. Beck, Warsow, pp. 90.

Rogozińska-Mikrut, J., 2010, *Basics of crisis management,* ASPRA, Warsaw, pp. 49–50.

Sienkiewicz, P. & Górny, P. 2001, *System analysis of crisis situations,* National Defence Academy, Warsow 2001, pp.32. www.mon.gov.pl.

The Act of 21 June 2002 on the state of emergency (Journal of Laws No. 113).

The Act of November 21, 1967 on the Universal Defense of the Republic of Poland (Journal of Laws No. 241, item 2416, as amended).

Żebrowski, A. 2013, *Crisis management in the security of the Republic of Poland,* Pedagogical University, Krakow 2012, pp. 33.

Production Management and Business Development – Mihalčová et al. (Eds)
© *2019 Taylor & Francis Group, London, ISBN 978-1-138-60415-5*

The living standard of the inhabitants of the Carpathian Euroregion

T. Piecuch & K. Chudy-Laskowska
Rzeszów University of Technology, Rzeszów, Poland

E. Szczygieł
"Centre for Education and Entrepreneurship Support" Association, Rzeszów, Poland

ABSTRACT: The article attempts to analyze the living standard of the Carpathian Euroregion inhabitants. The main objective of the study was to identify groups within the Carpathian Euroregion that are similar in terms of their residents' living standards, as well as an attempt to interpret obtained data, which has been gathered through selected indicators and using selected taxonomic methods. The article contains information on the essence and mode for measuring the living standard, along with the results from the statistical analysis of the studied phenomenon formulated with the use of data from the Polish Central Statistical Office. An attempt was also made to interpret the results, which is difficult due to the large diversity in the analyzed area and the inconsistency of the data. The obtained results allowed estimating the standard of living in the analyzed area, however, they also emphasised difficulty in an objective evaluation of this phenomenon.

1   INTRODUCTION

The living standard is one of the most important subject matters in public statistics. It allows to identify areas characterized by low and high standard of living, which consequently results "... the conclusions of an application nature that may indicate problem regions. This makes it easy (...) to lead an appropriate policy, which could counteract the deepening difficulties or the emergence of new problem areas" (Winiarczyk-Raźniak 2014). Thus, to this, the elimination (or limitation) of development disparities, contributing to sustainable development is possible.

The study presents an analysis and an attempt to interpret the living standard. This concept is the basic research category used in social statistics. It means a kind of well-being assessed by the individual based on objective conditions or subjective feelings (Piecuch & Chudy-Laskowska 2017). This is the satisfaction level of human needs, which results from the consumption of material goods and services (Świecka 2008). The concept of the living standard is often understood as the conditions of life. It is worth noting, however, that the concepts are different. The living conditions, in general, define the entirety of factors determining the satisfaction of human needs, while the living standard refers to the degree of satisfaction of these needs (US Łódź 2010). The living standard can be treated as the synonym of the broadest meaning of living conditions (Piasny 1993). It is

measured with the use of various quantitative indicators, most often grouped into categories relating to, among others: the labour market, health and social care, communication and economic infrastructure, housing, education and culture, the state of the environment, security, income and expenditure, household budgets (Majka 2014, Dziubińska-Michalewicz 2002, US Łódź 2010, Migała-Warchoł 2010).

The area of the Carpathian Euroregion, which was established on 14th of February 1993 by the decision of representatives of the cross-border regional authorities of four countries: Poland, Ukraine, Slovakia and Hungary (Romania joined in 1997), is quite diverse in many respects, which on the one hand is very interesting cognitively, but on the other hand, the analysis of such a diverse area poses a lot of problems. In many cases there is lack of "... comparable data characterizing the social or economic situation at similar levels of aggregation. The problem also arises from the extensive administrative divisions in individual countries, whose areas are part of the Carpathian Euroregion" (US Rzeszów 2012, 2015). This causes several problems that hinders the process of comparison of studies or to formulate appropriate conclusions. The study is based on available data on the living standard, published by the Polish Central Statistical Office. In total, 11 indicators were considered, including: GDP per capita, population growth per 1 thousand inhabitants, employment rate, unemployment rate and others. The main objective of the study was to identify groups within the Carpathian Euroregion that are similar in terms of their residents' living standards, as well as an attempt to interpret obtained data, which has been gathered through selected indicators and using selected taxonomic methods.

2 THE ANALYSIS OF SPATIAL DIVERSIFICATION OF LIVING STANDARDS IN THE CARPATHIAN EUROREGION

For the study of living standards in the Carpathian Euroregion, 11 diagnostic variables were selected: natural increase per thousand. population (x_1); flats completed for use in thousand people (x_2); university students for 10,000 people (x_3); medicine doctors for 10,000 people (x_4); beds in hospitals for 10,000 people (x_5); accommodation users for 10,000 people (x_6); expenditure on R&D in% of GDP (x_7); GDP per capita (€) (2012) (x_8); recorded crimes established per thousand people (x_9); employment rate (x_{10}); unemployment rate (x_{11}). The availability of variables accounted for the above choice. The analysis was carried out for year 2013 (the most recent available data). Using descriptive statistics, the indicators used for the study were characterized, as well as, checked was whether the accepted for the research features significantly differed in levels among the studied area (Table 1)[1].

The average natural increase in the studied regions has negative values, the smallest recorded in Hungary, in Észak-Magyarország region (–4.8), and the highest in Slovakia—Vychodne Slovensko

Table 1. The basic descriptive statistics of the examined diagnostic variables.

$(x \pm \sigma)$	Me	Min	Max	Vx	p
x_1 (–0.6 ± 2.2)	–0.8	–4.8	2.9	–378	0.05014
x_2 (2.0 ± 1.1)	2.1	0.3	4.4	54.4	0,17301
x_3 (273.9 ± 108.9)	254	171	548	39.8	0.48934
x_4 (37.4 ± 15.2)	31.4	20.2	61.3	40.6	0.00854**
x_5 (70.1 ± 12.5)	69,9	47.8	03.6	17.8	0.02720*
x_6 (374.5 ± 237,0)	347	130	790	63.3	0.14873
x_7 (0.5 ± 0.4)	0,44	0.16	1.27	69.8	0.01639*
x_8 (4775.4 ± 2551.9)	5800	1415	9200	53.4	0.00045***
x_9 (16.6 ± 11.4)	15.2	5.7	41.1	68.5	0.00004***
x_{10} (52.4 ± 6.3)	55	42.2	58.8	12.1	0.04203*
x_{11} (10.2 ± 5.1)	7.8	4.1	18.4	49.9	0.00250**

1. The results of the ANOVA test, as differences between the size of indicators and a given country, are included in the last column in Table 1.

(2.9). The coefficient of variation of natural increase assumes the highest value for all examined characteristics—as much as –378%, which indicates a very large diversity of the regions studied in this respect. The probability level is close to 0.05, which indicates that there are differences in the natural increase in the studied regions. The analysis of the number of dwellings completed per 1,000 population shows that in the analyzed year, an average of 2 flats were completed. The lowest value of the indicator was recorded in Hungary, in Észak-Magyarország region (0.3), and the highest in Ukraine, in Ivano-Frankivsk region (4.4).

The average level of the number of university students per 10 thousand inhabitants amounted 274 people. The largest number of students is in the Lviv region (548 students), and the smallest (171) in Romania, in the Nord-East region.

Two variables concerning health care considered in the analysis of the living standards of the inhabitants of the Carpathian Euroregion are the number of medicine doctors and the number of beds in hospitals per 10 thousand inhabitants. They differentiate the investigated regions, as demonstrated by the results of the ANOVA test (in both cases p<α). The highest number of medicine doctors for 10,000 inhabitants was identified in Ukraine in the Czerniovce region (61), and the highest number of beds for 10,000 inhabitants was also in Ukraine, however in the Lviv region (94). The smallest values of indicators referring to medical care and the number of hospital beds were recorded in Poland, in the Sub Carpathian region (respectively 20 and 48).

The highest number of lodging was in Romania, in Centru region – 790 people for 10,000 inhabitants. The region that is the least frequented by tourists is in Ukraine, namely the Czerniovce region (130 people per 10,000 inhabitants). The levels of the next two variables characterizing the level of expenditure on R&D and GDP per capita, were also significantly diverse in the studied regions, which the ANOVA test proved (p<α). The largest share of expenditure on R&D was in Poland, in Sub Carpathia (1.27), and the lowest in Ukraine, in Zakarpatsky region (0.16). The highest GDP per capita was recorded in Slovakia (9,200€) and the lowest, in Ukraine in Czerniovce region (1,415€).

The level of citizens' safety affecting the living standard has been characterized by the indicator of recorded crimes per thousand people. The largest number of crimes was recorded in Hungary in the Észak-Magyarország region (41.1) and the least—in Ukraine, in Ivano-Frankivsk region (5.7).

Two variables referred to the labour market—employment rate and unemployment rate. Both were significantly different between the regions, which the ANOVA test proved (p<α). The highest employment rate in the studied areas of the Carpathian Euroregion was recognized in the Lviv region in Ukraine (58.8), and the lowest in the Észak-Magyarország region in Hungary (42.2). The highest unemployment rate in the analyzed year occurred in Slovakia (18.4%), and the lowest in Romania, in Nord-Vest region (4.1%).

The studied areas of the Carpathian Euroregion were subjected to hierarchical cluster analysis with the use of the Ward's method. The purpose of this procedure was to distinguish groups of regions that are like each other in terms of diagnostic characteristics selected for the study. In this way, four groups of regions were created, ones like each other in terms of accepted characteristics which may indicate the level of regional development. The results of the clustering analysis are presented in Table 2.

For separate clusters, a group-average analysis was carried out aimed to check which characteristics accounted for the grouping. The "a" group included areas from Poland and Slovakia. They are characterized by high rates of: natural increase, and R&D expenditures, as well as, GDP per capita. Unfortunately, the unemployment rate is also high in these regions. The lowest values are assumed here by indicators regarding: health care (i.e. the number of hospital beds and medicine doctors per 10,000 inhabitants). The levels of analyzed indicators for all clusters are shown in the Figure 1.

In the group "b" there are two Hungarian and one Romanian (Centru) regions. These areas are characterized by a very low rate of natural increase, the fewest number of flats given for use and the level of employment was the lowest of all surveyed variables. On the other hand, the most significant indicator was that of reported crimes. The unemployment rate was also high. While, as a positive aspect of the "b" group it can be considered the indicator of tourists using accommodation for 10,000 people, expenditure on R&D and GDP per

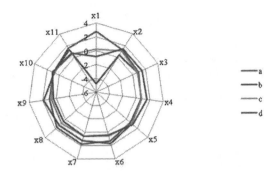

Figure 1.   The indicators of group averages in analyzed clusters.
Source: Own elaboration.

capita. These reached the second largest place after the "a" group, in which the indicator reached the highest level.

The "c" cluster is composed of two Romanian regions and one belonging to Ukraine. Almost all indicators in this group assume values below the global average. The level of health care, the number of university students per 10,000 people, GDP per capita and expenditure on R&D are low. However, the employment rate is high, and the unemployment rate is the lowest in this area.

The last one group "d" consists of regions belonging to Ukraine. The highest values among variables note the indicators concerning health care, the number of flats per thousand inhabitants and the employment rate. The highest is that indicator concerning education (the numbers of university students for 10,000 people). The lowest level is achieved by two indicators: the expenditure on R&D and GDP per capita; there was also the least number of reported crimes per one thousand people and the number of accommodation users for 10,000 people.

3   THE ATTEMPT TO ASSESS THE LIVING STANDARD IN THE CARPATHIAN EUROREGION

Based on the conducted analysis, attempts were also made to assess the standard of living based on indicators selected for the analysis. It has been found that regions belonging to Ukraine are surprisingly positive assessed. As many as 6 out of 11 presented indicators achieve high levels for Ukraine. This applies for the largest employment rate in the Carpathian Euroregion (58.8), also the highest number of: university students (548); medicine doctors per 10,000 people (61); beds in hospitals per 10,000 people (94). In Ukraine, there were also the least reported crimes per one thousand inhabit-

Table 2.   The assignment of regions to the appropriate group.

Group	State	Region
a	Poland	Sub Carpathia
a	Slovakia	Vychodne Slovensko
b	Romania	Centru
b	Hungary	Észak-Magyarország
b	Hungary	Észak-Alföld
c	Romania	Nord-Vest
c	Romania	Nord-East
c	Ukraine	Zakarpatsky
d	Ukraine	Czerniovce
d	Ukraine	Ivano-Frankivsk
d	Ukraine	Lviv

ants. On the other hand, it is widely known that the living standard in Ukraine compared to Poland, Slovakia or Hungary is much lower. For example, in Human Development Index (Human Development Data, 2016) created by the United Nations in 2015, Poland ranks 36th, while Ukraine is at a very distant 84th position. The remaining countries, whose regions belong to the Carpathian Euroregion, found themselves accordingly—Slovakia on 40th position, Hungary on 43rd and Romania on 50th. Moreover, research shows that in year 2015 the living standard in Ukraine has reached the lowest rates throughout the whole period previously observed. The assessment of living standards has fallen for all ages, social and gender groups, likewise forecasted for the future (Research: Poziom życia Ukraińców... 2016)[2].

In view of the above, the authors would like to emphasize that based on the indicators used in the study, it is difficult to provide a clear and objective assessment of the living standards of the inhabitants of particular regions of the Carpathian Euroregion. This is mainly due to the lack of available data. To assess the level and quality of life in the literature a number of different indicators is used (about 30, 40). This allows such analysis to be more reliable and present the real situation in a more objective way. The analysis presented in the study, due to the lack of complete data, has been based only on 11 indicators. In an attempt to assess the examined indicators, it can be assumed that their number and chosen types are not sufficient enough. In statistical research, the issue of selection, also the available amount of data, is very important, because "even a small lack of completeness of statistical material may cause a serious distortion of the result" (Michalski 2004). In effect, the information ultimately obtained is not an accurate reflection of reality (Michalski 2004). Such a situation took place in the case of the analysis carried out for the purposes of the study.

4 CONCLUSION

The study presents an analysis of the spatial diversity of the living standards of the inhabitants of the Carpathian Euroregion. Considerations of this type are extremely valuable for the fact that, thus to them "... it becomes possible to indicate the distance separating particular regions, distinguishing groups with a similar level of living, as well as grasping the similarities and differences between (...) specific administrative units or determining the threat of a given region" (Majka 2014). It also allows regional authorities and decision-makers to apply appropriate instruments aimed at smoothing out differences and contributing to the sustainable development of individual areas. A significant drawback of this type of analysis is the lack or limited access to relevant data, which may cause that the obtained results do not fully reflect the actual state of the studied areas in the analyzed issues. This situation applies to the presented study. To analyze the living standards, several dozen different indicators are used; most often they are grouped into certain categories. In the present study, due to the difficulties in the availability of data, the analysis was limited to 11 variables, thus receiving quite surprising information. The Carpathian Euroregion compromises countries that are members of the European Union (Poland, Slovakia, Hungary, and Romania) and also non-associated countries (Ukraine), which additionally makes it impossible to compare the data. The conducted analysis proved, with certainty, that the Carpathian Euroregion is much diversified in many respects, while the assessment of the standard of living based on a limited number of indicators is not possible for presenting the exact state of situation, as well as, it can cloud judgement or even falsify the formulated conclusions. In this situation, the solution would be to broaden the analysis with indicators of quality of life (objective living conditions do not always go hand in hand with a subjective assessment of life quality), which, by reference to the emotional layer, would enable a more accurate and comprehensive assessment of the general well-being of residents of such a diverse area as the Carpathian Euroregion.

---

2. The condition of roads also looks very bad in Ukraine. Although it is almost twice as large a country than Poland, its road network is more than twice smaller, and their density more than four times lowers. The quality of roads also leaves much to be desired. A study by the Gallup Institute from 2012 showed that Ukrainian roads are among the worst in the world. According to the drivers' assessments, Ukraine was placed 133 out of 148 countries surveyed. Equally unfavorable are, for example, expenditures on research and development, GDP per capita, life expectancy rates, high housing prices, the fact that the Ukrainian economy is strongly monopolized, also very high prices, high inflation, low wages (including very low pensions, low wages of young well-educated Ukrainians), enormous corruption, the growing gray economy will create a very unfavorable overall picture of the Ukrainian economy. 80% of citizens live below the poverty level (a statistical Ukrainian lives like a Polish poor man), and according to the National Report, the standard of living of residents is falling (Muszyński 2013; Konecka 2016).

REFERENCES

Badanie: Poziom życia Ukraińców pobił wszelkie rekordy. 2016. (online: https://pl.sputniknews.com/gospodarka/201601061788598-badanie-poziom-zycia-ukraina/).

Dziubińska-Michalewicz, M. 2002. *Wybrane wskaźniki poziomu życia – analiza porównawcza Polski i RFN,* Warszawa: Kancelaria Sejmu, Biuro Studiów i Ekspertyz, Wydział Analiz Ekonomicznych i Społecznych, Informacja nr 895, (Pobrane ze strony: http://biurose. sejm.gov.pl/teksty_pdf/i-895.pdf).

Human Development Data. 2016. (on-line: http://hdr. undp.org/ en/data).

Koniecka, A. 2016, *Dokąd zmierza Ukraina, a dokąd Ukraińcy? Analiza,* (on-line: http://www.biznesistyl. pl/biznes/polityka-i-biznes/4255_dokad-zmierza-ukraina,-a-dokad-ukraincy!-analiza.html).

Majka, A. 2014. Przestrzenne zróżnicowanie poziomu życia ludności województwa podkarpackiego. *Nierówności społeczne a wzrost gospodarczy,* 39(3): 408–418.

Michalski, T. 2004, *Statystyka.* Warszawa: WSiP.

Migała-Warchoł, A. 2010. Ocena zróżnicowania poziomu życia mieszkańców województwa podkarpackiego. In Bolesław Borkowski (ed.), *Metody Ilościowe w Badaniach Ekonomicznych, tom XI/2,* Warszawa: Wydaw. Szkoły Głównej Gospodarstwa Wiejskiego.

Muszyński, M. 2013. *Jak się żyje na Ukrainie,* (on-line: https://www.forbes.pl/wiadomosci/poziom-zycia-na-ukrainie-jak-naprawde-wyglada/s4795yd).

Piecuch, T., Chudy-Laskowska, K. 2017. Jakość życia przedsiębiorców ze szczególnym uwzględnieniem kobiet prowadzących działalność gospodarczą, *Studia i Materiały. Miscellanea Oeconomicae,* 21 (3/I): 343–354.

Świecka, B. (ed.) 2008. *Bankructwa gospodarstw domowych. Perspektywa ekonomiczna i społeczna.* Warszawa: Difin.

US Łódź. 2010. *Zróżnicowanie regionalne poziomu życia ludności w świetle wybranych wskaźników z badań Statystyki Publicznej,* (on-line: http://stat.gov.pl/cps/rde/ xbcr/lodz/ASSETS_referat_zroznicowanie_regionalne_poziomu_zycia.pdf).

US Rzeszów. 2012. *Potencjał społeczno-gospodarczy Euroregionu Karpackiego 2008–2010.* Rzeszów: Urząd Statystyczny w Rzeszowie.

US Rzeszów. 2015. Potencjał społeczno-gospodarczy Euroregionu Karpackiego 2011–2013. Rzeszów: Urząd Statystyczny w Rzeszowie.

Winiarczyk-Raźniak, A. 2014. Wymiary poziomu życia w *Polsce* w świetle wybranych wskaźników. In: Elżbieta Kaczmarska, Piotr Raźniak (ed.), *Społeczno-ekonomiczne i przestrzenne przemiany struktur regionalnych,* Vol. I. Kraków: Oficyna Wydawnicza AFM.

Production Management and Business Development – Mihalčová et al. (Eds)
© 2019 Taylor & Francis Group, London, ISBN 978-1-138-60415-5

Supply chain management sustainability

M. Pružinský & B. Mihalčová
Faculty of Business Economics, University of Economics in Bratislava with seat in Košice, Bratislava, Slovak Republic

ABSTRACT: The authors introduce the concept of sustainability to the field of supply chain management. There are relationships among environmental and economic performance within a supply chain management. The products and manufacturing process are under more scrutiny than ever before. Many B2B operations are required to demonstrate their environmental performance as part of sustainable supply chain management. For most companies, demonstrating that they are part of a sustainable supply chain is becoming a common component when dealing with their customers. Many organizations are demanding proof of what goes into the manufacture and delivery of products and services, including both the materials and processes. The paper introduces sustainability to the field of supply chain management and expands the conceptualization of sustainability beyond the triple bottom line to consider key supporting facets and evaluate supply chain management and provide few recommendations to help deliver this proof, or to evaluate company's vendors.

1 INTRODUCTION

We must respect and react to present business environment, which is in many ways controversial but first very competitive. The consequences of that is that we may often hear questions like—Where are your materials coming from? Of course, we can evaluate our suppliers and learn what goes into making their materials, which become a part or our product or supply chain. Sustainable supply chain management means looking at as all materials to learn what kind of "ingredients" our product is using.

Other question posed is—How does our process stack up? Our facility has a big impact on our product. We must benchmark our current environmental performance footprint and reduce it. How efficient our facility is can directly affect our standing in client's eyes, and their future interest in doing business with you.

Other problem touches us is how we do confirm our sustainability commitment? Can we provide tangible, credible commitment to sustainability, such as a sustainability certification, or an ISO 14001 environmental management system? If not, then we supposed to do it as soon as possible, because the only way to bring our facility to the next level through environmental programs and sustainability is certifications. This is our goal to have a more sustainable, profitable business. Even know this is not end of state, because certification is never ending story due to the obligation to get recertification in regular terms.

Besides all of relations between providers and customers, there is the most important the trust between any organizations involved as well as with

its member and product users. The most important precondition of this is communication building. Our honest communication with commitment to others must be clear and efficient. Through transparent and credible sustainability reporting, we can communicate our commitment to the environment as well as profitable business practices. Additionally, our products might benefit from tangible and credible environmental product declarations. These factors are key since in today's world of our customers, community, shareholders, and employees. All of them demand proof that our facility is operating in a sustainable manner while producing environmentally friendly products.

2 THEORETICAL BACKGROUND

2.1 *The beginning of sustainable supply chain management*

Although there exists a divergence of definitions of sustainability, these differences are not as great as one might initially believe. Sustainability is significant part of the social, economic and environmental impact of an organization occurs within its SC (Nikbakhsh 2009, Brandeburg et al. 2014). This is an increasingly important area of SCM research and is likely to become more important in years to come as organizations must respond to new governmental and international regulations, increased social and customer awareness, and changing market needs (New, 2010). Although the SCM literature has made a great contribution to understanding the environmental aspects of sustainability and incorporating them into SCM theory and practice, there is still a considerable lack of effective attention to social issues.

Most definitions of sustainability incorporate a consideration of at least environmental and economic concerns, and even CSR conceptualizations and operationalizations consider the intersection of social and environmental issues. Furtherly we may simply find varying definitions of a construct during the embryonic stages of its adoption in practice or its development in a field of scholarly inquiry (Kuhn 1996). As noted by Gladwin et al. (1995), "definitional diversity is to be expected during the emergent phase of any potentially big idea of general usefulness." The triple bottom line concept suggests that organizational sustainability, at a broader level, consists of three components: the natural environment, society, and economic performance. Figure 1 shows a visual representation of these three components.

This perspective corresponds to the idea of the triple bottom line, a concept developed by Elkington (1998, 2004), which simultaneously considers and balances economic, environmental and social goals from a microeconomic standpoint. Within this context, organizations recognize that sustainability:

✓ ... Is not simply a matter of good corporate citizenship—earning brownie points for reducing noxious emissions from your factory or providing health care benefits to your employees.
✓ ... Sustainability is now a fundamental principle of smart management (Savitz & Weber 2006).

Thus, the triple bottom line suggests that at the intersection of social, environmental, and economic performance, there are activities that

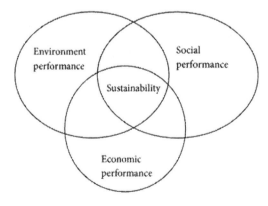

Figure 1. Sustainability: The triple bottom line.
Source: Google images. Retrieved from: https://www.researchgate.net/publication/275556774/figure/fig3/AS:319985432973312@1453301880209/The-triple-bottom-line-of-sustainability-19.png.

organizations can engage in which not only positively affect the natural environment and society, but which also result in long-term economic benefits and competitive advantage for the firm.

There are additional variables treated as causal antecedents, modifiers, or outcomes of sustainability. *Risk management*. While not a part of operational definitions of sustainability in the extant literature, the concept of risk and the management of risk was identified as a reoccurring theme in the sustainability literature (e.g. Shrivastava 1995). He stresses that within the context of sustainability, an organization must manage not only short-term financial results, but also risk factors such as harm resulting from its products, environmental waste, and worker and public safety.

Based on contents of above paragraphs we may define supply chain risk management as the ability of a firm to understand and manage its economic, environmental, and social risks in the supply chain. Corporations are increasingly recognizing that risk management is a part of their sustainability. Supply chain risk management can occur through contingency planning and by building more resilient and agile supply chains. As part of its sustainability, Motorola (2005) attempts to address potential supply chain disruptions via crisis teams that have:

✓ Developed preparedness plans to ensure that its response will be effective and its recovery swift. Teams conduct annual tests of their plans and capabilities to improve coordination, sharpen employee skills and discover potential trouble spots before an emergency happens.

Risk management also includes product stewardship issues related to being able to swiftly and efficiently recall damaged or tainted products (Corbett & Klassen 2007).

Sustainable supply chain management has emerged as a growing topic, receiving increasing interest in the sustainability and supply chain management area. While earlier publications that address related topics stated the major stream of research on sustainable supply chain management started in about the mid-1990s (Seuring & Müller 2007). The papers of Drumwright (1996) on "socially responsible organizational buying" and Murphy et al. (1994) on "management of environmental problems in logistics" marked the wide range of aspects taken into account later on. Issues addressed we may group according to different criteria, based on whether they deal with supply chain management or with sustainability management.

On the supply chain side, this includes research driven by different subthemes. The first subtheme is Purchasing (Min & Galle 2001, Zsidisin & Siferd 2001) and supply management (Bowen et al. 2001) form the basis towards what kind of additional criteria we must consider. Bowen et al. (2001) distinguish between "greening the supply process", where e.g. criteria for supplier selection are identified, and "product based green supply". The latter one aims to green the product itself, where frequently life-cycle assessment-based criteria consideration (Lamming & Hampson 1996, Pesonen 2001, Seuring 2004).

The second subtheme: The field of logistics has also contributed to this. Abukhader & Jönson (2004) presented detailed literature review on environmental issues in logistics.

The third subtheme is operations according Kleindorfer et al. (2005). The fourth subtheme is supply chain management formulated by Rao and Holt (2005) and Zhu et al. (2005). The economic impact is addressed through e.g. decision making (Sarkis 2003), cost management (Seuring 2001) or performance management (Hervani et al. 2005). On the sustainability side, the evaluation involves addressing environmental (Lamming & Hampson 1996, Roberts 2003) or social (Carter 2005) problems, but also related green product design (Baumann et al. 2002) and how sustainability issues might be integrated into supply chain management (Koplin et al. 2007). Vachon & Klassen (2006) studied the impact of cooperative supply chain environmental management.

2.2 Sustainable supply chain management

Assuming the literature review there are four major topics within sustainable supply chain management:

1. pressures and incentives for sustainable supply chain management,
2. identifying and measuring impacts on sustainable supply chain management,
3. supplier management (particularly addressing issues at the supplier–buyer interface) and
4. supply chain management (dealing with issues across all companies involved in the supply chain).

Simply we may say any supply chain subject has commitment to its Business' Success. Nevertheless, different firms have their own operations and processes. Both are unique. The reasons for that raise from the fact the companies tailor their services for each facility or organization they work for. Their business must run smoothly and protect the health of employees, the local community, and the planet, whenever possible. The company goal is to see its business rise above the competition, to become more sustainable and profitable. Company's experts implement extensive experience dealing with sustainable supply chain management, and excel at delivering results in an approachable, understandable manner.

2.3 Developing a supply chain of sustainable businesses

In nowadays entrepreneurship, the cooperation between suppliers, firm and customers is day-to-day changing environment. The key for success all of shareholders is their loyalty, openness and trust. It becomes quite normal in trust promotion between the partners they provide as well as share information necessary in building good relations. The company asks also information of third parties. By obtaining such demanding information document from partners the companies may concern since it could come from their primary customer. It would be difficult if they lost this customer, they would be in real trouble. There is only way they would have to review this form carefully, and maybe making some real changes to retain this customer's business.

That is the idea! Do business with the better organizations and stop doing business with those who act as if it is the 1950s. Corporate pressures, collectively, will make the companies more sustainable. In fact it is not important what company's line of business is, if company have not gotten one of these forms, company will. Soon. Moreover, when company does, if its value this customer's business, company too may have to make some changes at its business to meet the demands of tomorrow's customers.

Understanding how best to do this requires a multidisciplinary framework that draws from various different academic disciplines (other than OM, logistics and purchasing) such as sociology, computing, economics, philosophy, political science, health, construction and psychology to understand the impact that SC decisions can have on the societies and environments in which they operate.

Understanding, where competition can emerge from, how to mitigate against it and how to respond to it are increasingly important questions as SCs become more complex, global, new technologies emerge, and resources become more accessible. Recent examples of competition emerging from within an SC (from a supplier or a customer). Traditional competition theories are still relevant but new ones need to analyze competitive landscape changes and develops. In addition, there are still important gaps in areas regarding multi-criteria analysis of competition as well as randomness/uncertainty of competition parameters.

3 FINDINGS

3.1 Focusing on sustainable supply chains

If a company sells a thing to a customer, it most likely has a supply chain. In addition, that supply chain impacts almost every other business function. If that were not the case, it would be difficult to answer some of the following questions:

✓ How can Sales sell without Supply Chain supplying products?

✓ How can Finance calculate the cost of goods (and your profitability) without Supply Chain managing supplier and manufacturing costs?

✓ How can Research and Development research and develop new products without Supply Chain sourcing new components?

Nevertheless, what are supply chain and supply chain management? Supply chain management is not just the management of products—it is also the management of information, time and money. Let us have a look from the far end of the chain and work by way forward.

Tier II Suppliers

Supply chain management does not start when company orders a product from its suppliers. Company should be managing its product supply when its suppliers are sourcing their suppliers. We call it Tier II supplier management. If company's suppliers are not practicing supply chain management with its suppliers, company's own supply chain performance will suffer. That is why so many factors influence supply chain management field practice especially in Tier II supplier management field.

However, how can company influence its Tier II suppliers? The answer takes us back to what supply chain management is. It is the management of product flow, information, time and money. Moreover, for Tier II supplier management, "information" is one of the key performance drivers. The information company's Tier II suppliers need is the demand information that company has provided to its suppliers—whether that is forecasts are firm orders.

Company's Tier II suppliers can use that information to do its own capacity planning and raw materials buys (i.e. practice its own supply chain management). By ensuring company's Tier II suppliers have what they need to deliver on-time and cost effectively to company's suppliers, and then the company is on its way to optimizing own supply chain.

3.2 Supplier management

The arena of supplier management includes the cost of goods negotiations, on-time delivery management, quality audits and management, new product development—to name a few areas of focus.

Company's supply chain team will work with its suppliers' customer service teams, engineering teams, quality teams and even supply chain teams. Just as if company's customers probably measure its performance, it is important that company and its suppliers work together to determine the right metrics to measure their performance. On-time delivery is the most common metric that is measured, but make sure that company and its suppliers

understand the precise definition of on-time delivery that company will be measuring. On-time delivery is not having black-and-white as some might think. There are original promised delivery dates that can (and often) change during an order's lifetime.

In addition, company is measuring the dock date or the ship date. Oftentimes that will depend on the payment Terms Company has negotiated with its supplier. If company's payment terms are FOB Plant, for instance, that means company is responsible for the shipping method once the product leaves its supplier's plant.

In that case, company's on-time delivery metric would likely bases on the ship date. However, if company's payment terms are CIF, i.e. company's supplier pays for the cost, insurance and freight to deliver it to the company—then company's on-time metrics would likely be based on date the shipment arrives at your dock.

Logistics and supply chain are not the same things. Logistics is the management of the movement of goods whereas supply chain management covers the many other areas. Nevertheless, logistics is a part of supply chain and that means whoever manages company's supply chain will be responsible for managing freight forwarders, shipping companies, parcel delivery companies (like DHL and UPS), customs brokers and third-party logistics providers (3PL).

Logistics providers should manage in the same way that company manages work with its suppliers. Costs and contracts is negotiable. Company can source freight forwarders the same way the company would source suppliers of the products that the company needs. Shipping and warehousing costs can be one of the largest expenses in company's supply chain and it is critical that logistics providers are subjects of measure and then is possible to manage control of those costs.

Inventory represents one of the largest expenses in company's supply chain. The difference between paying for logistics and paying for inventory is that when company incurs the expense for logistics—it has received that benefit. A logistics provider ships something to the company and company pays them. Company has incurred the expense for a service rendered.

However, inventory is a double-edged sword. Often, company will pay its suppliers for its inventory and company will have the product company just paid for—but company has not received the benefit of that product. That benefit comes when company sells it. Moreover, that is where the inventory management aspect of supply chain management becomes critical.

There is supply chain management conundrum: Company needs product to sell to company's customers, but company will not have those products until company incur the expense of acquiring that product. Company needs to have enough inventory on hand to supply its customers what they want, when they want it—but company cannot have too much inventory on hand or company will have paid (possibly) too much money out of pocket.

There is the added risk that company can build too much inventory. Because company's suppliers might have minimum order quantities (MOQ), because company thoughts it would sell more than company did, or because something changed in the marketplace—company might end up paying for inventory that company can never sell.

Let us say company sells cases for smartphones. Moreover, not long ago, company acquired 10,000 pc of a Samsung 8 case that it planned to sell to Samsung, Nay, Datart, Alza and the other Samsung accessory retailers. Moreover, addition, after company sold 1,000 of them, Samsung launched the Samsung 9. Moreover, suddenly there was no market for company's Samsung 8 cases. Too much inventory. Money Company spent that will never recoups.

Inventory is a terrible balancing act. Company need enough, but not too much, – and company must make the decision on how much to acquire based on unreliable information. In such situation, it is much better to relay on experts in the field of supply chain management.

It is common to believe that supply chain is purchasing, but that is not accurate. Purchasing is a part of supply chain management, but it is not the totality of all that supply chain management. It is like saying that Slovak hockey is sports. While Slovak hockey is a subset of all sports, sports is so much more. Based on hockey analogy we may see the purchasing is a lot of blocking and tackling. While some purchasing teams are giving sourcing and negotiating responsibility, most of what a purchasing team does is transactional. Choosing the lowest priced supplier and cutting a purchase order does not constitute strategic supply chain management—although it is important for the day-to-day operations of any company.

Buyers and purchasing managers can grow into supply chain professionals, but it takes an understanding that the transactional activity of purchasing is only a small slice of what supply chain management is.

In some companies, some experts do not consider customer service as a part of supply chain. However, if company looks at the scope of supply chain management's definition in any industry the supply chain is not complete until company's product end user is using it. While company's supply chain may not reach all the way to a consumer, it should include what it takes to deliver company's product to its customer's dock. Customer service functions is the voice of the customer at company. If company receives this voice than it may clearly, answers

such questions: What shipping method does customer want? What size boxes does company need to pack product in and how many units per pack? Company's customer can drive those answers, especially if its customer is a big box retailer.

Company's customer service team drives company to deliver what customers want, and when customers want it. Since on-time delivery—both inbound and outbound—is one of the primary functions of supply chain management, customer service belongs in supply chain.

Managing the cost of company's products reflects the value of its overall inventory and logistics expenses—that is all company's CFO is going to want to know company's supply chain leadership is managing. Supply chain management is uniquely in position to be the cost monitor at the company.

Accuracy bases on an idea, that none of the cost analyses or metrics are any good if they are not accurate. Supply chain management needs to make sure the underlying data that drive on-time delivery reports and other supplier performance data is accurate. That requires audits of company's internal processes and audits at its suppliers.

Inventory accuracy is one of the most critical elements of valuing a company. Supply chain management team should be driving daily cycle counts of company's inventory. Then—at least once per year—company should be conducting a 100 percent physical inventory of everything on its books. If company has more than a 1 percent variance between what company's system tells it and what company's, physical count tells—that means company must work to do to get to 100 percent inventory accuracy.

At the end of the day, supply chain management assumes when company is delivering what its customers want, when they want it and doing that by spending as little money as possible. Cost of goods management, inventory control and manage company's entire supply chain from its Tier II suppliers to company's customers will get company on the right track.

4 CONCLUSION

SCM has been one of the most important management philosophies since 1982 as it has gained considerable attention from both practitioners and academics around the world. Although logistics is the main building block of every supply chain, SCM differs from logistics in requiring an integrated and coordinated approach to managing flows of material, information and money in competitive environments.

The main results of this article is showing trends of different areas within SCM, as well as most prominent techniques and philosophies in SCM. Then, we elaborated on implementation of SCM concepts, practice and introduced some promising future research areas within SCM. We underlined an important issue how organizations should manage security, insourcing, sustainability, competition, risk/disruption and human behavioural issues within their supply chains. We paid an attention to necessity of understanding the particular practices, challenges and opportunities. SCM academics and professionals to redefine the focus point of their research and application of SCM could use these recommendations.

REFERENCES

Abukhader, S.M. & Jönson, G. 2004. Logistics and the Environment: Is it an Established Subject? International Journal of Logistics: Research and Applications 7(2): 17–149.

Baumann, H. et al. 2002. Mapping the green product development field: engineering, policy and business perspectives. Journal of Cleaner Production 10(5): 409–425.

Bowen, F. E, et al. 2001. The role of supply management capabilities in green supply. Production and Operations Management 10(2): 174 189.

Brandeburg, M. et al. 2014. Quantitative models for sustainable supply chain management: developments and directions. Eur. J. Oper. Res., 233, 299–312.

Carter, C.R. 2005. Purchasing social responsibility and firm performance: the key mediating roles of organizational learning and supplier performance. International Journal of Physical Distribution and Logistics Management 35(3): 177–194.

Corbett, C.J. & Klassen, R.D. 2007. "Extending the horizons: environmental excellence as key to improving operations", Manufacturing and Service Operations Management, Vol. 8 No. 1, pp. 5–22.

Drumwright, M. 1996. "Company advertising with a social dimension: the role of noneconomic criteria", Journal of Marketing, Vol. 60 No. 4, pp. 71–87.

Elkington, J. 1998. Cannibals with Forks: The Triple Bottom Line of the 21st Century, New Society Publishers, Stoney Creek, CT.

Elkington, J. 2004. "Enter the triple bottom line", in Henriques, A. and Richardson, J. (Eds), The Triple Bottom Line: Does It All Add up?, Earthscan, London, pp. 1–16.

Gladwin, T.N. et al. 1995. "Shifting paradigms for sustainable development: implications for management theory and research", Academy of Management Review, Vol. 20 No. 4, pp. 874–907.

Google images. Retrieved from: https://www.researchgate.net/publication/275556774/figure/fig3/AS:319985432973312@1453301880209/The-triple-bottom-line-of-sustainability-19.png.

Hervani, A. et al. 2005. Performance measurement for green supply chain management. Benchmarking: an International Journal 12(4): 330–353.

Min, H. & Galle, W.P. 2001. Green purchasing practices of US firms. International Journal of Operations and Production Management 21(9): 1222–1238.

Murphy, P.R. et al. 1994. Management of environmental issues in logistics: current status and future potential. Transportation Journal 34(1): 48–56.

Kleindorfer, P.R., et al. 2005. Sustainable operations management. Production and Operations Management 14(4): 482–492.

Koplin, J., et al. 2007. Incorporating sustainability into supply policies and supply processes in the automotive industry – the case of Volkswagen. Journal of Cleaner Production 15(11): 1053–1062.

Kuhn, T.S. 1996. The Structure of Scientific Revolutions, 3rd ed., University of Chicago Press, Chicago, IL.

Lamming, R.C. & Hampson, J.P. 1996. The Environment as a Supply Chain Management Issue. British Journal of Management 7 (Special Issue): 45–62.

Motorola 2005. Motorola Corporate Citizenship Report, Motorola, Schaumburg, IL.

New, S. 2010. The transparent supply chain. Harv. Bus. Rev. 88, 76–82.

Nikbakhsh, E. 2009. Green supply chain management. Logistics and Supply Chain Management in International, National and Governmental Environment (R.Z. Farahani, N. Asgari & H. Davarzanieds). Berlin: Springer, pp. 195–220.

Pesonen, H.L. 2001. Environmental management of value chains. Greener Management International 33: 45–58.

Rao, P. & Holt D. 2005. Do green supply chains lead to competitiveness, and economic performance? International Journal of Operations and Production Management 25(9): 898–916.

Roberts, S. 2003. Supply chain specific? Understanding the patchy success of ethical sourcing initiatives. Journal of Business Ethics 44(2): 159–170.

Sarkis, J. 2003. A strategic decision framework for green supply chain management. Journal of Cleaner Production 11(4): 397–409.

Savitz, A.W. & Weber, K. 2006. The Triple Bottom Line, Jossey-Bass, San Francisco, CA.

Seuring, S. 2001. Green supply chain costing – joint cost management in the polyester linings supply chain. Greener Management International 33: 71–80.

Seuring, S. 2004. Industrial ecology, life-cycles, supply chains – differences and interrelations. Business Strategy and the Environment 13(5): 306–319.

Seuring, S. & Müller, M. 2007. Core Issues in Sustainable Supply Chain Management—A Delphi Study. Available from: https://www.researchgate.net/publication/227704125_Core_Issues_in_Sustainable_Supply_Chain_Management-A_Delphi_Study [accessed Jun 24 2018].

Shrivastava, P. 1995. "Ecocentric management for a risk society", Academy of Management Review, Vol. 20 No. 1, pp. 118–37.

Vachon, S. & Klassen, R.D. 2006. Extending green practices across the supply chain – the impact of upstream and downstream integration. International Journal of Operations and Production Management 26(7): 795–821.

Zsidisin, G.A. & Siferd, S P. 2001. Environmental purchasing: a framework for theory development. European Journal of Purchasing and Supply Management 7(1): 61–73.

Zhu, Q., Sarkis J. & Geng Y. 2005. Green supply chain management in China: pressures, practices and performance. International Journal of Operations and Production Management 25(5): 449–468.

Production Management and Business Development – Mihalčová et al. (Eds)
© *2019 Taylor & Francis Group, London, ISBN 978-1-138-60415-5*

Post-truth—a new trend in marketing management

M. Rzemieniak & M. Maciaszczyk
Faculty of Management, Lublin University of Technology, Lublin, Poland

ABSTRACT: Post-truth is an outcome of technological changes in the marketing environment. The phenomenon of post-truth has a huge impact on the marketing activities of enterprises and on entrepreneurial attitudes. The objective of the study is to characterise the impact of the newest trends in the marketing environment on marketing and entrepreneurship in general. The article presents the results of research on the influence of post-truth on the marketing strategies of business organisations. The study is supplemented with examples and makes use of research focussing on secondary sources obtained through the desk research method and participating observations carried out by the authors.

1 INTRODUCTION

Post-truth is a trend currently observed in our surrounding reality. The term appears in the context of an increased impact of digital reality on consumer behaviour in the real world. Post-reality is when consumers buy subscriptions to have continuous access to products without having to deal with the distribution, storage or maintenance of real products, etc. Technological solutions enable the co-existence of digital and physical reality. For many users this is completely natural (for instance, numerous filters on Snapchat). The technological options of controlling the acoustic reality are used in the business practice to eliminate unwanted sounds (e.g. baby's crying on an airplane). In medicine the scenarios of managing people's future by genetic control are becoming reality (TrendBook, pp. 34).

The survey was carried out with a CAWI (Computer-Assisted Web Interview) method—responsive electronic questionnaires available through a website and email. Opinions of 1112 Internet users were collected. The survey was implemented from 3 to 9 March 2017. The structure of the sample consisting of Internet users was adjusted with an analytical weight and corresponded to the structure of Polish internauts aged 15 or more broken down by gender, age and size of their place of residence. Only complete questionnaires were used in the analysis. The survey was performed by the Mobile Institute (Hermann 2017, pp. 6).

2 POST-THRUTH—THE ESSENCE OF CREAVITY AS A NEW TREND IN MARKETING MANAGEMENT

Creativity is a very crucial characteristic of human capital. It can be defined as creating useful and valuable products, services, ideas, procedures or ideas by entities collaborating with each other. Creativity may also be an important feature of all aspects of decision-making in business. The phenomenon of inspiring new thoughts, reformulating the existing knowledge and analysing assumptions to express new theories and paradigms or raising awareness. This is a process which involves identifying, selecting, exchanging and linking facts, ideas and skills (Proctor 1998, pp. 34). The world-famous psychologist M. Wertheimer described creativity as "division or reorganisation of thoughts on a given subject to obtain a new, deeper insight in its nature" (Wertheimer 1959, pp. 49). In turn, T. Rickards defined creativity as "an escape from stagnation in thinking" (Rickards 1998, pp. 121–123), emphasising the role of creative thinking in decision-making and problem-solving (Proctor 1998, pp. 36).

There is evidence to confirm a direct link between creative thinking and the effectiveness and productivity of organisations (The European Report 2010, pp. 45). A creative approach also makes it possible to solve organisational problems, encourages employees to introduce novel solutions, motivates them and helps them develop their skills, and also enhances team work (Sato 2017, pp. 223).

Creativity is also very crucial in marketing and in designing the global operating strategies of businesses (John 2017, pp. 117–129). With the constant flow of ideas about new products and services and the concept of streamlining processes in an organisation, its competitive edge increases as well (Blank 2015, pp. 117–129).

Contemporary enterprises are increasingly often focussing on activities having their source in human creativity, which not only gives rise to original ideas, novel solutions and variety, but also becomes a crucial economic development factor.

Creativity becomes a distinguishing factor between creative business and regular companies.

3 THE CONTEMPORARY IMAGE OF MARKETING MANAGEMENT AND ENTREPRENEURSHIP

The notion of entrepreneurship has been the subject of numerous disputes among researchers and society. It has been broadly discussed in the literature on the subject, where its meaning and essence has been considered. In a contemporary perspective, entrepreneurship can be defined as a combination of several characteristics and skills such as the ability to take up risks, innovative thinking, recognising needs and opportunities, creativity in action, flexibility and dynamism in decision-making, as a result of which business entities come into being and are able to develop. Entrepreneurship was first described by the French economist R. Cantillon, who defined it as hunting for opportunities everywhere there is a market imbalance which may bring extraordinary profit (Kangsoo 2017, pp. 212). He also claimed that entrepreneurship is an ability to project into the future and to take risks (Robinett 2017, pp. 111). J.B. Saya talked about concentrating on emphasising the significance of work capital and entrepreneurial activity factors in "combining means of production" (Piecuch 2005, pp. 162). A. Smith and D. Ricardo attached lesser significance to entrepreneurship, claiming that entrepreneurs do not have an impact on the economy, which is governed by "the invisible hand of the market", at the same time associating businesspeople with greedy capitalists. According to J. Schumpeter entrepreneurship and entrepreneurs are an innovation destroying the market balance and enabling it to reach a higher level of development. Through combining means of production entrepreneurs create new products and technologies which they introduce in the economy regardless of their capital (Schumpeter 1983, pp. 66). Contrary to the above theory, I. Kitzner claimed that entrepreneurs use the arbitration function on the market to adjust prices, thanks to which they contribute to market balance. They respond to the arising opportunities instead of creating them (Kirzner 1973, pp. 73). A bridging theory between the two was presented by F. Knight, who considered the compensation for uncertainty and risk as the source of profit. Currently a number of descriptions refer to the definition presented by P. Drucker (a follower of Schumpeter's line of thought), who presented entrepreneurship as purposeful and systematic work based on innovativeness, preceded by seeking change, responding to it by treating it as opportunities, and, in consequence, all these activities should be reflected in a new economic activity. Innovation is regarded as an instrument which provides resources with a new ability to create wealth, new products and processes, the result of which is creating a new market, generating demand and acquiring new customers (Drucker 2007, pp. 25–29). J. Siekierski supported these views, presenting entrepreneurship as an ability to get involved in a given process individually or as a team. In his opinion, the inseparable elements of entrepreneurship are innovativeness and creating new business endeavours, which require new creative approaches (Liu 2017, pp. 150–151). Furthermore, J. Timmons emphasised that money and access to resources are not a guarantee of success, and many undertakings do not require considerable outlays. Entrepreneurship is a creative act of the entrepreneur, who devotes their time and energy to create a company or organisation, not being limited to observing, describing and analysing it (Timmons 1990, pp. 5). The interpretation of this definition may cause some controversies because it downplays the significance of resources, which entrepreneurs may obtain thanks to their knowledge, skills and connections, i.e. intangible resources (Liu 2017, pp. 187–189). The European Commission defined entrepreneurship as "(…) an individual's ability to turn ideas into action. The notion encompasses creativity, innovativeness and risk-taking, as well as the ability to plan and manage projects to meet objectives" (Robinett 2017, pp. 132).

Currently start-ups are the most recognisable form of entrepreneurship, often associated with garage entrepreneurship. Garage entrepreneurship is an essence of entrepreneurial activities, with innovative ideas, passion and dedication of businesspeople, thanks to whom new business undertakings launched in garages develop dynamically and reach impressive sizes (Witmer 2017, pp. 220). The characteristics of start-ups include innovativeness, creativity, high risk, originality, focus on the future, flexibility, dedication, resilience and resistance to failure. The examples of successful start-ups which have turned into real businesses are Google, Amazon, PayPal, Facebook, Airbnb, and the relatively new Uber. These are enterprises which decided to create unique services. Before Google the online advertising market was practically non-existent; the same applies to online sales (Amazon), online payments (Paypal), social media (Facebook), hospitality services (Airbnb) and Uber, which is a real competition for taxis. Steve Blank created the most recognisable definition of a start-up. According to him a start-up is an organisation which seeks a profitable, scalable and repeatable business model (Blank & Dofr 2012). Eric Ries describes start-ups as organisations which creates products and services under the conditions of extreme uncertainty (Ries 2012). Currently start-ups are associated with innovation, which is the main driver of the economy. This is evidenced in the presence of numerous national and local government institutions supporting innovativeness and the processes of creating and developing new enterprises.

An enterprise which has survived the difficult transformation period, after reaching the profitability threshold is trying to enter the market. However, contemporary organisations are constantly competing. Extremely strong competition, excessive supply, the quick ageing of products and the necessity to immediately satisfy customer expectations are just a few reasons why traditional, established organisations are becoming a relic of the past (Maige & Muller, 1995). In the ever-changing, dynamic surroundings with growing complexity and intensive competition, relying on proven solutions leads to the premature ageing of organisations (Probst & Raisch 2005, pp. 90–105). Therefore, to stay on the market, entrepreneurs must make use of marketing as a management tool. An effective market presence requires enterprises to get involved in marketing activities and to adjust to the needs, possibilities and requirements of their industry (Witmer 2017, pp. 1162). A marketing orientation necessitates an individual selection of organisational entities and creating a system of internal and external links (John 2017, pp. 99). Changes in the business environment indicate that marketing is becoming increasingly important for enterprises in the process of achieving their goals, which is why marketing should become the key factor in determining the strategic direction for enterprise development (Jung 2017, pp. 114). The crucial role of marketing in creating the value of businesses is reflected in the new definition of marketing adopted by the American Marketing Association in 2013. Marketing is the activity, set of institutions, and processes for creating, communicating, delivering, and exchanging offerings that have value for customers, clients, partners, and society at large.

4 RESEARCH RESULTS AND OVERVIEW

4.1 New trend in marketing management—findings

The phenomenon of sharing objectively false information online (post-truth) take several forms, such as *clickbait, phishing* and *website spoofing*; however, in the recent year *fake news* became the most powerful carrier of post-truth.

Fake news blossomed during the US presidential campaign in 2016. False articles were produced on a mass scale, attracting significantly more readers than information published by renowned media. Apart from that, today the traditional media do not offer a guarantee of truthfulness. Early 2017 brought a new kind of fake news – *alternative facts.* Alternative facts are a linguistic construct coined by Kellyanne Conway, Counsellor to the US President, to explain the vast differences between measurable data and information released by the White House.

The phenomenon of post-truth is mostly connected with the media market. However, it was observed that trust towards public institutions, NGOs, companies and brands is decreasing—the level of trust in each of these categories has never been so low (Edelman 2016, pp. 68).Therefore, it is possible to state that the phenomenon of post-truth is a prelude to a major global crisis of trust.

One of the basic mechanisms determining the escalation of the post-truth phenomenon are social media (in particular Facebook and Twitter). The ease of sharing information, articles, films and animations leads to fake news appearing side by side with real information. Their verification is currently very difficult and often impossible.

However, political propaganda is not the only justification of such an abrupt development of the trend. Most clickbait articles (which attract readers with a misleading title and a miniature photo) are motivated by the profit generated by each display of AdSense ads on the website after opening it. Here the truth often loses with the number of clicks. Profit is the most frequent motivation for spammers, scammers and fake news creators. The owner and editor of one of the most influential websites disseminating fake news, Ovidiu Drobota, runs a portal on American politics named EndingTheFed because in America it is possible to earn more for clicks than in Eastern Europe. Post-truth also develops because of human tendencies to reaffirm their views, to be malicious and envious. The impact of fake news is amplified by its enormous reach and the possibility of spreading information in social media, following and blocking specific sources and the progressing automatic personalisation of content, search results, etc. The effect is referred to as *social echo chamber*.

Despite the fact that the presence of post-truth, fake news and alternative facts is the strongest in the media and politics, their impact is visible in a number of sectors. The yearly Edelman Trust Barometer, carried out regularly since 2001, points to a global crisis of trust concerning not only governments and politicians but also institutions, private companies, NGOs, the media, and even friends and acquaintances.

The conclusions drawn from the report point to the required changes and the necessity to adapt the marketing strategies used by enterprises. In the congestion of false and manipulated information people have lost their faith in authority—out of 28 surveyed countries CEOs are perceived as unreliable (they are trusted by on average 37% of respondents). The most trustworthy spokespeople of enterprises are ordinary employees, whose reliability is assessed up to five times higher than that of actual press spokespersons. Information published through official channels is also approached with reserve—the surveyed declared that their trust towards uncontrolled information leaks was almost twice as high. Interestingly, a similar proportion was recorded for trust towards adverts (38%) in comparison to the reliability of announcements published in social media (62%).

The results point to the need of cooperation between brands and influencers—people who are closer to the customers, perceived as honest, spontaneous and uncorrupted. Unfortunately, the recent months have brought a number of examples of influencers using methods typical for post-truth in their activities.

The media market requires particularly firm action—even the esteemed media companies with a strong position recorded a 5% decrease in trust in 2017, reaching an unprecedentedly low global result of 43%. The average is lowered by, i.e. the US, where only 32% of the respondents trust the media, and the percentage is continuously dropping. The results of research carried out among Polish Internet users for the TrendBook indicate a similar level of trust. Among the traditional channels, television is considered the most reliable (22% of the respondents), while radio is trustworthy for 10% of the surveyed. Online news is trusted by 21% of the respondents, and social media content—by 17% (Hatalska 2017, pp. 76–79).

5 CONCLUSIONS

Special attention should be drawn to educating children and adolescents in the critical analysis of information and its sources. The problem of differentiating between verifiable truth and manipulation is becoming increasingly difficult. It seems essential to develop data search skills to be able to support the information presented in the media.

One of the most effective weapons against fake news and declining trust seems to be transparency presented by enterprises and institutions, i.e. publishing real news about their operations. During a global crisis of trust and disillusionment with the current system, the younger generations expect brands to be transparent. This refers to the production process, to applying responsible environmental strategies, to employee attitudes and to the remuneration system, etc. Paradoxically, the remedy to the post-truth issue is very simple—this is the fairness and transparency of enterprises, organisations, brands and individuals.

REFERENCES

American Marketing Association 2013. www.ama.org. (18.02.2018).

Blank, S. & Dorf, B. 2015. *Podręcznik startupu. Budowa wielkiej firmy krok po kroku.*, Wyd. Helion, Gliwice.

Drucker, P.F. 2007. Innowacja i przedsiębiorczość, Elsevier, Oxford.

Edelman 2016. *Trust Barometer*, Global Report, Edelman.

Hatalska, N. 2017. *Trendbook*.

Herrmann, E. et al. 2017. *Accelerating statistical human motion synthesis using space partitioning data structures*, "SPECIAL ISSUE PAPERS Computer Animation and Virtual Worlds", Version of Record online: 12 MAY 2017.

John, N.W. et al. 2017. *The Use of Stereoscopy in a Neurosurgery Training Virtual Environment*, Presence-Teleoperators and Virtual Environments, Posted Online March 15, 2017.

Jung, S. et al. 2017. *Age-related gait motion transformation based on biomechanical observations*, "SPECIAL ISSUE PAPERS Computer Animation and Virtual Worlds", Version of Record online: 12 MAY 2017.

Kangsoo, K. et al. 2017. *The effects of virtual human's spatial and behavioral coherence with physical objects on social presence in AR*, "SPECIAL ISSUE PAPERS Computer Animation and Virtual Worlds", Version of Record online: 21 MAY 2017.

Kirzner, I. 1973. Competition and Entrepreneuship, The University of Chicago, Chicago.

Liu, Ch. et al. 2017. *Sky detection- and texture smoothing-based high-visibility haze removal from images and videos*, "SPECIAL ISSUE PAPERS Computer Animation and Virtual Worlds", Version of Record online: 3 MAY 2017.

Maige, Ch. & Muller, J.L. 1995. *Walka z czasem. Atut strategiczny przedsiębiorstwa*, Wyd. Poltext, Warszawa.

Probst, G. & Raisch, S. 2005. *Organizational crisis: The logic of failure*, Academy of Management Executive, 19(1).

Proctor T. 1998. *Zarządzanie twórcze*, Wyd. Gebethner & Ska, Warszawa.

Raport Europejski 2010. *Rok Kreatywności i Innowacji w Polsce*, Fundacja Rozwoju Systemu Edukacji, Warszawa.

Rickards, T. 1998. *Creativity and Innovation: A Transatlantic Perspective. Creativity and Innovation Yearbook*, Vol. 1. Manchester Business School, Manchester.

Ries, E. 2012. *The Lean Startup*, Wyd. Helion, Gliwice.

Robinett, W. 2017. *Technological Augmentation of Memory, Perception, and Imagination—From the Viewpoints of 1991 and 2017*, Presence-Teleoperators and Virtual Environments, Posted Online March 15, 2017.

Sato, S. et al. 2017. *Age-related gait motion transformation based on biomechanical observations.* "SPECIAL ISSUE PAPERS Computer Animation and Virtual Worlds", Version of Record online: 3 MAY 2017.

Schumpeter, J.A. 1983. *The Theory of Economic Development*, NewBrunswick, New Jersey.

The European Report, 2010.

Timmons, J. 1990. *New Venture Creation*, Irvin, Boston.

TrendBook 2017. *Trendbook, Hatalska Natalia*.

Wertheimer, M. 1959. *Productive Thinking*, Harper & Row, New York.

Witmer, B.G. & Singer, M.J. 2017. *Measuring Presence in Virtual Environments: A Presence Questionnaire*. Presence-Teleoperators and Virtual Environments, Posted Online March 13, 2016.

Production Management and Business Development – Mihalčová et al. (Eds)
© 2019 Taylor & Francis Group, London, ISBN 978-1-138-60415-5

Soft management factors and organizations—outcome of research

A. Rzepka
Faculty of Management, Lublin University of Technology, Lublin, Poland

ABSTRACT: The purpose of this article is to identify those public sector organizations as well as other entities such as business associations, local government bodies, research centers which are helpful for the development of entrepreneurship. The thesis of the article is an assumption that inter—organizational cooperation promotes the creation of soft management factors, and that this cooperation will improve the effectiveness of public sector organizations. The author attention has been drawn to such soft factors as trust, social capital, and organizational capital. The article presents the results of research with the use of such methods as: the sociological survey, interview, case study. According to the author, soft factors have a significant impact on the effectiveness of public sector organizations by intensifying cooperation as a result of increased confidence, growth of social capital, etc., which fosters the broadening of innovation of cooperating bodies.

1 INTRODUCTION

The purpose of this article is to identify the differences and similarities between commercial and non-commercial organizations, their inter-dependencies and interactions. Attention has also been paid to the role and importance of soft management factors such as trust, intellectual capital, and knowledge. It was tried to prove that these factors are necessary to enhance this cooperation, thereby fostering the innovation of cooperating organizations and enhancing their competitiveness. Hence, another research area emerges which is an identification of and an attempt to measure soft factors.

2 THE IMPORTANCE OF THE PUBLIC SECTOR

The public sector has been present since the formation of nations, however, the approach towards its role, functions and scope of activities public sector organizations has been considerably changed. It can be argued that by the eighteen century the public sector's activities were generally limited to legal and financial ones and partly to provide the public with social assistance and safety. This was due to a classic economy approach, taking into account the leading role of the invisible market hand as a mechanism for allocating resources and the satisfaction of society. Then, in the nineteenth century, the attempts were made to increase the involvement of the public sector in economy. "Public sector services have increased rapidly since the late nineteenth century as successive governments have undertaken the obligation to provide social security benefits, pensions, health, education, defense and a myriad of other services for their citizens" (Singh 2010).

Public expenses were increased to meet the objectives of the wider collective needs. This has also been reflected in the activities of many countries that have begun to regulate economic processes and mitigate social processes. As a result, various forms of welfare state and in XX century were formed and the so-called social market economy as well. The engagement of the nation in this respect fostered the development of the public sector and the scope of its activities but at the same time this resulted in an increase in expenditure. In this context, in economies of a market character there has been a growing interest in public sector reform activities since the seventies of the twentieth century. The model of administrative management of the economy has been questioned and an expanded public sector was criticized. The public authorities of the countries, especially those affected by the recession, faced the need to reduce public spending while preserving the quality of services. The attention has been drawn to the management of the public sector, based, as in the private sector, on established work standards and indicators of its effectiveness, control of the prepared plans and the results of the activities carried out, the impact and dependence factors existing in the public sector.

Public administration in the 21st century is undergoing dramatic change, especially in advanced economies, but also in many parts of the developing world. Globalization and the pluralization of service provision are the driving forces behind these changes. Policy problems faced by governments are increasingly complex, wicked and global, rather than simple, linear, and national in focus (Robinson 2015).

3 PUBLIC SECTOR ORGANISATIONS

Management in the public sector differs significantly from management in commercial enterprises. The main purpose of this management is to provide people with a particular service or good. Public sector organizations operate in certain market dependence, such as the comparability of costs, wages, investments, renovations, purchases, maintenance of equipment, but their action is determined by the imperative of meeting the needs of population.

The public sector is characterized by a considerable dependence on the current policy, and the decisions taken are of a temporary or even of business nature. To a greater extent, it concerns (1) state administration, or local government, to a lesser extent (2) universities, hospitals, and cultural institutions, to the least (3) non-governmental organizations (NGOs).

In total, by examining the possibility of management in these three groups of organizations, it is advisable to respect the principle of effectiveness and efficiency (efficiency) in a holistic approach to organization (Roberts 2008, Kożuch 2004, Hensel 2016).

4 ROLE AND IMPORTANCE OF SOFT FACTORS

The interest in soft factors began in the 1990s, with the development of computer science and the increasing role and importance of innovation in improving the competitiveness of companies. It seems that originally the problems of information management and knowledge were of primary importance (Davis & Botkin 1994).

The second area of interest was the phenomenon of intellectual capital (Steward1999). The third area of interest was the research over trust and the inclusion of psychological and sociological issue (Szompka 2007) to management research (Grudzewski & Hejduk 2007).

One of the first attempts to characterize soft factors and their measurement was made by Stachowicz. Together with a team of experts, he conducted a research over the clusters of enterprises in Silesian Voivodeship, using the Likiert scale, and by applying the sociological survey (Stachowicz 2006).

The notion of soft factors was shaped in the opposition of hard factors such as: raw materials, material, goods, machinery, buildings, etc. The phenomenon which characterized soft factors is that the more often they are used, the more of them are being created. In contrast to the hard factors, the more often they are used, the easier they are depleted, decreased and used and have to be recycled.

The phenomenon of creation of soft factors and their use by society creates new perspectives for the economy, allowing expecting a pervasive prosperity (Rifkin 2017).

The emergence of soft factors in inter-organizational networks is of particular importance. Such networks are conducive to the flattening of organizational structures, their decentralization, which promotes the growth of self-reliance of workers, increases their creativity and innovation, promotes the development of process management and self-management (Holacracy) (Bernstein 2016).

It is clear that the decentralization of organizational structures reduces the possibility of exerting pressure, but at the same time enhances the effect of cooperation, favors tolerance and openness, which encourages the generation of soft factors (Olesiński & Rzepka 2017).

5 SOFT FACTORS MEASUREMENT

The measurement of soft factors is a measurement of a sociological or even psychological nature. It is the measurement of certain reactions, behaviors that manifest themselves, or opinions. Relatively, the most easily certain data on the quantitative nature of the soft factors can be obtained, in the course of the interview or by developing a case study.

Basically, it involves arrangement of spoken opinions by their comparison, for example which statement has been spoken more bluntly, decisively, profoundly or gently.

Some data can be easily accessed by asking respondents about the frequency of relationships with individuals or organizations and the intensity of these relations. This method was used during the implementation of research grant of the Scientific Research Committee no. 2HOZDO2122 (Olesiński 2005).

78 organizations including research centers, local government bodies, government agencies, media were examined on account of their cooperation. Data obtained are presented in the table below.

Out of 290 respondents, only 139 people can indicate the names of organizations that are in relationship with their parent company. The names

Table 1.   Juxtaposition of the frequency of contacts with chosen organisations according to respondents.

Name	Number of indications as "key words"	Very often contacts	Help obtained often or very often in task implementation
Voivodship office	11	67	28
Marshal's Office	1	51	24
Municipal Office	5	108	34
Local authority government unit	6	101	27
Agency for Restructuring	0	17	3
Fundation for the Promotion	0	24	17
A business incubator in Starachowice	1	12	18
Media	0	78	40
Schools	14	86	34
Banks	103	162	61
Business entities	141	113	76
Local authority government unit:			
Commune self-government unit	10	Lack of data	33
Regional self-government unit	5	Lack of data	33
Voivodship self-government unit	5	Lack of data	20

Source: Z. Olesiński, zarządzanie w regionie…, p. 57.

Table 2.   Nature of connections between groups of organizations.

Names of groups of organizations	Higher schools	Business support organisations	Companies	Entreprenauship	Local government units	Offices
Offices	4	4	4	4	4	4
Local government units	5	6	4	5	2	
Companies	2	4	2	2		
Banks	2	2	2			
Business support organisations	5	5				
Higher schools	2					

Where 1 – connection of an unfriendly nature, 2 – connection of a competing nature, 3 – connection of a neutral nature, 4 – connection of a friendly nature, 5 – connection of a partner nature, 6 – connection of a cooperative nature, 7 – very strong cooperation.
Source: Olesiński 2005, pp.70.

of these organizations were used 418 times by 139 respondents. Most of the examined companies, especially the linear employees were unable to indicate any organizational names from the environment. On the other hand, those who pointed several or a dozen of names of organizations from the environment indicated them correctly, as it was evidenced by the high recurrence of each organization, almost 3 times among 139 names of a total of 418 indications.

Of the 143 mentioned organizational names, 69 are the names of companies, 31-banks and related organizations, 14 are business support organizations (associations, foundations), 9-offices, 8-regional authorities, 8-names of countries, 3-names associated with the European Union and 1-name of the international trade organization.

A larger number of names, were enumerated by a group of 50–60 respondents from different groups of organizations. It was found that the indications of very frequent contacts (practically daily) indicated a much higher number of respondents (see column 3) than the number of respondents who mentioned these organizations (see column 2). On the other hand, the question concerning the frequency of contacts in the parent organization of the respondent with the selected organization group, in order to benefit from the cooperation in carrying out the task (column 4) indicated as frequent (once a week) and very often (practically every day), it was less than in the third column.

6 THE INFLUENCE OF SOFT FACTORS ON COOPERATION OF A PRIVATE SECTOR WITH PUBLIC SEKTOR

An important area in the public sector is the essence of cooperation. Cooperation is demonstrated by the ability to create ties and interactions with others, ability to work in a group to achieve common goals, to perform tasks in a team and to solve common problems.

The authors presented below the results of their own studies carried out in the private sector (Research were carried out ina period of 10.2016–02.2017 in enterprises of the Podkarpackie voivodeship. (Olesinski et al. 2017). Based on the results of the research, it can be said that mutual cooperation exists in two sectors.

According to diagram 1, representatives of other types of organizations in which a significant advantage have the representatives of education organizations, most often cooperate with other organizations/institutions. Only in the case of cooperation with the consultancy firms they had to give priority to the representatives of industrial

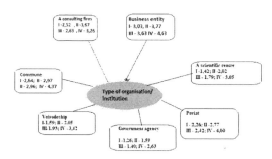

Figure 1. Model which shows a frequency of cooperation of examined companies with other institutions/organizations.
Source: Own study based on Rzepka 2017.

Figure 2. A model that shows the size of cooperation of examined companies with other organisations/institutions.
Source: Own study based on Rzepka 2017.

production. In general, the cooperation of all companies is mostly undertaken with the commune or other companies (even several times in a quarter), while the least often with a government agency (once in a few years or never).

Figure 2 shows the size of cooperation among analyzed companies. It turns out that it is very dependent on the type of organization with which cooperation is undertaken. As far as cooperation with companies is concerned, commercial companies are leading here—on average each of them cooperates with six other companies. In case of other organisations, the advantage of one company over another is not so significant, but it is worth noting that organisations of different nature (mostly of educational nature) cooperate with the highest number of consultancy companies and research centres whereas the representatives of the service companies cooperate with government agencies.

7 CONCLUSION

The aim of the article was to identify the impact of the soft management factors on the effectiveness of public sector organizations. The content of the article includes attempts to identify public sector organizations such as business associations, local authorities, national institutions, schools, universities, scientific and research centers that may and are able to cooperate with each other and business entities.

Soft factors are information and knowledge, intellectual capital, trust and cultural conditions.

The article contains the results of research conducted by author, ways of measurement of soft factors using a sociological survey and comparison of outcome.

The author has proven that inter-organizational cooperation fosters the creation of soft management factors, which improve the effectiveness of public sector organizations. On the basis of the studies presented above, it should be noted that without the participation of soft factors the growth of these factors would not be so explicit and their role would not be so important.

REFERENCES

Bernstein, E. et al. 2016. *Beyond the Holarcacy hype*, [In:] Harvard Business review, July- August, pp. 38–049.
Davis, S. &. Botkin, J. 1994. *The Coming of Knowledge Based Business* Harvard Business Reviev, no. 5, p. 166.
Frączkiewicz-Wronka, A. 2004. *Poszukiwanie istoty zarządzania publicznego*, [In:] *Zarządzanie publiczne – elementy teorii i praktyki scholarly (and critical)* editing A. Frączkiewicz- Wronka, p. 31.

Grudzewski, W.M. et al. 2007. *Zarządzanie zaufaniem w organizacjach wirtualnych*, Publisher: Difin, Warsaw.

Hensel, P. 2016. *Sektor publiczny – specyfika i metody zarządzania*, [In:] B. Glonka, M. Kostera, *Nowe kierunki w organizacji i zarządzaniu; organizacje, konteksty, procesy zarządzania*, Publisher: Wolter Kluwer business, vol. II, Warsaw, p. 173.

Kożuch, B. 2004. *Zarządzanie publiczne w teorii i praktyce polskich organizacji*, Publisher: Placet, Warsaw, p. 50.

Matusiak, K.B. 2006. *Rozwój systemów wsparcia przedsiębiorczości – przesłanki, polityka i instytucje*, Wydawnictwo Instytutu Technologii Eksploatacji PIB, Radom- Łódź, p. 137.

Olesiński, Z. 2005. *Zarządzanie w regionie; Polska-Europa-Świat*, Publisher: Difin, Warsaw, p. 57 and next.

Olesiński, Z. et al. 2017. *Zarządzanie międzyorganizacyjne zwinnymi przedsiębiorstwami*, Publisher: Texter, www-texterbooks.com, Warszawa.

Rifkin, J. 2017. *Reguły rynkowej gry się zmieniły*, interview H. Skalika w *Rzeczpospolita -Plus, minus*, no. 53 (10691) 4–5.03.2017, pp. 8–9.

Roberts, N.C. 2008. *Organizational Configurations; Four The Challenge of Development, World Development Report* 1991, World Bank, Publisher: Oxford University Press, New York.

Robinson, M. 2015. *From Old Public Administration to the New Public Service Implications for Public Sector Reform in Developing Countries*, GSPSE Publication, Signapore.

Rzepka, A. 2017, *Inter-organizational relations as a one of sources of competitive advantage of contemporary enterprises in the era of globalization*, Procedia Engineering, 174, ss. 161–170.

Singh, T. 2010. *The service sector and economic growth: some cross-section evidence*, Applied Economics Volume 42, Issue 30, p. 7.

Stachowicz, J. 2006. *Zarządzanie kapitałem intelektualnym w regionalnych się ciach innowacyjnych*. Raport merytoryczny z realizacji projektu badawczego, maszynopis powielany, Warsaw 2006.

Stachowicz, J. 2006. *Zarządzanie kapitałem społecznym, procesem organizowania i rozwoju klastrów, doświadczenie z prac nad organizowaniem klastrów przemysłowych w województwie śląskim*, [In:] scholarly (and critical) editing E. Bojar,2006. *Klastry jako narzędzie lokalnego i regionalnego rozwoju gospodarczego*, Publisher: Politechnika Lubelska, Lublin.

Steward, T.A. 1999. *Intelectual Capital*, Bantam Doubleday Publishing Group, New York, pp. 91–99.

Szompka, P. 2007. *Zaufanie; fundament społeczeństwa*, Publisher: Znak, Cracow 2007.

Production Management and Business Development – Mihalčová et al. (Eds)
© 2019 Taylor & Francis Group, London, ISBN 978-1-138-60415-5

Large-volume collection of municipal waste

M. Stričík, M. Bačová & M. Čonková
Faculty of Business Economics with seat in Košice, University of Economics in Bratislava, Košice, Slovak Republic

ABSTRACT: In 2016, nearly 2 million tons of municipal and small construction waste were generated in Slovakia, of which less than 34% was recovered and more than 66% of the waste was landfilled. In our contribution, in accordance with valid legislation and positive examples from selected Slovak municipalities, we point out the possibility of applying the mixed municipal waste collection and charging based on the quantity instead of the flat-rate charging. The resulting effect of this system is to reduce the production of municipal waste and, in particular, to reduce the amount of municipal waste landfilled and to increase the amount of sorted and subsequently recovered municipal waste. We consider it to be a step that will improve achieving the current targets that are set for the Slovak Republic in the area of municipal waste management to reach the 50% of the municipal waste recycling rate by 2020.

1 INTRODUCTION

In a developing consumer society, the degree of environmental pollution caused by high waste generation and pressure for excessive use of natural resources increases. Along with the large volume of waste, there is another problem that is the way the waste is handled. A complete system for waste reduction, collection, composting, recycling, and disposal is required to tackle the growing challenge of Municipal Solid Waste Management (Asefi & Lim 2017).

Slovakia is a land where waste landfilling is predominant. More than 60% of mixed municipal waste or municipal solid waste (MSW) goes to landfills. However, landfilling is considered to be the most environmentally unsuitable form of the MSW handling. It is necessary to prevent this negative trend, in particular by increasing the level of waste sorting. MSW, once the province of relatively autonomous local authorities concerned with the most economically efficient collection and disposal of waste, is now a complex process in which a range of international institutions, national, regional and local government agencies and non-state actors have a degree of influence and responsibility (Bulkeley et al. 2005). The European Commission has set a target for Slovakia to recycle at least 50% of household waste by 2020. The European Union has set a clear waste management hierarchy for the Member States, but it cannot be complied with. The effectiveness of the actions depends to a large extent on the legal standards and the waste management system.

According to Act No. 79/2015 Coll. on waste and amendments to certain acts, the waste is defined in § 2 as: "a movable object or substance which the holder discards or intends or is required to discard under this Act or a specific regulation".

The Slovak definition is based on Directive 2008/98/EC of the European Parliament and of the Council on Waste.

In his Waste Management Practices: Municipal, Hazardous, and Industrial, Pichtel (2014) freely defines waste as a rigid material that has a negative economic value, suggesting that it is cheaper to discard than to use it.

As stated in Directive 2008/98/EC of the European Parliament and of the Council: The waste management hierarchy is a binding order of the following priorities:

- Prevention.
- Preparation for re-use.
- Recycling.
- Other recovery, e.g. energy recovery.
- Disposal.

On the basis of this hierarchy, individual Member States are taking actions that will lead to the best possible environmental outcome. (Article 4(1) of Directive 2008/98/EC of the European Parliament and of the Council of 2008 on waste).

Based on the fact that waste is not only a negative source of pollution but has a high economic potential, and if it is effectively used, there is a need to create a closed cycle of substances from production to consumption. (Chmelievská & Kuruc 2010).

When dealing with waste, it is very important to ensure its recovery. The Waste Act defines waste recovery as "an activity of which main purpose is to make beneficial use of waste for replacing other materials in the production or wider economy or to ensure the readiness of the waste to perform that function" (Section 3, Paragraph 13 of Act No. 79/2015 on waste).

The Slovak Republic (SR) also sets its own objectives in the area of waste management. The main objective of waste management by 2020 is to "minimize the negative effects of the production and management of waste on human health and the environment".

The strategic objective is: "a major diversion of waste from its disposal by landfilling, especially for MSW". (Program odpadového hospodárstva Slovenskej republiky na roky 2016–2020 2015).

The goal by 2020 is to increase the recycling of waste from households and from other sources that contain similar waste as households to at least 50% by weight. In order to meet this objective, it is necessary to increase the level of sorted collection of recyclable parts of MSW. These parts are mainly paper, cardboard, plastic, metal, glass and biodegradable waste. As individual sorted MSW components are not fully recyclable, the targets for the extent of the sorted MSW collection exceed the recycling target itself. Targets for the sorted waste collection extent are 20% in 2016, 30% in 2017, 40% in 2018, 50% in 2019 and 60% in 2020.

For the past period, the low rate of sorted waste was characteristic, so it is necessary to monitor and evaluate this rate every year so that measures can be taken to support waste sorting immediately when any signs of a negative development trend appear.

Environmental pollution due to the generation of waste can be reduced in two ways: by the development of more sophisticated and cost-effective wasteless technologies or by the organized waste collection, together with their environmental assessment and recycling. (Bigoš et al. 2008).

When dealing with waste, it is important to ensure the individual logistics activities. Logistics means "the organization, planning, management and performance of flows beginning with development and purchase, ending production and distribution by end-customer to meet all the requirements of the market with minimal cost and minimal capital expenditure." (Ceniga & Šukalová 2012).

– In US legislation, we can see the abbreviation PAYT – Pay As You Throw. The people are then charged for the MSW, based on the amount of the waste they have dumped. This system is designed to create a direct economic stimulus for recycling more waste. Traditionally, residents pay for waste collection by means of property tax or they pay a fixed fee regardless of how much waste they generate. In case of PAYT, households pay a variable rate that depends on the amount of waste handed in. Most communities that use this system pay for each discarded waste suck; in the case of smaller communities, fees are charged to residents on the basis of the weight of the waste. This system is especially popular for simplicity and justice. The "PAYT" MSW management system has also found support for Environmental Protection Agency (EPA), which is committed to ensuring that waste is managed in an environmentally sound manner through a number of international initiatives, because it includes three mutually correlated components that are the key to successful community programs. These are the following components (EPA 2016):

– Environmental sustainability – communities using the PAYT system have noticed an increase in recycling and reduction in waste amount. This brings a lower need for extraction of natural resources. Another benefit of PAYT is a reduction of greenhouse effect gas emissions associated with the production, distribution, use and subsequent disposal of products, also due to the increased recycling and waste reduction supported by PAYT. This slows the production of greenhouse gases in the atmosphere changing the global climate.
– Economic sustainability – it is an effective tool for communities that try to cope with rising spending on MSW management.
– Justice – inhabitants really pay only for what they discard. Apart from the US, the PAYT system is yet in place only in some European cities and villages, despite the fact that it contributes to a significant reduction of mixed MSW and an increase in recycling rates, which is a goal of the European environmental policy. (Šauer et al. 2008).

2 MATERIAL AND METHODS

The object of the research is the handling of MSW in the Slovak Republic in comparison with the European Union and its economic efficiency. When comparing the economic efficiency of MSW management, we arise from the effect of implementing a token system for MSW management in selected Slovak municipalities.

The aim of the paper is to evaluate the development of MSW, unsorted MSW and sorted waste collection in municipalities with applied token system for MSW management and to evaluate the economic efficiency of waste management before and after the implementation of token system in monitored municipalities in Slovakia.

Another objective is to compare the data on the MSW token system with the average waste amounts in Slovak municipalities per capita and on the basis of learned results to propose the improving actions, which could lead to a reduction of mixed MSW generation and to an enhancing in sorted waste in Slovakia.

Reliable waste management data provides an all-inclusive resource for a comprehensive, critical and informative evaluation of waste management options in all waste management programs (Hancs et al. 2011). Our data for the analytical part of the paper was obtained from the statistical web portals, mainly from the Statistical Office of the Slovak Republic and Eurostat, as well as from the Information Portal of the Ministry of Environment of the Slovak Republic – Enviroportal.

Information on the token system of MSW management was obtained from primary sources through personal consultation with mayors and employees of municipal offices. We have received complementary information from the websites of these municipalities, in particular through published documents such as the general binding rules about MSW and small construction waste handling, the general binding rules about local charges for MSW and small construction waste, municipal budgets, the municipal annual reports and final financial statements.

Within the framework of the analysis, we have paid attention to the token MSW handling system in selected Slovak municipalities. These are Liesek, Veličná, Pucov, Párnica, Istebna, Oravska Poruba, Rudno nad Hronom and Dedinky. The general characteristics of municipalities are presented in the following table.

A sample of examined municipalities consists of 8 Slovak villages from, 3 counties, 4 districts and 4 size groups according to the number of inhabitants.

If the waste collection based on the quantity is implemented in the municipality, the fee is set as a product of the frequency of the waste take-offs, rates and volume of the collecting bin that the ratepayer uses in accordance with the established MSW collection system.

- In case the quantity collection is not implemented in the municipality, the municipality will use the following method to determine the fee for a period (Bosák et al. 2016):
- The product of the charge rate and the number of calendar days in the period during which the ratepayer has a permanent residence or temporary stay in the municipality or is entitled to use the property.
- The product of the charge rate, the number of calendar days in the period and the indicator of daily MSW production.

Table 1. Basic characteristics of selected municipalities.

Municipality	Population Number	Area ha	District	Region	County
Dedinky	246	364	Rožňava	Horný Gemer	Košice
Istebné	1360	1129	Dolný Kubín	Dolná Orava	Žilina
Liesek	2904	3090	Tvrdošín	Horná Orava	Žilina
Oravská Poruba	1046	1320	Dolný Kubín	Orava	Žilina
Párnica	894	5199	Dolný Kubín	Orava	Žilina
Pucov	860	995	Dolný Kubín	Orava	Žilina
Rudno nad Hronom	531	1929	Žarnovica	Nová Baňa	Banská Bystrica
Veličná	1273	2930	Dolný Kubín	Dolná Orava	Žilina

Source: Own processing according to Statistical Office of the Slovak republic and e-obce.sk (2018).

The municipality levies its MSW charges in two ways:

- Flat-rate fee – sets the fee per person per calendar year.
- According to the amount of waste produced for a given time (so-called quantity collection), the fee per liter or dm³ of waste is set.

3 RESULTS AND DISCUSSION

Most MSW per capita was produced in Denmark in 2016. Overall, it is 777 kg of MSW produced yearly by one inhabitant. In Malta, 647 kg of MSW was produced per inhabitant and 640 kg of MSW per inhabitant was produced in Cyprus. On the contrary, the countries with the lowest production of household waste per capita in 2016 were Romania with a total of 261 kg of MSW per inhabitant, Poland, where 307 kg per inhabitant were generated in 2016, and the Czech Republic with 339 kg MSW pre inhabitant. In Slovakia, 348 kg of MSW was produced per inhabitant in 2016. An average of 482 kg of MSW is per 1 EU inhabitant.

In most of the European countries, most of the MSW is landfilled or incinerated. The goal of EU policy is to reduce the landfill rate in European countries, because landfilling is considered to be the most environmentally unsuitable way of dealing with MSW. Most of MSW is landfilled in Malta, up to 92% of the total processed waste, in Greece (82.46%), Cyprus (81.35%), Romania (79.8%) and in Croatia, 44%). In the Slovak Republic, 65.92% of MSW was landfilled in 2016.

The least rate of landfilling among the EU countries is in Sweden (0.64%) and Belgium (0.81%). In Denmark, Germany and in the Netherlands, landfills are also minimal, a little above 1% of the total processed MSW. For the EU as a whole, 24.53% of the total processed MSW was landfilled in 2016. The aim of the EU and each Member State is to increase the recycling rate of MSW what is an effective way of handling MSW. In 2016, they achieved the highest recycling rate of recyclable waste in Germany, where up to 48.11% of total MSW was recycled. Other countries significantly lag behind. For the EU as a whole, the recycling rate in total was 29.80% in 2016. The lowest amount of municipal waste is recycled in Romania (7.40%) and Malta (7.84%). In 2016, 15.52% of the total MSW was recycled in the Slovak Republic. Since 1995, this has been an increase of 14%. A growing trend was also observed in the field of waste incinerating with the energy recovery and composting of MSW. In 2016, 10.51% of the total MSW amount was processed with energy recovery and 7.63% was composted.

In order to reduce the generation of municipal waste and to increase the level of its sorting, a quantity collection of MSW using tokens was implemented in several Slovak municipalities. The token system for MSW handling in selected municipalities in Slovakia. A positive example of how to achieve reduction of the mixed MSW generation and to motivate people to recycle waste is the implementation of a token system for MSW handling.

This system has been implemented in some municipalities in Slovakia. The economic impact and the development of the amount of MSW after the implementation of the token system in selected municipalities will be described.

The obtained data on the evolution of the total MSW, mixed MSW and sorted MSW per inhabitant of the municipality were averaged by the weighted arithmetic mean, where the weighting factor is the number of inhabitants, and we compared the resultant values with the same indicators for the whole SR population. In addition to results expressed in absolute values, we have specified also the degree of sorting in municipalities with established token system for MSW handling also by material recovery's percentage. The calculation was based on the share of the quantity of separated MSW per inhabitant and the amount of the total MSW per inhabitant. Since the token system has been implemented in different municipalities for varying lengths of time, only the data after the token system implementation, which we have highlighted in the table by italics, were used for the computation the MSW average in municipalities. The result values can be seen in Table 2.

If we compute the average amount of produced MSW per capita in municipalities with the token system for MSW handling and compare it with MSW generated per capita in whole Slovakia, we will find that token MSW system generates about half an amount of MSW per capita in whole Slovakia. Mixed municipal waste per capita in municipalities with token system forms less than half of mixed municipal waste per capita in the whole SR.

Table 2. Comparison of municipalities with a token system for handling of MSW and Slovak MSW averages.

Municipality	Municipal waste kg per capita			Mixed municipal waste kg per capita			Sorted municipal waste kg per capita			Material's recovery % of total MSW		
	2015	2016	2017	2015	2016	2017	2015	2016	2017	2015	2016	2017
Dedinky	388.58	165.00	212.47	335.93	130.35	145.53	52.65	34.65	66.94	13.55	21.00	31.51
Istebné	209.11	201.34	221.80	140.71	128.77	135.16	32.36	36.61	52.07	15.47	18.18	23.48
Liesek	90.80	102.39	120.81	67.97	63.81	71.83	22.83	38.59	48.98	25.15	37.69	40.55
Oravská Poruba	178.60	188.79	144.59	100.98	99.03	103.25	41.52	52.25	46.96	23.25	27.67	32.47
Párnica	240.32	300.31	307.08	154.45	156.72	168.23	41.36	83.27	96.75	17.21	27.73	31.51
Pucov	193.29	192.73	204.24	72.21	71.20	90.01	121.07	121.53	97.84	62.64	63.05	47.90
Rudno nad Hronom	172.73	165.77	166.21	152.03	143.68	135.42	20.70	22.09	30.79	11.98	13.32	18.52
Veličná	–	–	144.31	100.44	96.81	99.09	–	–	45.22	–	–	31.34
Weighted arithmetic mean	145.50	169.82	178.54	88.07	95.31	105.56	43.86	55.20	57.41	30.14	32.50	32.15
SR	348.34	360.01	–	220.18	218.33	–	40.57	60.42	–	11.65	16.78	–

Source: Own processing according to documents from municipalities (2018).

In 2015, 30.15% of the total MSW was recovered in the villages with the token MSW system, and 32.50% in 2016, what is more almost by half the Slovak average MSW recovery percentage. Here we can see the greatest benefit of the implementation of the token system if SR aims to increase even more the recycling rate.

The Ministry of the Environment of the Slovak Republic, at the end of 2015, argued that Slovakia would not meet the valid recycling target for 2020, which is the recycling of 50% of municipal waste. In 2015, despite the efforts of the Ministry, only 14.9% of the MSW was recycled. The Ministry plans at least to mitigate this negative situation with the new act on higher landfill charges. The act is designed to motivate municipalities to maximize the sorting of MSW, that is, "the more you sort, the less you pay". This act will enter into force in January 2019.

The European Commission adopted on 2nd December 2015 a package of measures in the field of the economy. All businesses are trying to make effective use of their available resources. Most of the natural resources are limited, therefore the world is looking for an economically viable way of using them. The primary objective of the circulation economy is to maintain as long as possible the value of the products and materials used in the production, which will not only minimize waste. but also make unnecessary use of new materials and resources. In practice, this means that at the end of the product's life cycle, it is not expected to be decommissioned with the sources that make it up, but it will be re-input for production to create a new value. This system completely replaces the original "take-make-throw" and, together with the increase in innovative activities, also brings new jobs in Europe. saves energy and reduces greenhouse gas emissions. (European Commission 2015).

The package of legislation was adopted, in particular, on the basis of statistics according to which Europe loses up to 600 million tons of materials a year found in the compartment. These materials could be reused or recycled. However, recycling also lags far behind, as according to European statistics about 40% of waste generated in EU households is recycled. It is precisely the transfer of waste to the source that is the basis for increasing the efficiency of resource utilization and the way it goes to the circulation of the economy. (Bosák et al. 2016).

The European Commission defined in 2015 Actions aimed to meet the objectives of the economy as follows (European Commission 2015):

– A common EU target of recycling 65% of MSW by 2030.

– A common EU target of recycling 75% of MSW from packaging by 2030.
– A binding target by 2030 to landfill the mixed MSW a maximum of 10% of all waste.
– Cooperation with Member States on the improvement of waste handling.
– Simplification and improvement of the definition of waste and harmonization of calculation methods.
– The use of structural funds to support the objectives of EU waste legislation.
– Minimum criteria for extended producer responsibility.
– Remuneration of producers producing more environmentally friendly products and who support the recovery and recycling of their products at the end of their life cycle.

4 CONCLUSION

On the basis of the analyzes carried out, we propose actions to improve the MSW handling in the Slovak Republic:

– At national level, for the more efficient MSW handling, we propose to adopt legislative actions concerning the implementation of the token MSW system or other motivational system for the MSW handling.
– Adoption of an act on the modification of landfill fee, as this is the lowest in the EU and its low value is not conducive for seeking options for the recovery of waste.
– Implementation of a back-up system for PET bottles and cans in the Slovak Republic.

We believe that the adoption of these actions will help to improve the handling of municipal waste in the Slovak Republic.

ACKNOWLEDGEMENT

This contribution is a partial output of VEGA project no. 1/0582/2017 "Modeling the economic efficiency of material and energy recovery of municipal waste" addressed at the Faculty of Business Economics of the University of Economics in Bratislava with seat in Kosice.

REFERENCES

Act No. 79/2015 Coll. on waste and amendments to certain acts.
Asefi, H. & Lim, S. 2017. A novel multi-dimensional modeling approach to integrated municipal solid waste

management. *Journal of Cleaner Production*. 166: 1131–1143.

Bigoš, P. et al. 2008. Materiálové toky a logistika II.: *Logistika výrobných a technických systémov*. Košice: Strojnícka fakulta TU.

Bosák, M. et al. 2016. Poplatok za komunálny odpad na Slovensku. Košice: OZ Gamajun.

Bulkeley, H. et al. 2005. Governing municipal waste: Towards a new analytical framework. *Journal of Environmental Policy and Planning* 7(1): 1–23.

Ceniga, P. & Šukalová, V. 2012. *Logistika v manažmente podniku*. Žilina: Žilinská univerzita.

Chmelievská, E. & Kuruc, J. 2010. *Odpadové hospodárstvo*. Bratislava: Príroda.

Directive 2008/98/EC of the European parliament and of the Council of 19 November 2008 on waste and repealing certain Directives.

EPA 2016. *Pay-As-You-Throw*. Available at: https://archive. epa.gov/wastes/conserve/tools/payt/web/html/index. html.

European Commission 2015. *Circular Economy Package: Questions* & Answers. Available at: http://europa.eu/ rapid/press-release_MEMO-15-6204_en.htm.

Hancs, A. et al. 2011. Composition and parameters of household bio-waste in four seasons. *Waste Management*. 31: 1450–1460.

Pichtel, J. 2014. *Waste Management Practices: Municipal. Hazardous and Industrial*. New York: CRC Press.

Program odpadového hospodárstva Slovenskej republiky na roky 2016–2020. 2015. Vestník Ministerstva životného prostredia SR (5) XXIII.

Šauer, P. et al. 2008. Charging systems for municipal solid waste: Experience from the Czech republic. *Waste Management*. 28(12): 2772–2777.

Production Management and Business Development – Mihalčová et al. (Eds)
© 2019 Taylor & Francis Group, London, ISBN 978-1-138-60415-5

Tender procedures and offers evaluation criteria, polish and EU law

E. Szafranko
Institute of Building Engineering, Faculty of Geodesy, Geospatial and Civil Engineering, University of Warmia and Mazury in Olsztyn, Olsztyn, Poland

ABSTRACT: Public procurement in Poland constitutes a very important component of economy. Tender procedures consist of a series of actions that both the awarding authority (the client) and the tenderer (supplier, contractor, service provider) must go through for a contract to be signed and implemented. The overriding objective of procurement procedures is to ensure that public funds are expended economically and purposefully. A tool that serves this purpose is the application of efficient methods for the evaluation of tenders, and the preparation of such selection criteria that would enable the choice of a tender that best satisfies the expectations of the procuring entity. This article presents a review of legal solutions that regulate public procurement in Poland as well as data demonstrating the popularity and effectiveness of various approaches. In addition, the author discusses some of the EU regulations, which Poland, by being an EU member state, is obliged to abide to.

1 INTRODUCTION

Public procurement in Poland is a very important component of economy. Public procurement procedures consist of a series of predefined actions that both the contract awarding authority and the tenderer must perform for a contract to be signed and executed (Wat et al 2010). In recent years, the European Commission and the EU member states have taken measures to create legal and institutional frameworks which will ensure efficient allocation of public funds and guarantee that the most economically advantageous tenders win the bids (Forysiak 2015, National 2010). The public procurement system can stimulate a demand for specific types of products and services, and can influence the rate of economic and social changes. Increasingly often a question arises how to include in public procurement notices solutions promoting innovative and cutting-edge technologies as well as social and environmental aspects. An instrument that can help to achieve this purpose is a system of the evaluation of tenders based on a properly constructed set of award criteria. Criteria for the assessment of tenders are among the most important elements of public procurement. They are constituents of an individually adopted measure which will eventually play a key role in selecting a tender that most faithfully matches the specification presented in the tender notice and is the most advantageous for the contracting authority (Criteria 2015).

2 CRITERIA FOR THE EVALUATION OF OFFERS IN LEGAL REGULATIONS AND THEIR APPLICATION

Public procurement procedures in Poland are legally regulated by the Act of Public Procurement Law (PPL), which came into force on 29 January 2004, and the related executive regulations. This document replaced an earlier Act on Public Procurement of 10 June 1994, and represents an implementation of the European Union's directives into Polish law. The public finance sector units as well as other units of a similar character or controlled by public sector finance units whenever they enter into contracts with suppliers for services, deliveries of goods or construction works are obliged to comply with the PPL.

In 2014, the basic value threshold of a contract at which the Public Procurement Law becomes obligatory corresponded to an amount of 14,000 euros converted to Polish zloty. Once the Act amending the Public Procurement Law and some other laws of 14 March 2014 (The Act of 2014 r., item 423) came into effect, that is since 16 April 2014, pursuant to Art. 4 paragraph 8 of this Act, the PPL does not apply to contracts and contests where their value expressed in PLN does not exceed an amount of 30,000 euros, i.e. about 125,247 PLN (according to the regulations, the currency exchange rate for Polish zloty to euro was 4.1749 as of 1 January 2016).

The Polish Public Procurement Law (PPL) does not provide a definition of an award criterion for tenders. The concept 'criterion for an evaluation of tenders' in the legal sense can be defined as an indicator used to assess tenders, an individual measure adopted by the contract awarding entity which will substantiate a decision about which of the solutions submitted by tenderers will satisfy the specified expectations to the highest degree. The Public Procurement Law and the EU directives contain examples of evaluation criteria other than the price (Saja-Żwirkowska 2015). In practice, however, contracting entities most often apply the price criterion and consequently choose an offer with the lowest price, frequently meaning worse quality, generating additional costs in the future and sometimes even at the stage of contract execution (Vademecum 2015). The Public Procurement Office in their publication issued in 2011 drew attention to advantages and disadvantages of selecting tenders based on the price solely or the price and additional parameters (Table 1).

A long-awaited change in regard of the tender evaluation criteria came with the amendment of the Act on Public Procurement of 29 August 2014. Article 91 paragraph 2 limited the role of a price as the sole selection parameter, adding other criteria in this respect. Likewise, changes were made with respect

to award criteria by supplying examples of social, innovativeness and environmental criteria. The amended act mentions: quality, functionality, technical parameters, environmental and social aspects, innovativeness, contract completion date and maintenance costs. A paragraph was added stating that a price can be the sole criterion only in the case when procurement items are widely available and have well-established quality parameters (excluding some of the awarding authorities that are obliged to specify in an attachment the information about how the description of the subject-matter of the contract in question provides for costs incurred during the whole life cycle of the said services or items).

Since the amended law came into effect, the most advantageous bid has been the one which presents the most beneficial balance of the price and other criteria indicated in the specification of essential terms of the contract or the one with the lowest price quotation. A catalogue of non-price evaluation criteria given in Art. 91 paragraph 2 is an open one and lists examples of parameters. In the Monitor (The Act 2015) no 1/2015, the Public Procurement Office published results of analyses into the application of award criteria in tender bids. These data are shown in Table 2 and Fig. 1.

Table 1. Advantages and disadvantages of selecting a tender based on the price alone or the price and other criteria.

LIST OF ADVANTAGES AND DISADVANTAGES OF METHOD FOR EVALUATION OF TENDERS

Using the price as the only criterion
FOR
- quick and easy to use
- safe
- effective acquisition of goods with specified quality parameters
- low cost of preparing and conducting the procedure
- possibility to implement a request-for-quotations procedure and electroning bidding procedure for contracts below the EU thresholds
AGAINST
- impossible to assign a higher score for desirable characteristics of the subject of the contract in question, including quality
- impossible to submit variant tenders
- competitive dialogue procedure excluded
- risk of purchasing goods expensive to use, technologically outdated, generating higher maintenance costs

Using the price and other non-price criteria
FOR
- adjustment of the selection of a tender to specific needs of the contracting authority
- better preparation of the specification of the contract subject-matter as the awarding entity must consider its significant characteristics for inclusion in the specification
- a possibility to assign a higher score for desirable properties of the subject, including quality and innovative solutions
- a possibility to submit variant tenders
- a provision for competitive dialogue rationalisation of expenses
AGAINST
- higher labour input into the preparation of a tender bidding procedure
- higher costs of preparation and execution of the proceedings (e.g. expert opinions, hire an specialist to evaluate solutions proposed in tenders)
- more complicated and longer procedure of the assessment of tenders
- a risk to the contract award procedure being described with an inadequate specification or a risk that the award criteria are questioned by contract tenderers

Source: The author.

Table 2. Changes in the use of a price as the sole criterion relative to the PPL amendment of 29 August 2014.

	Year 2014			
	Notices in the Public Procurement Office		Notices in the EU Official Journal	
	Before	After	Before	After
Price – the only criterion	93%	31%	85%	33%
Price and other criteria	7%	69%	15%	67%

Soucre: The author based on the Monitor of the Public Procurement Office no 1/2015.

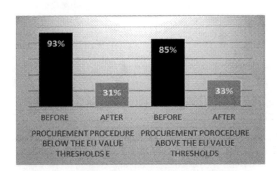

Figure 1. Percentage of procurement procedures in which a price was the sole criterion, prior and after the amendement of the Act on Public Procurement.
Source: The author's analysis, based on data provided in the Public Procurement Office Monitor no 1/2015.

The price remains a necessary criterion in the evaluation of tenders. The legislator does not state what per cent value relative to other selected criteria the price can correspond to, as this is for the contracting authority to decide, same as the criteria and priorities they will adopt for the subsequent procurement procedure steps.

Monitor of the Public Procurement Office no 1/2015 also provides information about the most popular criteria, their number and average weights assigned to these criteria, after the Act on Public Procurement was amended. These data were gathered from the Public Procurement Newsletter and pertained to procurement procedures for contracts below the EU value thresholds. This information is given in Tables 3 and 4 as well as Fig. 2.

While analysing the above data, it emerges that the procurement calls where other criteria were applied most often restrained the range of parameters to just one more criterion next to the price, which most frequently was the contract completion date or the warranty period. Yet, the weights assigned to such additional criteria, which the contracting authorities can choose freely, are typically around a few per cent, which means that the contract is ultimately awarded to a bidder offering the lowest price.

Table 3. Most popular award criteria and their average weights in public procurement procedures after the amendment of the PPL, 29 August 2014.

Most popular non-price criteria	Percentage of procurement procedures	Average weight
Date of contract execution/ date of delivery	29%	11%
Warranty/guarantee	25%	10%
Terms/terms of payment	10%	7%
Quality/functionality/ technical parameters	8%	18%
Knowledge/experience	7%	18%
Service response time	3%	9%

Source: The author based on the Public Procurement Office Monitor no 1/2015.

Table 4. Number of criteria applied to evaluation of tenders adopted in public procurement procedures after the amendment of the PPL, 29 August 2014.

Number of criteria in a procedure (data as of 2014)	Percentage of procedures (data as of 2014)
Two	92,06%
Three	6.19%
Four	1.18%
Five and more	0.57%

Source: The author based on the Public Procurement Office Monitor no 1/2015.

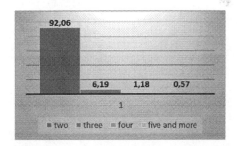

Figure 2. Number of criteria included in public procurement procedures after the amendment of the PPL Act.
Source: The author's analysis, based on data provided in the Public Procurement Office Monitor no 1/2015.

2.1 Application of the price as a criterion

The definitions of a price and a unit price under the Public Procurement Law were amended on 25 July 2014. In line with these definitions, a price means the value expressed in monetary units that the buyer is obliged to pay to the trader for the goods or services, whereas a unit price of the goods (services) means the price set for a unit of specific goods (services), the value or amount of which is expressed in measurement units as understood in the regulations on measurements. The price includes a tax on goods and services and an excise duty, should the sale of a given service or goods be subject to these taxes.

The price is also considered as a tariff rate, meaning that economic turnover participants who apply the provisions of the Public Procurement Law are obliged to take into account gross prices, including the tax, VAT and excise tax in conformity with separate legal regulations. Bidders are also obliged to quote the final price responsibly and to make every effort to ensure that the tender they submit relies on true and not abnormally low prices. Attention should be drawn that the awarding entity which handles public funds because, pursuant to Art. 44 paragraph 3 item 1 of the Act on Public Finances, it should manage public funds in a way that is purposeful, economic and adheres to the principles of good economy and efficiency. The contracting party should be aware that attaining some of the essential parameters of the contract may incur higher costs of the contract's performance.

The evaluation of tender bids is associated with the problem of abnormally low prices, which can be of particular importance when public procurement procedures are initiated to award contracts for construction and civil engineering works. The procuring entity can request a bidder to provide explanation, in conformity to Art. 90 paragraph 1 of the PPL, if the price relative to the object of the procurement procedure seems abnormally low or raises doubts whether the contract can be performed in compliance with the requirements (especially if it is 30% lower than the value of the contract or the arithmetic mean price of all submitted tenders). If the tenderer does not provide explanation within the specified period of time, or if the review of the explanation provided confirms that the quoted price is abnormally low, the procuring entity rejects the tender pursuant to Art. 90 paragraph 3 of the PPL.

2.2 Application of non-price criteria

When other criteria are applied, apart from the price (pursuant to Art. 36 paragraph 1 item 13 of the PPL), a detailed description of these criteria including their importance and the method used to evaluate submitted tenders is a mandatory part of the specification of essential terms of contract (the Polish acronym SWIZ). It is worth mentioning that if the tender evaluation criteria are also included in the procurement notice, there must be complete agreement between these criteria and their significance and the ones specified in the SWIZ. Lack of concordance will be perceived as a change in the criteria applied to evaluating tenders, which is unacceptable according to the Public Procurement Law and consequently leads to the procedure being declared null and void.

The specification should also contain the information how the tenders shall be evaluated according to the defined criteria (cf. Art. 36 paragraph 1 item 13 of the PPL). The legislator does not specify precisely the format of this information. It may be assumed that this part of the notice should describe accurately what the selected criteria apply to and how the tenders will be compared so as to assign to them measurable scores. This description should leave no room for doubt when interpreting the information, and particularly when deciding which characteristics of the works, supplies or services to be contracted are desirable from the point of view of the contracting party, which will be scored highly and which will play a role in terms of the lowest price. The way these criteria are to be applied should limit to the minimum subjective feelings and preferences of the persons who are to evaluate tenders (Król 2015). It is essential to ensure proper verification of the evaluation of tenders by suppliers and organs authorized to verify the compliance of procurement procedures with the Public Procurement Law.

The freedom which the awarding party enjoys in terms of the application of non-price criteria for the evaluation of tenders is limited (Korytarowa 2004) so as to ensure that the criteria are applicable to the works, services or supplies contracted and compliant to the provisions of Art. 7 paragraph 1 of the PPL. Considering the obligation of equal treatment of all bidders, the criteria designed for evaluation of tenders must be relevant to the subject of the contract, as well as being objective and non-discriminating. The ban to create award criteria which relate to the object of the contract does not apply to procedures which are conducted in order to award public contracts for services that are considered non-priority ones (e.g. auxiliary and additional transport services, educational and training services).

3 CRITERIA FOR EVALUATION OF TENDERS IN THE EU LAW – EUROPEAN DIRECTIVES

The European Union is also in the process of reforming the public procurement system. The key objective is to overcome the habit of awarding contracts on the basis of just one criterion, such as the lowest price (Olejarz 2014). These efforts had a direct influence on the amendment of the Public Procurement Law of 29 August 2014 (The Act of 2014, item 1323) in Poland. Currently, the legal regulations governing the evaluation of tenders are comprised in the provisions of Art. 53 paragraph 1 of the classical directive, i.e. Directive 2004/18/EC of the European Parliament and Council, of 31 March 2004, on coordinating public procurement procedures for awarding public contracts for building works, supplies and services, and in the analogous provisions of Art. 55 of the sector directive, i.e. Directive 2004/17/EC.

On principle, the new directives are to create a change in the trends of selecting tender evaluation criteria and to encourage procuring entities to implement multi-criteria evaluation systems. The classical directive 2004/18/EC, which is still binding law, is to be repealed within 24 months after the new directive comes into effect. Provisions of the new directives were to be implemented into the national law starting on 18 April 2016. The assumptions underlying the new classical Directive 2014/24/EU are that the choice of a tender should be motivated not only by economic considerations, as it was implicated in Directive 2004/18/EC, but also by social and ecological aspects. Public procurement contracts, having linked the reform of the public procurement system with the Europe 2020 strategy, are expected to support innovative and ecological solutions (Bowis 2012). The regulations proposed in the new directives regarding public procurement modify the contributions of criteria developed on the basis of Directive 2004/18/EC and also define 'the most economically advantageous tender'. This term, from the point of view of contract awarding authorities, enables them to determine criteria for awarding a contract based on the price or cost (cost effectiveness, life cycle costing), or based on the best price-quality ratio, estimated in relation to the relevant social, qualitative or environmental aspects associated with the subject-matter of the public contract in question (Skowron 2014). The new directive clarifies that by restricting the possibility of applying the price or the cost criterion alone it hopes to encourage a greater quality orientation of public procurement. Article 67 paragraph 2 of this Directive provides a model catalogue of criteria serving to evaluate tenders in a public procurement procedure including the best quality-price ratio approach. The catalogue was ordered according to the classes; qualitative criteria, criteria regarding properties of tenderers, and criteria referring to customer service. For the first time, a legal document directly includes social aspects as applicable in the best quality-price ratio approach. Another example of a new criterion is

to allow contracting authorities to evaluate qualifications and experience of the staff responsible for the performance of a contract in question (which is when qualifications of the staff have influence on the contract's performance level and quality) and to request specific labels that will prove that building works, services and supplies, for example, satisfy their specific environmental, social or other requirements.

Another rule concerning tender evaluation criteria is contained in Art. 67 paragraph 4 of the new classical directive, stating that the contract award criteria cannot confer an unlimited freedom of choice on the procuring entity, nor should they result in limiting effective competition. Criteria applied to evaluating tenders should be logical and understandable. The contracting authority should provide tenderers with the specification that will enable them to effectively interpret the information given in terms of how they satisfy the award criteria.

A significant change made in 2014 arises from the provisions regulating the life cycle costing, specified in Article 68 of Directive 2014/24/EU. Life cycle costing can cover part or all of the costs over the life cycle of a product, service or building works. They are inscribed as costs borne by the contracting authority or other users (costs relating to the acquisition of the subject of the contract, its use, maintenance), as well as costs assigned to environmental external conditions, as long as their monetary value can be determined and verified. If contracting authorities estimate costs in line to a life-cycle costing approach, they are obliged to indicate the data that tenderers will have to provide as well as the method which the contracting authority will employ to determine the life-cycle costs.

4 CONCLUSIONS

In order to promote a wider use of non-price criteria and the implementation of the EU directives, the Act on Public Procurement in Poland was amended in October 2014. The amended act described more precisely the problem of criteria to be applied in procurement procedures. However, the statistics presented by the Public Procurement Office justify the claim that the amended act and modifications of the regulations it offers have resulted in only apparent changes. The contracting authorities comply with the binding law, but most often add just one more criterion, to which they assign a relatively low weight. Consequently, the lowest price remains the factor that most frequently decides which tender is awarded the contract. This may happen because of the lack of firmly rooted practice, knowledge and experience in using additional criteria. A fear of being accused of wasting public funds, and consequently being at risk of control checks and questions whether the contract was awarded correctly is another reason why contracting authorities are not willing to include more criteria in procurement notices.

REFERENCES

Bovis, C. 2012. *EU public procurement law*. Edward Elgar Publishing.

Criteria for the evaluation of offers after the amendment of the Public Procurement Law, Wydawnictwo Wiedza i Praktyka sp. z o. o. 2015.

Directive of the European Parliament and the Council of Europe 2014/24/UE, 26 February 2014 r. on public procurement.

Forysiak, J. (ed.). 2015. *Criteria for the evaluation of offers*. Presscom Sp. z o.o., Wrocław 2015.

Korytarowa, J., & Ticha, A. 2004. The Assessment of the Public Order's Tender. *Prace Naukowe/Akademia Ekonomiczna w Katowicach*:183–188.

Król, B. 2015. Public procurement: Lowest price – why not worth it? Non-price criteria – why it is worth it? *Inżynieria Bezwykopowa*, 86–87. Nr1/2015.

Monitor no 1/2015, the Public Procurement Office nr 1/2015.

National Action Plan on sustainable public procurement for 2010–2012. U. Z. P. 2010.

Sadowy, J. (ed.). 2011. *Criteria for the evaluation of tenders in public procurement procedures – examples and application*. Public Procurement Office. Warszawa 2011.

Saja-Żwirkowska, K. (ed.). 2015. *Criteria for the evaluation of offers after the amendment of the PPL act*. Wydawnictwo Wiedza i Praktyka Sp. z o.o., Warszawa 2015.

The Act of 29 January 2004 Public Procurement Law.DZ. U. z 2014r. p. 2164.

Vademecum. 2016. *Criteria for the evaluation of publishing offers*, Presscom sp. z o.o. 2015.

Watt, D.J. et al. 2010. The relative importance of tender evaluation and contractor selection criteria. *International Journal of Project Management*, 28.

Production Management and Business Development – Mihalčová et al. (Eds)
© 2019 Taylor & Francis Group, London, ISBN 978-1-138-60415-5

Invention process modelling to assess innovation performance

P. Szaryszová & L. Štofová
Faculty of Business Economics with seat in Košice, University of Economics in Bratislava, Košice, Slovak Republic

ABSTRACT: Current managerial conceptions are based on the integrated process assessment approach, but only a few enterprises in general are trying to monitor innovation processes or concretely invention processes to assess their innovation performance. The process of inventions creation phase is represented by processes connected with impulses capture, recording, evidence and transformation, with which have small and medium sized enterprises operating in Slovakia bigger or smaller complications. Therefore their attention should be centred on the primary phase of the innovation process. These enterprises could have better possibilities to use their innovation potential on the creation of new inventions and so gain higher possibilities on more successful innovation implementation and better results from innovation performance assessment. The research published in this paper was realised with the aim to propose and monitor the process of inventions creation performance in form of the causal model using the software Vensim PLE.

1 INTRODUCTION

New research centers have emerged in recent years; respectively organizational components in enterprises with aim to define business processes that will help drive innovation processes.

Even recently, innovation has been seen mainly from the economic point of view (inputs and measurable outputs), but less time has been devoted to how innovation is organized and managed to provide lasting benefits and economic growth (Allaire et al. 2012, Sinha et al. 2013). At present, innovation centers focus on what is happening, which roles/actors the system needs with which competencies and knowledge, and how to organize optimal relationships to advance the system and develop it successfully.

Recently, there have been many publications on innovation and innovation systems. Also, many professional journals, such as the Research Policy, the Strategic Management Journal, the International Journal of Technology Management, the Organization of Science, the Academy of Management Review, the Innovation Journal, and Technovation, are devoted to innovation, their resources, organization and management. However, these publications have three major deficiencies:

1. The innovation describe as a phenomenon from different perspectives of the author or the environment in which the successful innovation has arisen.
2. Introduce own terminology, which is mostly valid only for the given context.
3. There is no exact and accepted specification of an innovation system with clear axioms and definitions that would provide the scientific basis for the effective building of innovation systems.

This state of art and absence of the methodology prevents the effective building of innovative ecosystems, especially in small and medium-sized enterprises (SMEs) that are considered as so called "spine of innovation potential" in actual Europe. According to company IPA Slovakia Ltd. research (2013) are in these enterprises applied inconvenient innovation process models, what signalize a need to modeling them for increasing their innovation potential and performance. This deficiency and social need create a unique opportunity for the breakthrough research of exact and structured innovation systems. Causes of non-success in the innovation field of SMEs already rest in unsystematic solutions and wrong decisions of employees and management in the first innovation process phase – the process of inventions creation.

The strategic orientation define phase is in many enterprises a narrow place so enterprises, which are able to react very fast gain the big competitive head start. The activities in the field of training of innovative managers (potential experts who will innovate systematically) are developing mainly two business entities in Slovakia: IPA Slovakia Ltd. organizing the Academy of Innovation and the Novitech Partner Ltd. organizing the Pearson Certified Course "Education (UK)" Innovation and Growth.

From practical view is known that about innovation processes are deficient analytical methods on the problem solution, but important are also psychological aspects needed for the innovation culture creation in the enterprise. Very important is also to develop employment's creativity and potential, without which is not created any invention or innovation solution.

These things cause that within our realised research was formulated the scientific problem as the process of inventions creation performance system monitoring in SMEs operating in Slovakia. The main aim of this research was to propose and monitor the process of inventions dynamics creation model for SMEs as a tool for unsystematic innovation impulses arrestment process, which increments inventions creation.

2 PROCESS OF INVENTION CREATION AS A BASE OF INNOVATION PERFORMANCE

The complexity in invention processes, in which new technologies are created, is growing as the processes engage an increasing number of people, organizations, regions, and existing technologies that may have many intricate interactions, and also tend to result in more complex interlinked technologies and systems. As such, the increasing connectivity and complexity of new technologies may be both an antecedent and a consequence of the increase of complexity of the related invention processes. In sum, there is a growing underlying complexity of both technological artefacts and the processes through which they are designed.

For SMEs is important rivet mainly on the innovations and innovation processes. In innovation definitions is mostly concerned characteristic of innovation process, enterprise's activities conduced to positive changes or product, service, process and system as a result of innovation process. The concept of innovation is in this research considered as output of innovation process as a new value for the customer and enterprise, which it has implemented. Founder of the innovation theory Schumpeter divided invention from innovation and later enlarged innovation on "commercialization of new product or process" (Nauwelaers & Wintjes 2008, pp. 3–4).

Interconnection of knowledge and inspiration according to Tidd et al. (2007) define the innovation process as the process of innovation from impulse identification to the invention implementation in form of innovation. Following Figure 1 is consisted from four phases of sequential impulse conversion.

To every of introduced four phases belongs certain output. The innovation process consists from 4I:

1. Impulse – the motive of invention existing in concrete information, which can come from internal or external enterprise's environment.

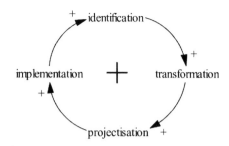

Figure 1. Innovation process reinforcing loop.

2. Invention – the realizable innovation idea created of filed impulses transformation.
3. Integration – the prepared innovation prototype or project intended on implementation.
4. Innovation – the product, process, system as a new value for the customer and enterprise, which has implemented that.

Today are very important exactly change strategies, because safeguard future by manage of sustainable changes in the enterprise's environment and infrastructure. Enterprise has to learn change, leave with it and use it so to bring in that, what market needs in the right place at the right time. The evolution of design processes may shape ability to invent next-generation technologies, systems and services. How do the design and invention process in general change over time? Is there any general pattern of change in both technologies and invention processes? Answers to these questions can guide the direction of future engineering design research and education for more inventive outcomes. However, such understanding is still rather limited. Current engineering design research and education are not informed to respond to the evolution of technologies and invention processes (Luo & Wood 2017).

The process of inventions creation funnel begins of many potential internal and external resources continues of the captured impulses depending up enterprise's innovation preparedness, consequently the filed impulses as the result of the captured impulses processing and follows into certain amount of inventions, from which could create and then implement innovations. In many cases but give out to wrong interpretation of the captured impulses and thereby to their loss, deficient transformation on inventions what causes quite lower amount of inventions. The process of inventions creation does not habituate to be a research object. It is very important part of the innovation process, because this phase is its start, which should be planned and manage systematically because of other consequent innovation process phases.

In order to be able to monitor the performance, it is necessary to set key performance indicators stemming from the company's strategic goals. Based on benchmarking, an enterprise monitors and evaluates the level of optimization as well as the current state of fulfillment of strategic goals with the possibility of predicting their future development. To processes measurement are using different systems as well as basic diagnostic tools used to manage the innovation process through the enterprise information system.

The first step of innovation process performance is to set up a self-evaluation team, in which the staff of the organization cooperates. It is necessary for selected staff to have qualified knowledge of the areas to be targeted. Team members have an obligation to study individual evaluation documents and methodologies, as well as evaluation criteria before collecting background material, followed by self-evaluation of the evaluators, presentation of results in the presence of all evaluators, processing of results, correction and revision of differences in results, finalization of self- presenting the results before management and the final step is to reconcile the results.

For the development of innovation potential, it is necessary to objectively determine the indicators whose application the enterprise can detect its critical locations, as well as benefit from a competitive advantage. The innovation performance of enterprises is dependent on all areas involved in the business environment. In order to find out to what extent the enterprise is innovating, we must focus our attention on the products offered, efficiently implemented production processes, organization and financial management of the company, the use of information technology, as well as the extent to which the company concentrates its insights on marketing and, last but not least, at what level are its supply relationships and networking. The Global Innovation Index (GII) provides detailed metrics about the innovation performance of 126 countries which represent 90.8% of the world's population and 96.3% of global GDP. Its 80 indicators explore a broad vision of innovation, including political environment, education, infrastructure and business sophistication (Cornell INSEAD WIPO 2018).

3 RESEARCH METHODOLOGY

Following the formulation of the scientific problem was the main aim of our research to propose and monitor the process of inventions creation model for SMEs doing business in Slovakia, given the interest to contribute by own proposals, respectively recommendations to improve their innovation process.

In the period 2014–2017 were in order to identify the relevant variables of the innovation process in practice realised these surveys:

1. Identification of relevant variables from state of art and innovation management knowledge.
2. Personal managed interviews and observation in selected enterprises.
3. Questionnaire survey no. 1.
4. Questionnaire survey no. 2.

The first survey used secondary data, information and knowledge from actual resources and references. Personal managed interviews were realized in three large enterprises of Prešov Autonomous Region of Slovakia. Its aim was to identify variables of the innovation process as a basis for creating questions for a questionnaire survey and gaining inspiration for drawing up the causal model for SMEs. The objective of on-line questionnaire of survey no. 1 has been collecting information from the field of innovation potential utilization and innovation management in companies in order to test the clarity of the questions generated by the personal experiences of a personal structured interview, and to obtain additional information on the course of the innovation process.

Randomly selected represented 0.06% of the enterprises investigated region. At the first survey participated together 77 questioned enterprises, including 58 small (75%), 13 medium-sized (17%) and 6 large enterprises (8%). Confirmation of the need to model the process of inventions creation and its detailed examination in order to identify its key variables of SMEs was the aim of questionnaire survey no. 2. A sample of 130 Slovakian SMEs operating in Košice and Prešov Autonomous Region (43% micro, 34% of small and medium-sized 23%) was obtained by filtering out correctly completed questionnaires from 142 the total collected. Both samples of on-line questionnaire surveys are so considered as relevant to identify the key variables of the proposed model.

For the creation of the proposed model were used causal relations of identified variables defined by other authors with the use of logical research methods to detect causal relationships based on self-knowledge gained by studying literature and carrying out own investigations. In order elements and links between them have worked without any problems, just need to reach their logical arrangement. As a tool for solving the identified scientific problem we chose a causal model of researched process of inventions creation, whereas the linear model cannot adequately explain the operation, respectively principles of the innovation process as accurately evaluated Kim & Choi (2009).

Dynamic and systematic thinking is believed to explain the behavioural pattern of problems as a lapse of time rather than to detect the cause of the problem for a specific time. Appropriate representation of the proposed mental model is a causal loop diagram (CLD), which helps to understand and communicate interactions determining the dynamics and performance of the system (modeled in software Vensim PLE). The links between the identified variables in the model are labeled as follows (Catalina Foothills School District 2003):

1. "+" – Both variables move in the same direction. If the first variable increases, the second variable will be greater than it would have been otherwise; a decrease in the first causes the second to be less than it would have otherwise been.
2. "–" – Two variables change in the opposite direction. If the first variable increases, the second will be less than it would have been otherwise; a decrease in the first variable causes the second to be greater than it would have been otherwise.

Cycles in the causal model can be amplified up to limits or offset the balance. This kind of model thus serves to express the tendency of system behaviour or its stabilization, when is pursued its dynamics innovation and performance. A CLD may be reinforcing and grow, or shrink, until acted upon by a limiting force or balancing and move toward, return to, or oscillate around a particular condition. Reinforcing loops are marked with a "+" in the centre; balancing loops are indicated with a "–" in the centre. Two short commas represent very important time delay.

4   MENTAL CAUSAL MODEL OF INVENTION PROCESS DESIGNED TO MEASURE INNOVATION PERFORMANCE

Common operation programmes collect research capacities and help to achieve results, which should not achieve countries of European Union individually. Innovation activities (as result of R&D) are in EU motive power of economics development, develop possibilities of future competitiveness in form of new knowledge, increase effectiveness and fighting power of economics mainly through SMEs. On the basis of information overview about pro-innovation environments, which were obtained from regional innovation strategies and own survey results was possible to identify some groups of factors, which influence enterprise innovation activity. In some cases or opposite situations can be negative factors of environment threats, but also opportunities for given business unit. The object of modeling was the process of inventions creation as the first part of the innovation process. The basic process of inventions creation reinforcing loop as well as its outputs is shown in Figure 2.

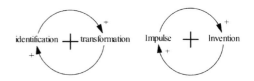

Figure 2.   The process of inventions creation reinforcing loops.

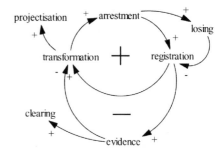

Figure 3.   The process of inventions creation flows/ reinforcing & balancing loop.

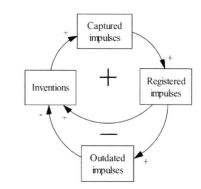

Figure 4.   The process of inventions creation stocks/ reinforcing & balancing loop.

The first phase of the innovation process (identification) is divided because of the detailed examination on the base of information from secondary and primary sources (personal interviews) to the sub processes: arrestment, losing, registration, evidence, clearing of impulses, projectisation of inventions as is shown in Figure 3. The sub processes are inherently related to impulses, which in the process of inventions creation acquire higher forms of their transformation.

Based on primary and secondary sources (personal managed interviews) have been identified outcomes of the process of inventions creation (Fig. 4), which are stock variables. The first three of them represent different stages of the researched process funnel:

1. Captured impulses – the number of impulses gained by their arrestment from internal and external resources.
2. Registered impulses – the amount of well-interpreted and subsequently registered or registered impulses recorded in the business evidence.
3. Inventions – the amount of viable innovative ideas generated by the transformation of registered impulses.
4. Outdated impulses – the number of registered impulses stored in the evidence that are not transformed to the inventions.

Identified variables affecting the process of inventions creation can be characterized as follows:

– Company size (by employees).
– Innovation team – the number of qualified employees intended by management in order to achieve the enterprise's innovation objectives.
– Internal information resources of impulses – the amount of used internal resources of impulses types (journals and books, in-house network or intranet, changes in business processes, etc.).
– Management and other employees – human resources outside the innovation team as internal resources of impulses.
– Internal resources of impulses – the number of internal information and human resources of impulses used by enterprise.
– External resources of impulses – the amount of used external resources of impulses (legislation, exhibitions and trade fairs, conferences, workshops, seminars, different types of networks, internet, customers, benchmarking, etc.).
– Inventions as internal resources of impulses – the amount of impulses resources transformed from created inventions.
– Resources of impulses – the amount of internal and external resources of impulses, among which we count to 1% generated inventions as an internal resource of impulses.
– Creative methods – the rate of use of creative methods and techniques in the creation of inventions,
– Interpretation – the degree of understanding or awareness of the captured impulse.
– Innovation potential of enterprise – the participation rate on impulses arrestment of other human resources outside the innovation team members.
– Innovation team member potential – the expected number of captured impulses by member of innovation team depending on his motivation, skills and knowledge.
– Need of impulses arrestment – the amount of impulses needed to capture on the innovation team member to achieve the planned amount of captured impulses.

– Utilized potential of innovation team – the number of impulses captured by an innovation team.
– Reaction time of employees – the time elapsed from the call to capture impulses with respect to the innovation objectives to the employees' reaction in the form of captured impulses.
– Registration time – the scheduled time that elapses from the captured impulse to its registration (save in the records or evidence).
– Time of evidence – the scheduled time that elapses from the registration of the impulse to its clearing from the evidence.
– Duration of transformation – the scheduled time that elapses from the registration of the impulse to its transformation to the invention.

Causal portrayal of identified variables in the form of CLD is the proposed model of inventions creation for SMEs (Fig. 5) designed on the base of these assumptions:

– The increasing size of the enterprise (by employees) increases the amount of captured impulses.
– The compilation of innovation team earmarking of human resources with the aim to manage the process of inventions creation.
– The process of registration aim is to achieve nearly the same amount of impulses recorded by staff captured in a certain period of time.
– At the registration process of captured impulses has positive impact their complete interpretation in terms of awareness of the objectives and strategies of enterprise.
– The utilization of creative methods and longer duration of registered impulses transformation supports the establishment of viable inventions.
– Inventions serve as a further internal resource of impulses and thus positively influence the impulses arrestment.
– The number of inventions defines a need to capture additional impulses from the business environment.

The described mental model reflects a causal dependence of selected variables on the process of inventions creation within the entire innovation process. The modeled process consists of a reinforcing (positive) cycle, and simultaneously of a balancing (negative) cycle. The first of them is formed by a process of inventions creation, at the end of which a transfer of created inventions occurs in the form of a feedback. The feedback has a form of an auxiliary variable – inventions as internal resources of impulses influence the amount of impulses resources. They represent one of the key variables that are the driving force behind the process of inventions creation. To maintain the balance of the dynamic system, it is

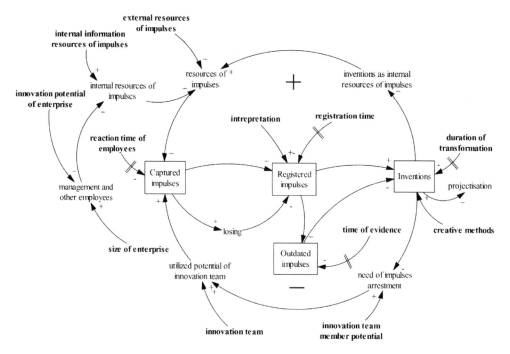

Figure 5. The process of inventions creation mental model.

necessary to include also a negative feedback of the process of inventions creation. The introduced relation is an inevitable part of the balancing cycle, which consists of two auxiliary variables: the need of impulses arrestment and the utilized potential of innovation team.

5 CONCLUSION

In theories of innovation, the strategic paradigm results from adoption of three basic assumptions regarding the functioning of enterprises. It assumes that the activity of companies is based on markets and resources, entrepreneurs look to the future and entrepreneurs make decisions with regard to the operational efficiency on the market. These conditions determine the decision on the need of formulating a strategy as a declaration of a specific behavior, that takes into account both all its resources and external conditions. In addition, a strategic approach to innovation and technology transfer encourages companies to focus on customer needs and customer demand. Including innovation in the development strategy is an essential factor to effective competition. An important element that entrepreneurs need to heed is the ability to turn knowledge into innovation. The greatest challenge of contemporary enterprises is the per-

ception of the role of business cooperation. It is this only, and not the traditional overtaking of the competition, that can determine market success.

Successful enterprises are about systematic process of the innovation impulses recognition and collection. They use a various concepts of impulses detection as for example the early recognition and the careful environment monitoring systems. Comparison and critical evaluation of theoretical approaches and also primary and secondary data analysis were the bases for processing of the practical innovation management implementation proposal. The main aim of research described in this paper was from introduced reasons to propose a process of inventions creation model for SMEs, what was reached. Methodology of the proposed model modeling provided despite of limitations its key variables identification based on the real process of inventions creation in surveyed enterprises.

In the Vensim PLE software the CLD model can be transformed into a simulated form and then parameterized the various variants of the proposed model variables. On this basis, the dynamics and performance of the inventions and other variables of the proposed model of the invention process can be monitored, which is one of the research activities of the authors' of this paper. The aim of the future research should be further modeling of others innovation process phases and their key variables assessment. These should represent amount of integrations (innovation projects) as accumulation variable and amount of the implemented innovations as innovation process expected output consistent with the proposed innovation process cycle.

ACKNOWLEDGEMENT

The article is written within the project of young scientists, young teachers and PhD students number I-18-109-00.

REFERENCES

Allaire, D. et al. 2012. An information-theoretic metric of system complexity with application to engineering system design. J Mech Des 134:100906-1.

Catalina Foothills School District 2003. Tips for Using System Dynamics Tools. [online]. 2003. [cit. 2018.03.27]. Available at: <http://www.clexchange.org/ftp/documents/Implementation/IM2003-12TipsUsingSDTools.pdf>.

Cornell INSEAD WIPO 2018. Available at: < https://www.globalinnovationindex.org/Home>.

IPA Slovakia 2012. Available at: <http://www.ipaslovakia.sk/udalost_view.aspx?id_u=201>.

Kim, S.W. & Choi, K. 2009. "A Dynamic Analysis of Technological Innovation Using System Dynamics", POMS 20th Annual Conference, Florida, 2009. [online] [cit. 2018.02.10]. Available at: <http://www.pomsmeetings.org/ConfProceedings/011/FullPapers/011-0622.pdf>.

Luo, J., & Wood, K.L. 2017. The growing complexity in invention process. Research in Engineering Design, 28(4), 421–435.

Nauwearles, C. & Wintjes, R. 2008. Innovation Policy in Europe: Measurement and Strategy, Edward Elgar Publishing, Cheltenham, Northampton.

Sinha, K. et al. 2013. Structural complexity: quantification, validation, and its systemic implications for engineered complex systems. In: Proceedings of international conference on engineering design, 19–22 August, 2013, Seoul, Korea.

Tidd, J. et al. 2007. Řízení inovací: Zavádění technologických, tržních a organizačních změn, Computer Press, Brno.

Total Quality Software, QFD 2000 for Customer Led Design, Lincolnshire, UK (1999), [Version 2.0 Windows 95/98].

Production Management and Business Development – Mihalčová et al. (Eds)
© 2019 Taylor & Francis Group, London, ISBN 978-1-138-60415-5

Social acceptance of retailing on Sunday in Poland—results of surveys

A. Szromnik
University of Economics, Cracow, Poland

E. Wolanin-Jarosz
The State Higher School of Technology and Economics in Jarosław, Poland

ABSTRACT: The Authors of the presented elaboration concentrated on time as a factor determining shopping behavior and on perception changes of this problem in the contemporary socio-economic environment. The Authors identified both external and internal factors influencing the process of "shopping on Sunday"—as a complex market phenomenon. The initiators of the new, more restrictive, legal framework for retail were presented through a detailed analysis of the main voices and arguments in contemporary discussions on the subject. The Authors presented the results of a direct survey conducted among the inhabitants of South-Eastern Poland. The respondents were answering questions regarding their level of acceptance of the restrictions on retailing on Sunday.

1 INTRODUCTION

The market freedom of enterprises' functioning is connected mainly to the fundamental right to freedom of choice of business partners—suppliers and recipients, in many cases it is limited in the form of top-down administrative regulations that impose special conditions on entrepreneurs and the scope of running their own business. Such restrictions apply to various sides and aspects of the implementation of business functions.

The time of functioning of enterprises, i.e. the time of personnel work, and thus the time of offering products to clients, are determined by the national legal norms included in the labor codes, employment and protection of employees. They also define social and sanitary conditions of performing work, including days off, number of working hours and breaks, a system of paid holidays and layoffs in various sectors, branches of the economy, in various types of enterprises and with different work organization systems.

Particular social interests concentrates on work standardization in service sectors. On the one hand, on public holidays, there is a growing interest from society in offer of service facilities and the possibility of using it at that time, and on the other hand, there is a growing awareness of work burdens during periods usually dedicated to leisure and recreation. There is therefore a contradiction between the needs of society and the social rights of service companies' personnel. In the emerging conflict of social interests, the owners of relevant enterprises are additionally involved, for whom the

functioning of facilities on non-working days is a source of additional financial benefits. Increasing, for many years, contradiction—the conflict of social and business interests in the service sector on non-business days focused on the problem of the functioning of trade on Sundays—trade in various organizational, institutional and technical forms.

The aim of this elaboration is to present the results of the research on the social acceptance of the possibility of shopping on Sunday, and thus the inclusion to a broad discussion about the conditions and purposefulness of the operation of retail trading posts on Sundays. Therefore, not only the results of one's own empirical research in South-Eastern Poland were presented and developed, but also the general premises and options of the subject were shown.

2 TIME FACTOR IN THE PROCESS OF PURCHASING CONSUMPTION PRODUCTS

In the market research of consumer behavior, various characteristics of purchasing process are the subject of interest, beginning with realizing the need to satisfy the needs and ending with the impressions and out-of-purchase assessments. Consumer's decision regarding the purchase of products is a multi-element structure of the entire decision-making process, which defines a set of basic characteristics of the purchasing activity, ordered logically according to the generality level. Purchasing as an operational expression of the orientation to meet the needs and consumer demand includes, therefore, reference to the subject and scale of purchase (what and how much to buy), brand and product model (selection of a specific article), place of purchase (town, district, housing estate, street and retail outlet) and the time the purchase and sale transaction was made. Time as a basic characteristic of a product purchase operation refers to its significant chronological dimension, from a general clarification of the moment of the paid takeover of the purchased good (year, month, week) up to its detailed reference to the time scale (day and time). The criterion of purchase time, in the literature to the subject and place of purchase, is not, however, a topic focusing the attention of a large group of consumption researchers, being even ignored in oriented on the main regularities of the analyses of buyers' market behavior. Query of the subject literary activity published in the main periodicals and monographs in the area of the market, marketing and consumption makes it impossible to indicate and cite here serious—representative and in-depth studies explaining time distributions of purchasing processes both in the cross-section of various business complexes, industries or product groups, types of commercial outlets, forms of sales organization, location. Meanwhile, a comprehensive approach to the model description of the correct behavior of clients in the final stage of satisfying their own and household's needs, enforces taking into account the time factor in various degrees of accuracy of expressing it (Rosa 2015).

The analysis of purchase chronology leading to the identification of a specific cycle of consumer shopping activity reflects a number of different buyers' characteristics, including among others:

– Changes of the needs intensification in the scale of the time unit considered.
– Diversification of consumption of household members in terms of time, for example on a monthly, weekly basis.
– Changeability of free time resources dedicated, among others, to shopping as a resultant of professional activity of the household members.
– Ways of spending free time, especially during weekends, including time being at home going away.

Moreover, the actual time of shopping in retail units is one of the main factors determining the internal organization and management system in trade. Diversified to a greater or lesser extent in chronological order, the trend of buyers and the accompanying changeability of operational processes resulting from the standard of customer service in retail trade forces the management of the point of sale adequate correction and mitigation of logistic and sales activities resulting from:

– Periodic shortage of shop personnel.
– Lack of goods on store shelves.
– Physical and mental overload of personnel.
– Queues to registration checkouts.
– Lack of full control over the sales area.
– General chaos and disruptions at work of a business unit.

The above-mentioned phenomena generating difficulties and tensions in the work of retail trade units are just one side of the problem. In the situation of a limited number of buyers, low number of customers in retail and low trade, there are other negative phenomena in the work of sales outlets—phenomena related to the incomplete use of the service potential. Work time management based on rational methods of preventing frictions in the cycle of providing commercial services becomes a real challenge for managerial staff. However, the basis for successful activities is full knowledge of consumer shopping habits (Jachnis & Terelak 1998).

3 DAYS OFF WORK—SUNDAY AS TIME TO DO SHOPPING

An important analytical cross-section of purchases is the weekly cross-section, which reflects the intensification of the consumer's commercial activity on the scale of the following weekdays, and thus the time of satisfying consumption needs. This popular reporting system in retail stores (store reports) explains the distribution of quantities and values of purchases done on individual days, and thus the structure of the buyers' trend in the analyzed retail units—stores, department stores, supermarkets, market halls, hypermarkets and shopping centers. This structure is influenced by, among others, the following factors:

– Frequency of shopping and the size of one purchase batch connected to it.
– Size of households—number of people.
– Availability of retail outlets (their reachability in pedestrian and mechanized traffic).
– Working time structure.
– Ways of spending free time at the weekends,
– Nutrition style—eating habits.
– A shopping model involving all family members.

The daily amount of cumulative sales at the retail outlet as the sum of the sales value of everyday purchase, frequent purchase goods (shopping every 3–5 days) and periodic and episodic goods purchase is clearly different in the weekdays scale. The phenomena that enforce the so-called out of turn shopping, related to family and personal celebrations, trips, meetings, visits, etc. (Świtała 2010).

Particular moments in explaining the changeability of the weekly shopping cycle are the first and last days of the week, which is outside weekend and pre-weekend days. In the first case (and this concerns Monday and partly Tuesday), above-average, increased turnover in retail trade is observed. It is as a consequence of the weekend, increased consumption of basic consumer goods (food), consumption exhausting gathered domestic stocks. In the second case, that is in relation to pre-weekend shopping, their increased sizes result from the "holiday" character of the weekend itself, from typical for those days (Saturday, Sunday) orientation on leisure, time without duties, time of relaxation with family and friends (Perchla & Włosik 2010).

Resignation from shopping on non-working days, and mainly on Sundays, is the result of many years of habits, practice and social norms, according to which it is a day without work and effort, a day for the family, a day for one's own interests and personal development (Michalski 2016). This traditional model of the weekend, especially Sunday, proper for Catholic culture, has undergone significant changes in the period of socio-political and economic transformation, mainly under the influence of such related to them phenomena as:

- Break with rigid working time norms in enterprises (flexible working time),
- Requiring from employees to be fully prepared to provide work and availability on all days of the week,
- Common phenomenon of "working after hours",
- Finding jobs in places considerably far away from the places of residence,
- Starting your own business (often as an extra one), meaning in practice work without time limits, the whole week.

As a result of changes on the labor market, conditions alteration, forms and rules of performing work, and ways of earning, the organization and norms of social life of people and families, including especially leisure time resources and its use, underwent a significant transformation (Rochmińska 2011). At the disposal of the working part of the society, especially young people, there was mainly free time on non-working days, that is on Saturdays and Sundays. In this way, there has been a temporary postponement in the week scale of cultural, educational, recreational and family-friendly realization of activities in the households. This also concerned the time spent on purchases and visits to retail centers connected to them (Bywalec 2017).

The growing role of non-working days in doing shopping for various consumption goods and services, and in particular the consequences of this phenomenon for all involved sides, had triggered a broad social discussion, which lasted until the final adoption of the law of Polish parliament—January

10, 2018. The main problem in the discussion was limiting and even banning large-area trade on Sunday. The arguments for and against formulated, based on the experience of several European countries (Austria, Germany, Norway), such entities as: trade unions as a representative of employees of large-area retail trade companies, representatives of large-area retail enterprises (e.g. Polish Trade and Distribution Organization), employers' corporations ("Lewiatan" Confederation), shop-trading organizations (e.g. "Społem"), social and religious organizations (among others, Catholic Action, Association of Catholic Families).

In discussions, protests, social campaigns and thematic conferences, there were also politicians, representatives of the government and parliament, but also scholars and hierarchs of the Church. The work of large-area retail on Sunday has become one of the most important social problems in Poland. Despite the new legal regulations introducing restrictions on trade on Sundays and holidays, the controversy around the problem has not expired.

4 THE OBJECTIVE AND METHODOLOGY

With reference to the initially characterized discussion about the issue of introducing restrictive restrictions on the functioning of retail trade on Sundays, an own attempt to diagnose the problem was made. The aim of the project was acquiring knowledge and measurement of the strength of social support or opposition to the introduction of trade restrictions in the cross-section of different groups and sub-groups of Poles.

The research was carried out in 2016–2017, in south-eastern Poland, in several municipalities (Kraków, Rzeszów, Dębica, Jarosław, Olkusz, Bukowno) and in one rural commune (Klucze). All of these enumerated towns were in the Małopolskie Voivodeship (3 cities and one village) and one Podkarpackie Voivodeship (3 cities).

The selection of respondents to the survey was not random, because the research was conducted among two social groups, namely:

- UTW students – "Universities of the Third Age" (Krakow, Dębica, Olkusz, Jarosław, Bukowno, Klucze), that is people "60+" (seniors).
- Full-time students (Kraków, Rzeszów), that is young people (first and second year of study).

The surveyed sample included a total of 544 people, thus 244 students (44.9% of the total) and 300 UTW students (55.1%).

As a method of diagnosing the Poles 'opinion concerning the functioning of trade and shopping on Sunday, a survey based on the Likert scale was elaborated. According to the relevant procedure for studies using the 7-point Likert scale (answers: 1 – definitely not, 2 – no, 3 – probably not 4 – I do not know (I have no opinion), 5 – I think so, 6 – yes, 7 – definitely yes) a set of 33 statements was developed, in the light of which one can recognize the attitude of respondents to shopping on Sunday. The proposed declarative sentences were selected deliberately in such a way that the proper targeting of their pronunciation could be an approximate measure of the strength of acceptance or non-acceptance of the studied phenomenon after summing the numerical evaluation of the answer.

5 SHOPPING ON SUNDAY—ANALYSIS OF OWN RESEARCH

Among 35 introduced statements (theses), all (except for one, statement 3) were deliberately focused on accepting purchases on Sunday, however, giving the respondents the opportunity to comment on "no" or "yes", according to the variant development of the Likert scale. The responses of all 544 people were subjected to statistical analysis, which in the first stage concerned the whole group (without separating the age or geographical sub-groups). Thus, the arithmetic mean $(\bar{x})$, median (Me), standard deviation (s), and coefficient of variation (V) were calculated for all responses.

The highest values of the arithmetic mean were observed in the case of finding 33 $(\bar{x} = 5.08)$. and finding 1 $(\bar{x} = 5.02)$. It results from that that these two theses, that is "Work in commerce is a necessity to work on Sunday" (No. 33) and "The need decides about shopping, not the day of the week" (No.1) obtained the highest level of acceptance of the respondents (although it is a weak acceptance because it equals the answer "probably yes"). From among the other statements, the lowest acceptance on the level between "no" and "definitely not" obtained theses:

- No. 5 "Sunday shopping is a ritual" – $(\bar{x} = 2.37)$.
- No. 18. "I could not do it without shopping on Sunday" – $(\bar{x} = 2,51)$.
- No. 7. "It is best to buy on Sundays" – $(\bar{x} = 2.65)$.
- No. 9. "On the remaining days there is not enough time to shop" $(\bar{x} = 2.68)$.
- No. 8. "On Sundays, there are no crowds in shops" – $(\bar{x} = 2.77)$.
- No. 11. "Sunday shopping is a good way to spend free time" – $(\bar{x} = 2.79)$.
- No. 29. "Only on Sunday I can refer to the commercial offer" – $(\bar{x} = 2.83)$.

It should be emphasized that the mentioned results were obtained as a result of researching the entire population of 544 people, of whom 300 are students of universities of the 3rd century, and the remaining 244 are students.

The numerical equivalents of the Likert scale, i.e. numbers from 1 (definitely not) to 7 (definitely yes), allowed to determine the median, thus the central value (second quartile). This value divides the entire examined group into two equal parts due to the answer to each thesis.

The highest median, as at level 6, occurred in the case of only two statements, that is sentence no. 1 – "The need decides about shopping, not the day of the week" and the last sentence, i.e. no. 33 "Work in commerce is the need to work on Sunday." This means that in the case of these opinions, the same number of people commented on the scale of 1–5, and 7. The high median (5 on the scale of assessments) was observed in the cases of 3, 13, 20, 22, 27, 28 and 32, which indicates moderate acceptance.

The standard deviation (s) explaining the average size of deviations from the arithmetic mean for all research results was between 1.47 (thesis 5) and 2.05 (thesis 13). In the case of sentences 13 and 5, the dispersion (diversity) of responses was the highest. These were the opinions:

- No.13 "Shopping does not interfere with religious life" (s = 2.05)
- No.5 "Sunday shopping is a ritual" (s = 2.02).

Significant differences in responses occurred in the case of no. 33, no.1, no.20 and 21, as well no. 5 and 18. In the first case, and therefore the opinion: "Work in trade means the necessity to work on Sundays" (33), "The need decides about shopping" not the day of the week" (1), "Sunday trade is a matter of business" (20), and "Do not interfere in the right to Sunday trade" (21), respondents were the most unanimous (V = 33.9–39.5%). The most diverse answers were obtained for statements: no.18 – "I could not do it without shopping on Sunday" (V = 67.0%), and no.5 – "Sunday shopping is a ritual" (V = 62.2%).

A ranking, according to the highest level of their acceptance, based on the average value of the assessment, can be obtained, that is from the thesis number 33, for which the respondents answered on average to more than 5 (exactly 5.08, which can be referred to as "probably yes") to the thesis number 5 (the smallest acceptance level, average response only 2.37).

Initial statistical analysis allowed distinguishing those opinions that were unequivocally evaluated and the ones clearly evoking various impressions among the studied population, which confirmed a significant dispersion of their assessments (calculations were performed using the STATISTICA program).

6 SOCIAL ACCEPTANCE SUMMARY GAUGE OF TRADE AND SHOPPING FUNCTIONING ON SUNDAY

The Likert scale used in the study allows to analyze the obtained results using various statistical measures. They express the distribution of responses to individual questions, their diversity and symmetry. An important advantage of the Likert scale is the possibility of making generalized measurements of attitudes, opinions or attitudes to the phenomenon under investigation. In this case, the verbally expressed 7-point scale of responses is replaced by its numerical equivalents in such a way that 1 means complete lack of support and 7 means full acceptance of the formulated view (thesis). Summing up all numerical assessments for each researched person, the group and the entire population studied, gives a measure of the degree of negative or positive support for the view under consideration. The gauge accepts extreme values equal to n × 1 (minimum value) and n × 7 (maximum value).

As a result of summing up the received grades for all 33 statements for all people participating in the research, that is 544 respondents, the following descriptive statistics characterizing the acceptance strength of the existing trade organization system .on non-working days—for the possibility of shopping on Sundays:

– Arithmetic mean – $\bar{x} = 122.9$ points, so the value is very close to the middle, neutral evaluation, corresponding to the "I have no opinion" or "Hard to say" rating 132 points.
– Median (the median value of the answer) – Me = 121 points, and therefore almost identical to the arithmetic mean, which indicates a symmetrical distribution of assessments that do not accept and accept the main thesis of the research.
– Standard deviation – s = 35.4 points.
– The first quartile $c_{25} = 96.5$ points (one quarter of the answers falls into the point range 33–96.5).
– Third quartile $c_{75} = 148$ (three-quarters of the total scores falls into the range of 33–148 points).
– The maximum value of the total measure in the cross-section of 544 people – xmax = 227 points.
– The minimum value of the total measure xmin = 39.

Both the descriptive statistics and the graphical representation of the distribution of the total measure testify to the almost perfect normal distribution of the opinion of the surveyed population. It corresponds to an even distribution of negative attitudes and positive attitudes towards the issue of "trade—shopping on Sunday". In the cross-section of the whole research and the results obtained for young and older people, an even dichotomous division of the studied population can be stated due to the attitude to the functioning of commerce on Sunday—as many people are against as the ones who support "trade-shopping liberalism".

7 CONCLUSION

The problem of trade restrictions on Sunday in Poland arouses lot of emotions and disputes among people. Discussions on this topic are largely influenced by exemplary legal regulations in several European countries, additionally stimulated by the opinions of various types of unions and social associations acting for the benefit of trade and small trade enterprises as well as employees' protection and safety (Oxford Economics (2015). However, the most important thing is social acceptance of this phenomenon (Reddy, 2012). In the absence of unequivocal social support, support of serious business circles, support of socially neutral non-governmental organizations, and even several important political parties in Poland, further strong argumentation for purposefulness and benefits due to restrictions introduced on the functioning of trade on Sunday and holidays should be discontinued or limited, and the social and economic effects themselves should be assessed after a few years of restrictions being in force.

REFERENCES

12 fałszywych argumentów za zakazem handlu w niedzielę (12 false arguments for the ban on trading on Sunday) 2016. Gazeta Prawna.pl., Praca i Kariera (Work and Career), 04.11.2016.
Bywalec C. 2017. Gospodarstwo domowe – Ekonomika, Finanse, Konsumpcja, (Household – Economics, Finance, Consumption). Published by Cracow University of Economics, Cracow.
Jachnis A. & Terelak J.F. 1998. Psychologia konsumenta i reklamy (Psychology of a consumer and advertising), Publishing House "Branta", Bydgoszcz.
Michalski T. & Juszkiewicz R. 2016. Nikt nie powinien mówić Polakom jak mają spędzać czas wolny (Nobody should tell Poles how to spend their free time) – interview, Onet, 21.12.2016.
Oxford Economics. 2015. Economic impact of deregulating Sunday trading. A Report for the Association of Convenience Stores, London, September.
Perchla-Włosik A. 2010. Czas wolny jako wyraz zachowań konsumenckich młodych Polaków (Leisure time as an expression of consumer behavior of young Poles). Ujęcie socjokulturowe (Sociocultural approach), Edited

by G. Rosa, A. Smalec, ZN University of Szczecin, Nr 594, Ekonomiczne problemy usług (Economic problems of services), Nr 594, Szczecin.

Reddy K. 2012. Price effect of shopping hours regulation; evidence from Germany, Institut of Economic Affairs, Blacwell Publishing, Oxford.

Rochmińska A. 2011. Centra handlowe – miejsca spędzania czasu wolnego Łodzian (Shopping centres – places of leisure time for Łódź residents), "*Acta Universitatis Lodziensis*", Folia Geographica Socio-Oeconomica, Nr 11.

Rosa G. (ed.). 2015. Konsument na rynku usług (Consumer on the services market), C.H.Beck Publishing House, Warsaw.

Świtała M. 2010. Psychologiczne uwarunkowania zachowań konsumentów w wieku starszym (Psychological determinants of elderly consumers' behaviour), in: *Konsument w Unii Europejskiej – Podobieństwa i różnice* (Consumer in the European Union – Similarities and differences), Ed. Z. Kędzior, R. Wolny, University of Economics in Katowice, Katowice.

Production Management and Business Development – Mihalčová et al. (Eds)
© 2019 Taylor & Francis Group, London, ISBN 978-1-138-60415-5

Modelling supplier risks in Slovak automotive industry

L. Štofová & P. Szaryszová
Faculty of Business Economics with seat in Košice, University of Economics in Bratislava, Košice, Slovak Republic

ABSTRACT: The twenty-first century business environment is characterized by organizations which have extended their enterprises by forming supply chain networks to counteract the effects of global competition. However, as organizations increase their dependence on these networks, they become more vulnerable to their suppliers' risk profiles. The aim of this paper is to use Bayesian networks for modelling and assessing suppliers' risk profiles of Slovak automotive company. Used networks provide a methodological approach for determining a supplier's external, operational, and network risk probability and are able to measure the potential revenue impact that supplier can have on the automotive company as measured by Value At Risk (VAR). In realised research were used supplier' risk profiles to determine risk events which have the largest potential impact on an organization's revenues and the highest probability of occurrence.

1 BAYESISAN NETWORKS IN CONTEXT OF SUPPLY CHAIN RISK MANAGEMENT

In an effort to counteract current market forces, increasing levels of global competition, demanding customers and employees, shortening product lifecycles, and decreasing acceptable response times, many organizations have extended their enterprises outside of their legal boundaries by forming competitive networks of organizations known as supply chains.

Sawhney et al. (2006) identified supply chains as a mechanism for fostering business innovation within organizations through the adoption of streamlined information flows, restructured business processes, and enhanced collaboration among network members. The associated financial and operational risks of supply chain disruptions represent a major concern to organizations competing in the global economy (Craighead et al. 2007). As organizations increase their dependence on integrated supply networks, they become more susceptible to supply chain disruptions.

Supply Chain Management (SCM) seeks to enhance the competitive performance of the network through the internal integration of an organization's functional areas, and by effectively linking them to the external operations of suppliers, customers, and other network members (Kim 2006). Kleindorfer & Saad (2005) note that due to events such as the the 2001 terrorist attack on the World Trade Center and the 2003 blackout in the Northeastern sector of the USA, organizations have placed an increased emphasis on Supply Chain Risk Management (SCRM). Moreover, the massive product recall and

production shutdown experienced by the Toyota Motor Corporation in January 2010 had an adverse impact on its supply chain as well as supplier and customer relations, also illustrating the need for effective risk management within supply chains.

Increased risks due to the 2008–2009 global financial crises mean a new challenge faced by supply chain managers in their quest to mitigate supply chain threats along with possible disruptions to their supply chains (Murphy 2009). Additionally, the long-run negative effect on an organization's stock price due to supply chain disruptions has been documented through a study by Hendricks & Singhal (2005), illustrating a negative 40% return two years after the date of the disruption announcement.

Cousins et al. (2004) argue that exist also important non-financial consequences of supply chain disruptions, such as a reduction in product quality, damage to property and equipment, lost reputation among customers, suppliers, and the wider public and delivery delays. Therefore, it has become increasingly important for organizations to manage the risks associated with their supply chains.

On modelling supplier risks not only in automotive industry are analogically used Bayesian networks (BN) which are based on the Bayesian statistics application and use a graphical model to represent a group of variables and their probable relationships. This network consists of nodes representing random variables and arrows connecting the main and subordinate nodes. They are used to identify causal relationships to help understand the nature of the problem and predict the consequences of the intervention. Bayes network analysis consists of defining system variables, defining causal relationships between variables, conditional and fundamental probability specifications, adding evidence to the network, performing proofreading and extracting results (Vernor 2010).

2 DATA AND METHODOLOGY

The Bayesian approach can be used to the same extent as classical statistics with a wide range of outputs. Bayesian statistics are based on Bayes' veto, which is a simple mathematical formula used to calculate contingent probabilities. Bayesian probability perception is associated with a certain degree of faith, and it is about measuring the validity of an event with incomplete information.

Bayesian networks are probabilistic graphical models in which random variables are represented by a directed acyclic graph. A material flow based supply network can readily be represented by such a graph: material flows have a direction and—assuming return flows and recycling are negligible—there are no cycles in the network. In a BN, an arc denotes causality between two nodes. In the supply risk context, the relationship A → B is interpreted as: disruption at A is a direct cause for disruption at B. We assume that a company downstream does not cause disruptions upstream. This is in line with typical supply network dynamics where materials flow downstream. In principle, a customer can cause a disruption at a supplier, but such a possibility is beyond the scope of this paper.

The purpose of this article is to introduce a methodology for modelling and assuming risks in supply chains, based on a study of 15 suppliers of Slovak automotive company. The main advantage of the Bayesian approach is the use of expert opinions as a robust statistical tool. The methodology uses Bayesian networks for the creation of risk profiles for each supplier. The methodology is offered as a tool to assist managers in the formulation of strategies and tactics to mitigate overall supply chain risks.

2.1 Building bayesian network model

Prior to building the Bayesian Network Model of Enterprise Risk Management, the three pre-processing steps are performed:

1. Risk identification.
2. Risk analysis.
3. Risk assessment.

There are steps when applying Bayesian Networks for risk analysis—to determine the risk status of each node. The status of node can be classified based on historical experience. First, set the threshold for each node and determine the level, which can be divided into three states: 1, 2, and 3 corresponding to the three levels: low, medium and high.

Bayesian networks were constructed to examine the probability of a supplier's impact on company revenues. Network, operational, and external risk levels were computed using the provided a priori probabilities for the identified risk events. These risk levels were then used to determine a supplier's probability of revenue impact on the company. In this study we used as the useful tool a diagram (Fig. 1) of the Bayesian networks.

Nodes represent variables in the Bayesian network. Each node contains states, or a set of probable values for each variable. They are connected to show causality with arrows known as "edges" which indicate the direction of influence. When two nodes are joined by an edge, the causal node is referred to as the "parent" of the influenced "child" node. Child nodes are conditionally dependent upon their parent nodes. Therefore, in Figure 1, the probability of suppliers experiencing network risks is dependent on the a priori probabilities associated with the following variables: disagreement of among interested; financial stress; leadership change. The a priori probabilities associated with the variables low quality, delivery problems, service problems, and HR problems directly influence operational risks. External risks are dependent upon the following variables: supplier locked-in, integration, and unexpected events. The joint probabilities of the computed network, operational, and external risks are then used to determine the probability that a supplier will have an adverse impact on the company's revenue stream.

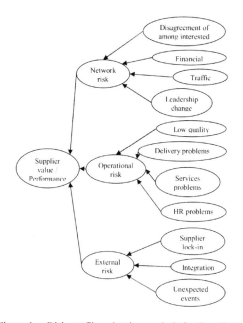

Figure 1. Risk profile reduction analysis for Supplier 1.

3 MODELLING RESULTS

3.1 *The risk profiles associated with a group of selected suppliers in the automotive industry*

This research examines VAR profit for the company based upon the risk profiles of each supplier. VAR is defined as the minimum loss expected on a portfolio of assets over a certain holding period at a given probability. The a priori probabilities for the 11 supply chain risk events which influence network, operational, and external risks are presented in Table 1 for each supplier. These values were used to generate a risk profile using Bayesian networks comprised of network, operational and external risk probabilities along with the supplier's probability of revenue impact on the company.

The table reveals that Suppliers 1, 3, 10 and 14 have the highest probability of revenue impact on the company, while Supplier 11 has the lowest probability of revenue impact.

3.2 *Risk reduction analysis*

To determine the effects of minimizing various combinations of risk events on company revenue was conducted a risk profile reduction analysis for each supplier. An illustration of risk reduction analysis for Supplier 1 is provided in Table 2.

The first row of values are network, operational, and external risk probabilities associated with Supplier 1 along with its probability of revenue impact, as illustrated in Table 1. This is referred to as the base case. The subsequent rows illustrate

Table 1. Supplier risk profiles.

Supplier	Network risk probability	Operational risk probability	External risk probability	Probability of revenue impact
1.	0.35	0.48	0.45	0.42
2.	0.20	0.24	0.39	0.28
3.	0.34	0.47	0.44	0.41
4.	0.22	0.24	0.40	0.29
5.	0.24	0.24	0.42	0.29
6.	0.25	0.31	0.44	0.33
7.	0.23	0.28	0.41	0.32
8.	0.23	0.28	0.41	0.32
9.	0.23	0.29	0.41	0.31
10.	0.35	0.47	0.46	0.42
11.	0.19	0.28	0.35	0.27
12.	0.29	0.36	0.34	0.33
13.	0.24	0.28	0.40	0.31
14.	0.34	0.48	0.44	0.42
15.	0.24	0.27	0.42	0.31

Table 2. Risk profile reduction analysis for Supplier 1.

Network risk probability	Operational risk probability	External risk probability	Probability of revenue impact
0.35	0.48	0.44	0.42
0.00	0.48	0.44	0.30
0.35	0.00	0.44	0.27
0.35	0.48	0.00	0.28
0.00	0.00	0.44	0.15
0.00	0.48	0.00	0.17
0.35	0.00	0.00	0.12
0.41	0.42	0.45	0.12
0,33	0.41	0.42	0.17
0.25	0.35	0.43	0.25
0.19	0.28	0.44	0.33

Table 3. Risk profiles and VAR reduction analysis.

Supplier	Network risk probability	Operational risk probability	External risk probability	Probability of revenue impact	VAR (%)
1.	0.35	0.48	0.45	0.42	73.2
2.	0.20	0.24	0.39	0.28	77.8
3.	0.34	0.47	0.44	0.41	72.5
4.	0.22	0.24	0.40	0.29	75.0
5.	0.24	0.24	0.42	0.29	79.3
6.	0.25	0.31	0.44	0.33	75.0
7.	0.23	0.28	0.41	0.32	72.4
8.	0.23	0.28	0.41	0.32	76.8
9.	0.23	0.29	0.41	0.31	76.7
10.	0.35	0.47	0.46	0.42	73.2
11.	0.19	0.28	0.35	0.27	76.9
12.	0.29	0.36	0.34	0.33	71.9
13.	0.24	0.28	0.40	0.31	73.3
14.	0.34	0.48	0.44	0.42	73.2
15.	0.24	0.27	0.42	0.31	73.3

the probability of revenue impact for Supplier 1 if it were possible to minimize a risk category (or a combination of risk categories) to the value of zero. The table shows that minimizing operational and external risk events reduces the probability of revenue impact from the base case of 48–12%.

While it may not be possible to reduce a risk event or category associated with a supplier's profile to a zero probability of occurrence, it may be possible to improve the profile by instituting proactive SCRM strategies and tactics in areas which will yield the maximum benefit. Thus, it is important for organizations to determine which risk categories, when improved, will provide the greatest risk reductions and benefits with respect to a particular supplier.

A comparison of supplier risk profiles using a priori risk event probabilities and the most favourable risk profile reduction combinations of network, operational, and external risks (excluding the combination where all three risks categories have a zero probability of occurrence), along with corresponding VAR results are presented in Table 3.

The first row of values corresponding to a given supplier represent its network, operational, and external risk probabilities along with its probability of revenue impact as displayed in Table 1. This represents the base case risk profile for the supplier. Also included in these rows are the corresponding monthly revenue impacts for each supplier and VAR results for the base case.

4 CONCLUSIONS

Bayesian networks can be used to develop supplier risk profiles to determine the risk exposure of a company's revenue stream for its supplier base. Based on these profiles, organizations can determine if it is in their best interest to either assist a supplier in improving their risk profile, or altering their relationship. The supplier risk profiles can be used to determine those risk events which have the largest potential impact on an organization's revenues, and the highest probability of occurrence. As part of a comprehensive supplier risk management program, organizations along with their suppliers can develop targeted approaches to minimize the occurrence of these risk events.

The use of Bayesian networks to model supply chain risks can be used as a tool to assist managers in determining a supplier's status in the supply network. Suppliers who have been shown to improve their risk profiles over time may be rewarded by an organization via the apportionment of more business. Overleaf, suppliers who have experienced increases in network, operational, and/or external risk events over time may be classified as "at risk" suppliers whose relationship may be subject to alteration. Ultimately, the alteration could result in removal from the supply network. This tool could not only be used to evaluate current suppliers, but also to examine the viability of potential suppliers based upon the generation of their risk profiles using Bayesian networks.

The methodology used in this study can be adopted by managers to formulate strategies and tactics which mitigate overall supply chain risks. This methodology can also be used as a means of monitoring risk in the supply network. These updates could be incorporated into a Bayesian network to create a new risk profile for each supplier. Risk management strategies, policies, and tactics could then be adjusted to reflect the new risk realities associated with the supply network. Thus, the methodology provides a proactive means of managing supply chain risks.

ACKNOWLEDGEMENT

The article is written within the project of young scientists, young teachers and PhD students number I-18-109-00.

REFERENCES

Cousins, P. et al. 2004. "The role of risk in environment-related Initiatives", International Journal of Operations & Production Management, Vol. 24, No. 6, pp. 554–65.

Craighead, C.W. et al. 2007. "The severity of supply chain disruptions: design characteristics and mitigation capabilities", Decision Sciences, Vol. 38, No. 1, pp. 131 -56.

Hendricks, K.B. & Singhal, V.R. 2005. "An empirical analysis of the effect of supply chain disruptions on long-run stock price performance and equity risk of the firm", Production and Operations Management, Vol. 14, No. 1, pp. 35–52.

Kim, S.W. 2006. "Effects of supply chain management practices, integration and competition capability on performance", Supply Chain Management: An International Journal, Vol. 11, No. 3, pp. 241–248.

Kleindorfer, P.R. & Saad, G.H. 2005. Managing Disruption Risks in Supply Chains. In Production and Operations Management Society. Volume 14, Issue 1, pp. 53–68.

Murphy, S. 2009. "Suppy Chain 2010: building on the lessons learned", Supply Chain Management Review, Vol. 13, No. 9, pp. 2–9.

Sawhney, M. et al. 2006. "The 12 different ways for companies to innovate", Sloan Management Review, Vol. 47, No. 3, pp. 75–81.

Vernor, J. et al. 2010. Identification of Emerging Risk Using Bayesian Conditional Probability. Enterprise Risk Management Symposium. Society of actuaries, Chicago, 2010.

Production Management and Business Development – Mihalčová et al. (Eds)
© 2019 Taylor & Francis Group, London, ISBN 978-1-138-60415-5

Managerial approaches to the sustainability challenges of cultural tourism

M. Tajtáková

School of Management/City University of Seattle in Trenčín, Bratislava, Slovak Republic

ABSTRACT: The paper reflects on managerial approaches intended to cope with current sustainability challenges of cultural tourism. Due to the unprecedented growth of the tourism sector in the last years the cultural tourism entrepreneurship has been challenged mainly by two principle dilemmas: contrasting perceptions of cultural assets' value by tourists vs. locals, and conservation vs. commodification of cultural heritage. Sustainable cultural tourism implies joint management of cultural heritage and tourism activities involving interests and economic benefits of all stakeholders to benefit both tangible and intangible cultural heritage conservation and tourism development. To achieve this, diverse managerial solutions were identified within operational, strategic, crisis and participatory management.

1 INTRODUCTION

Tourism is generally regarded as one of the world's largest industries. Cultural tourism has been recognised as a separate product category since the late 1970s (McKercher 2002) and has been considered to be a particularly advancing sector (Bywater 1993, Bendixen 1997, Hughes 2002, Richards 2007). It emerged as a consequence of the very development of the tourism market and its need for diversification (Richards 1996, Bendixen 1997, Bonet in Towse ed. 2003). However, it has been only since the late 1990s when an increased number of cultural tourism studies were published, building mainly on a pioneer report by Greg Richards ed. (1996) entitled *Cultural Tourism in Europe*.

Early studies on cultural tourism focused mainly on identifying the nature of rapport between the two sectors. Mutual benefits of merging into a symbiotic relationship between culture and tourism —based on their complementarity—were highlighted (Richards 1996, Bendixen 1997, Hughes 2002). From marketing perspective, tourism was considered as a tool for bringing visitors to cultural sites and venues, and culture as a source of attractive opportunities for cultural experiences and challenges to tourists for cultural discoveries (Bendixen 1997, pp. 21). However, the unprecedented growth of tourism industry in the last years drew attention to another phenomenon—the cultural tourism sustainability. A desire of quick profits in the tourism industry has often neglected the ability of cultural sites to withstand increased visits. Bucurescu (2012) points out that the promotion of cultural attractions for tourism has been

considered as most important, while the assessment of their capacity to resist and absorb negative impacts from tourism has been seen as a secondary issue to be solved afterwards.

Yet, the relevance of the tourism sustainability questions has been recently highlighted on a global institutional level. The World Tourism Organisation (UNWTO) declared *The International Year of Sustainable Tourism 2017*. This initiative was believed to be a unique opportunity to raise awareness on the contribution of sustainable tourism to development among public and private sector decision-makers and the general public, while mobilising all stakeholders to work together in making tourism a catalyst for positive change (UNWTO, 2016). This was followed by *The European Cultural Heritage Year 2018* proposed by the European Commission. The latter one was intended to activate and make visible the many positive effects of cultural heritage activities on other areas of life, society and the economy, including tourism (EC 2016).

2 CULTURAL TOURISM AND SUSTAINABILITY

2.1 *Trends in the tourism industry*

The tourism industry generates about 10% of the world's GDP, and is a key sector contributing to job creation, sustainable consumption and production, and the preservation of world's natural and cultural resources (UNWTO 2017, pp. 7–11). In 2017, tourism has grown above average, at around 4% per year, for eight straight years. A comparable sequence of uninterrupted solid growth has not been recorded since the 1960s. In total, 393 million more people travelled internationally for tourism between 2008 and 2017 (UNWTO 2018, pp. 12). Moreover, the trend of international tourist travels is growing. It is estimated that cultural tourism accounts for around 40% of all international tourist arrivals (UNWTO 2016a).

Up to one third of EU travellers indicate that cultural heritage is a key factor in choosing a travel destination (EC 2014). Europe is one of the world's regions with the largest concentration of cultural heritage (EC 2010). Heritage—together with the arts—are considered to be 'primary elements' of cultural tourism due to their superior status in visitor interests (ETC 2005). This is particularly important for Europe which has been recognised as the world's No 1 tourist destination (EC 2010).

2.2 Defining sustainable tourism

Debates on sustainable tourism began at the beginning of 1990s. The concept of sustainable tourism was proposed by the *World Tourism Organization* (UNWTO) and defined as 'the tourism that meets the needs of current tourists and host populations, while enhancing opportunities for the future' (UNWTO/McIntyre et al. 1993). Cultural aspects have been included into sustainable tourism concerns from the very beginning pointing out 'cultural integrity' (UNWTO 1993), 'tourism as a contributor to the enhancement of cultural heritage' (UMWTO 2001), 'cultural spheres and built environment', and encouraging to 'respect the socio-cultural authenticity of host communities, conserve their built and living cultural heritage and traditional values, and contribute to inter-cultural understanding and tolerance' (UNEP & UNWTO 2005). A landmark in sustainable tourism debate is considered *Rio+20 Conference on Sustainable Development* in 2012 where the UN's ST policy was formulated.

However, there is a certain ambiguity in the very term 'sustainable tourism'. This lies in the potential conflict between the meaning of the two words: *Sustainable* implies a state that can be maintained, is ongoing, perhaps even unchanging, whereas *tourism* implies the dynamic process of change to suit consumer demands (Nasser 2003). In addition, Bramwell & Lane (2005, pp. 53) suggests to distinguish between *sustainable tourism* and *tourism sustainability*. The authors claim that sustainable tourism should not become 'an excuse for tourism to compete for scarce resources in order to sustain tourism; rather, it should be an approach that seeks the most appropriate and efficient shared use of resources, on a global basis, within overall development goals'. This ambiguity is also reflected in the academic literature, where the concept of sustainable cultural tourism has been approached from different perspectives. As a result, it has gained its proponents, as well as, opponents.

Three different perspectives through the lens of capital were identified—a focus on *resources* (limits of cultural and natural capital), *activities* (economic capital invested in tourism) and *community* (the role of social capital in the local context) (Saarinen 2006). In addition, two schools of thought were distinguished (Nasser 2003): The *functional approach* (Ashworth 1994, 1995, Butler 1997, Wall 1997, Ashworth & Tunbridge, 2000, McKercher & Cros du 2002) emphasising the considerable economic importance of the industry to all participants, while looking for ways to improve its efficiency and minimise its adverse effects through good management and appropriate policy measures; and the *political-economy approach* (Lea 1988, Rees 1989, Cater 1994, Orbasli 2000) calling for more financial responsibility for the long-term maintenance of the heritage resources on which it depends, by allowing governments and local communities to hold higher stakes in tourism and in the management of their historic resources.

2.3 Sustainability challenges of cultural tourism

Early studies on sustainable tourism highlighted two major issues: the *'sustainability trinity'* (Farrell 1999) and the *'paradox of sustainability and tourism'* (Butler 1997). The 'sustainability trinity' aims at the smooth and transparent integration of *economy, society* and *environment* (Farrell 1999). It should be added that in the context of sustainable cultural tourism the environment to consider is primarily built and cultural, although cultural tourism may effect also the natural environment. This refers mainly to the behaviour and consumption patterns of tourists who use and consume local natural assets (e.g. water resources, pollution). As with any economic activity, Nasser (2003, pp. 472) points out that tourism entrepreneurship makes use of resources and produces an environmental impact that amounts to exploitation if the quantity and quality of those resources are degraded. According to Bramwell & Lane (1993) sustainable tourism implies the effort to reconcile the tensions and friction created by the complex interactions between the partners in the triangle, and to ensure equilibrium in the long term.

Within the 'paradox of sustainability and tourism' Butler (1997) argues that tourist destinations are deliberately changing in anticipation of, or to reflect changes in, customer preferences brought on by the competitive nature of tourism. Such a pattern of induced change runs both counter to, and in sympathy with the principles of sustainable development. Moreover, the author introduced the concept of the *'tourist area life cycle'*, which describes the way destination areas change and frequently obliterate or change overwhelmingly the inherent features that first made them attractive to visitors. Butler (1997) attributes the decline in the tourist destination cycle to the unchecked development of the destination until it exceeds its innate capacity to absorb tourism and its associated development. After this point, problems emerge, which if not addressed satisfactorily would result in subsequent visitor decline, and further in the inevitable failure of tourism entrepreneurship.

Moreover, it has been observed that with the emergence of a greater number of destinations competing for unique tourist experiences, traditional historic places are undergoing a redefinition and reinterpretation of their cultural heritage in order to be competitive and attractive. By doing this heritage places are responding to the commercial forces of consumer demand, and in many cases conservation and cultural values are being compromised (Nasser 2003, pp. 468). From the sustainability perspective, the need to consider the ability of a heritage site to withstand increased visits and/or a change in visitor profile without causing undue damage to tangible and intangible values has to be highlighted (Cros du 2001).

In addition, potential conflicts between tourists and local stakeholders may arise from different perceptions of the cultural assets' value, in particular by focusing primarily on its extrinsic appeal as a product to be consumed (McKercher et al. 2004). However, when culture is shared, tourism and heritage coexist in harmony so that tourism revenues can be used to sustain and conserve environments of heritage value. In contrast, when culture is exploited or created, there is an explicit dominance of commercial values over conservation values as tourism becomes central to the local economy (Newby 1994).

In 2013, a report entitled *Sustainable tourism as driving force for cultural heritage sites development* was published under the CHERPLAN project (Ruoss & Alfarè 2013). The report highlighted two main problems – 'carrying capacity' (the number of individuals a given area can support within natural resource limits and without degrading the natural, social, cultural and economic environment for present and future generations.), and 'Hit-and-Run' tourism (tourists visiting the site for few hours to continue their travel to other destinations with more attractive accommodation and recreational facilities). These problems generate negative impacts on heritage sites (dealing with increased waste generation, water consumption and traffic) while the income is almost absent.

It should be noted that the tourism industry is conscious of the need to maintain the social, cultural, environmental, and economic attributes that are basic to its positive development (Edgell 2015, pp. 25). Benet (in Towse ed. 2003, pp. 191) points out that an effort to preserve the quality of cultural and patrimonial resources and to avoid triviality must be made alongside the sustainable development of tourism. It is believed that if the tourism sector is well managed it can foster inclusive economic growth, social inclusiveness and the protection of cultural and natural assets (UNWTO 2016).

3 MANAGERIAL SOLUTIONS TO ACHIEVE SUSTAINABLE CULTURAL TOURISM

Tajtáková (2017, pp. 3) argues that 'sustainable cultural tourism implies joint management of cultural heritage and tourism activities involving interests and economic benefits of all stakeholders to benefit both tangible and intangible cultural heritage conservation and tourism development'. In general, discourses on sustainable tourism management have been oscillating between two broadly interpreted models of 'top-down' approach characterised by institutional measures, infrastructure provision and inward investment, and 'bottom-up' approach based on best practices and practical managerial tools on how to cope with current sustainability challenges.

However, it should be emphasised that risks generated from numerous factors can be most conveniently managed through the shared responsibilities of government, authorities, heritage sites managers, tourism operators and the tourists themselves. Hassan & Rahman (2015, pp. 213–214) claim that the effective policy planning is essential for the systematic development of tourism entrepreneurship with a proper assessment and management of risks, their impact on cultural heritage and opportunities for sustainable, mutual growth. In this respect, several managerial solutions have been developed in order to achieve sustainable tourism development. They encompass measures within operational management, strategic management, crisis management and participatory management. Main managerial solutions are listed in the Table 1.

Managerial solutions to achieve sustainable cultural tourism development are intended to reconcile two principal dilemmas of cultural tourism development: (1) Contrasting perceptions of cultural assets' value by tourists vs. locals, and (2) Conservation vs. commodification of cultural heritage.

First, while tourists tend to prioritize the extrinsic appeal of cultural heritage as a product to be consumed (economic value), the local community perceives cultural assets' value rather as an embodied heritage of their past (cultural, symbolic and social value).

Table 1. Managerial solutions for sustainable cultural tourism.

Management level	Objective	Tool
Operational	To control the amount and flow of tourists	Visitor management Crowding management
Strategic	To assess potential of cultural heritage sites for tourism development	Carrying capacity Potential matrix
Crisis	To limit tourism development	No-growth strategy
Participatory	To encourage local community involvement within cultural tourism development	COBACHREM model Community involvement mode

Second, due to the increased competition among heritage sites, in many cases, cultural heritage managers prioritise destination image and promotion over the assessment of its robusticity (the capacity to resist and absorb negative impacts from tourism). In addition, the profits of commodification do not always translate to a circular economy, with sustainable financing for investment and value creation.

3.1 *Operational management*

On the operational management level simple solutions as visitor management and crowding management have been adopted. Their objective is to limit the number of tourists and facilitate their flow in the area of heritage sites. By doing this, cultural assets are less exposed to uncontrolled crowds of visitors, and the risk of their deterioration is diminished. The 'Visitor management' is applied primarily within the management of protected areas where number of tourists and their behaviour needs to be controlled in order to prevent damage to vulnerable heritage sites. The 'Crowding management' is a method applied to control crowding issues as a part of a tourism destination implicit image and tourism sustainability. The level of crowding can also be used as an indicator of effective management practices.

3.2 *Strategic management*

Solutions on the strategic management level serve mainly to assess the ability and potential of heritage sites to cope with tourism development. The 'Carrying capacity' (Ashworth 1994, 1995) concept represents a managerial approach assessing the maximum use of any place without causing negative effects on its tangible and intangible heritage

and other resources, and the subsequent loss of visitor satisfaction. The 'Market Appeal/Robusticity Matrix' (called also Potential Matrix) (McKercher & Cros du 2002) analyses the interdependence of the two aspects: *Market appeal* reflecting the attractiveness of the site for tourism, and the *robusticity* determining the capacity to cope with increasing tourism. The authors believe that by adopting a correct assessment of the tourism potential of cultural assets one can avoid future risks resulting from overdeveloped or underdeveloped tourism.

3.3 *Crisis management*

The tension between the interests of stakeholders from tourism industry and culture may result into situations in which tourism might not be considered as an appropriate use of resources compared with other development options or to no development at all. This solution has been adopted at the crisis management level and labelled as 'no-growth' strategy or reduced activity scenarios (Bramwell & Lane 2005, pp. 53). Actually, the same approach is advocated by McKercher & Cros du (2002) within their *Market Appeal/Robusticity Matrix*. The authors identified a specific segment characterised by a moderate/high market appeal, but a low robusticity. It means that tourists may be very interested to visit a particular cultural site, however, its physical state is too fragile, or its cultural values are sensitive to high visitation levels. Therefore it is suggested to limit extensive tourism activities and to ensure that an existing visitation does not harm the cultural values of the asset.

3.4 *Participatory management*

Finally, the participatory management has been recognised as a new managerial approach within fields with contrasting interests of diverse stakeholders. True participation means that everyone has a voice which must be acknowledged. Participatory approaches to the management of tourism activities encompass a greater involvement of public bodies, civil societies, citizens and local community, besides tourism entrepreneurs. The COBACHREM model 'Community-based cultural heritage resources management model' has been initiated as a new approach that outlines the symbiosis between cultural heritage, environment and various stakeholders, with the aim to create awareness about neglected conservation indicators inherent in cultural resources (Keitumetse 2013). The 'Conceptual model of community involvement for sustainable heritage tourism' synthesises the constructs of organisational motivation, community empowerment, community involvement, and sustainable tourism operations in an integrated framework. (Li & Hunter 2015). Both models aim to achieve an integrated framework for sustainable tourism management highlighting the role of local communities as the holders of cultural assets for tourism entrepreneurship.

4 CONCLUSION

The growth of tourism industry in modern society resulted into an increased debate on sustainable tourism entrepreneurship in the last two decades. Approaches towards sustainable cultural tourism are grouped around management models improving the efficiency and minimising the adverse effects of tourism, and around new models and policies allowing for a higher involvement of different stakeholders. Two principal dilemmas of sustainable tourism entrepreneurship were identifies: (1) A potential conflict between tourists and local stakeholders arising from different perceptions of cultural assets' value, in particular, by focusing primarily on its extrinsic appeal as a product to be consumed; (2) An increased competition among cultural heritage sites leading to the **prioritization of** destination image and promotion over the assessment of its robusticity (commodification vs. conservation of cultural heritage).

Major challenges of sustainable tourism management encompass:

- *Sustainability trinity* (Farrell, 1999) – smooth and transparent integration of economy, society and environment;
- *The paradox of sustainability and tourism* (Butler, 1997) – deliberate changes in tourist destinations to reflect customer preferences;
- *Tourist area life cycle* (Butler, 1997) – the way destination areas change inherent features that first made them attractive resulting in a subsequent visitor decline;
- *'Hit-and-Run' tourism* (Ruoss and Alfarè, eds., 2013) – tourists visiting the site for few hours to continue their travel to other destinations with more attractive accommodation and recreational facilities, resulting in increased waste generation, water consumption and traffic, while the income for the place is almost absent.

To cope with the identified challenges of sustainable tourism entrepreneurship several managerial solutions were identified. They include tools at the operational management level intended to control the amount and flow of tourists (visitor management, tourism crowding management); at the strategic management level to assess potential of cultural heritage sites for tourism development (carrying capacity assessment, Market Appeal/ Robusticity Matrix); at the crisis management level to limit tourism development (no-growth strategy); and finally at the participatory management level to encourage local community involvement within cultural tourism development (COBACHREM and Community Involvement Model). The identified tools represent bottom-up solutions based on best practices and practical managerial approaches towards current sustainability challenges.

REFERENCES

Ashworth G.J. & Tunbridge J.E. 2000. *The Tourist-Historic City. Retrospect and Prospects of Managing the Heritage City*, Pergamon, Elsevier.

Ashworth G.J. 1994. From history to heritage: From heritage to identity: In search of concepts and models. In *Building a new heritage: Tourism, culture, and identity*, G. J. Ashworth and P. J. Larkham (eds.). London: Routledge.

Ashworth, G.J. 1995. Environmental quality and tourism and the environment. In *Sustainable tourism development*, H. Coccossis and P. Nijikamp (eds.). Aldershot, UK: Avebury.

Bendixen, P. 1997. Cultural Tourism—Economic Success at the Expense of Culture? *The International Journal of Cultural Policy*, Vol. 4, no. 1, p. 21–46.

Bonet, L. 2003. Cultural tourism. In: *A Handbook of Cultural Economics*, R. Towse, (eds.), Edward Elgar, p. 187–193.

Bramwell, B., & Lane, B. 2005. From niche to general relevance? Sustainable tourism, research and the role of tourism. *Journal of Tourism Studies, 16*(2), 52–62.

Bucurescu, I. 2012. Assesment of tourism potential in historic towns. Romanian case studies. *V. International Conference 'The role of Tourism in Territorial Development'*, Gheorgheni University, October 10, 2012, Proceedings p. 100–118.

Butler, R. 1997. Modelling tourism development: Evolution, growth and decline. In S.Wahab & J.J. Pigram (eds.), *Tourism, development and growth: The challenge of sustainability* (pp. 109–125). London: Routledge.

Butler, R. 1999. Sustainable tourism: A state-of-the-art review. *Tourism Geographies, 1*(1), 7–25.

Bywater, M. 1993. The market for cultural tourism in Europe. *Travel and Tourism Analyst*, No. 6, 1993, p. 30–46.

Cater, E. 1994. Ecotourism in the third world—Problems and prospects for sustainability. In *Ecotourism: A sustainable option?* E. Cater and G. Lowman (eds.). Chichester, UK: Wiley.

CHERPLAN. n.d. *Enhancement of Cultural Heritage Through Environmental Planning & Management*. [online]. [Accessed 2017-01-05]. Available at http://www.cherplan.eu/.

Cros du, H. 2001. A new model to assist in planning for sustainable cultural heritage tourism. *International Journal of Tourism Research* 3, 165–70.

EC 2010. *Europe, the world's No 1 tourist destination—a new political framework for tourism in Europe*. Communication from the Commission to the European Parliament, the Council, the European Economic and Social committee and the Committee of the Regions. Brussels, 30.6.2010, COM(2010) 352 final. [on-line]. [Accessed 2017-01-05]. Available at http://eur-lex.europa.eu/legal-content/EN/TXT/PDF/?uri=CELEX:52010DC0352&from=EN.

EC 2014. *Towards an integrated approach to cultural heritage for Europe*. Communication from the Commission to the European Parliament, the Council, the European

Economic and Social committee and the Committee of the Regions. Brussels, 22.7.2014, COM(2014) 477 final. [on-line]. [Accessed 2017-11-15]. Available at http://ec.europa.eu/assets/eac/culture/library/publications/2014-heritage-communication_en.pdf.

EC 2016. *European Year of Cultural Heritage proposed for 2018.* News 30/08/2016. [on-line]. [Accessed 2017-01-05]. Available at http://ec.europa.eu/culture/news/20160830-commission-proposal-cultural-heritage-2018_en.

Edgell, D. L. 2015. International Sustainable Tourism Policy. *The Brown Journal of World Affairs,* Vol. XXII, Issue I, Fall/Winter 2015, p. 25–36.

ETC 2005. *City tourism and culture: the European experience.* [on-line]. [Accessed 2017-01-05]. Available at http://81.47.175.201/stodomingo/attachments/article/122/City-TourismCulture.pdf.

Farrell, B. H. 1999. Conventional or sustainable tourism? No room for choice. *Tourism Management, 20*(2), 189–191.

Hassan, A. & Rahman, M. 2015. World Heritage site as a label in branding a place. *Journal of Cultural Heritage Management and Sustainable Development.* Vol. 5 No. 3, 2015, pp. 210–223.

Hughes, H. L. 2002. Culture and tourism: a framework for further analysis. *Managing Leisure*, vol. 7, 2002, p. 164–175.

Keitumetse, S. O. 2013. Cultural Resources as Sustainability Enablers: Towards a Community-Based Cultural Heritage Resources Management (COBACHREM) Model. Sustainability. [on-line]. [Accessed 2017-01-05]. Available at www.mdpi.com/2071-1050/6/1/70/pdf.

Lea, J. 1988. *Tourism and development in the third world.* New York: Routledge.

Li, Y. & Hunter, C. 2015. Community involvement for sustainable heritage tourism: a conceptual model. *Journal of Cultural Heritage Management and Sustainable Development,* Vol. 5 No. 3, 2015, p. 248–262.

McKercher et al. 2004. Attributes of popular cultural attractions in Hong Kong. *Annals of Tourism Research*, 31(2), 393–407.

McKercher, B. 2002. Towards a classification of cultural tourists. *International Journal of Tourism Research* 4, 29–38.

McKercher, B., & Cros du, H. 2002. *Cultural tourism: The partnership between tourism and cultural heritage management.* New York: The Hawthorn Hospitality Press.

Nasser, N. 2003. Planning for Urban Heritage Places: Reconciling Conservation, Tourism, and Sustainable Development. *Journal of Planning Literature,* Vol. 17, No. 4 (May 2003), p. 468–479.

Newby, P.T. 1994. Tourism: Support or threat to heritage? In G.J. Ashworth & P.J. Larkham (eds.), *Building a new heritage: Tourism, culture, and identity in the New Europe* (pp. 206–228). London: Routledge.

Orbasli, A. 2000. *Tourists in historic towns: Urban conservation and heritage management.* London and New York: E & FN Spon.

Rees, W. E. 1989. *Defining sustainable development.* Center for Human Settlements research bulletin. Vancouver, Canada: Center for Human Settlements, University of British Columbia.

Richards, G. 1996. *Cultural Tourism in Europe.* CABI, Wallingford, re-issued in 2006 in electronic format by the Association for Tourism and Leisure Education (ATLAS). [on-line]. [Accessed 2017-01-05]. Available at www.atlas-euro.org.

Richards, G. 2007. *Global Trends in Cultural Tourism.* In: Richards, G. (ed.) Cultural Tourism: Global and Local Perspectives. Routledge 2007. ISBN 0-78903-117-5.

Ruoss, E. & Alfarè, L. (eds.) 2013. Sustainable tourism as driving force for cultural heritage sites development. *Planning, Managing and Monitoring Cultural Heritage Sites in South East Europe.* CHERPLAN. Enhancement of Cultural Heritage Through Environmental Planning & Management. [on-line]. [Accessed 2017-01-05]. Available at Eurpehttp://www.cherplan.eu/sites/default/files/public_files/Sustainable%20tourism%20in%20SEE.pdf.

Saarinen, J. 2006. Traditions of sustainability in tourism studies. *Annals of Tourism Research, 33*(4), 1121–1140.

Tajtáková, M. 2017. *Inventory and analysis of the main tools currently available to cultural sites and authorities with regard to sustainable cultural tourism on a transnational level (EU / Council of Europe/ UN).* The study carried out in the framework of The European Expert Networks on Culture and Audiovisual (EENCA) for The Directorate General for Education and Culture (DG EAC) based on the request of the European Commission.

Tajtáková, M. 2017a. *Sustainable Cultural Tourism.* The study carried out in the framework of The European Expert Networks on Culture and Audiovisual (EENCA) for The Directorate General for Education and Culture (DG EAC) based on the request of the European Commission.

UN 2012. *Rio+20 Conference on Sustainable Development.* [on-line]. [Accessed 2017-01-05]. Available at https://sustainabledevelopment.un.org/rio20.html.

UNEP/UNWTO 2005. *Making Tourism More Sustainable: A Guide for Policy Makers.* [on-ine]. [Accessed 2017–01–05]. Available at http://www.unep.fr/shared/publications/pdf/DTIx0592xPA-TourismPolicyEN.pdf.

UNWTO 2001. *Global Code of Ethics for Tourism.* Resolution adopted by the General Conference 21 December 2001 (A/RES/56/212). [on-line]. [Accessed 2017-01-05]. Available at http://www2.unwto.org/en/content/full-text-global-code-ethics-tourism.

UNWTO 2016. *International Year for Sustainable Tourism for Development 2017 garners support from the sector.* Press release. 05 Dec 16. [on-line]. [Accessed 2017-01-05]. Available at http://media.unwto.org/press-release/2016-12-05/international-year-sustainable-tourism-development-2017-garners-support-sec.

UNWTO 2016a. *UNWTO congress to discuss the links between cultural heritage and creative tourism.* Press release. 23 Nov 16. [on-line]. [Accessed 2017-01-05]. Available at http://media.unwto.org/press-release/2016-11-23/unwto-congress-discuss-links-between-cultural-heritage-and-creative-tourism.

UNWTO 2017. *UNWTO Annual Report 2016.* [on-line]. [Accessed 2017-11-15]. Available at http://cf.cdn.unwto.org/sites/all/files/pdf/annual_report_2016_web_0.pdf.

UNWTO 2018. *UNWTO Annual Report 2017.* [on-line]. [Accessed 2018-06-25]. Available at http://www2.unwto.org/publication/unwto-annual-report-2017.

UNWTO/McIntyre et al. 1993. *Sustainable tourism development: guide for local planners.* UNWTO, Madrid.

Wall, G. 1997. Sustainable tourism—Unsustainable development. In *Tourism, development and growth*, S.Wahab and J. J. Pigram, (eds.). London: Routledge.

Production Management and Business Development – Mihalčová et al. (Eds)
© 2019 Taylor & Francis Group, London, ISBN 978-1-138-60415-5

Indebtedness of selected enterprises with regard to sectoral aspects

M. Taušová, L. Domaracká, M. Shejbalová Muchová & P. Tauš
Technical University of Košice, FBERG, Košice, Slovak Republic

ABSTRACT: Indebtedness is currently in general, often addressing the issue, which affects the viability and future growth businesses. The aim of this contribution is to analyze key indicators of indebtedness in a correlation with selected sector-specific indicators of asset structure through an analysis of 100 selected industrial enterprises. For the purpose of the analysis, a database of 100 supporting enterprises from the industry was created according to the SK NACE classification with the representation of the production and services enterprises and the division into the heavy and light industry. These segmentations will be crucial in looking for factors affecting the financial stability of enterprises. Key indicators of debt and equity rating were analyzed through a regression and correlation analysis using JMP Pro software support. The results of the analysis point to the increased indebtedness of Slovak enterprises compared to the European average, which highlights the need to address this issue.

1 INTRODUCTION

The specific corporate indebtedness and capital structure is fundamentally a complex process dependent on a large variety of determinants; and the chosen financial strategy, therefore, depends on the particular decisions of individual firms (Bolfíková et al. 2010). A severe debt overhang problem, either public or private, the analysis of the factors that influence companies' leverage reveals essential, in particular for the high-indebted firms. Also, it is important to define accurately enterprise indebtedness, because it is used in the calculation of financial ratios, serving for evaluation of enterprises financial performance (Ishchenko 2013). Internal factors were supposed to be: the corporate philosophy, the cost of the capital, and the financial health and indebtedness of a business, so the final capital structure of a company is the result of its own decision-making, or rather a result of various external factors, thus tends rather to the predominance of the internal factors, performance monitoring has positive impact on business performance by Teplická (2015). The findings of the study by Iatridis & Kilirgiotis (2012) provide evidence that also the firm size is positively related to indebtedness and fixed asset revaluation. González & Jareño (2014) carry out an analysis of four key financial variables: percentage of indebtedness, volume of equity, overall liquidity, and returns on equity, concluding that some expected relationships are confirmed—such as the logical exchange between equity and borrowed capital—as well as other less obvious relationships—like the positive relationship between the returns and the volume of equity. Kudlawicz et al. (2015) studies the existence

of fit between the capital structure and economic performance leading companies to position themselves on the efficient frontier. The results are indicating that the efficiency increases the performance of the company and still more companies, close the efficient frontier, have a higher economic performance and in addition, lower levels of indebtedness.

The aim of this paper was to show a view of the indebtedness of Slovak enterprises by examining the basic financial statements of 100 enterprises at the level of 20 branches. The debt ratios have been put in relation to indicators that characterize enterprise background assets such as liquidity, golden funding rule and ROA.

2 METHODOLOGY

The main method of searching is a method of financial rate indexes, allowing to express rate among own and foreign capital. Indexes measures extend of debts using.

Indexes serve also as indicators for determination of risk level, but indebtedness does not mean always negative characteristics. A Certain level of indebtedness is profitable for the company, which should try to have a financial structure with minimal cost of capital and correspondent structure of its assets. Searched indexes of indebtedness are as follows: Total indebtedness – IND (debt ratio):

$$Debt\ ratio = foreign\ capital/total\ assets \qquad (1)$$

Debt ratio (total indebtedness) expresses percentage part of foreign sources from total assets of the company. In case total indebtedness is lower, there is an assumption for greater financial stability and profitability. Recommended value is 30–60%, depending on the sector, in which company makes business and market situation.

Leverage ratio – LR:

$$Leverage\ ratio = total\ assets/equity \qquad (2)$$

Leverage ratio testifies about how big amount of assets forms own capital, value 2 explains the same amount of own and external capital. The acceptable limit of the external capital is 70% (two thirds), according to given relation, it should be the value 3.

In relation to the profitability, there is the rule: in case profitability of invested capital is higher than a price of interested foreign sources, financial leverage is positive and vice versa.

Insolvency – INS:

$$Insolvency = commitment/receivables \qquad (3)$$

Insolvency is a measure of a company's ability to pay off its incurred debt. The value bigger than 1 refers to primary insolvency, a value lower than 1 is defined as secondary insolvency.

In addition to debt ratios, it is necessary to examine the relationship between the enterprise's assets and the sources of coverage and, consequently, the ability of the enterprise to generate profits. The most important rules that, in terms of maintaining solvency, ie long-term payability, include the "Golden Balance Rule" – GBR.

The golden balance rule of funding requires that long-term assets be funded by capital that is available to the enterprise on a long-term basis and that short-term assets be financed by capital that is available only for a short time.

The relationship that expresses the golden balance rule can be interpreted as follows:

$$Long\ term\ asset < Own\ capital + Long\text{-}term\ foreign\ capital \qquad (4)$$

Respectively

$$Long\ term\ asset - (Own\ capital + Long\text{-}term\ foreign\ capital) < 0 \qquad (5)$$

This means that total long-term assets should be less than the amount of financial resources available over the long term.

Liquidity—available liquidity – LI

Available liquidity compares the relationship of financial assets to short-term liabilities. It points to the solvency of the subject being analyzed. It is important that the organization under analysis has as many funds as possible so that it is able to pay its due liabilities. The recommended value varies considerably from one sector to the next, ranging from <0.2; 1>, and that was the subject of our investigation

$$LI = Financial\ asset/Short\text{-}term\ liabilities \qquad (6)$$

Return on equity – ROE

Return on equity provides information on equity interest. The level of return on equity depends on the ratio of profitability of total capital to that of foreign capital. We calculate it as follows:

$$ROE = net\ profit/own\ capital \qquad (7)$$

Optimum is the value that means capital reproduction (own) for the period of 4–5 years at 0.25–0.20.

Mentioned indicators had been searched in Slovakian companies, analyzed in the frame of choosing industrial sectors. Every sector included five chosen companies, where internal data served for interpretation of their financial situation. Consequently according to obtained data from financial reports during 2009–2016, searched indicators had been calculated for every company individually. Calculated values of giving indexes in choosing sectors had been evaluated by graphs, serving for final evaluation of indebtedness in the 100 companies in the frame of chosen sectors.

The calculated indicators were then analyzed by analyzing ANOVA, examining the variability of the indicators achieved with respect to the individual sectors. Subsequently, a multidimensional analysis was carried out using software support JMP Pro, where a pair correlation analysis was carried out at sector level. The results of the correlation coefficients were compared in a sectoral manner in order to identify the common features of selected sectors.

3 ANALYSIS OF FINANCIAL INDICATORS

Based on the data collected from the publicly available financial statements of the balance sheet and the profit and loss statement, the financial indicators for the business entities were calculated, the results of which varied widely (Table 1) and the standard deviation size indicates the need to examine the individual indicators separately for each sector.

3.1 Analysis of variability

The ANOVA analysis examined the variability of the resulting values of the calculated financial indicators per sector. For all indicators, the statistically significant variability of the achieved values was confirmed by the choice of the sector. As shown in the analysis sample in Figure 1 when analyzing the ANOVA of

Table 1. Univariate simple statistics.

Indicator	Mean	Std Dev	Min	Max
ROE	0.0488	0.2666	−4.3724	0.8838
LI	0.6372	2.0397	−0.0010	32.7990
GBR	−8.0575	36.0480	−624.13	3.0984
Indebtedness	0.6604	0.3206	0.0000	2.8905
Levarage ratio	8.8636	36.0574	−188.08	540.590
Insolvency	1.7833	4.9441	0.0000	75.9369

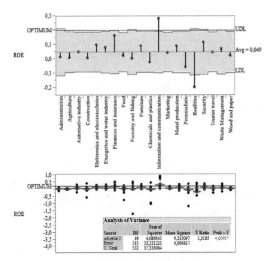

Figure 1. ANOVA—ROE.

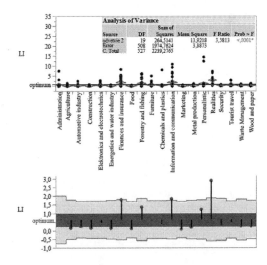

Figure 2. ANOVA—LI.

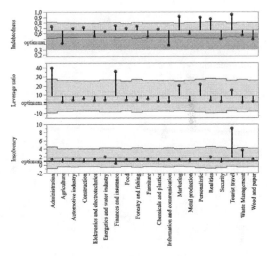

Figure 3. ANOM—Insolvency, leverage ratio, indebtedness.

the liquidity indicator LI, it can be stated that the average liquidity value for all the examined sectors is 0.6 which belongs to the optimal interval <0.2, 1>.

However, most sectors are located at the lower end of the range or below the optimum level in the period 2009–2016, only five sectors are at the upper end of the range and show excessive liquidity, including realities, Information and communication, Finance and insurance, Forestry and fishing a Personalistics.

Each of the indicators analyzed showed statistically significant variability of the achieved values by the influence of the industry, at the same time it can be noted that the impact of the sector on individual indicators is different. Branches that are above average in one pointer in another pointer are below average of what we see in Figure 2. In analyzing the return on equity indicator, the optimum set at 0.2 exceeds only the information and communication sector, which also shows above average liquidity, but on the other hand significantly lower than average results were recorded in Realities, which was significantly above the previous indicator.

The GBR indicator, represented by the requirement to finance long-term assets with long-term

capital, was met in all sectors, as is evident from Table 1 with values ranging from about <624; 3>.

The analysis of corporate indebtedness results through ANOVA analysis also points to statistically significant differences in the average indebtedness of individual sectors. For the sake of clarity, we present the results of the ANOM analysis, which represents the analysis of deviations from the average at the level of the indicators (Fig. 3).

The following facts have been identified in a detailed examination of each indicator. The average value of the indebtedness indicator for all sectors surveyed is shifted above the optimum interval of

<0.3, 0.6> to the level of 0.66, which indicates the overall level of indebtedness of Slovak enterprises. Only eight of the 20 industries surveyed show the value of this indicator at the optimum interval or optimum border. These are the sectors Agriculture, Information and Communication, Security, Wood and Paper, Electronics and Electrotechnics, Furniture, Metal Production, Waste Management. These sectors also show positive results in other debt ratios.

3.2 *Parallel correlation analysis*

The results of the variability analysis have shown a significant impact of sectoral peculiarities on the results achieved in the property and debt ratios.

Our goal was to verify the interdependence between the indicators and compare the impact of the industry on the strength of these dependencies by analyzing the pair correlation. The pair correlation analysis was performed at the level of each industry and the results were summarized in the following tables (Tables 2 and 3).

The results of this analysis also show the strong impact of the sector on the interrelationships between the indicators. Significant differences in correlations between the indicators were demonstrated. There is a very strong negative correlation with a correlation coefficient in the range of <–0.92; –0.7> between ROA and the indebtedness of the sectors—Finance and Insurance,

Table 2. Negative of the pair correlation of selected indicators at sector level.

SECTOR	ROE* LI*	ROE* GBR*	ROE* IND*	LI* GBR*	LI* IND*
Electronics and electrotechnics			–0.60		–0.61
Wood and paper			–0.75		
Information and communication		–0.83		–0.72	
Administration	–0.67			–0.95	–0.71
Construction		–0.70			
Forestry and fishing			–0.66		
Personalistic					–0.74
Finances and insurance			–0.80		
Marketing			–0.92		
Realities		–0.81	–0.86		
Energetics and water industry		–0.79			

*ROE – Return on equity, LI – Available liquidity, GBR – Golden Balance Rule, IND – Total indebtedness.

Table 3. Positive of the pair correlation of selected indicators at sector level.

SECTOR	ROE* LI*	GBR* IND*	GBR* LR*	GBR* INS*	IND* LR*	IND* INS*	LR* INS*
Electronics and electrotechnics					0.80		
Security					0.91	0.64	
Wood and paper		0.60	0.75				0.67
Metal production						0.67	0.70
Agriculture					0.96		
Information and communication	0.75	0.66		0.60	0.90		
Waste Management	0.60						
Construction						0.77	
Furniture					0.70	0.61	
Chemicals and plastics		0.81			0.64		
Food						0.64	
Energetics and water industry					0.85		

*ROE – Return on equity, LI – Available liquidity, GBR – Golden Balance Rule, IND – Total indebtedness, LR – Leverage ratio, INS – Insolvency.

Marketing, Reality, Wood and Paper (Table 2), and Second Sector whose correlation was not confirmed with a correlation coefficient in the range of <–0.49; 0.49>. A positive correlation can be seen in the assessment of the relationship between the debt ratios themselves, with the strongest correlation between the indicators of the indebtedness and the leverage ratio with the correlation coefficient in the range of <0.85; 0.96> in Electronics and Electrical, Security & Protection, Wood & Paper, Metalworking, Agriculture, Information & Communication, Energy & Water Management (Table 3). The subject of further investigation will be the classification of the common features and segmentation of the sectors based on the analysis of the sensitivity indicators.

4 CONCLUSION

At present, most Slovak companies have a too high value for debt indicators, which may be threatening in the long period. However, indebtedness cannot be perceived globally, irrespective of the specificities of individual sectors, which often display a very different asset structure resulting from different technological claims on the sector itself. Based on this analysis, the impact of individual sectors on debt ratios was assessed, as confirmed by the ANOVA analysis, and then examined the intensity of the relationship between debt ratios and asset and profitability indicators. Even in this second part, the sector's marked impact on the intensity of dependence between indicators was evident, opening up further possibilities for review.

ACKNOWLEDGEMENT

This contribution is the result of the project implementation KEGA No. 002TUKE-4/2017 – Innovative didactic methods of education process at university and their importance in increasing education workmanship of teachers and development of students' competences.

REFERENCES

Bolfíková, E., Hrehová, D. & Frenová, J. 2010. Manager's decision-making in organizations—empirical analysis of bureaucratic vs. learning approach. In *Zbornik Radova Ekonomskog Fakultet au Rijeci*, 28(1): 135–163.

González, C. & Jareño, F. 2014. Financial analysis of the main hotel chains of the Spanish tourism sector. *Regional and Sectoral Economic Studies*, 14(2): 91–108.

Iatridis, G.E. & Kilirgiotis, G. 2012. Incentives for fixed asset revaluations: The UK evidence. *Journal of Applied Accounting Research*, 13(1): 5–20.

Ishchenko, M. 2013. Mining and beneficiation companies liabilities figures correction. *Economic Annals-XXI*, 11–12 (1): 58–61.

Kudlawicz, C., Senff, C.O. & Bach, T.M. 2015. The economic performance and capital structure: Brazilian companies to light efficiency frontier. *Journal Globalization, Competitiveness and Governability*, 9(3): 40–52.

Teplická, K., Daubner, M. & Augustínová, E. 2015. Analysis of causal relationships between selected factors in process of performance management in industrial companies in Slovakia. *Ekonomicky casopis*, 63(5): 504–523.

Production Management and Business Development – Mihalčová et al. (Eds)
© 2019 Taylor & Francis Group, London, ISBN 978-1-138-60415-5

Economic aspects decisive about entry into the global alliance

I. Vajdová, S. Szabo & S. Szabo Jr.
*Department of Air Traffic Management, Faculty of Aeronautics, Technical University of Košice,
Košice, Slovak Republic*

ABSTRACT: Business alliances have been two of the major tools for companies to achieve a global dimension in the last three sharply globalizing decades. At the same time, global alliances are among the most watched manifestations of economic globalization. A specific feature of air transport is the creation of a transport system that operates on the multilateral cooperation of air carriers. This article deals with the origins of bilateral and multilateral agreements between airlines. The contribution points in particular to global alliance cooperation between air carriers, with emphasis being placed on the legal and economic reasons for the decision to join the Alliance. The article is more focused on the economic advantages and disadvantages accruing airline of this kind of cooperation. On the example of the airline CSA, it points to the specific changes in selected indicators that have occurred in the company after its entry into the global SkyTeam alliance.

1   INTRODUCTION

It is important for each business to follow current trends and adapt to market conditions to achieve competitive advantage and gains. So how currently dominated supermarkets and hypermarkets over a small private shops in air transport is dominated agreements between airlines both bilaterally but especially on the international global level. As well as private businessmen in a small shop cannot compete with its offer to offer of supermarket chains also the only airline cannot offer to passengers such product which offers them a variety of cooperating airlines.

2   THEORETICAL BACKGROUND

The economic development of the previous decades is characterized by a sharp increase in global activity. One of the basic variables of the complex globalization equations are international companies which with their activities contribute significantly to the continued densification of global economic sphere. At a certain stage in the development of economic globalization, they are necessarily struggling, and the number and variety of forms of their interactions are growing sharply. In particular, the Alliance makes strategic the fact that such a move will affect the long-term competitiveness of the business and require its long-term engagement. (Javor 2005).

Transnational corporations have many advantages over local businesses. Their size gives them the opportunity to achieve considerable savings in the scale of product and product development. Their global presence expands them more strongly to new ideas and opportunities.

However, in addition to all the benefits which brings them a large dimensions, there are also potential threats of cumbersome and bureaucratic. International trade and global pressures make alliances of multinational corporations often not only effective, but sometimes necessary.

3   AIRLINE COOPERATION

A specific feature of air transport is the creation of a transport system that operates on the multilateral cooperation of air carriers. The operation of this system is based on cooperation in commercial, operational, technical, technological and security fields, both at the level of cooperation between the two contractual partners and at the level of multilateral cooperation at national and international level. (Pruša 2008) International cooperation is made possible by the existence of international agreements and activities of governmental and non-governmental organizations such as ICAO, IATA and others.

4   ECONOMICS ASPECT OF ALLIANCE COOPERATION

Deregulation of the market has prompted a wave of cooperative agreements and alliances between airlines. These are primarily intended to achieve

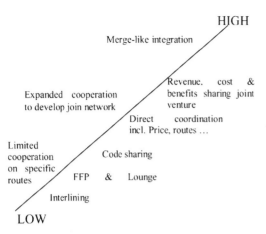

Figure 1.   The spectrum of airline cooperation.
Source: US DOT and European Commission.

Figure 2.   Different level of cooperation within the Global Alliance of Airlines.
Source: IATA Economics Biefing. 2012.

fleet rationalization, widening and rationalizing the network structure, greater use of cost savings on the scale of transport and reducing costs through joint purchasing, joint marketing, and the like (Begera 2015).

4.1   Legal and economic reasons for the decision to join the alliance

Passengers use air transport to move between major hubs but more often they move between smaller cities and airports. In this case, it is a problem for a single airline to offer the passenger a sufficient service by using only his aircraft fleet. Research suggests that a company that would have more than 50 aircraft in its fleet would be able to fully cover the offer of passengers in smaller cities. Companies operating on these markets are forced to use alliance cooperation and use the networks of other airlines.

Another key economic reason for the use of cooperation within the airline alliance is the importance of savings from the flow density of passengers. Savings on the scale of operating activities appear to be limited, but by creating a heavier flow of passengers, the use of seat capacity increases, making it possible to reduce aircraft unit costs. Low-cost carriers increase the flow density of passengers by using low prices, attracting cost-oriented passengers to smaller cities at prices that increase the catchment area of these small towns. The international alliance between the airlines has become the second best solution to achieve the benefits of closer economic cooperation and services integration. (Douglas & Tan 2017).

Closer airline cooperation means lower prices for passengers and the higher services. Price reductions are due to increased use of the capacity of co-operating airlines, on the basis of which they can afford to lower prices. (Wang 2014).

Empirical evidence suggests that the total cost of a transfer ticket is up to 27% lower for Alliance partners than for non-cooperating airlines. Horizontal cooperation can be a means of distributing risks, saving costs, increasing investment, sharing know-how, increasing the quality and diversity of products, and accelerating innovation.

4.2   Selected economic advantages and disadvantages of cooperation between air carriers

"Economic benefits of the alliance"

1. Lower fares for mutual recognition of travel documents for passengers
By combining two carriers in price cooperation, both airlines influence prices and complementary products along the entire route, leading to a reduction in the overall price and increased satisfaction of both airlines and passengers.

2. Lower tariffs resulting from traffic density savings
Because of a broader degree of cooperation, space for service integration and the maximization of traffic-density savings is limited.

3. Passengers can easily combine fare on their route
This kind of advantage belongs to the limited offer of non-price advantages of airlines. Consequence of the cooperation of the carriers is an increase in the number of routes at lower prices from which passengers can choose in the framework of the alliance cooperation of carriers.

4. Airlines offer their passengers a much wider range of travel schedules
Cooperation between the Alliance carriers may also improve schedules with a higher frequency of routes, more choice and coordination of arrivals

and departures and shorter downtimes. Important in this case is the clustering of services around the time of the highest demand.

5. Benefits from the experience of passengers resulting from seamless services and similar products
As the alliance builds the value of its brand, the airlines' motivation to harmonize and improve the standards for customer service is increased.

"Economic disadvantages of alliances"
The airlines alliance raises fundamental questions about the impact on aviation competition:

– The effect of aviation alliances on competition depends on the nature of network cooperation. The Alliance can considerably restrict competition on overlapping routes, where allied airlines have once been the main competitors. Even where the two networks are not overlapping in the markets on which they operate, the alliance may have serious injurious effects on competition by reducing or eliminating competition on the route.
– In addition, the alliance between airlines operating within the hub-and-spoke network to increase demand for the network as a whole and increase the market power of the network, especially at their hub airports. This entails the risk of heavier entry into the market of this network at the expense of international and domestic competition.

4.3 Other advantages and disadvantages of alliance cooperation

The benefits of alliance cooperation can be divided into two categories, namely marketing benefits related mainly to the market prevalence due to the expanded network and the financial benefits mainly related to cost reductions and increased revenues.
Advantages for airlines stem from:

– Network extensions: this is often done through code share agreements. Many alliances began with this kind of cooperation.
– Reduce costs by sharing:
  – Business Offices.
  – Device maintenance.
  – Operating equipment, e.g. catering or computer systems, e.g. land-handling workers, check-in and boarding staff.
  – Investments and purchases, e.g. in order to agree on further quantitative discounts.

Disadvantages for airlines may arise from:

– Possible increase in overheads.
– Increased costs for unification of processes and IT systems.
– Slowing down decision-making processes.
– Worsening the image of the whole alliance in worsening the image of one airline.

– The impossibility of independent development of the airline.
– Deterioration of the position in bilateral cooperation with non-Alliance members.

5 COMPARISON OF SELECTED INDICATORS OF CZECH AIRLINES (CSA) OF VIEW OF ACCESS TO THE GLOBAL ALLIANCE

Based on the assessment of selected indicators of the Czech Airlines, we point out some of the benefits that the airline has shown in terms of its entry into the global alliance of airlines.

In the following table, we point to a comparison of selected Czech Airlines (CSA) indicators before and after entering the SkyTeam alliance. The company entered the above alliance on March 25, 2001.

The number of aircraft has decreased after 2010, due to the streamlining of the aircraft fleet composition and the aircraft fleet unification. The number of destinations offered is within their own network, within the SkyTeam alliance, CSA can offer its passengers flights to all available SkyTeam destinations and locations through alliance partners.

As we can see in terms of reducing the number of destinations since 2003 as a result of more efficient network use, timetabling, and cooperation with other member airlines of the alliance, Czech Airlines' revenues are still increasing thanks to the offer of destinations not only within its own network.

Since joining the alliance in its annual reports, Czech Airlines describes its entry into this alliance as an advantageous strategic step and states: "Thanks to the membership of CSA in the SkyTeam alliance, our company is part of a global system that offers to the public more than 510 destinations in 110 countries of the world over 8000 SkyTeam Airlines daily departures" (ČSA Annual Report 2002).

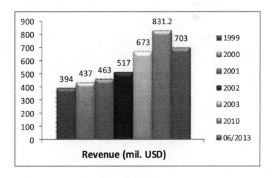

Figure 3. Change in revenue over the reference period. Source: (ČSA Annual Reports).

Table 1. Comparison of selected CSA indicators after joining the SkyTeam alliance in 2001.

	'99	'00	'01	'02	'03	'10	06/'13
Revenue (mil. USD)	394	437	463	517	673	831.2	703
Economic outturn after tax. (mil. USD)*	2.8	29.5	7.8	14.6	19.5	3.8	–
Destination	54	58	59	59	66	56	47
Country	38	38	39	38	40	37	27
Fleet	27	27	30	31	35	39	31
Passengers (annual in mil.)	2.06	2.46	2.87	3.065	3.59	5.06	4.2

*According to international standards
Source: (ČSA Annual Reports).

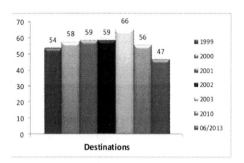

Figure 4. Change in destinations offer over the reference period.
Source: (ČSA Annual Reports).

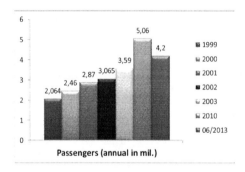

Figure 5. Change in passengers carried over the reference period.
Source: (ČSA Annual Reports).

6 CONCLUSION

Global alliances are now indispensable from a strategic point of view for any competitive multinational enterprise. Associating businesses of a different business focus to remain competitive on the market is nowadays a matter of course. Based on the analysis of the data and information we can say, the emergence of alliances in air transport is currently a positive phenomenon. Alliances offer many benefits not only for airlines included in the alliance but also for passengers who use the services of these airlines.

Unification fleet, reduce costs, increase offered by the network, and these are the advantages offered by cooperation within the alliance. As we have seen in the example of CSA in the observed years—reducing network destinations and reducing the number of aircraft, the revenues of this airline have continued to increase thanks to cooperation in the SkyTeam alliance.

However, if we are looked at alliances in the long term in the future, the problem of distortion of the basic market conditions and of competition may arise, which would have a negative impact on transport, which would be disadvantageous for passengers. In determining the terms of this cooperation and capturing this fundamental negative impact on regulators, alliances will also be a good choice for the future in the future.

REFERENCES

Begera, V. 2015. The comparison of multilateral, bilateral and global alliance cooperation of airline operations. Nase More. 62: 237–241.
ČSA Annual Reports 1999, 2002, 2003, 2010 and 2013. Available on: <http://www.csa. cz/cs/portal/quicklinks/ news/vyrocnizpravy.html>.
Douglas, I. & Tan, D. 2017. Global airline alliances and profitability: A difference-in-difference analysis. Transport Research Part A-Policy and Practice,103: 432–443.
European Air Law Association 1999. 11th Annual Conference. Recent developments in European air transport law and policy. Lisbon, Friday 5 November 1999 Available on: http://ec.europa.eu/competition/speeches/text/sp1999678_en.html.
IATA Economics Biefing. 2012. Available on: http://www.iata.org/whatwedo/Documents/economics/Economics%20of%20 JVs_Jan2012 L.pdf.
Javor, M. 2005. Globálne strategické aliancie a akvizície. Acta Oeconomica Pragensia, (4)13: 20–39.
Pruša, J. et.al. 2008. Svet leteckej dopravy. Galileo CEE Service ČR s.r.o., ISBN 978-80-8073-938-6.
US DOT and European Commission (Nov 2010) 'Transatlantic Airline Alliances: Competitive Issues and Regulatory Approaches'.
Wang, W.S. 2014. Do global airline alliances influence the passenger's purchase decision? Journal of Air Transport Management. 37: 53–59.
Žihla, Z. et al. 2010. Provozování podniku letecké dopravy a letišť, CERM, Praha.

Production Management and Business Development – Mihalčová et al. (Eds)
© *2019 Taylor & Francis Group, London, ISBN 978-1-138-60415-5*

Using of neuromarketing in communication with young consumers

J. Wyrwisz
Lublin Technical University, Lublin, Poland

ABSTRACT: The purpose of the article is to describe neuromarketing as contemporary, effective marketing tool enabling to identify requirement and reaction of the customer. In the area of marketing processes, neuromarketing is appropriable in the marketing communication of the organization and products. Neuromarketing consists of using neurological and physiological method to estimate and analysis of customer reaction to the marketing stimulus. Dissertations in the article are being kept around the thesis: under the conditions of the pervasive digitization of the communication of the organization, neuromarketing can be tool of creating the bond with customers representing young generation. The article presents a research approach leaning against preliminary research of the writing and empirical research were presented. The article indicates the definition of the neuromarketing, characteristics and kinds of method of neuromarketing as eye-tracking, galvanic skin response, face emotion recognition and nanomarketing. Also an extensive profile of young customers was presented.

1 INTRODUCTION

Contemporary consumers are characterized by high activity in terms of acquiring more and more products; moreover, they are bombarded by thousands of advertising messages almost every day. Therefore, they expect a wide range of emotional experiences. To be effective, the messages reaching the consumer should be more decisive and comprehensive, involving several senses at the same time (Skowronek 2014). Communication with consumers based on emotions is currently visible in almost every product category. It is distinguished by an attractive message and is effective from the point of view of the brand. (Kuropatwa 2016)

Every second, the human senses receive about 11 million pieces of information. The vast majority of stimuli reach the brain through eyesight, but the senses of hearing, touch, smell, taste and balance are not without significance. The conscious mind processes only a fraction of this information. The rest is subject to analysis at the subconscious level. (Pradeep 2010)

A rational and conscious cognitive process has a marginal impact on consumer decision making. Obviously, it is often used in marketing messages, ignoring the area of emotions and the non-verbal subconscious. This, however, does not translate into the effectiveness of a message reaching the client. (Dooley 2015)

While not underestimating the conscious and rational elements, marketing communication, especially with the young consumer, should be based on the emotions and unconscious needs of the consumer. In the area of solutions that allow effective communication resulting from understanding the customer's nature, neuromarketing is found. From the perspective of neuromarketing, knowledge about the customer's needs refers to the understanding of the consumer's model of reality and neural processes. (Woźniak 2012)

Neuromarketing provides a spectrum of tools and measurement methods that can be applied both before and after advertising.

2 BASIC ASSUMPTIONS OF NEUROMARKETING

The neuromarketing area is based on the knowledge indicating that the vast majority of consumer behavior is determined by their subconsciousness. They are not able to explain, and they do not understand why they make specific choices on the market. (Dooley 2015) Thus, consumers make decisions on the basis of models of reality, which include life experiences, knowledge, beliefs and collected resources. (Woźniak 2012)

The model sets directions for undertaking actions; however, it is not reality itself. The brain focuses on some part of the experience. This is related to selective attention, selective memorization and distortion, which means that part of the experience is ignored because it is considered invalid. The model of reality, being the basis of the consumer's decision, is important from the point of view of marketing activities, in particular communication activities. (Woźniak 2012)

The subject literature does not indicate clearly what neuromarketing is and what it is not. In a narrow sense, this term refers to marketing analysis of the magnetic resonance imaging of the brain. In a somewhat broader sense, neuromarketing also includes other technologies such as eye tracking, or testing of pulse, breath, and sweating. Neuromarketing encompasses behavioral studies and strategies based on behaviourism. It aims to understand how the brain works regardless of the technology used for this assessment. (Dooley 2015)

It focuses on measuring tools, consumer behavior and scientific psychophysiological research. Neuromarketing analyzes decision making in the process of shaping communication with the market, (Ohme 2018) in particular how the client's mind reacts to the advertising message.

Properly used neuromarketing techniques allow for creating properly tailored advertising messages and adequate products, which results in increased customer satisfaction. (Dooley 2015)

The concept of neuromarketing emerged with new discoveries in the field of knowledge about the structure and function of the brain and the formation of new research methods. This fact gave rise to the development of various fields of science, including marketing, thereby creating its new direction neuromarketing. This was also influenced by the fundamental need to enrich marketing research with more precise, credible and practical knowledge, useful for making business decisions. (Pradeep 2010)

A breakthrough in this area has also been entering into the era of digital technologies and the combination of the EEG method with computers of adequate computing power. This gave scientists the opportunity to observe and learn the mechanisms of brain functioning. However, to this day, man has not been able to fully understand it. (Pradeep 2010)

The origins of neuromarketing are connected with studies conducted by Zaltman, marketing professor at Harvard University, in the late 1990s. His studies using functional magnetic resonance imaging proved that 95% of thoughts, emotions and learning processes occur unconsciously. (Zaltman 2003)

At the same time, Pradeep states that 99.99% of decisions are subconscious (Pradeep 2010). Discrepancy in the results confirms that it is an extremely difficult area to study and determination of the exact number is rather impossible. Nevertheless, scientists agree that people's actions are based on subconscious or unconscious decisions. (Dooley 2015)

From a marketing point of view, it is extremely important since, during a decision making process, a consumer will be guided by their needs and emotional values, which they attribute to a given product, than its real value or price.

The development of neuromarketing research resulted in a significant increase in the interest in advertising, especially in the context of its psychological and neurobiological conditions. Particular attention was paid to attitudes, moods and emotions. (Wąsikowska 2016)

Attitudes depict positive or negative feelings encoded in human memory. More complex and intensified feelings create emotions. Emotions, apart from negative or positive assessment, are accompanied with reaction of the body, namely faster heartbeat, a specific facial expression, or sweating. (Ohme 2018)

Research conducted within the scope of neuromarketing enables gaining deeper knowledge about the customer, which in turn helps in the precise development of product offer or marketing message. Knowledge in the area of advertising psychology and consumer behavior in confrontation with neurobiological conditions enables better identification of marketing communication conditions, which directly translates into communication effectiveness. (Wąsikowska 2016)

3 NEURORESEARCH IN MARKETING COMMUNICATIONS

Neuromarketing as a marketing concept allows for a better understanding of consumer desires and, as a consequence, creation of adequately prepared product offer, also in the area of the communication of the offer. Neuromarketing, using scientific knowledge about the brain, its structure and work, is part of neuroresearch. This research involves tracking brain activity in order to identify reactions to provided marketing stimuli. It uses specialized tools, appropriate methods and procedures, as well as multifaceted software for the assessment and analysis of acquired data on human reactions. (Tarczydło 2017)

The most frequently used neuromarketing techniques include: (Golczyk 2018)

- Eyetracking. This method uses a special camera to track the way of perception of elements. The camera records even the smallest subconscious and conscious movements of the eyeball. For the marketing purposes, points where the eyes have been cast as well as eye movements from one point to the other are recorded. The method enables the identification of where the subject focuses, which element they focus on for the longest period of time, which element draws their attention first, and the order in which the subject focuses on the particular elements of the product, advertising or store shelf.
- Measurement of galvanic skin response, in other words, electrodermal response, psychogalvanic reflex, or skin conductance. It is a measure of changes in skin electrical resistance dependent on the degree of skin hydration caused by changes in the activity of sweat glands. As sweating increases, skin electrical resistance decreases. Experiencing emotions by people leads to changes in electrical resistance of their skin. Registering these changes

enables the assessment of what reaction is triggered by a given factor in the subject.
- Non-invasive functional magnetic resonance imaging (fMRI) is a method consisting in the observation of metabolic processes taking place in the brain. It is a specialized imaging method thanks to which increase in blood flow and oxygenation of the active area of the brain are measured, allowing for the identification of structures in the brain that are responsible for particular actions.
- Electromyography is the study of electrical activity of muscles and peripheral nerves. It is also an analysis of facial muscle expression which consists in the recording of the currents of muscle activity due to the fact that emotional stimulation is characterized by greater muscle contraction.
- Electroencephalography (EEG) is a non-invasive method of recording the electrical activity of cerebral cortex neurons using electrodes placed on the scalp with 4 reference points: the bony process in the centre of the occiput, the nasal bridge, and small bone mounds over the ears. This technique allows for the assessment of the impact of advertising on the human subconscious, andidentifies whether the message is received positively, negatively or indifferently.

Neuromarketing tools can be used primarily to analyze the effectiveness of advertisements and to modify them in accordance with the recipients' reactions. Analysis of brain waves allows for describing the advertisement with the accuracy of a fraction of a second and identifying scenes and images which evoke the strongest emotions with complete omission of the recipient's opinions. The use of the EEG method enables description of the recipient's reactions to individual elements of the advertisement that is sound, text, image, or animations. (Ohme 2018) Table 1 includes selected emotions used in advertisements.

On the basis of research and knowledge, effective ways of reaching customers with an advertising message are developed. It is known which communication channels evoke specific reactions desirable from the point of view of the advertiser. Both positive and negative emotions can effectively draw attention, which will be justified in the case of a specific advertising creation. (Bucki 2015a)

Table 1. Type of emotions in advertising.

Type of emotions in an advertising	
Positive	Negative
curiosity, humor, longing, surprise, pleasure, joy, bliss, love, happiness, nostalgia	anxiety, anger, guilt, disgust, contempt, worry, shame, revenge, jealousy, fear, envy, hatred

The content and form of the message must be consistent in terms of emotions evoked. Based on neuromarketing research, it is possible to objectively determine to what extent the advertisement evokes emotions and what kind of emotions these are. The final step of the research is to determine what the viewers felt in every second, during which of the scenes they were joyful and what caused their anger. The research provides information on how they react to the appearance of the brand. These methods are extremely effective for the tactical improvement of commercial spots. They give detailed and valuable knowledge that cannot be obtained from the recipient's opinions. (Kuropatwa 2016)

Among the disadvantages of research in the field of neuromarketing, the costs should be indicated. Research requires the participation of high-class specialists, research teams and agencies, whose tasks significantly go beyond the scope of work of creative agencies. (Bucki 2015b)

4 NEUROMARKETING AND MARKETING COMMUNICATION WITH YOUNG CONSUMER

Young consumers are a very diverse social group with a different developmental and economic potential, as well as various interests and activities that are reflected in purchasing decisions. The advertising message addressed to young audiences must stand out to draw attention of this demanding group, distrustful and resistant to suggestions, changeable in terms of trends and moods. Humor and non-standard action are important in communicating with young consumers because their lifestyle is characterized by freshness and fun. An important limitation for advertisers is the fact that young people do not believe in the content of the advertising message and treat it with caution and distance.

Research using neuromarketing techniques allows for an objective assessment of how the recipient reacts to messages and what emotions these messages evoke. Such research eliminates the issue of declarativeness. The use of EEG makes it possible to check the impact of advertising on the human subconscious, that is determine whether it receives it positively, indifferently or negatively. It is possible to determine in which areas the reactions caused by stimuli presented to the subject occur.

The research was designed to evaluate marketing communication with a young consumer using neuromarketing techniques. Its aim was to assess the reaction of a young consumer to a selected advertising message and to determine whether selected advertisements affect the emotions of recipients. The research was carried out in April 2014. The technique of objective assessment of advertisement used was the EEG test. It was conducted in the Department of Complex Systems and Neurodynamics at in Lublin. A sample of 20 people (10 women and 10 men) aged 24, who were residents of the Lublin voivodeship, participated in the research.

The subject of the research was 10 commercial spots on various topics. The content of the subsequent commercials involved entertainment and humor, love, children, food, politics and social problems. The commercials assessed in the research included:

– WoW video game commercial with Chuck Noris.
– Evian mineral water commercial "Baby & Me".
– Danone's Danio homogenized cheese with the character called Small Hunger.
– McDonald's "Classic duet" commercial.
– KFC commercial.
– Law and Justice (PiS) party campaign ad.
– Lublin city promotion campaign.
– SYNAPSIS Foundation commercial "The child will not tell you they have autism".
– Social commercial encouraging parents to vaccinate children "Vaccinate me".
– KNGF Geleidehonden commercial addressed to war veterans "Buddyhond".

Based on the conducted experiment, the most important findings from the research were formulated:

– Advertisements affect the emotions and mood of the recipients, this impact is varied for each material presented and for individual recipients.
– Correlation of the declaration of preferences concerning various aspects of the presented advertising materials with the subjective assessment of the commercials after watching them is 78%.
– The subjects are not aware of the subconscious reactions of their brains—it can not be said that any subject was aware of their attitude to all issues.
– Men demonstrate greater awareness of their objective responses to advertising materials than women.
– Women are more emotionally affected by the content presented to them; in men, advertisements stimulate other areas of the brain to a greater extent.
– The subjects are not aware of the impact of advertising on their brains, they often overestimate or underestimate their impressions.
– Men demonstrate a greater level of awareness of the strength of their feelings than women.
– The subjects react subconsciously in a very different way.

5 CONCLUSIONS

The use of neuromarketing gives wide possibilities of diagnosing consumer responses to external stimuli related to marketing activities for products and brands. Emotions are a response to external factors, such as a promotional message. Reaching all consumers, it determines their behavior, including purchasing behavior. However, this does not mean that everyone reacts to it in the same way.

Neuromarketing creates great opportunities to assess the impact of advertising on consumer behavior and to choose the right messages from the point of view of effectiveness.

REFERENCES

Bucki, P. 2015a. Marka dla zmysłów. *Marketing w Praktyce* 206(4): 84–85.
Bucki, P. 2015b.Wzmacniacze rzeczywistości. *Marketing w Praktyce* 207(5): 65–67.
Clow K.E. &Baack D. 2016. Integrated Advertising, Promotion and Marketing Communications. London: Pearson Education Limited.
Dooley, R. 2015. Neuromarketing. 100 szybkich, łatwych I tanich sposobów na przekonanie klienta, Warszawa: Wydawnictwo Naukowe PWN.
Fill Ch. & Turnbull S. 2016. Marketing communications—discovery, creation and conversations. London: Pearson Education Limited.
Golczyk, P. 2018. Neuromarketing, czyli różnica między prawdą a kłamstwem, http://golczyk.com/neuromarketing-czyli-roznica-miedzy-prawda-a-klamstwem/l/, (20.04.2018).
Hulten, B. et al. 2009. Sensory Marketing, London: Palgrave Macmillan.
Kuropatwa, A. 2016. Od neuromarketingu do zwykłej rozmowy. *Marketing w Praktyce* 218(4): 39–41.
Neuromarketing, https://pl.wikipedia.org/wiki/Neuromarketing, (20.04.2018).
Neuromarketing, jak techniki marketingowe są wspierane przez naukę?, https://poradnikprzedsiebiorcy.pl/-/neuromarketing-jak-techniki-marketingowe-wspierane-sa-przez-nauke, (20.04.2018).
Ohme, R. 2018. http://neurohm.pl/, (20.04.2018).
Piech, O. 2018. Emocje w reklamie. Czy wszystko jest na sprzedaż. https://nowymarketing.pl/a/17235,emocje-w-reklamie-czy-wszystko-jest-na-sprzedaz, (20.04.2018).
Pradeep, A.K. 2010. The Buying Brain: Secrets for Selling to the Subconscious Mind, Hoboken NJ: John Wiley&Sons.
Skowronek, I. 2014. Zmysły dla zysku. Marketing sensoryczny w praktyce, Warszawa: Wydawnictwo Poltext.
Szymusiak, H. 2012. Neurobiologiczne techniki stosowane w biznesie, Poznań: Wydawnictwo Uniwersytetu Ekonomicznego w Poznaniu.
Tarczydło, B. 2017. Neurobadania skuteczności reklamy—przykłady zastosowań. *Zarządzanie i Marketing* 49(3): 85–93.
Woźniak, J. 2012. Neuromarketing 2.0. Wygraj wojnę o umysł klienta, Gliwice: Wydawnictwo Helion.
Wąsikowska, B. 2016. Elektroencefalografia (EEG) w badaniu efektywności komunikacji reklamowej. *Przedsiębiorczość i Zarządzanie* 11: 407–422.
Zaltman, G. 2003. How Customers Think, Boston: Harvard Business Press. https://pl.wikipedia.org/wiki/Neuromarketing, (20.04.2018).

Production Management and Business Development – Mihalčová et al. (Eds)
© *2019 Taylor & Francis Group, London, ISBN 978-1-138-60415-5*

Knowledge acquisition by manufacturing firms in European Union countries

J. Wyszkowska-Kuna
University of Lodz, Lodz, Poland

ABSTRACT: Along with the development of economies based on knowledge, the importance of knowledge input in production processes has been increasing. There are two main ways for manufacturing enterprises to acquire knowledge input, i.e. (1) by employing highly qualified specialists; or (2) by purchasing knowledge from external specialists. The aim of the paper is to examine the importance of both methods, and to compare their changing role with changes in productivity performance. It is based on data from the World Input-Output Database (WIOD), Eurostat and EU KLEMS. Thanks to the availability of relevant data, the analysed period covers the years 1995–2016. The study demonstrates the growing importance of the development of an internal knowledge base in the periods before and after the recent global financial crisis, while the role of knowledge acquisition from external specialists (other firms) has been decreasing, especially in the case of the EU-15.

1 INTRODUCTION

In today's knowledge-based economies operating in a competitive global landscape, knowledge is an essential asset, a key for firms' profitability and survival, to a greater extent than traditional production factors (Nonaka 1994, Dean & Kretschmer 2007). Thus, the ability to create and apply new knowledge, is one of the primary sources of competitive advantage (Nonaka 1991, Mu et al. 2008).

Firms need to acquire new knowledge from numerous internal and external sources in order to constantly generate innovations and maintain their competitive edge (Cotic Svetina & Prodan 2008, Santamaria et al. 2009). Moreover, the development of knowledge-based economies, the information and communications technology (ICT) revolution, and increased competition in markets have resulted in the need to reorganize production processes in order to increase their efficiency (Jones & Kierzkowski 1990, Baldwin 2014). As a result, it has been possible to observe the growing demand for business services (those related to new technologies and knowledge, which are called "knowledge-intensive business services" – KIBS), as well as the tendency to outsource and offshore business services. In the light of this phenomenon, the growing importance of knowledge input acquired from external sources should be expected.

The aim of the paper is to examine the changing role of the internal knowledge base and the acquisition of knowledge from external sources in manufacturing enterprises. I proposed two indicators to measure the importance of internal knowledge base, and one indicator to measure knowledge acquired from external sources. Finally, the average annual growth rates of all indicators are compared with average annual productivity growth in the manufacturing sector, measured by total factor productivity (TFP). To take into account the impact of the recent financial crisis, the analyzed period is divided into two sub-periods: 1995–2007 and 2008–2015.

2 INTERNAL AND EXTERNAL SOURCES OF KNOWLEDGE

High-skilled, professional employees represent the most important internal source of knowledge (Divanna & Rogers 2005, Gabcanova 2011). Based on their internal knowledge base, firms acquire knowledge through in-house R&D activities and by learning from continuous improvements in business processes. Firms may also develop their knowledge base through education and training.

If firms do not have an appropriate knowledge base inside the firm, they can acquire it externally by cooperating with customers and suppliers, as well as other firms. Among the external sources of knowledge, inter-firm collaboration has received the most widespread research attention, as a consequence of the dynamic development of outsourcing and offshoring of business services since the 1980s. Nowadays, in order to bring new products, processes and services to the market, firms must mobilise a broad set of skills, which are often beyond their internal capabilities and which include not only technical skills but also market analysis, logistics, and behavioural sciences. Outsourcing and cooperating with other firms enable enterprises to specialise and enhance their competitive advantage (Abramovsky et al. 2004), using their internal knowledge resources optimally and combining them with their partners' specific competencies. In recent years, the range of business services that have been subject to these processes, has extended from simple, routine, and standardised tasks to KIBS, such as IT applications, finance and accounting, engineering, R&D, and human resources (Massini & Miozo 2010, Berchicci 2013, Garavelli et al. 2013).

Firms may acquire knowledge from other private or public firms. In the first case knowledge input is delivered by firms from the KIBS sector, while in the second case by universities or research institutes (Keeble & Wilkinson 2000). KIBS are increasingly recognized as important carriers of new knowledge developed in upstream sectors, and then diffused into manufacturing industries (Schricke et al. 2012), which determines their value added and productivity (Tomlinson 2000, Baker 2007). KIBS may also be used by manufacturing firms to translate codified academic knowledge into practical and accessible know-how, to enhance product differentiation, and they may help companies to reduce costs by providing services more cheaply (Di Cagno & Meliciani 2005).

3 METHODOLOGY AND DATA

Two indicators are used to measure an internal knowledge base, and one indicator is used to measure the acquisition of knowledge from external sources. In the second case, the study refers only to knowledge acquired from other firms.

The first indicator takes the form of the share of hours worked by high-skilled persons engaged in total hours worked (HHS). The values of this indicator are presented in WIOD (2013), but they are available for individual manufacturing industries. Thus, it was necessary to calculate it for the whole manufacturing sector, according to the formula:

$$HHS^M = \frac{\Sigma_{i=C10-c33}HHS_i \cdot HEMP_i}{\Sigma_{i=c10-c33}HEMP_i} * 100\% \quad (1)$$

where $HEMP$ = total hours worked by persons engaged; M denotes the manufacturing sector; and i denotes divisions according to NACE Rev. 1.1. The term 'persons engaged' is wider than the term

'employees' as it also includes self-employed and family workers (O'Mahony & Timmer 2009).

The second index (PROFS) shows the share of Professionals in total employment in the manufacturing sector (Eurostat 2017). It can be calculated for the period 2008–2016.

The third indicator, measuring knowledge acquired from other firms, takes the form of the share of KIBS input in total intermediate inputs. It is calculated according to the formula:

$$IIKIBS^M = \frac{\Sigma_{i=J62-63,M69-73}II_i^M}{\Sigma_{i=A01-T}II_i^M} * 100\% \quad (2)$$

where II = intermediate inputs derived from Use tables; and i denotes divisions according to NACE Rev. 2. KIBS are defined as including the following divisions: Computer programming, consultancy and related activities; information service activities (J62-63); Legal and accounting activities; activities of head offices; management consultancy activities (M69-70); Architectural and engineering activities; technical testing and analysis (M71); Scientific research and development (M72); Advertising and market research (M73) (Schnabl & Zenker 2013). This indicator measures the acquisition of all types of knowledge input (not only R&D), as well as knowledge input acquired from both private and public enterprises.

Finally, the growth accounting framework (O'Mahony & Timmer 2009) is used to calculate changes in TFP. The contribution of TFP (value added based, in 2010 prices) is calculated on the basis of data derived from the EU KLEMS database (2017) for the periods 1995–2007 and 2008–2015. Because of the lack of data on capital input for Belgium, Ireland, Portugal, Bulgaria, Latvia, Croatia, Cyprus, Malta, and Romania, it was not possible to calculate TFP growth for these countries.

The values of HHSM and IIKIBS Mare calculated based on data from the WIOD database. It covers the period 1995–2009 (the WIOD 2013 Release), and 2000–2014 (the WIOD 2016 Release). The values of the HHS index are available only in the WIOD 2013 Release. To enable the comparison of this index with the TFP growth in the years before the recent global financial crisis, I calculated its average annual growth rate for the period 1995–2007, but I also presented its values in 2009. The values of the IIKIBS index can be calculated for both periods. One should note, however, that the WIOD 2013 Release was developed based on NACE Rev. 1.1, while the WIOD 2016 Release is based on NACE Rev. 2. Moreover, data in the WIOD 2016 Release are more disaggregated than those in the WIOD 2013 Release. This changes the definition of KIBS, thus making the results incomparable. Finally, one should note that the definition of KIBS according to the WIOD 2016 Release is more relevant as, to a larger extent, it includes only those services that are knowledge-intensive, and therefore used data from the WIOD 2016 Release (for the period 2000–2014, which is also divided into two sub-periods 2000–2007 and 2008–2014).

4 EMPIRICAL STUDY

In Table 1, the values of the two indicators used to measure the internal knowledge base in the EU countries in 2007 (2009) and 2016, as well as their

Table 1. The share of hours worked by high-skilled persons and Professionals in manufacturing.

Country	HHS* (in %)	PROFS** (in %)		
	2007 (2009)	1995–07	2016	2008–16
AUT	14.9 (15.4)	5.7	8.7	11.4
BEL	13.1 (14.6)	2.3	10.4	3.4
DNK	21.8 (25.3)	3.6	13.1	5.8
FIN	29.6 (32.0)	3.0	22.5	7.6
FRA	25.0 (27.3)	4.3	11.3	0.7
GER	21.1 (23.5)	1.6	12.2	3.4
GBR	27.4 (26.5)	4.7	18.4	7.2
GRC	14.9 (14.2)	4.2	8.7	6.7
IRL	32.4 (38.0)	6.5	14.7	3.7
ITA	7.1 (8.0)	6.6	5.2	5.1
LUX	17.8 (23.0)	1.7	–	–
NLD	20.4 (22.4)	4.2	15.1	5.9
PRT	4.2 (5.8)	4.4	5.8	10.5
ESP	28.1 (30.8)	5.2	8.0	7.0
SWE	16.4 (16.9)	5.6	12.9	5.0
BGR	4.2 (5.8)	4.4	5.4	1.6
CYP	15.2 (17.0)	−0.3	6.2	12.3
CZE	7.3 (8.5)	1.8	4.6	3.9
EST	23.3 (24.9)	1.0	7.9	3.3
HRV	– (–)	–	5.7	1.5
HUN	9.7 (12.0)	2.0	7.9	4.6
LTU	19.9 (22.1)	2.0	8.5	1.7
LVA	15.9 (17.8)	1.6	9.1	6.2
MLT	4.2 (5.8)	4.4	5.0	−0.2
POL	12.5 (15.0)	4.9	7.6	4.2
ROU	4.2 (5.8)	4.4	9.0	1.9
SVK	7.7 (8.3)	1.4	2.6	−2.1
SVN	11.4 (14.6)	2.9	11.0	6.4

*The share of hours worked by high-skilled persons engaged in total hours worked (in 2007 and 2009, and the average annual growth rate in the period 1995–2007).
**The share of Professionals in total employment by type of occupation (in 2008, and the average annual growth rate in the period 2008–2016).

changes in the analyzed periods (1995–2007 and 2008–2016), are presented.

Both indicators increased their values in the EU countries (HHS decreased slightly only in Cyprus, while PROFS in Slovakia). The strongest increase in the HHS index took place in Italy and Ireland, while the lowest was in Estonia. The HHS value ranged from 32.4% (Ireland) to 4.2% (Portugal, Bulgaria, Malta and Romania) in 2007, which proves a high variation within the EU countries. The values for the EU-15 were considerably higher than those for the EU-12, with a tendency to increase this disparity. In both groups, one can notice some exceptions—Portugal and Italy reached the lowest values among the EU countries, while in Estonia and Latvia the situation was the reverse. In the subsequent two years, the index was still on the increase (except for Greece), with a significant improvement in most countries. The second index reached the highest value in Finland (18.4%), and the lowest in Slovakia (2.6). The growth rate was still stronger for the EU-15 than the EU-13, though the highest one was achieved by Cyprus. Even though the period for which the growth rate of the PROFS index was calculated covers the years of the recent global financial crisis, it was higher than the growth rate of the HHS index that was calculated for the period before the crisis—such a situation occurred in most of the EU-15, and in half of the EU-12 countries.

Table 2 presents the values of the index measuring the acquisition of knowledge from other enterprises.

KIBS input decreased its share in total intermediate inputs in most of the EU-15 countries, while in the EU-13 countries the tendency was usually reversed. In most countries, this decline took place in the second period, though in some countries it already started in the first period. The exceptions are Luxembourg and Malta where a downward trend occurred only during the first period. Belgium, Ireland, Bulgaria, the Czech Republic, Romania, and Slovakia are the countries with an upward trend through both periods. Romania recorded the highest average annual growth rate (in both periods), whereas Ireland experienced the highest total growth (5.8 percentage points). Ireland was also distinguished by the fact that this growth took place mainly in the second period. In general, KIBS input played a much more significant role in total intermediate inputs in the EU-15 than in the EU-13 countries, with a tendency to decrease this disparity. The dynamics of this index was usually lower than of the two indexes presented in Table 1.

Figure 1 shows the average annual growth rate of TFP in 19 out of the 28 EU countries in

Table 2. The role of KIBS input.

Country	IIKIBS/II* (in %)		IIKIBS/II** (in %)	
	2000	2014	2000–07	2008–14
AUT	5.7	4.8	0.3	–3.4
BEL	4.6	5.8	0.9	3.2
DNK	4.2	3.9	–0.4	–4.8
FIN	14.8	9.8	–2.8	–4.3
FRA	9.8	6.4	0.6	–7.6
GER	7.9	6.5	–0.7	–2.2
GBR	4.8	5.0	1.2	–0.8
GRC	6.0	4.8	2.3	–5.7
IRL	8.2	14.0	0.9	8.6
ITA	7.6	6.3	–0.6	–2.4
LUX	3.3	1.9	–5.7	0.9
NLD	10.6	4.0	0.05	–14.3
PRT	2.7	2.8	1.8	–1.3
ESP	3.6	2.9	–0.3	–3.1
SWE	12.8	7.9	–2.2	–5.0
BGR	1.4	2.0	2.5	2.6
CYP	1.3	1.5	2.1	–1.1
CZE	1.5	3.0	5.8	3.5
EST	4.2	3.6	–1.0	–1.0
HRV	3.8	5.5	6.1	–0.3
HUN	2.8	2.8	3.2	–4.2
LTU	2.0	1.9	4.2	–1.0
LVA	2.5	2.7	2.5	–1.0
MLT	7.5	5.3	–5.9	2.4
POL	3.9	3.4	–0.5	–2.5
ROU	2.3	4.7	6.4	5.5
SVK	2.5	2.7	2.4	–1.4
SVN	3.6	4.4	1.1	1.5

*The share of KIBS input in total intermediate inputs in 2000 and 2014.
**The share of KIBS input in total intermediate inputs—the average annual growth rates in the periods 2000–2007 and 2008–2014.

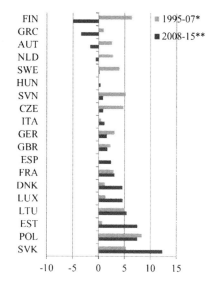

Figure 1. TFP average annual growth rate. The results were put in descending order according to the period 2008–2015.
*NLD 2000–07; EST, LTU 2000–07; POL 2003–07; SVK 2004–07, SVN 2000–07.
**GBR, GRC, ITA, SWE, CZE, EST, LTU, POL 2008–14; HUN 2011–14.

the periods 1995–2007 and 2008–2015 (or as described below Figure 1). The comparison of all indexes shows that two countries stood out. First, Ireland reached the highest values of HHS and IIKIBS, and a high value of PROFS, with a steady upward trend in each case. This proves that the manufacturing sector in this country has been increasing its knowledge base dynamically through knowledge acquisition from both internal and external sources, but with significantly higher dynamics with respect to external sources in the recent period. Unfortunately, it is not possible to compare it with TFP growth in this country. The opposite trend is visible in the case of Finland. The Finish manufacturing sector recorded the second highest value of HHS, the highest value of PROFS (with a steady upward trend), and the highest value

of IIKIBS, but only initially. In subsequent years, the last index decreased its value significantly, though it was still quite high in 2014. As far as the TFP growth in the Finish manufacturing sector is concerned, it recorded the highest growth rate among the 'old' EU countries in the first period, but then it declined at an almost equally high rate.

Among the other 'old' EU countries, the example of Great Britain can also be mentioned. The British manufacturing sector improved its productivity performance in both periods, mainly thanks to the relatively high importance and dynamics of its internal knowledge base.

In the group of 'new' EU member states Estonia and Lithuania achieved quite high TFP growth, mainly due to the relatively high importance of their internal knowledge base, while knowledge acquisition from external sources was among the lowest. In Slovakia and Poland, the highest rates of TFP growth seem to be determined more by other factors than those covered by the study.

Finally, I used the Pearson correlation coefficient to examine the correlation between the average annual growth rates of each index and TFP. The results proved that the growth rate of KIBS input was positively correlated with TFP, but what came as a surprise is that the correlation was negative in the case of both indexes measuring internal knowledge base. This may be explained as follows:

the growing share of high-skilled hours worked and of professionals in total employment resulted in a disproportionate growth of labor input costs, thus leading to the growing contribution of labour input and the decreasing contribution of TFP to valued added growth. One should note, however, that there are many different factors affecting the TFP growth.

5 CONCLUSIONS

Based on the study carried out in this paper, a few conclusions can be formulated:

1. Knowledge base, developed through both internal and external sources, played a significantly more important role in the EU-15 than the EU-13, with a tendency to decrease these disparities only in the case of knowledge acquisition from other firms.
2. The role of an internal knowledge base increased significantly in the period before and after the outbreak of the recent global financial crisis, while the role of knowledge acquisition from other firms decreased, particularly in the EU-15. The second finding is not in line with the subject literature on KIBS and outsourcing. The employment of professionals recorded the highest growth rate.
3. Variation within the EU countries is high, especially in the case of HHS.
4. Ireland and Finland stood out with the highest importance of knowledge acquired through both methods (Ireland also by the highest dynamics). In Finland it seems that the declining role of knowledge acquisition from other firms negatively affects the TFP growth of the manufacturing sector.
5. TFP growth was positively correlated with the growth rate of knowledge acquired from external sources, while negatively with the growth of knowledge developed internally. This suggests that the acquisition of knowledge from external sources was less expensive, and therefore the manufacturing sectors from those countries, which to a larger extent based their knowledge acquisition from external sources, achieved better results in productivity performance.

REFERENCES

Abramovsky, L., Griffith, R. & Sako, M. 2004. Offshoring of business services and its impact on the UK economy. *IFS Brieffng Note BN51, AIM Brieffng Note*.
Baker, D. 2007. The impact of business-services use on client industries: evidence from input output data. In

L. Rubalcaba & H. Kox (eds.), *Business Services in European Economic Growth*: 97–115. New York: Palgrave MacMillan.
Baldwin, R.E. 2014. Trade and Industrialisation after Globalisation's Second Unbundling: How Building and Joining a Supply Chain are Different and Why it Matters. In R.C. Feenstra & A.M. Taylor (Eds.), *Globalization in an Age of Crisis: Multilateral Economic Cooperation in the Twenty First Century*: 165–212. Chicago, IL: University of Chicago Press/NBER.
Berchicci, L. 2013. Towards an open R&D system: internal R&D investment, external knowledge acquisition and innovative performance. *Research Policy* 42(1): 117–127.
Cotic Svetina, A. & Prodan, I. 2008. How Internal and External Sources of Knowledge Contribute to Firms' Innovation Performance. *Managing Global Transitions* 6(3): 277–299.
Dean, A. & Kretschmer, M. 2007. Can ideas be capital? Factors of production in the post-industrial economy: a review and critique. *Academy of Management Review* 32(2): 573–594.
di Cagno, D. & Meliciani, V. 2005, Do inter-sectoral flows of services matter for productivity growth? An input/output analysis of OECD countries. *Economics of Innovation and New Technology* 14(3): 149–171.
Divanna, J.A. & Rogers, J. 2005. *People – the new asset* on the *balance sheet*. New York: Palgrave Macmillan.
EU-KLEMS. 2017. Growth and Productivity Accounts: Statistical Module, ESA 2010 and ISIC Rev. 4 Industry Classification. Luxembourg: European Commission.
Eurostat. 2017. Labour market: Employment by occupation and economic activity. Luxembourg: European Commission.
Gabcanova, I. 2011. The Employees—The Most Important Asset in the Organizations. *Human Resources Management & Ergonomics* V(1).
Garavelli, A.C. et al. 2013. Benefiting from Markets for Ideas—An Investigation Across Different Typologies. *International Journal of Innovation Management.* 17(6): 1340017.
Jones, R.W. & Kierzkowski, H. 1990. The role of services in production and international trade: a theoretical framework. In R.W. Jones, A. Krueger (eds.), *The Political Economy of International Trade*: 31–48. Oxford: Basil Blackwell.
Keeble, D. & Wilkinson, F. (eds). 2000. High-technology clusters, networking and collective learning in Europe. Aldershot: Ashgate.
Massini, S. & Miozzo, M. 2010. Outsourcing and Offshoring of Business Services: Challenges to Theory, Management and Geography of Innovation. *Manchester Business School Research Paper* 604.
Mu, J. et al. 2008. Interfirm networks, social capital, and knowledge flow. *Journal of Knowledge Management* 12(4): 86–100.
Nonaka, I. 1991. The knowledge-creating company. *Harvard Business Review* 69(6): 96–104.
Nonaka, I. 1994. A dynamic theory of organizational knowledge creation. *Organization Science* 5(1): 14–37.
O'Mahony, M. & Timmer, M.P. 2009. Output, Input and Productivity Measures at the Industry Level: the EU KLEMS Database. *Economic Journal* 119(538): F374-F403.

Santamaria, L. et al. 2009. Beyond formal R&D: Taking advantage of other sources of innovation in low—and medium-technology industries, *Research Policy* 38(3): 507–517.

Schnabl, E. & Zenker, A. 2013. Statistical Classification of Knowledge-Intensive Business Services (KIBS) with NACE Rev.2. *evoREG Research* Note #25.

Schricke, E. et al. 2012. *Knowledge-Intensive (Business) Services in Europe* (No. EUR 25189: 52). Luxembourg: European Commission.

Tomlinson, M. 2000. The contribution of knowledge-intensive services to the manufacturing industry. In B. Andersen, J. Howells, R. Hull, I. Miles & J. Roberts (eds.), *Knowledge and Innovation in the New Service Economy*: 36–48. Cheltenham: Edward Elgar Publishing.

World Input-Output Database. 2013. *Socio Economic Accounts*. Luxembourg: European Commission.

World Input-Output Database. 2016. *National Input-Output Tables*. Luxembourg: European Commission.

Author index